P9-CDC-924

Larchmont Public Library
Larchmont, New York

THE RISE AND FALL
OF THE LEAGUE
OF NATIONS

THE
RISE AND FALL
OF THE LEAGUE
OF NATIONS

GEORGE SCOTT

Macmillan Publishing Co., Inc.

NEW YORK

341.22
S

Copyright © 1973 by George Scott

All rights reserved. No part of this book may be reproduced
or transmitted in any form or by any means, electronic or
mechanical, including photocopying, recording or by any
information storage and retrieval system, without
permission in writing from the Publisher.

Macmillan Publishing Co., Inc.
866 Third Avenue, New York, N.Y. 10022
Collier-Macmillan Canada Ltd.

Library of Congress Catalog Card Number: 73-20179

FIRST AMERICAN EDITION 1974

Printed in the United States of America

ACKNOWLEDGEMENTS

It has been a great help to me in trying to recapture the atmosphere of Geneva, and to gain some understanding of the dramatic events enacted there during the life of the League, to have been able to draw on the memories of many who were themselves involved or who were there as journalists. In particular, I must express my gratitude to Don Salvador de Madariaga and to W. N. Ewer for talking so freely to me.

My wife gave me invaluable assistance with research and we both owe much to the staff of the Public Record Office for their guidance in the use of the Cabinet papers. I am also grateful to the librarian and staff at Chatham House, to Miss Tindall, formerly Reform Club librarian, and to Mrs. Audrey Tester, who not only typed this book but made numerous helpful suggestions as well.

The release of the Cabinet papers for the years between the wars has enabled me to add new information to what was already known of the story of the League and, I hope, to throw some new light on the circumstances in which certain British government decisions were taken and the motives behind them. But no one can approach this subject without consulting *A History of the League of Nations*, written by F. P. Walters, who was a member of the secretariat from the beginning and was deputy secretary-general during the first year of the war. I want to acknowledge my own debt to his book, published in 1952 by the Oxford

University Press under the auspices of the Royal Institute of International Affairs.

I am grateful to the following for permission to quote from published works: Macmillan, London and Basingstoke, *Diaries, Letters and Papers* of Gustav Stresemann, edited and translated by Eric Sutton; Cassell and Company Ltd, *The Eden Memoirs: Facing the Dictators*, by the Rt. Hon. the Earl of Avon, K.G., P.C., M.C.; J. C. Smuts and Cassell and Company Ltd, *Jan Christian Smuts*, by J. C. Smuts; Lord Salter, *Personality in Politics*, published by Faber and Faber; Hodder and Stoughton, *Memoirs of Cordell Hull*; the Executors of the Estate of Viscount Cecil of Chelwood, *A Great Experiment*, published by Jonathan Cape Ltd; Hutchinson Publishing Group Ltd, *On Active Service in Peace and War*, by Henry L. Stimson and McGeorge Bundy. I must also thank the University of Birmingham Library for permission to quote from letters of Sir Austen Chamberlain, which appear in *Life and Letters of Sir Austen Chamberlain*, by Sir Charles Petrie, published by Cassell and Company Ltd; the Royal Institute of International Affairs for allowing me to use quotations from a speech made by Sir Austen Chamberlain at Chatham House on February 4th, 1930, the text of which appeared in the March, 1930, issue of the Journal of the RIIA; the British Broadcasting Corporation, for a quotation from *Peace in the Family of Man*, the 1968 Reith Lectures given by Lester Pearson and published in *The Listener*. Transcripts of Crown-copyright records in the Public Record Office appear by permission of the Controller of H.M. Stationery Office.

CONTENTS

PART ONE

The Rise

'Mankind is once more on the move'

The Peace Conference which met at Paris in January, 1919, provided a far from perfect environment for the birth of the League of Nations. The delegates who met there, the political leaders and the victorious generals of the Allied powers, were in a hurry. They were driven by the demands of their war-sick peoples. It was their job to usher in the new era, when, all over the world, there would be peace. Peace, but little enough goodwill. The four years of war had not only left millions of dead on the battlefields of Europe; it had also maimed the minds of those who still lived. The war had exalted nationalism, enthroned hate, nourished a huge appetite for revenge. The Germans must be punished, the Germans must pay. The Germans must be made impotent; never again could they be allowed to take up arms to march against their neighbours. The bureaucrats at Paris, the representatives of the Foreign Office and the Quai d'Orsay, were sceptical and intolerant of new concepts for conducting the affairs of man, such as a world forum and an international court. They knew that the old ways, the tried ways in which they had been trained and to which they were dedicated, were the best ways, nation talking to nation, secretly, behind closed doors, in the language of diplomacy. Everyone at the Conference wanted peace all right, but, in all but a few, the dominating ideas of how that peace should be achieved, of what the new world should look like, of the materials with which it should be built, gave little hope that man had learned his lesson.

Not that the occasion lacked great men and brave words. Because we know how the story ended, it would be wrong to accuse the men who met together at Paris of wanting it to end that way. Their desire for peace was genuine enough. Like the people they led, they were weary of war. They, too, could choke at the sight of the blind, the crippled, the crazed heroes, who had shambled back from the trenches. They wanted to make a world fit for them to live in. But even among the statesmen, who embraced each other in public, there was distrust in private.

President Woodrow Wilson was not the first, nor the last American to believe it was his mission to straighten out the wayward Europeans. Wilson was an idealist and he had a vision, a noble vision, of how man should live and his code for international standards of behaviour was no less exacting than that for individuals. Woodrow Wilson personalised the aspirations of mankind. This lofty, arrogant sermoniser inspired ordinary men and women to the hope that all the misery and grief had been worth while. He embraced their inarticulate yearnings in his own giddy oratory, lifting up their hearts with his talk of 'eternal principles of right and justice,' telling them that life need not be what it had always been before, showing them a world where man had been cleansed of envy and greed and lust, and where statesmen would greet each other as brothers and would work together to advance, not the selfish interests of their individual nations, but the transcendent interest of all mankind. Wherever Wilson had gone, in those first few weeks after the armistice of November, 1918—to Paris, to London, to Rome, to Milan and Turin—there had been cheers and flowers and banners of tribute. Wilson was the deliverer, even 'the god of peace.' But some of the qualities which made him the darling of the crowds made a less endearing impression upon the other Allied leaders at the Paris Conference.

There was, for instance, his didacticism: the former Princeton professor could never lose the habit of lecturing, no matter how eminent the company, and this, frequently, in high moral tone. The French Prime Minister, Georges Clemenceau, 'le père Victoire,' as he was known to his people, a man in his eightieth year when the Peace Conference began, observed Wilson with a savage derision. He nicknamed him 'Jupiter.' They clashed many times. On one occasion, Clemenceau walked out of the Conference, giving Wilson no indication when, or, indeed, whether, he would return. When an emissary suggested to the Frenchman that, at least, he should talk things over with the President, Clemenceau replied, 'How can I talk to a fellow who thinks himself the first man in two thousand years to know anything about peace on earth?' Wilson was a man of courage, but it was a quality which sometimes declined into obduracy. This Wilson may have called, 'sticking to his principles'; others saw it only as pig-headedness, and it was not only the European leaders who found it offensive. It also helped to alienate powerful men in the United States, whose friendship, or, at worst, neutrality, he was to need. At Paris, when it came to a digging in of toes, Clemenceau could be a fair match for Wilson.

Like Clemenceau, David Lloyd George, the British Prime Minister, felt that he and his countrymen had done their share towards victory. Well aware though he was of the power of the United States, of what her entry into the war had meant and of the role she must now assume, he, too, found Wilson's assumption of moral superiority and omniscience exasperating. Lloyd George, no less than Wilson, was a man who could transport an audience with his images of glory and goodness, but he was also a realistic politician, who knew the perils that could befall nations, as well as maidens, who were seduced by golden words. Lloyd George was anything but convinced that to translate all the American President's fine principles into action was going to be in the interests of Great Britain. Nor was he uncritical of Wilson's personal abilities.

At a meeting of the British War Cabinet on the 1st of March, 1918, the possibility of a separate peace with Austria was in the air and ministers discussed how the negotiations could best be handled. There was general agreement in the Cabinet that President Wilson should be kept out of it, even though they knew very well he wanted to be the great man of any peace conference. The Prime Minister said 'he was somewhat apprehensive of President Wilson's intervention in this question. President Wilson was not making a success of his own war administration. All accounts agreed that matters were very behindhand in regard to the raising of men, construction of aircraft, shipbuilding, the provision of railway material for France, and the organisation of the American railways. In these circumstances, there was a real danger that the President might want to end the war, and might agree to conditions that we could not accept. It was plain from the proposals made through the King of Spain that President Wilson's conditions could be interpreted in a sense hostile to us.' The Foreign Secretary, Arthur Balfour, did point out that the President's four conditions 'were really platitudes, which could equally easily be interpreted in our favour.' What is interesting now is not the detail of those discussions, or the substance of Wilson's 'four conditions,' but the light thrown upon the attitudes prevailing within the British leadership. At a further meeting of the War Cabinet four days later, Balfour was to be found urging that Wilson should be kept informed 'with complete candour' of any action Britain might take over Austria, but it was pointed out that the President's interests 'were not identical with ours, and the interests of the British Empire were so vital, and concerned so many self-governing states, that the British Government could not devolve them upon anyone else.'

When the delegations assembled in Paris, then, there was, particularly among the British and French, this distrust of the President's intentions and a resentment of his intellectual and moral arrogance. Nevertheless, although Clemenceau presided over the main conference, Wilson's role as the great peacemaker was freely conceded. It was under his chairmanship that a committee was set up to draft the Covenant of the League of Nations, the statement of aims, responsibilities of membership, the rules by which it should conduct its business and the prescription for corporate action, which was at once the foundation-stone of the League and also the holy book to which, throughout its life, members so often turned for guidance and authority. The creation of the Covenant was the supreme work which had brought Woodrow Wilson to Paris. The word, 'Covenant,' he chose himself, because, he said, 'I am an old Presbyterian.' It was he who insisted that the drafting of the Covenant and the setting-up of the League of Nations should be an integral part of the business of the Peace Conference, indeed that it should be given major priority, taking precedence over even the most pressing of all the massive and bitter problems associated with the redrawing of borders and the award or surrender of territory. It was Wilson who said that there should be no distinction between the Covenant and the Versailles Treaty. They could not be considered as separate entities; nations which ratified the Treaty pledged themselves to observe the terms of the Covenant.

Given the haste with which the delegates were expected to put the world to rights and the animosities which were already beginning to fester, it would not have been surprising if the Covenant had been a shoddy, inadequate thing. The chances of its commanding universal confidence were not improved by the restriction of membership of the drafting committee to representatives of the Allied powers. Initially, too, it was weighted heavily in favour of the five great powers, the United States, France, Italy, Japan, and the British Commonwealth, each of which had two spokesmen, while five other countries, Belgium, Brazil, China, Portugal and Serbia, were allowed just one each. It was only after these smaller powers had protested that four more representatives, from Greece, Poland, Czechoslovakia and Rumania, were admitted. There was no question of neutrals being included, and even when they were consulted later it was only informally. The defeated had no say whatsoever. The way in which the Covenant was drafted and the League established lent substantial justification to the charge, which was frequently to be levelled by Germany, that the League of Nations was really no more than 'a victors' club.'

Yet the Covenant which that committee produced stands today, no less than it did in 1919, as a testament to the aspiration of man to govern his affairs by reason, to assert the concept of justice into the settlement of international disputes and to enshrine the collective interest of all nations a supreme above the interests of any group of nations or of any individual nation. It entrusted to the League the tasks of preventing disease and of fighting the evils of slavery, drug trafficking and prostitution. It envisaged international conventions which would oblige members to strive for the provision, throughout the world, of fair and humane conditions of labour. It advanced as 'a sacred trust of civilisation' the wellbeing and development of the people of former colonies, a trust which was to be undertaken by mandatory powers on behalf of the League. Seen against the background of history, and, not least relevantly, the recent history of Europe, it represented the magnificent endeavour of man to make a fresh start and to enter upon a new phase of his evolution as an intelligent animal. The Covenant was not a blueprint for Utopia; although it was certainly and consciously idealistic, it offered a framework for practical and effective co-operation between nations for their common good. That nations and individual statesmen did not live up to the standards set by the Covenant; that, ultimately, the aggressors spat upon it, does not debase it, nor diminish the achievement of those who conceived it.

The Covenant was of such a quality because of the quality of so many of the men who comprised the drafting committee, men of exceptional intellectual, professional and political talents. Outstandingly, there were Woodrow Wilson himself and Colonel Edward House, the President's closest associate and adviser; the two British Commonwealth representatives, General Smuts and Lord Robert Cecil; Léon Bourgeois for France, by then an old man but still an impressive influence, and the Italians, Orlando, the Prime Minister, and Vittorio Scialoja. The committee was also lucky to have two highly gifted legal advisers, one American, David Hunter Miller, and one British, Sir Cecil Hurst.

Many of the men serving on that committee had already given a lot of detailed thought to the idea of a League of Nations, for, although Wilson's advocacy of it was a decisive influence in its creation at the Peace Conference, no one man can be credited with the original concept. The notion evolved and developed over perhaps hundreds of years and derived new strength at times when men despaired most at the waste of war. Lord Robert Cecil, when receiving the Nobel Peace Prize in 1938, quoted what his father had said more than forty years before:

'The one hope that we have to prevent this competition from ending in a terrible effort of mutual destruction which will be fatal to Christian civilisation, the one hope we have is that the Powers may be gradually brought together to act together in a friendly spirit on all questions of difference which may arise until at last they shall be welded in some international constitution which shall give to the world as a result of their great strength a long spell of unfettered and prosperous trade and continued peace.'

Along similar lines was Theodore Roosevelt's statement in 1910: '. . . it would be a master-stroke if those great powers bent on peace would form a league of peace, not only to keep the peace among themselves, but to prevent, by force if necessary, its being broken by others.'

Norman Angell has told* of the formation in 1914 of the Union of Democratic Control, of whose executive committee Ramsay MacDonald, later to be the first Labour Prime Minister, was an original member. The Union said that the governing principle of British foreign policy should 'not be aimed at creating alliances for the purposes of maintaining the balance of power, but shall be directed to the establishment of a Concert of the Powers and the setting up of an International Council whose deliberations and decisions shall be public, part of the labour of such Council to be the creation of definite Treaties of Arbitration and the establishment of Courts for their interpretation and enforcement.' Norman Angell, undoubtedly, both by his writings and his personal contacts, through Colonel House, with Woodrow Wilson, stimulated the growth of the League idea. During the war, he fed Wilson several memoranda on the subject. That was at the time when American interest had been formalised in a 'League to Enforce Peace,' a movement to which leaders of both the Democratic and Republican parties subscribed and which sprouted branches throughout the United States.

Its counterpart in Britain was the League of Nations Society, which was founded within a few months of the outbreak of war. The idea gained ground within the political parties. In 1916, Lord Robert Cecil, then Minister of Blockade, wrote a memorandum, 'On proposals for diminishing the occasion of future wars' out of which grew eventual British Government support for the League concept; it also contributed substantially to the shape and substance of the Covenant. But, before he saw his ideas bear such fruit, Cecil had to suffer a deal of discouragement from his Government colleagues, which was only a foretaste

* *After All*, Hamish Hamilton, 1951. p. 192.

of what he was to endure during the years when he represented Britain at Geneva.

There were, for instance, two meetings of the Imperial War Cabinet (the British War Cabinet, strengthened by representatives of the Dominions) in the spring of 1917, at which the report of a committee set up under Lord Milner was discussed. Those discussions anticipated the arguments that were to continue for the next twenty years, arguments about how to achieve international disarmament or a limitation on armaments, and about what kinds of sanction could be imposed to enforce the decision of a League of Nations. At the first of the two meetings, on April 26th, 1917, the Prime Minister, Mr. Lloyd George, commented that the report had 'rather thrown cold water on the idea of a League,' which was not unexpected, coming from a committee dominated by that redoubtable imperialist Lord Milner, a Minister without Portfolio in the War Cabinet, a man now in his seventies and generally, though not invariably, reactionary in his opinions.

The Prime Minister said the committee had not dealt at all with the questions of disarmament or sanctions, and he considered there would be great disappointment if it were thought, at the end of the war, that nothing could be done. Cecil, who was acting Foreign Secretary at that moment, pointed out that he had advocated limitation of armaments in his memorandum, 'but he confessed that he had been driven out of his position by the criticisms in an examination of that memorandum by Sir Eyre Crowe.' Sir Eyre was an assistant under-secretary at the Foreign Office and his severe criticisms were reflective of the predictable scepticism of the professionals. In their exchanges, the members of the Imperial War Cabinet showed how well they appreciated the practical difficulties of achieving effective disarmament. There was the question of setting the level at which armaments were to be limited. They recognised that while 'the existence of our own dominating sea-power, coupled with the sea-power of America, was undoubtedly the best guarantee for peace,' one of the very first things which members of an international body would agree to cut down would be precisely that sea-power. They also perceived that the powers which were most likely to use their armaments to further their ambitions were the ones least willing to fall in wholeheartedly and honestly with any scheme for the limitation of armaments.

Dealing with the question of a League of Nations, Lord Robert said there were two main alternatives, either an international court of arbitration or a system of international conference and consultation. But even Cecil, who was to prove himself so dedicated a worker for the international idea, could then go on to say he did not believe that 'matters affecting the vital interests of the British Empire could possibly be submitted to the decisions of an international tribunal.'

Lord Milner said he did not believe any attempt to establish an international court would be successful or be a good thing in itself. He did, however, go along with Cecil's idea that no nation should go to war without submitting its case to a conference of all the powers. He thought that failure to do so should be a cause of war for all the powers which signed the next peace treaty. He considered that such a conference would have prevented war in 1914. Yet he also held that the conference could not be a court binding the nations which took part in it to enforce its decisions. Sir Robert Borden, the Canadian Prime Minister, reckoned that world public opinion must be the real basis of future peace; the war they were now fighting had demonstrated, he said, the futility of treaties and conventions when nations were determined to violate them—a truth which was to be learned again within less than a generation. Sir Robert considered that the United States and the British Empire could do more than anything else to maintain the peace of the world.

The Imperial War Cabinet continued discussing the Milner Committee report a few days later, and Cecil proposed that a clause should be inserted in the peace terms by which, in the event of any difference or controversy, a conference should be summoned forthwith. No action should be taken until the conference had deliberated, or for three months after its meeting, and each of the high contracting powers should bind itself to enforce this agreement by cutting off all financial and commercial intercourse from an offending power. General Smuts suggested that the precise nature of the sanction to be imposed would have to be worked out later and that, meanwhile, it would be sufficient if the Imperial War Cabinet expressed itself generally in favour of the principle of a sanction, and his colleagues agreed.

In what were to be the last months of the war, the discussions within the British War Cabinet and the Imperial War Cabinet about the League took on some sense of urgency. By this time, too, their ideas had taken more definite shape, following upon the report of another committee, under Lord Justice Phillimore, to which Lord Robert Cecil's memorandum had been referred. From this committee came a series of positive, detailed proposals for the creation of a League, but when the Imperial War Cabinet met on August 13th, 1918, the report of the committee, which had been submitted the previous March, had still not been published, because President Wilson had said he did not wish it to be, before making known his own views. In the discussions at that meeting of the IWC, Cecil showed his irritation at the delays and his apprehension about the kind of ideas to which they might be subjected from people who had just discovered an enthusiasm for the League concept. Cecil was always an idealist, but he was a politician, too, who wanted to see the scheme for a League, presented by the Phillimore Committee, make progress quickly.

'Of course,' said Cecil, 'I am very violently in favour of this scheme, but I am very anxious that we should not be left merely at the mercy of the various schemes put forward by people who have not thought very much about the subject, and who merely sit down and write a scheme of a League of Nations. Anyone can do that, and make a fairly good scheme; but it is only the people who have been into it who know what the practical difficulties are, who are in a position to do it satisfactorily. I do not say that the scheme we have is perfect, or that it is right or the best scheme, but I do think that it is a scheme that has been very carefully thought out and considered by competent men. It is moderate and goes only a little way, and if it is found possible to go further no one would be better pleased than I. What I am afraid of is that we shall be driven into a welter of faddist schemes which have no practical value at all, and that the whole idea will perish under that flood. I do think it would be of great importance now to have this as a kind of standard for people to work to, and to consider something which would stabilise and settle discussion on the subject. I quite agree we must not do anything which will antagonise or annoy the President in a matter of this kind, but I do think we ought to try and see now whether, on those kind of lines, he would object to its publication. I think it is important, and I am not sure that if you leave it to the Americans we shall do very well, because I do not think they have been able to give very much attention to it.'

'Very little,' agreed Lord Reading, the British Ambassador in Washington.

'And they do not know the atmosphere,' added Cecil, 'the immensely difficult atmosphere in which any scheme must be launched—in Europe, at any rate.'

'Before any publication takes place,' said Hughes, the Australian Prime Minister, 'I assume that it will be discussed here, and that the Government will have a policy on it?'

'You are very sanguine, Mr. Hughes,' said Cecil.

'. . . I only want to make this observation,' Lord Reading said, 'that the President, for some time, I do not mean at all for the future, but for some time, has been very cool about the League of Nations. He has definitely, to my knowledge, stopped a very big meeting which was to have taken place, and at which Mr. Taft, the president of the League to enforce Peace, and President Lowell, of Harvard University, and a number of very distinguished men, were going to speak, and he stopped it. In consequence, the meeting which had been called turned into what was called a "Win the War Convention," and, instead of a League of Nations meeting, you had a loud beating of drums for war. That has gained strength in America, and the other has lost strength as the war progresses . . .'

It would not have taken a very sensitive man to detect a lack of enthusiasm for the League at that Cabinet, and Cecil was not deceived by the lip-service paid to the idea, the protestations of support.

'I am afraid,' he said, 'it is only too evident that some of my colleagues do not want this scheme put forward.' But he had the general support of the Canadian Prime Minister.

'Even if I thought the proposal for a League of Nations was absolutely impracticable,' said Sir Robert Borden, 'and that statesmen a hundred years hence would laugh at it as a vain attempt to accomplish the impossible, nevertheless, I would support the movement because of its supreme purpose and because it might succeed. I think we ought to do our utmost to support it. I am heartily in support of it, but I do see the force of what the Prime Minister has said about the publication of the Phillimore Report, and I think we ought not to publish it at present if the President so requests.'

'That is only a question of a few weeks,' said Lord Reading, shifting his ground rather rapidly, 'but I know he is at work on it.'

'Does he propose to publish his memorandum?' asked Borden.

'No,' said Reading.

'Do you think he has got a desire to be the first on the platform?' Bonar Law, the Chancellor of the Exchequer, wanted to know.

'I don't think so,' said Reading. 'If he did, it would be——'

'Not improper,' Lord Balfour, the Foreign Secretary, cut in, 'but natural.'

'It would be improper,' said Reading, 'to hold us and prevent our publishing it until he has had the opportunity of publishing his.'

The Prime Minister then raised a point of fundamental importance to the League—the question of whether Germany was to be admitted to membership from the beginning. The answer to that question was to determine what kind of League was to be formed, and it was to have a considerable influence upon European history, certainly that of the next few years. In German minds, above all, it was to assume symbolic importance, for it involved the question of status, of equality with other nations.

'I have got the quotations which were sent me by a Member of the House of Commons from President Wilson's speeches about the League of Nations,' said Lloyd George, 'and they bear out what you said. I read them only yesterday. I was surprised to see him take the line he has taken. If these mean anything they mean the exclusion of Germany from the League of Nations until Germany has become a democracy in the British sense.'

'I think,' said Reading, 'that is very likely what you will find President Wilson will put forward.'

At a further meeting of the Imperial War Cabinet only two days later, the Prime Minister returned to the question of how to treat Germany, and expressed himself in terms oddly at variance with his previous sentiments. The tone he set now was the one which would be taken up more and more loudly in the months to come.

'I believe you will inflict upon them,' said Lloyd George to his colleagues, 'such a defeat as will enable you to dictate terms, and the terms that should be dictated ought, in my judgement, to be such as will mark the view which humanity takes of the heinousness of the offence committed by Germany. That is the only basis of any League of Nations. The League of Nations will start here. You will say: now this is the thing that will happen to any nation which repeats this offence in future. Unless you are able to do that this war is not won . . .'

It is plain from the evidence of the exchanges which took place within the British and Imperial War Cabinets that, with a very few exceptions, little hard thought had been given to the League. Questions, objections, platitudinous sentiments there were in plenty, but detailed proposals and constructive analysis were lacking. When the British Cabinet met on October 2nd, 1918, a memorandum about the League, written by the Labour politician, George Barnes, another Minister without Portfolio in the Coalition War Cabinet, was considered. Barnes was urging the practical examination of the idea of the League, and the achievement by the Allies 'of mutual understanding' on the subject. At present, he said, no precise views had been formulated. Meanwhile, the Germans were exploiting the idea, and it might be dangerous, he thought, to let them be the first in the field with definite proposals. Barnes believed that 'if the scheme of a League of Nations admitted the adherence of a democratic Germany, and this were made known to the German people, it might bring a satisfactory ending to the war appreciably nearer.'

Balfour said the main difficulty was the President of the United States; they were waiting to hear his views. Lord Reading said that he himself, like the President, attached great importance to the desirability of the question being discussed in the first instance between Great Britain and the United States alone, so that they could arrive at a working basis, before the matter went further.

Then the Cabinet turned again, briefly, to look at the question of how to enforce the will of the League, of what sanctions to apply against an aggressor. It was the question which was to be asked in one way or another, over and over again during the lifetime of the League; no satisfactory answer to which all member-nations could agree was ever found. At that meeting on October 2nd, Lord Reading saw the 'final sanction' as the crux, although he did not see it as a matter of principle. The difficulty, he said with prescience, was how to enforce the decrees of any international council or tribunal. The fact that Lord Curzon, a member of the inner Cabinet, should have asked for 'an early opportunity' for ministers to express their considered views 'on many difficult points raised in the Phillimore Report' is further evidence of how little serious discussion about the League there had been. The Phillimore Committee had rejected the idea of an international court, whose decisions would be enforced. Instead, the Committee recommended that international coercion should be applied only to enforce the holding of a conference, whose purpose would be to try to arrive at a pacific settlement of international disputes. Curzon felt, justifiably, that a number of vital questions were left hanging in the air: How were the decrees of the conference to be enforced? Was the necessary pressure to be military or economic in character? If it was to be military, was it to be mounted on an international basis? He also reverted to the problem of how to control armaments, military supplies and the like, which had concerned the Prime Minister at an earlier meeting. Then there was E. S. Montagu, the Secretary of State for India, who thought that, apart from sanctions, the most difficult problem was how the Allies were going to treat their enemies. 'Are we to have no peace with the Hohenzollerns, and are we to state that the German peoples are not to be admitted to the League at present, but might be later when deemed fit for admission?' Britain's colonies, said Montagu, would also have to be considered, and they would certainly not wish the Germans to be allowed to enter the League until they had given acceptable guarantees of their future good behaviour. The Cabinet generally agreed that any considerable delay in arriving at some positive conclusions about the League would be regrettable and decided to hold an early, informal meeting of ministers at the Foreign Office to explore the subject of the League, which would also give Lord Reading the chance to acquaint himself with the trend of Government views before his return to the United States. Lord Robert Cecil was asked to prepare another memorandum as a preliminary to that meeting, and Lord Reading was to do all he could, as soon as possible after arriving back in Washington, to talk privately and unofficially with the President, making it quite clear to Wilson that their conversations would not commit His Majesty's Government to any agreement, nor to any definite line of action.

There were many apprehensions and reservations in the minds of the Government about the price Britain would have to pay for belonging to the League, and, as the war neared its end and the Allies prepared for their discussions at Paris, the suspicion that what Woodrow Wilson was aiming at was not necessarily congenial to British interests showed no sign of fading. At its meeting on October 26th, 1918, for instance, the War Cabinet was unanimous in its opposition to the principle of 'freedom of the seas.' This was one of the famous Fourteen Points, defined by Wilson, in his address to Congress of January 8th, 1918, as the chief war aims of the United States. These points included general provisions for the setting up of a League 'for the purpose of affording mutual guarantees of political independence and territorial integrity to great and small states alike.' Trade barriers were to be removed, armaments cut down, diplomacy conducted out in the open where the people could see and hear what was being done in their name. All but one of the President's Fourteen Points came to be accepted by the Allied powers, though not without misgivings which were to be revived later. One point, however, was never accepted; Britain was determined that Wilson's call for 'freedom of the seas,' except where League action might close them, should not be one of the principles to which the League of Nations should be committed.

At that Cabinet meeting just a couple of weeks before the war ended, the only question was how to tell the President without hurting his feelings too much. Lloyd George and his colleagues agreed it would be better not to try to do so in a telegram, and so they decided that the Prime Minister and Balfour should sound out the views of the other Allies and sense the general atmosphere of the Paris Conference on the subject, and then, at their discretion, 'make it perfectly clear to the Conference that we do not accept the doctrine of the freedom of the seas and that a notification to this effect must be made in some form to Germany before we enter into peace negotiations.' Not that the British were under any illusion about the likely reaction of their Allies on this point. As Balfour said during the discussion, he pictured the position at the Conference 'as a difficult one.' All our Allies, he said, were grateful for British sea-power, but they were also afraid of it. The tradition of all continental jurists had been that naval international law was made to suit our sea-power. 'They have always tried to limit it,' said Balfour, 'first at the Conference at Paris in 1856, and later at the Conference at London. Moreover, all the permanent officials in the Chancelleries, who have great influence, are opposed to us on this point.' Nevertheless, the British resolved to stand firm. They would go a long way with Wilson, but when it came to essential British interests they reckoned they had a better understanding of them than he had. The Foreign Office was given the job, in advance of the Paris Conference, of combing through Wilson's Notes to Germany in which he laid down the bases for peace negotiations. The purpose of the search was to 'ascertain whether there were any more doubtful points besides the freedom of the seas and the clause dealing with economic considerations, which were either ambiguous or harmful to the interests of this country.'

Yet another indication of how little serious forethought was given to the League is to be found in the Prime Minister's remarks to the Imperial War Cabinet on November 26th, 1918:

'We want to know your views as to the kind of League of Nations which we ought to recommend,' said Lloyd George. 'The Government has no views apart from the War Cabinet. All we have done is to commit ourselves to the principle, but we have no definite scheme as to how to carry it out . . . Therefore, it is open for anyone to make suggestions.' One man had several suggestions to make, chiefly concerned with what kind of League it should not be: the uninhibited Australian Prime Minister, William Morris (Billy) Hughes, the enemy of all visionaries, among whom he gave high priority to H. G. Wells. Hughes was a Welshman, who emigrated to Australia when he was twenty, and worked as a farmhand, a seaman and a labour organiser, before entering the Australian parliament. His speech was as bluff as his background suggests, and he was the kind of aggressive imperialist which Australia used to breed so incomparably and so prolifically. The Cabinet minutes do not record any expressions of sympathy with his views, but nor do they show any sense of outrage among his colleagues. They may well have found some private amusement in him, but it is also likely that, though he carried opposition to Wilsonian ideas to the extreme, he gave voice to opinions which others there would have liked to express had they not been more conscious than he of the practical politics of the forthcoming Paris Conference.

'I will put my views forward for what they are worth,' said Hughes, with a momentary but scarcely credible gesture of humility. 'It is a big question . . . I object altogether to President Wilson's scheme of a League of Nations. Where does it end? I don't know. It would appear that there is no substantial difference between his view and that of Wells. That is to say, he wants some sort of world-state, in fact a Utopia, in which all nations would have to surrender some of their self-governing rights. There is to be an international police and there is to be a navy and an army, and so on, for this purpose. But it will not bear examination for ten minutes. It is a very obvious thing that no country will allow for a moment its vital interests to be decided by anybody but itself. I speak with some considerable experience of what nations will do in that direction, and those who shout loudest for international arbitration will stand most rigidly on their own rights when a vital right is threatened.'

The last thing Hughes could ever be accused of was hypocrisy, as he showed as he went on to illustrate the dangers of a League of Nations to the land closest to his heart, Australia. He knew the kind of Australia he wanted, and he wanted no interference with it by any international body.

'Let us ask ourselves,' he said, 'if Great Britain would agree to interference by any council of nations as regards the size of her navy. Certainly not. I will take the case which affects Australia with regards to this League of Nations. You have Japan and China, which are desirous that their people should be allowed to settle in Australia, which is a continent capable of holding 100

million people. There are, at present, only five million. We have
no moral right at all to refuse any more than you have in regard
to India. We have got Australia and we are going to hold it, and
we say to the world in respect to this 100 million of people, "You
shall not come in here," but we have no moral right to say anything of the sort. This is all right now, Great Britain's navy and
the power of the Empire keeps out the Japanese and the Chinese,
but the League of Nations, as I interpret what is meant, would
absolve these things, and moral right would become the only
touchstone by which every claim would have to be met. The
white Australia policy would come up, for example, and Japan
would say, "We want to come into your country," and we
would reply, "No." The question would then be taken to the
League of Nations. By what right can five million people usurp
territory that would feed 100 million? You have no moral right
at all. Therefore, they come in. But whilst Australia had a leg
to stand on she would fight . . .

'The right of Great Britain to India might come up. What
sort of right is it? It comes up before the League of Nations, and
200 million make their voice heard. They say, "What right have
you now to India, since we have had this war for liberty? We
want to govern ourselves, not by the methods of Montagu, which
is to come by degrees, but by a decision of the Council of
Nations." You cannot agree,' Hughes told his colleagues, 'to
any League of Nations which might do anything of the sort. The
League of Nations which we could agree to would be a League
binding together the United States and Great Britain—I don't
care how closely—and possibly France and Italy and such other
nations as you may think proper. If America and Great Britain
were to stand together the peace of the world would be assured.
If France would come in, it would be trebly assured, and there
would be no danger of any war and no danger of any friction . . .
I do not care what sort of a League you have; and you could have
a great Anglo-Saxon Empire if you liked. That would assure the
peace of the world. I think it would be workable, and we should
be bound together, not by any Utopian scheme, but by ties of
blood, of common history and of common purpose. You would
find that the American thinks very nearly like the Englishman.
At any rate, he thinks very much like the Canadian and the

Australian, and we are all cousins.' As he came to the end of his magnificent exhibition of jingoism, he obviously repented his earlier concession to certain, relatively acceptable foreigners, for he added:

'It seems to me that, if necessary, a League of Nations might leave France out of account and also Italy. The League of Nations, in my opinion, that will ensure the peace of the world, is the League of Nations whose history and traditions and ideals are nearly alike, and a League which will not interfere with the internal government of each particular member.'

Happily, from the point of view of the League, at any rate, there was, within the Imperial War Cabinet, another representative of the British Commonwealth, a man of very different outlook from Hughes, and a man whose views were to influence deeply, not only the British Cabinet, but also President Wilson and the Peace Conference itself. That man was Jan Christian Smuts. Smuts was born in Cape Colony, and it was in that territory, as supreme commander of the Boer forces, that he proved himself an audacious commando leader in the war against the British. But Smuts was not anti-British, and all his inclinations were to work to bring together the peoples of the world—or the white peoples, at least. After fighting in the campaign in German South-west Africa, and commanding the Allied troops in German East Africa, it was as his country's defence minister that General Smuts came to Britain in 1917 to join the Imperial War Cabinet. This short, sparely-built man, with the little beard, a man of first-class intellect and relentless physical self-discipline, was to emerge as an outstanding world figure.

The decisive contribution which Smuts made to the creation of the League of Nations was a 'brilliant pamphlet,' as Cecil was to describe it, in which he took up the several proposals for the League, including Cecil's own, and elaborated them, giving them a new strength, a new comprehensiveness, which derived from his own encompassing and mountain-top vision of mankind's progress. His pamphlet was called, 'The League of Nations: A Practical Suggestion.'* It is worth quoting substantially from it, both to show the quality of Smuts's mind, and also to show

* Quoted in *Jan Christian Smuts* by his son, J. C. Smuts, Cassell, 1952. pp. 214-18.

what kind of organisation the League of Nations might have been.

'If the League is ever to be a success it will have to occupy a much greater position, and perform many other functions besides those ordinarily assigned to it . . .

'. . . It is not sufficient for the League merely to be a sort of deus ex machina called in in very grave emergencies when the spectre of war appears; if it is to last, it must be much more. It must become part and parcel of the common international life of States, it must be an ever visible, living, working organ of the policy of civilisation. It must function so strongly in the ordinary peaceful intercourse of States that it becomes irresistible in their disputes; its peace activity must be the foundation and guarantee of its war power . . .

'The new situation does not call for a new talking-shop. We want an instrument of government which, however much talk is put into it at the one end, will grind out decisions at the other end . . .'

When he came to consider what sanctions should be applied against an aggressor nation, General Smuts recognised, as the statesmen of the 1930s did not, or would not, that there could be no limit, if there was to be an effective deterrent. It could not be confined even to a complete trade and financial boycott:

'. . . I do not think the League is likely to prove a success unless in the last resort the maintenance of the moratorium is guaranteed by force. The obligation of the members of the League to use force for this purpose should therefore be absolute, but the amount of the force and the contribution from the members should be left to the recommendation of the Council to the respective Governments . . .

'. . . Mankind is once more on the move. The very foundations have been shaken and loosened, and things are again fluid. The tents have been struck, and the great caravan of humanity is once more on the march. Vast social and industrial changes are coming, perhaps upheavals which may, in their magnitude and effects, be comparable to war itself. A steadying, controlling, regulating influence will be required to give stability to progress, and to remove that wasteful friction which has dissipated so much social force in the past, and in this war more than ever before. These great functions could only be adequately fulfilled by the League of Nations. Responding to such vital needs and coming at such a unique opportunity in history, it may well be destined to mark a new era in the Government of Man, and become to the peoples the guarantee of Peace, to the workers of all races the great International, and to all the embodiment and living expression of the moral and spiritual unity of the human race.'

Whatever the causes of the eventual failure of the League of Nations, it was not a lack of vision to guide it from the outset. But of the three most powerful men at the Peace Conference, Lloyd George, Clemenceau and Wilson, one seemed to change his image of the League, though not his general support for some sort of League, almost from day to day; the second was profoundly sceptical of grandiloquent sentiments and inspirational visions, but was prepared to go along with any proposition which seemed to serve the one thing that mattered to him, the achievement of French security from future invasion; the third was, without doubt, impelled by a passionate belief in his own destiny as the man of peace, the man chosen to sire the League of Nations, a message of moral uplift never far from his lips, for so long curiously infirm in his thoughts about just what kind of League there ought to be and what powers it ought to possess, and then, later, disastrously rigid about it.

A brief exchange between Lloyd George and Curzon at the Imperial War Cabinet meeting of November 20th, 1918, following conversations in Paris the previous week between Curzon and Clemenceau, was illuminating about all three men's attitude towards the League. Clemenceau, Curzon reported, favoured a trial of the ex-Kaiser.

'As we all hoped that a League of Nations would emerge from this war,' said Curzon, 'would it not be really a great act of initiation if the first step that would really call the League of Nations in an effective manner into being should be an act of justice taken by the world as a whole . . .'? A few moments later, Lloyd George picked up the idea of the League as an instrument of justice.

'. . . With regard to the question of international law,' said the Prime Minister, 'well, we are making international law, and all we can claim is that international law should be based on justice. I think if we demanded this man, if he is not responsible, he could then make his case. The League of Nations is a committee either of diplomats or statesmen, but this ought to be a judicial tribunal which should be set up by the Allies. . . .'

'It was M. Clemenceau's view,' said Curzon, 'that if the nations set up this tribunal a League of Nations will be in existence, and this will be its first act. . . .'

On December 13th, 1918, just over four weeks after the signing of the armistice, President Wilson, escorted by a vast array of American and French warships, welcomed by 21-gun salutes and military bands, sailed into Brest harbour. The Peace Conference was not ready for him—and perhaps he was not really ready for it—but he soon bent himself to enriching European audiences with his thoughts. By now, the Imperial War Cabinet had held several long and serious discussions about the establishment of the League, with impressive contributions from both General Smuts and Lord Robert Cecil. At one of these meetings, just before the end of the year, the IWC considered a report in the *Observer* of an address on December 21st at the Sorbonne by President Wilson, acknowledging the conferment of an honorary degree:

'My conception of the League of Nations is just this: that it shall operate as the organising moral force of men throughout the world, and that whenever, or whatever, wrong and aggression are planned or contemplated, this searching light of conscience will be turned upon them, and men everywhere will ask, "What are the purposes that you hold in your heart against the fortunes of the world?" Just a little exposure will settle most questions. If the Central Powers had dared to discuss the whole purposes of this war for a single fortnight it never would have happened, and if, as should be, they were forced to discuss it for a year, war would never have been conceivable.'

Winston Churchill, then Minister of Munitions, offered a characteristic comment. A League of Nations, he said, could be no substitute for national defences. He believed in a complete and intimate understanding between France, America and Great Britain, which would be a basis on which a League could be erected. Lord Reading reckoned that too much was being asked of the League at the start. He wanted the idea of a League to be treated seriously as something which would lead to the prevention of wars in the future, but to try to guard at this stage against the causes of future wars was to doom the League of Nations to failure. No country, said Reading, would give up her complete security without knowing how the League was going to work. When the Prime Minister tried to sum up he showed, whatever his own uncertainties, his awareness of the extent of popular feeling for the League. He agreed with Cecil, he said, that if it were not set up, as a result of the Peace Conference, there would be profound disappointment in this country, even profound anger. Any Government that dared to set up a League that was not real would be sternly dealt with by the people, and 'sooner rather than later.' If the League did not include some provision for disarmament it would be regarded as a sham. Without some check on armaments there would be the greatest disappointment among the people. Disarmament, said Lloyd George, would be regarded as the real test of whether the League of Nations was a farce, or whether business was meant. He did not agree with those who considered that the League would not stop war. In his own lifetime there had been three great European wars; in his opinion all three would have been stopped if a League of Nations such as he contemplated had been in existence. Of the war that had just ended, the Prime Minister said that if regular, permanent international machinery had existed, Germany could not have refused a summons to attend. Could anyone, he asked, imagine that in those circumstances the dispute would not have been settled? But in summing up the views of the Imperial War Cabinet about what the extent of the League's powers should be, he said there was, if not disagreement, at least considerable hesitation and doubt about how far it should go. Lloyd George himself did nothing to give a lead.

On December 30th, Lloyd George reported to the IWC on the conversations he and Balfour had had with Woodrow Wilson, during the President's triumphal visit to Britain.

The President, said Lloyd George, had opened at once with the question of the League and had given the impression that that was the only thing he really cared much about. His mind was apparently travelling in very much the direction of the proposals advocated by Lord Robert Cecil and General Smuts. Wilson had no definite formal scheme in mind, said the Prime Minister, and was certainly not contemplating anything in the nature of giving executive powers to the League. But the President was anxious that the League of Nations should be the first subject discussed at the Peace Conference. Both he (the Prime Minister) and Balfour were inclined to agree, on the ground that this would ease other matters, such as questions of the 'freedom of the seas,' the disposal of the German colonies and economic issues. The President, having attained his object, could then say that those matters could be left to be worked out by the League of Nations. Also the President might have to go back to America before the Conference concluded; if so, he would want to be able to tell the American people that he had achieved his purpose of creating the League.

The Australian Prime Minister once more gave his colleagues the benefit of his trenchant views. If we were not very careful, said Hughes, we should find ourselves dragged quite unnecessarily behind the wheels of President Wilson's chariot. He readily acknowledged the part which America had played in the war. But it was not such as to entitle President Wilson to be the 'god in the machine' at the peace settlement and to lay down the terms on which the world would have to live in the future. The United States, said Hughes, had made no money sacrifice at all. They had not even exhausted the profits which they had made in the first two and a half years of the war. Their sacrifices in men were not even equal to Australia's, and, relatively, their sacrifices had been nothing like as great as those of Australia. America had given neither the material nor the moral help which entitled her to come before France. The blunt Mr. Hughes was, indeed, laying it on thick, and he must have regretted the lack of any American in his audience. He hoped, he said, that Great Britain and France, which had both sacrificed so much, would defend their own interests and not let their future be decided for them by one who had no claim to speak even for his own country.

Referring to the general election—the so-called Khaki Election —held in Britain earlier that month, Hughes said that the British Prime Minister had received an overwhelming vote from his fellow-countrymen, not only in recognition of what he had done, but because of their confidence that he would see to it their sacrifices had not been made in vain. In taking up that line at the Peace Conference, Lloyd George would have not only all England, but more than half America behind him. He and Clemenceau could settle the peace of the world as they liked. They could give to America the respect due to a great nation which had entered the war somewhat late, but had rendered great service. It was intolerable, however, Hughes considered, for Wilson to dictate to them how the world was to be governed. If the saving of civilisation had depended on the United States, he said, it would that day have been in tears and chains. The Australian premier again gave it as his view that, if a League of Nations was to endure and weather the storms of time, it would have to be a thing like the British Empire, framed in accordance with historical associations and practical needs. President Wilson, on the other hand, said Hughes, had no practical scheme at all, and no proposals which would bear the test of experience. The League of Nations was to him what a toy was to a child—he would not be happy till he got it. The President's one idea was to go back to America and say he had achieved it, and then everything else could be left for the League to complete. The Australian Prime Minister did not consider that the peace of the world could be settled on terms of 'leave it all to the schedule.' To start with a League of Nations and then continually refer everything to this League would mean giving up the substance for the shadow. The League, said Hughes, 'should be the gilded ball on the dome of the cathedral, and not the foundation-stone.'

On this occasion, Hughes found support from no less a figure than Curzon, who thought the Australian's views were also shared by many other members of the Imperial War Cabinet. In particular, Curzon thought that Lloyd George should remember the power he possessed, not merely as a result of the recent election, but of all the sacrifices made by the British Empire and of the interests it had at stake all over the world. While holding the opinion, said Curzon, that the future fortunes of the world must largely depend on co-operation between England and America, he did feel that, if Wilson persisted in the line he had been reported as taking, then it might be necessary, on some issues at any rate, for the British Prime Minister to work at the Conference in alliance with Clemenceau.

Those, then, were the kinds of opinion being expressed by British and Commonwealth leaders. They were convinced that President Wilson's determination to see the League set up was so obsessional—'a matter of life and death to him,' as Lloyd George described it—that, provided they went along with him on that, he would make concessions on the things that mattered most to them. But what did ordinary people really expect the Paris Conference to achieve? Lloyd George, who professed to understand popular feelings and knew the way to exploit them better than most, spoke often of the deep desire for a League and for disarmament. But, if he were to reflect truly the emotions of his countrymen, he was also going to Paris to satisfy their craving for revenge. During the election, candidates of all parties had outbid each other in their promises to see that Germany was wiped off the map, squeezed dry, rendered penniless, made to suffer every conceivable humiliation, as her punishment for having made war. Lloyd George had submitted to the popular mood; indeed, he could justly be said deliberately to have inflamed it to ensure his own victory. 'They must pay to the uttermost farthing, and we shall search their pockets for it,' he had said, although in the privacy of Cabinet meetings he expressed his doubts about Germany's capacity actually to pay 'all the indemnity we had a right to demand.' Because Lloyd George was anything but a fool, he must also have acknowledged to himself that the consequence of forcing Germany economically to her knees could only be one of general disaster.

The theme of retribution was one which Clemenceau and the French were entirely content to pursue. The old enemy must be bled. Above all, whether it be through the League of Nations or by any other means, France must be guaranteed her security from German aggression. It was France which had suffered. It was French land which had been invaded and ravaged. It was French villages and towns which had been shattered. It was France, not the United States or Britain, which knew what living next door to Germany really meant. All Clemenceau cared about was making sure that France would never again be the victim of German invasion. The old French leader stayed outside any discussions about the League; he was content to leave French participation in its formation to others, in particular to Léon

Bourgeois, for many years the champion of the League idea, and the author, as early as 1908, of a book called *Société des Nations*. At the Paris Conference, Bourgeois pressed time and again for the Covenant to contain a provision for the establishment of an international force to back up League decisions and act as the deterrent which Smuts had seen as necessary. But, despite Smuts's presence on the drafting committee, Bourgeois was unable to persuade the British or American delegations to agree, and neither would they accept his lesser claim for an international general staff, at least, capable of preparing for military action in support of the Covenant.

The mood of the Paris Conference induced deep pessimism in many who observed the bitter insistence on vengeance, the squalid prosecution of national interests, the petty wranglings between men from whom a more than human greatness was demanded. It was not a scene to inspire hope for the future. Yet it did produce the Covenant of the League of Nations.

2

'A living thing is born'

When Woodrow Wilson said of the Covenant, with his instinct for forging the historically memorable phrase, 'A living thing is born,' he was speaking prematurely in more than one sense. He said it of the first draft for a League produced by the committee set up under his chairmanship. Remarkably, that draft had been agreed within eleven days of the committee's first meeting, but it had now to come before the plenary conference, presided over by Clemenceau, and before it was to be adopted it had to undergo considerable changes; the League itself was not to be born until a year later. Furthermore, when at last the League of Nations was born, Wilson was not there to see it, and the United States had no part in it. Some historians have argued that it would have made no difference to the League or the history of Europe even if the United States had assumed the role, the pre-eminent role in the League, Wilson had always envisaged for it; but that is wilful cynicism. Had America been fully involved in the League and had accepted all the responsibilities and obligations that would have entailed, France would not have suffered from that chronic sense of insecurity which was a major influence in shaping international relationships up to the time when Hitler took over in Germany. Nor would the League have lacked the power and the will to deter military adventures or to enforce its decisions. One need only make the obvious comparison with American policy after the Second World War to prove what might have been. If Woodrow Wilson had not become President of the

United States in 1916, there might never have been a League of Nations at all. For all the significance of the work done by Smuts and Cecil and others, it was the insistent, driving power of Wilson, as President, which forced the question of the League into its priority position at the Paris Conference. How far the other Allied leaders would have pursued the idea, not merely at Paris, but, earlier, within their own Cabinets, if there had not been American pressure, is extremely doubtful. Yet, paradoxically, if Woodrow Wilson had not been President, the United States might have accepted the Treaty of Versailles and joined the League.

Quite simply, Woodrow Wilson put people's backs up. He could make men and women adore him, he could move them to tears, he could lift his finger and they would follow him, but he could also be insufferably pig-headed and his presumption of superior knowledge and divine guidance often outraged those who had to do business with him. There was, for instance, the occasion at Paris, when the Peace Conference had been meeting for nearly four months and tempers were eruptive. Wilson always claimed to understand 'the people' better than other statesmen, not just the American people but all peoples. He had spent only three days in Italy in the whole of his life, but that did not stop him, at one particularly touchy moment, from snapping at Orlando, the Italian Prime Minister, 'I know the Italian people better than you do.' That was the authentic voice of the American crusader, the man who said, 'I know that Europe is still governed by the same reactionary forces . . . But I am satisfied that if necessary I can reach the people of Europe over the heads of their rulers.' All suffered alike, Orlando, Clemenceau, Lloyd George, he riled them all, lecturing them, chiding them for the narrow selfishness of their demands. None denied him the judgement seat, however. He was the great peacemaker, to whom all the world brought its problems. The persecuted, the dispossessed, the greedy and the ambitious, they all came to court his favours, and it seemed at times as though just that one man was remaking the map of the world. He had little time even for his own advisers. When others took time off from the fevered conference rooms, Wilson went on working, day after day, week after week, and the harder and longer he worked, the more strained and tetchy and intolerant of argument he became, splintering his relationship with the great men of Europe. He held them there with him, in the last resort, by threats to pack up and quit the Conference They took the threat seriously, for, whatever their resentment of the American President, they knew they must put up with him, his person represented the promise of continuing American involvement in Europe, the security of American military strength and the insurance of American wealth. And so it was that, despite all the wrangling, the frequent ruptures, the bitterness and the anger, the Versailles Treaty was made, the world put to a sort of rights, and the Covenant adopted. But Woodrow Wilson could not keep the promise on which so much of it depended. Some have seen the story of Wilson's failure to carry his people with him into the League of Nations as a noble tragedy. It was a tragedy, certainly, but it is hard at this distance, knowing the consequences of Wilson's inflexibility, to appreciate the nobility of it. The tragedy was much of his own making, but its effects were to engulf all mankind.

If the United States were to enter the League of Nations, President Wilson must first sell the Covenant, and the Treaty, of which it was part, to a Congress where he faced Republican majorities in both the Senate and the House of Representatives. That fact did not mean he was bound to be defeated. There were many moderates among the Republicans in the Senate—which is where the crucial battles had to be fought—who might be persuaded to give the President the support he needed, and there were others, among them ex-President William Howard Taft, who were positive advocates of the League. But, undoubtedly, it was a question of the President winning votes, and Wilson had done as much as any one man could to lose sympathy among Republicans. During the mid-term elections in 1918, he broke a wartime political truce between the parties by making an appeal to the American people to send him to Paris with a Democratic majority in both the House and the Senate. The Republicans resented his action and so, too, apparently, did the American people; at any rate, it was the Republicans who triumphed. Then there was Wilson's failure to take a single major Republican with him in the delegation to the Peace Conference. Had he taken one, Wilson might well have ignored him, as he ignored his Democratic advisers, but at least he would have acknowledged, by his gesture, that the Republican party had a right to share in the making of the peace. Consequently, the principle and the substance of the Covenant apart, there was a personal hostility towards the President among the Republican senators. There was, also, as Wilson discovered when he made a brief trip to the United States at the end of February, 1919, a growing opposition, both in Congress and in the country, to the idea of America being involved in the League of Nations, and there was one man, above all others, who was determined to foster that opposition, to canalise and direct it, to bring about the defeat and the humiliation of Woodrow Wilson. That man was Senator Henry Cabot Lodge, the chairman of the Senate Foreign Relations Committee —a key role—and Wilson's implacable enemy.

Lodge's hatred of Wilson—which was reciprocated—is usually attributed to a personal clash at an earlier stage in their lives and aggravated by Lodge's jealousy of Wilson's success. As politicians, their relationship had been characterised by the sharpest of conflict. Now Lodge, an outstandingly clever man and one who was a master of political in-fighting, planned and organised his revenge, while Wilson, in Paris, haggled and drove himself on into the deepest exhaustion. By the time the President returned to the United States in July, his work in Europe finished at last, he found the opposition much stronger and much more vocal. It came from many different quarters and sometimes joined together, temporarily, those who, on any other issue, would have been hostile to each other. It ranged from those professing extreme isolationism, believing that the concern of the United States should begin and end on the American continent, to those who held that the Covenant agreed at Paris was too weak an instrument for the enforcement of peace. In between came groups objecting to particular aspects of the peace settlement, such as the one allowing Japan to hang on to rights and concessions in Shantung which she had seized from Germany. The Italian-Americans said the President should have backed Italy in its demand to be given the port of Fiume; the Italian delegation had walked out of the Paris Conference in protest when it failed to get what it wanted. The German-Americans were far from alone in their shock and indignation at the severity of the treatment Germany was to receive from the Allies.

When President Wilson went to the Senate in that summer of 1919 to ask for approval and ratification of the Treaty and the Covenant, he did so in a way which played further into Lodge's hands. He had not come to persuade, but to receive the grateful affirmation of the Senate. The time for arguing was over; he, the President, had done all the arguing at Paris, and he, the President, had agreed the terms on behalf of his countrymen. His opponents he lashed with contempt, deriding their 'poor little minds,' refusing to demean himself by contact with them.

Lodge played his hand well. He refused to commit the folly, urged upon him by extremists like Senator William Borah, of calling for an outright rejection of Wilson's peace terms. What Lodge did was to formulate a number of amendments and 'reservations'; there was a provocative mockery about his catalogue of precisely fourteen reservations. Those amendments and reservations were incorporated in a majority report of the Foreign Relations Committee, which examined the Treaty and Covenant, before they were considered by the Senate as a whole: the report was prepared by Lodge. The Senate was not prepared to go all the way with Lodge. Indeed, it rejected each of his formal amendments by a clear majority. But there was considerable sympathy with certain of his reservations and the way Lodge chose to oppose the President was the way likely to cause Wilson the maximum political embarrassment. What he did was to frame a resolution calling upon the Senate to ratify the Treaty and, at the same time, to accept his fourteen reservations. Senator Borah feared that Wilson, and hence his supporters in the Senate, would be willing to accept these reservations for the sake of getting the United States into the League. But Lodge, who was just as determined as Borah to keep America out of the League, knew his man. Woodrow Wilson would, in any event, have been loath to compromise. He felt he had made concessions enough in the horse-trading he had had to do with his Allies at Paris, and the idea of going back to them again, asking them to agree to changes in the Treaty he himself had done so much to frame, would have been most unpalatable to him. The identification of those changes with Lodge made it certain that he would reject them. Similarly, although Lodge was a resolute opponent of America's commitment to the League, and he was ambitious of attaining the highest office himself, he might have been less ruthless and less destructive had the President been other than Woodrow Wilson.

To be fair to Wilson, some of Lodge's reservations were so substantial it is doubtful whether he would have been able to get the Allies to accept them. One of them would have taken away the right, which the British Empire delegation had won in the face of strong resistance, including Wilson's, for the self-governing dominions to vote as individual members of the League. Another would have deprived Japan of the former German rights in Shantung. But whatever his feelings about those and lesser reservations, there was one which Wilson felt would destroy the League as he had conceived it. Lodge wanted to water down drastically American obligations under Article 10 of the Covenant. Article 10 read:

'The Members of the League undertake to respect and preserve as against external aggression the territorial integrity and existing political independence of all Members of the League. In case of any such aggression or in case of any threat or danger of such aggression the Council shall advise the means by which this obligation shall be fulfilled.'

The British Empire delegation had mounted strong, but unsuccessful, opposition to the wording of this article at the Conference. They considered it too rigid in its perpetuation of the *status quo*, no matter what pressures and good reasons there might be for peaceful change and the revision of treaties. Wilson was adamant. This was the fulfilment of his aim to bring the protection of the League to the weak and defenceless nations against the mighty and greedy ones. It glorified him in the image of the Great Father. Cabot Lodge interpreted Article 10 as placing the United States under a comprehensive obligation to send American troops to all parts of the world as League of Nations policemen. There is no doubt that France and other countries represented at the Peace Conference saw it in much the same way, for they joined Wilson in rejecting the British arguments. In the United States, there were many, who, while wanting America to join the League, were anxious about the general nature of the commitment under Article 10. Lodge proposed that it should be the right of Congress to examine each and every case where American action might be called for.

Wilson would have nothing to do with the reservations. Close associates, like the faithful Colonel House, urged him to compromise to save his League of Nations. Wilson spurned compromise, because compromise was ignoble and because compromise would murder the League. He tried to win over enough individual senators to give him the votes he needed, but too many of them told him he must make concessions to carry the Senate. He still refused. He would not bend his knee to Lodge; he would fight him.

The President had boasted that he could reach the people of Europe over the heads of their rulers. Now he decided he must reach the people of the United States over the heads of the men they had elected. He would force the Senate to ratify the Treaty and the Covenant, as they stood, by rallying public opinion behind him. He must make the people understand how precious was this League of Nations, which the politicians were threatening to cripple with their compromises. He was aware, through newspaper editorials and reports that came to him privately, of the mounting success of Lodge's campaign: the people were turning against their President. The President, then, must go to his people and show them once more the road, the right road, they must follow.

However vainglorious Woodrow Wilson may seem today, there is no denying his great courage. The months at Paris, and now the political struggle in the broiling, enervating heat of a Washington summer, had drained him of his strength. What he needed was rest. What he chose was the daunting challenge of a four weeks' speaking tour, living in the Presidential train, covering nearly ten thousand miles, one big, set speech virtually every day, plus several whistle-stop speeches, a programme which demanded that he give himself to the people, hour after hour after hour. There was, unquestionably, a grandeur about the sacrifice this grey, gaunt, asthmatic of sixty-four prepared to make, as, with his wife, a small band of personal and political servants, his team of bodyguards and an attendant corps of pressmen, he boarded his train to head west. His wife, his doctor, his friends, had all told him he should not go; Woodrow Wilson had said he must.

The people came to their President. He shook their hands, he listened to their stories of sons lost in battle, he offered them a message of hope. He told them why there must be a League of Nations, and why the United States must have a leading part in it. That was what America had fought for, the League of Nations was the justification and the reward for the loss of their sons' lives. He reached out to their hearts over the heads of his enemies. Often, they were waiting for him, waiting to mob him as their heroic leader. Sometimes, he had to face their jeers and taunts, for Lodge and Borah and their followers had also been out at work among the people. He became more and more tired, his voice grew weaker, but he bullied himself on, rejecting suggestions that he should break his tour and rest.

It was at Pueblo, Colorado, where he spoke to a crowd of some ten thousand that he was struck down by a thrombosis. It was his twenty-fourth day aboard the train, and he was nearing the end of the tour. He never finished it. The train turned back to Washington. A few days after he had returned to the White House, he suffered a second thrombosis. He was completely paralysed on his left side. For weeks afterwards, he could do no more than whisper. His mind was also affected. Whether this was the second or third thrombosis—it was thought later that he had suffered a first one in April at the Peace Conference—his doctor considered that the President's brain had been seriously damaged. The story of Wilson's last seventeen months in office has been told in dramatic detail by the American historian, Gene Smith.* What concerns us here is only how the President's illness affected America's relationship with the League of Nations, and the truth seems to be that if there had ever been the slightest chance of Wilson agreeing to any form of compromise, it was now gone. On the rare occasions he received anyone during the first weeks of his illness—crucial weeks in the Senate battle for the League—he refused to listen to any talk about making concessions. 'No compromise,' he insisted in his hoarse voice. 'No compromise.' His old associate, Colonel House, wrote to him, urging him to accept the reservations, arguing that they would not prevent the League from developing into 'a workable machine.' The President never even saw House's letters. Mrs.

* *When the Cheering Stopped*, Hutchinson, 1964.

Wilson never gave them to him. The First Lady protected her husband from anything which might agitate and perturb him. She knew his mind, and she interpreted his wishes to the outside world. She, too, said there could be no compromise. Astonishing and alarming though the story is of her behaviour during the time Wilson's illness was at its worst, there is no reason to suppose that, even if he had been given House's letters, and had been able to read them and understand them, it would have caused him to modify his attitude in any way. Even when he had recovered sufficiently to take a personal hand in affairs again, infirm hand though it was, he remained inflexible. The Senate might have been willing to ratify the Treaty if he had agreed to reservations less injurious to the League than those demanded by Lodge. Ex-President Taft drew up such a list in the hope of preventing the defeat which became more and more certain. But Wilson showed no more readiness to deal with Taft than with Lodge. When Senator Hitchcock, the Democratic minority leader, came to plead with him to accept the reservations, Wilson said, with tragic magnificence, 'Better a thousand times to go down fighting than to dip your colours to dishonourable compromise.'

Woodrow Wilson went down fighting—twice. The first time was on November 19th, 1919, when the Senate refused to approve the Treaty with the Lodge reservations and then also rejected the Treaty as it stood. The battle was not over. Those who wanted the United States in the League demanded that the issue be put to the test again, and on March 19th, 1920, after four months of desperate campaigning either to persuade the President to change his mind or persuade enough of his loyal supporters to accept the Lodge reservations, the Senate voted again. A majority was in favour of the Lodge resolution, but it was not a big enough majority for ratification. Forty-nine voted for it, thirty-five against. Another seven votes were needed for the required two-thirds majority. America's entry into the League was blocked, however, not by the League's opponents, but by its supporters. Only twelve of those who voted against the resolution were Republican opponents. Twenty-three were Democrats, faithful to their President, obeying his instruction to reject the Lodge reservations.

The last chance of reversing that decision lay in the election of the Democratic candidate, James Cox, to succeed Wilson in the White House. But in the November election, Cox was defeated, and Warren Harding, the Republican, became President. Before he was elected, some believed that Harding, too, wanted to see America in the League of Nations, but as soon as he took office he made clear he intended to keep the United States free of any such involvement with the rest of the world's troubles. Thus started the twenty years during which America isolated itself, twenty years for which the whole world, including, eventually, the Americans themselves, were to pay such a terrible price.

According to certain American writers, Wilson's culpability lay not only in his refusal to make the concessions which would have allowed the United States to enter the League, but also in his failure to explain to the American people the real reasons why they had gone to war. Because of that he failed also to convince enough of them it was any business of theirs to help to keep the peace. That is the argument put forward by Walter Lippmann,* for instance, writing in the middle of the Second World War, when the consequences of Wilson's conduct during and after the first one were being brought home:

'The war was certainly not engaged in to overthrow the Kaiser and to make Germany a democratic republic: if the Germans had not broken into the Atlantic and threatened the whole structure of our Atlantic defences, private citizens would still have made faces at the Kaiser, but the nation would not have made war upon him. The United States did not go to war because it wished to found a League of Nations; it went to war in order to preserve American security. And when the war was over, the nation would almost certainly have accepted in some form or other the scheme of the League of Nations if President Wilson had been able to demonstrate to the people that the League would perpetuate the security which the military had won for them. Mr. Wilson failed to make this demonstration. He failed because in leading the nation to war he had failed to give the durable and compelling reasons for the momentous decision. The reasons he did give were legalistic and moralistic and idealistic reasons, rather than the substantial and vital reason that the security of the United States demanded that no aggres-

* *U.S. Foreign Policy*, Hamish Hamilton, 1943.

sively expanding imperial power, like Germany, should be allowed to gain the mastery of the Atlantic Ocean.

'Because this simple and self-evident American interest was not candidly made explicit, the nation never understood clearly why it had entered the war. As time went on, the country was, therefore, open to every suggestion and insinuation that the nation had fought for no good reason at all, that its victory was meaningless, that it had been manœuvred into a non-American war by the international bankers and the British diplomats. And so, having failed to make plain that the war was waged for a vital American interest, President Wilson had no way of proving to the nation that his settlement of the war really concerned the United States. The war had been fought without a foreign policy, and neither President Wilson nor the nation had the means, therefore, of judging whether the League was merely a foreign or was also an American interest.

'Thus the longer the Senate debated the Treaty of Versailles with its Covenant, the more the people felt that there was no compelling connection between their vital interests and the programme which President Wilson offered them. They saw that the League imposed upon the United States the unprecedented commitment to help enforce the peace of Europe. They saw only what they were asked to contribute. For they had not been taught to understand what British and French power meant to the security of America's vital interests all over the world . . . The legalistic, moralistic, idealistic presentation of the war and of the League obscured the realities—caused it to appear that for what we were asked to give to our allies, we were to receive nothing from them. It was made to seem that the new responsibilities of the League flowed from President Wilson's philanthropy and not from the vital necessity of finding allies to support America's vast existing commitments in the Western Hemisphere and all the way across the Pacific to the China Coast. . . . After the rejection of Wilson's settlement, American foreign relations were conducted for twenty years without any indication that the nation had any conception of its commitments.'

Walter Lippman argues that people can be persuaded to accept apparently uncongenial policies if only they are taught to recognise the realities of their situation and to perceive their self-interest. There can be no doubt that Wilson encouraged the delusion that the United States went to war altruistically, as a crusading knight, and that made it all the easier for the League's opponents, the isolationists, to sell the notion that Wilson was the dupe of the cunning British. That was the ultimate product of Woodrow Wilson's idealism. Yet idealism need not ignore or distort reality. Nor need an idealistic politician find it impossible to make concessions, if that is the only way he can achieve his objective, or go a long way towards achieving it. That is what politics is about; that is how things get done. Obviously, before striking a bargain, the politician must be sure that his concessions will not so debase what he is trying to achieve that it is no longer worth doing at all. That is what Woodrow Wilson believed would be the effect of agreeing to Lodge's reservations, or any reservations. But that was where Wilson's legalistic approach did him and the world a disservice. His idealism and his legalism could be satisfied only by the right form of words, and once he had found it, he believed it could not be changed without grievous harm. That was to mistake the wrapping for the thing itself, a mistake no effective politician makes. The words were important, the structure of the Covenant was important, but the idea of the League was greater than any particular form of words and, if America had entered it, it could certainly have survived and overcome the disabilities caused by the Lodge reservations.

Woodrow Wilson's vision never faltered. It was a vision of the American people showing the rest of mankind how to live as brothers. It was a vision, as we have seen, whose overweening expression was often resented in Europe, but it was a generous, creative vision, characteristic of the American people at their greatest. On May 30th, 1919, at the American army cemetery at Suresnes, Wilson spoke of the sacrifice made by the men who lay there in their graves, of the idealism which, as he believed, had inspired them, and of what they would expect of those who had survived.

'We command you,' said the President, 'in the names of those who, like ourselves, have died to bring the counsels of men together, and we remind you what America said she was born for. She was born, she said, to show mankind the way to liberty. She was born to make this great gift a common gift. She was born to show men the way of experience by which they might realise this gift and maintain it. Make yourselves soldiers once for all in this common cause, where we need wear no uniform except the uniform of the heart, clothing ourselves with the principles of right, and saying to men everywhere: "You are our brothers and we invite you into the comradeship of liberty and peace." '

That 'great gift' was never bestowed. Instead, the American people put their hands in their pockets and turned their backs on Europe. Woodrow Wilson's vision perished and we are left with a tarnished, grotesque memory of the man. It was after he had left the White House, when he was in retirement, still paralysed and now losing his sight, that Lord Robert Cecil went to visit him. They talked of the hopes they had shared, and Cecil told him of the League of Nations, as it was now working, without America. As Cecil was leaving, Woodrow Wilson said to him, 'Remember, no compromise.'* He died early in 1924. He had kept his integrity. He had kept faith with his vision. But he had failed the world.

* This incident is told by Arthur Salter in *Personality in Politics*, Faber and Faber, 1947. p. 150.

3

'An obscure corner of the Black Sea'

The world waited for the League of Nations to start work, and as it waited the earlier enthusiasm and expectations wilted. Jubilation at the ending of the war and hope for a new world gave way to disillusion and bitterness. Nation was still fighting nation and tensions were mounting which would explode into new wars, Russian against Pole, Russian against Persian, Pole against Lithuanian, Greek against Turk. Large parts of the world were sick with disease, hunger and poverty, and the League of Nations had not even met for the first time. The other great powers had been waiting for America to ratify the Treaty and the Covenant, and their peoples had watched Wilson's struggle with disbelief. Even when the League did begin work, it was still on the assumption that the United States would soon be joining in.

The Council of the League met for the first time on January 16th, 1920, six days after the Versailles Treaty came into force. As required by that Treaty, the Council was convened by the American President. It met in Paris, in the Quai d'Orsay, and occupied itself almost exclusively with amiable and rhetorical formalities to mark the occasion. Representatives of Great Britain, France, Italy and Japan were there; with them were those of the four lesser powers which had been nominated for membership of the Council until the Assembly had held elections for those four non-permanent seats: Greece, Belgium, Spain and Brazil. A conference of ministers held at 10, Downing Street, under the Prime Minister's chairmanship, some two months before, had decided that the British Government would not agree to any business being discussed at that first meeting of the Council other than the one item for which it had been summoned: the appointment of a three-man commission to carry out the delimitation of the frontier between the Saar territory and Germany.

The Council's second meeting, in London, a month later, set the pattern for future meetings. It opened and closed with a public session. All the real argument and work was done in private. While recognising the extreme importance of publicity, said Balfour, who took the chair, if the work of detailed discussion was to be done efficiently, it must be carried on with perfect freedom, which meant in private. The Council met in the picture gallery of St. James's Palace, the representatives wearing uniform black coats, sitting at a red-covered table, under a portrait of Henry VIII. It was a lofty and spacious apartment, with chairs set out for one hundred and sixty distinguished guests, ambassadors and ministers of Allied, associated and neutral powers, and fifty-six British and foreign pressmen at a long table on the window side of the gallery. On that first morning Léon Bourgeois took the chair, before proposing that Balfour, sitting on his right, should preside over their activities in London. The Secretary-General of the League, Sir Eric Drummond, sat on the chairman's left. Once the public posturing was disposed of, the Council got down to three days of useful work.

It took the first step towards setting up the Permanent Court of International Justice under Article 14 of the Covenant by sending an invitation to twelve international jurists, including Elihu Root, the former American Secretary of State, to form a committee to prepare plans. If the Court were established, said the invitation, 'on sound and statesmanlike principles, it can contribute perhaps more than any other single institution to maintain the peace of the world and the supremacy of right amongst the nations.' The Court was one of the finest achievements of the League, although the big powers long resisted the idea that its jurisdiction should be compulsory.

That second meeting of the Council also took the necessary initial action which was to lead on to the creation of two other institutions within the League, the Health Organisation and the

Organisation for Communications and Transit. (The International Labour Organisation—the ILO—had already held its first conference and the International Labour Office had begun work. Under its first director, the Frenchman, Albert Thomas, a former socialist politician, it claimed for itself more and more autonomy and built up a high reputation, after overcoming early suspicions in some quarters that it was anti-capitalist. The ILO, which still exists, has done a great deal to eliminate the exploitation of labour and generally to improve working conditions throughout the world.)

The Council also passed a resolution which made it possible for Switzerland to become a member of the League despite her traditional neutrality. That meant finding a formula which would excuse Switzerland from any obligation to participate in military operations undertaken by the League, while still committing her to share in the imposition of economic sanctions. Before Switzerland could join the League, she would also have to hold a referendum later that year among her own people, and ahead lay a bitter political conflict on the issue. But, in February, in London, the Council did its part, and in view of all the prevarications and humiliating capitulations to aggression which were to come later, it is incidentally interesting to note the terms of its resolution and to see how seriously the possibility of employing force on behalf of the League was then contemplated.

'The Council of the League of Nations,' ran the resolution, 'while affirming that the conception of neutrality of the members of the League is incompatible with the principle that all members of the League will be obliged to cooperate in enforcing respect for their engagements, recognises that Switzerland is in a unique situation . . .

'The members of the League of Nations are entitled to expect that the Swiss people will not stand aside when the high principles of the League have to be defended. It is in this sense that the Council of the League has taken note of the declaration made by the Swiss Government . . . in accordance with which Switzerland recognises and proclaims the duties of solidarity which membership of the League of Nations imposes upon her, including therein the duty of co-operating in such commercial and financial measures as may be demanded by the League of Nations against a Covenant-breaking State, and is prepared to make every sacrifice to defend her own territory under every circumstance, even during operations undertaken by the League of Nations, but will not be obliged to take part in any military action or to allow the passage of foreign troops or the preparation of military operations within her territory.' As *The Times* commented, 'The Covenant imposes on all members the duty of military assistance in enforcing certain obligations upon States who have broken them.'

At that same meeting, the Council dealt briefly with two issues which were to give the League repeated headaches—the Saar and the Free City of Danzig. The Council took the questionable but, in view of French influence, probably inevitable decision to make a Frenchman chairman of the Saar Commission. The Commission, the Peace Conference had agreed, was to govern the territory for the next fifteen years, after which a plebiscite would be held to find out what the Saarlanders themselves wanted—whether to become part of Germany again, to become part of France, or stay under the League. The Council appointed a High Commissioner in Danzig, which was to retain independence in its internal affairs, but to be heavily subordinate to Poland in most other respects.

The Council had held an unspectacular but workmanlike meeting, and *The Times* said, appropriately, in a leading article: 'None of the questions on which reports were received is of first-class importance, and no decision was made which will arouse immediate expectations of a new heaven and a new earth. The first labours of the Council have been modest; the more arduous problems are reserved until it has attained experience and confidence.' Balfour, in his concluding public address, treated the distinguished guests and journalists to somewhat loftier and more flatulent sentiments:

'... In Paris,' he said, 'the greater part of the work ... had to be done by the representatives of the great powers. They were assisted by the representatives of other Allies on certain rare and fixed occasions. Here, for the first time, we have not merely representatives—I am sorry to say in this case four, not five, of the great powers—but we have also representatives ... of allied powers, and more important perhaps than all—more novel, at all events, we have the valuable assistance of representatives of neutrals. This is a great, and I believe, a happy and beneficent innovation, and if the nations of the earth, not merely those who were engaged in hostilities, but those who—not so many after all—were not involved in this world cataclysm—if we could all assemble and meet together and discuss in future in some business-like, friendly and conciliatory spirit . . . I cannot doubt that the service which the League of Nations is capable of rendering in the future to mankind is almost incalculable and certainly is beyond computation at the present moment.'

That speech of Balfour's was in sharp contrast to what he had said in the House of Commons the day before, when he had made mock of the Council. It was the Paris Conference all over again, he had said, exactly the same gentlemen 'called by a different name.' He could not conceive why they should be more efficient under the new name than under the old one, or at St. James's Palace rather than the Quai d'Orsay. People said they had failed totally in 1919. He could not, for the life of him, Balfour had said, see why they should do any better in 1920. The next day he had to issue a statement saying his remarks in the Commons had been misunderstood, and that what he had said at the end of the Council represented the proper expression of his views. Which was just as well, for Balfour was to represent Britain at the Council, whenever possible, for the next three years. Arthur Salter who, along with Jean Monnet and Salvador de Madariaga, was one of the most able of the earliest recruits to the League Secretariat, described Balfour's chief characteristics as 'lethargy alternating with intense energy; sceptical indifference with strong purpose.'* Balfour's contribution to the growth of the League was a valuable one, but there were moments when he could not resist bringing his companions down to earth and his mode of expression was often interpreted as cynicism or sheer flippancy.

At its meetings in the months which followed, the Council, convening in the capitals of the great powers, in London, Paris or Rome, did a deal of useful, if unspectacular, work. It was at its most useful and most effective when it showed itself conscious of its limits. It did itself and the League no good at all when,

* Op. cit. p. 34.

responding to public pressure, it overreached itself. It was unfortunate, for instance, that the first appeal to the League for help from a member-state was one which exposed its weakness. The appeal came from Persia, whose Caspian Sea port of Enzeli (Pahlevi) had been bombarded and occupied by Bolshevik troops. A special meeting of the Council was summoned in London on June 14th. The *Manchester Guardian* looked forward to the meeting which, it said, 'may be a turning-point in the history of Europe.' In the House of Commons, Lord Robert Cecil and Mr. George Barnes, the Labour MP who had served in the wartime coalition, pressed the Prime Minister himself to represent Britain at the Council. Several branches of the League of Nations Union—an organisation which was to develop very considerable influence—passed resolutions like the one from Kidderminster, calling on Lloyd George to attend and for prompt action to be taken 'to make the League of Nations an effective force for the maintenance of peace.' In the event, the Council meeting was a let-down. It was Curzon, not Lloyd George, who took the chair on behalf of Great Britain; apart from the Japanese, the other representatives lacked distinction, as the *Daily News* noted:

'The Prime Minister yesterday told Mr. Barnes he would seriously consider the suggestion that he himself should sit on the Council of the League of Nations. An hour later there was assembling a meeting of the Council, consisting of Lord Curzon, Viscount Chinda, and six diplomatic nonentities whose names are about as familiar to the ordinary, well-informed man as the names of the last six Princes of Liechtenstein . . . the Council of the League of Nations was not meant to be manned by chargés d'affaires.'

Nor was the Council's action any more impressive, although entirely realistic. It noted that the Soviet authorities had already ordered the evacuation of Persian territory and that negotiations were going on between the two governments. The Council decided to wait and see what happened, 'before advising upon the means by which the obligations prescribed by the Covenant shall be fulfilled.' *The Times*, in a scathing editorial, expressed a common sense of indignation at what it called the 'pompous farce.' 'A few more sittings of the Council of the League of Nations like that over which Lord Curzon presided at St James's

Palace yesterday would go far,' it said, 'to kill the very idea of a League, were that idea destructible.' The leading article scoffed at Curzon's declaration of sympathy for Persia, expressed 'in his most opulent style.' As for the decision to await the result of Soviet promises, 'a peal of Homeric laughter must rise from unregenerate throats throughout the world. If ridicule could kill,' said *The Times*, 'it would kill the Council of the League and Lord Curzon with it.' In view of the part this same newspaper was to play in helping and promoting the appeasement of the next decade, the force of its criticism in 1920 has a special interest.

'Yet this matter of the League is no farce,' the leader went on, 'but a tragedy. A real League alone could stand, in one form or another, between the nations and a renewal of war waged upon a scale and with means involving the very downfall of civilisation. As yet the League is but a babe, and a crippled babe to boot. Why, save in malice, seek to feed it with meat too strong for the strongest adult digestion? It needs to be nursed with care and fed with discreet affection. None can nurse it into health and strength, through these early hours of its life, but Great Britain and France, to whom the people of the United States may presently lend some aid. To this end, and to many others, France and England must cease to drift apart and must get together and agree. For theirs is now the effective trusteeship for the League of Nations and, through it, for the best hopes of humanity.'

The Times was derisive of the Council's decision to wait upon Russia, because Russia's hostility to the League had been made clear. The Russians saw the League as the creation of countries which had helped the White armies; it was a tool of capitalism. Earlier in 1920, the Council of the League had proposed to the Bolshevist Government that a commission of inquiry should be allowed to enter Russia and be given official help to find out what conditions were really like. The Russians laid down such terms about the composition of the commission that their reply was in effect, a refusal. If Curzon, in particular, had retained any illusions—which was most unlikely—they were soon totally dispelled.

In 1920, war had broken out between Poland and Russia, a war which at one time saw Polish troops in occupation of the Ukrainian capital, Kiev, and then Russian troops advancing into

Poland and reaching the outskirts of Warsaw before being driven back. The British Government offered to mediate to bring about peace between the two countries. The Soviet Commissar for Foreign Affairs, Chicherin, sent a message to Curzon in July which Curzon laid before the Cabinet. It told Great Britain that Russia was quite capable of conducting her own peace negotiations with Poland. But Chicherin went on to attack the League in much more vehement language. 'The Soviet Government,' he said, 'considers still less admissible the interference in the cause of peace between Russia and Poland of the group of governments called the League of Nations. . . . The Russian Government has never received from the so-called League of Nations any communication as to its creation and existence and it has never had the opportunity of adopting a decision about recognition or non-recognition of this association of states. When acquainting itself from unofficial press sources with the Covenant of the so-called League of Nations the Soviet Government could not leave unnoticed the fact that according to Article 17 the non-members in case of conflict with members of the so-called League can be invited to submit to its decision as if they were members. The Soviet Government can in no way agree that one group of powers should assume the role of supreme body over all the states of the world and watching over the full inviolability of the sovereign rights of the Russian labouring people the Soviet Government absolutely rejects the pretensions of any foreign groups of powers claiming to assume the role of supreme masters of the fate of other nations. It absolutely rejects therefore every immixation of this association in the cause of peace between Russia and Poland . . .'

The essence of the criticism of the Council by *The Times* at the time of the Persian appeal had been that, by pretending to concern itself with matters beyond its control or influence, the Council was damaging the League. The Council, at any rate, if not the League as a whole, did not make the same mistake over Armenia, whose brief independence was threatened by both Turkey and Russia. The Supreme Council of the Allies suggested that Armenia should be considered like a mandated territory, whose protection would be entrusted to the League. The League Council refused to accept the responsibility, pointing out that individual states, not the League itself, undertook mandates; the League could not do so, unless the Allies provided the necessary arms and troops and money. That was in April, 1920. Anxiety about Armenia grew throughout that year, but the Council always refused any commitment to intervene, because it recognised the impossibility of doing so effectively.

The Council was more successful, however, in tackling the massive problem of repatriating Austrian, Hungarian and other prisoners of war captured by the Russian armies and still in Siberia. Or, rather, Dr. Fridtjof Nansen, the famous Norwegian explorer and scientist, was successful; it was the Council's good fortune that Nansen accepted the invitation to take on the task. Only a Nansen could have done it, a man who, once he had committed his energies, refused to give up. He had not only to organise the physical transport of the prisoners over land and sea; he had also to persuade the Soviet, Polish and German Governments to co-operate with him and his Red Cross teams, and he had to persuade other governments, including the British and French, to make funds available out of the money at the disposal of the International Committee on Relief Credits. When Philip Noel-Baker went to the Cabinet meeting on July 15th, 1920, to press the case on behalf of Nansen and the League, the British Government agreed to pay their share only on condition that other European powers paid theirs and that none of it was used to repatriate German prisoners. Nansen overcame all those difficulties. The first boat had sailed on May 14th, 1920, and the September Council meeting learned that some 100,000 prisoners had been returned to their homes. In all, in the two years he was engaged on the work, Nansen helped more than 425,000 to go back home. Nansen, a humanitarian of the rarest and greatest kind, whose ideals were matched by his actions, was an outstanding figure in the early years of the League, not only in his own achievements but in the way he so often became the conscience of the League, impatient of excuses for not doing what he knew ought to be done. He was the hero of the smaller powers, a man of dignity and enormous influence, his speeches corrosive and challenging.

If individual governments were reluctant to make funds available to Nansen, they were even less ready to give money to help Poland to fight epidemics, especially of typhus, although it was ultimately in their own interests to check the spread of disease. The League Council appealed to members in May, 1920, for £2 million. In September, Balfour, in the name of the Council, appealed again for governments to provide at least an immediate £250,000. The effect was negligible.

The Council could claim at least one positive success during 1920, although the proof of it was not to come until the following year. A dispute between Finland and Sweden over which country should own the Aaland Islands in the Baltic had reached such an intensity that there was a real danger of war between them. As so often in such cases, there was a certain amount of right on both sides. The islands were part of Finland, but in all else the islanders were Swedish and wanted to be joined with Sweden. On the initiative of the British Government the issue was referred to the Council of the League. The islanders wanted a plebiscite to decide their future, but Finland denied the League's right to intervene in a matter of internal jurisdiction. The Council appointed a small panel of jurists to examine the question and then, later, having decided that it was competent to deal with the matter, set up a neutral commission to investigate on the spot. The British Government was asked whether it had any objection to a distinguished British statesman being nominated to the commission. The Cabinet, meeting on September 30th, showed itself disinclined to have any more to do with the issue, feeling that Britain had already incurred enough responsibility by referring it to the Council in the first place; it was highly contentious and it was better not to be mixed up in it. In the end, the Cabinet agreed to the nomination of a British representative, but not unless a French one of equal distinction was also nominated, and they were all in favour of trying to get an American to join the commission. The commission took its time, but at length advised that, despite the islanders' own wishes, the Aalands should remain part of Finland. Sweden felt strongly about the decision to this effect announced by the Council in June, 1921, but, with a loyalty to the League characteristic of the Scandinavian countries, she accepted it. So, too, did Finland which had to admit that the League had a continuing concern to ensure that the rights of the Swedish-speaking minority in the Islands were protected.

The League's efforts to settle a dispute between Poland and Lithuania over the city of Vilna, the old capital of Lithuania, were less happy, although it did seem for a while that they would bring about a peaceful settlement. Vilna lay in the path of the warring Russian and Polish armies in 1920 and it changed hands several times, but when Russia signed a peace treaty with Lithuania, the city once more became the seat of government of the newly independent country. That was in July. Soon afterwards, in pursuit of the fleeing Russian army, the Poles advanced towards Vilna. The Lithuanians defended what they considered to be their frontiers, as agreed with the Russians. The Poles accused the Lithuanians of helping the Russians and called upon the Council to act to prevent war between themselves and the Lithuanians. They also laid claim to Vilna, where, it is true, there were at that time more Poles than Lithuanians.

The League Council considered the issue at its September meeting in Paris. Poland was represented by Ignacy Paderewski, whose world reputation as a musician was matched by his statesmanship. His appearance and manner were much in contrast with those of the Lithuanian, Professor Augustinas Voldemaras; so, too, was his brevity of argument. But the Council was able to bring them to agreement on a ceasefire and a demarcation line between the armies of the two countries, which was to be safeguarded by a military commission set up by the League. The question of what was to happen to Vilna itself could be settled later. Léon Bourgeois, as president, said the ninth Council had made it very clear that 'the League was no longer at the stage of talk but at the stage of action, successive, repeated, and methodically linked together.' It was, he said, 'the best augury for the future of the great task confided to it by the Versailles Treaty.' Paderewski turned to the Lithuanian delegate, referring to him as 'my colleague and not adversary,' and offered him his hand 'as a symbol of the lasting friendship which should reign between our two countries.' The two men congratulated themselves on the happy solution and the spectators of this public reconciliation applauded. 'Bravo, the League,' said the London evening newspaper, the *Star*. 'League's first score,' said the *Morning Post*.

A multi-national military commission reached the demarcation line about a fortnight later, and on October 7th, the Poles and

Lithuanians signed a formal agreement to respect the line and the ceasefire. It was broken almost immediately in the most flagrant way. A Polish army led by General Zeligowski crossed the line into Lithuanian territory and seized Vilna. The Polish Government denied that Zeligowski was acting on orders; his action was a wilful, headstrong one taken on his individual initiative, without authority or approval. It became clear later that Zeligowski was doing exactly what he had been ordered to do by Marshal Pilsudski, the romantic, hot-tempered soldier-statesman, the sometime revolutionary socialist who had become the benevolent dictator of Poland; it was probably true, however, that other members of the Government knew what was going to happen. Lithuania now asked the Council to intervene and although it did not hold a special meeting, Bourgeois, acting on its behalf, called upon the Poles to withdraw their troops and to honour their agreement. The Polish Government professed the best of intentions, but nothing actually happened: Zeligowski stayed in Vilna. In London, at a conference of ministers, some ten days after the Poles had occupied Vilna, the Foreign Secretary told his colleagues he was not yet satisfied that the Polish Government had connived at the occupation. The general feeling was that if it became clear in the course of the next few days that the Polish troops in the city were being reinforced or sustained from Poland, then it would be plain that Poland was 'defying the Allies and the League of Nations.' The proper course would then be to 'turn her out of the League and decline any longer to preserve her territorial integrity.'

When the Council did meet later in October at Brussels, the atmosphere was very different from the conciliatory, or at least courteous, one in which the Polish and Lithuanian delegates had come together in Paris. Paderewski's place had been taken by a man of sullen belligerence. The Council imposed its will, however, successfully as it seemed at the time, although it incurred a lot of criticism for not taking more drastic, disciplinary action against Poland. Even had the Council decided that such action was the best way of dealing with the situation, it would have been quite incapable of enforcing its decision. As it was, the Council said the decision about whether Vilna should belong to Poland or to Lithuania should be made by the people who lived there. The League would administer a plebiscite; the Polish troops would withdraw and an international force, responsible to the Council, would go in. Several member-countries agreed to send troops as part of the force, and when the Cabinet met on November 17th, it heard that H. A. L. Fisher, the Minister of Education, who was representing Great Britain at the current Council meeting in Geneva, had telegraphed asking the Government to hurry up with arrangements for sending three hundred British troops; the French contingent, he said, was already on its way. It looked as though all was going ahead as the Council had proposed. In fact, the international force never took up its responsibilities in Vilna. Zeligowski, far from withdrawing, was soon on the march again, apparently with the aim of taking over the rest of Lithuania. But the Lithuanians resisted and there was fighting for several weeks. During that time, preparations still went ahead for raising the international force and for holding the plebiscite. Early in the New Year, the Poles turned their thoughts to a peaceful settlement once more, promising the withdrawal of their troops as soon as the League's force arrived, and full co-operation in the plebiscite. But the Council had to face new difficulties. First, there was a new obduracy on the part of the Lithuanians, and then an objection by Russia to the entry of foreign troops—those raised by the League, that is—into Lithuania. In March, 1921, the Council gave up the idea of holding a plebiscite and sought an agreement between the two countries by negotiation. It tried throughout the rest of that year, but it failed. Polish troops remained in Vilna, sporadic fighting between the two sides continued year after year. The Conference of Ambassadors awarded Vilna to Poland, but Lithuania went on fighting. It was December, 1927, before the Council managed to get the two nations to accept peace. Even that peace was a sour, queasy one.

The Vilna issue was just one example of the complex, seemingly intractable problems with which the Council was to be faced during the lifetime of the League. Its proceedings were rarely to recapture the frivolity which must have inspired the resolution it passed in May, 1920, when it ordered its permanent military commission to study measures regarding the military and naval forces of the republic of San Marino. But it was not only the

Covenant-breakers or the hostility of non-members like Russia or the exclusion of the United States which impeded the development of the League. Blame for its deficiencies lay also with the great powers themselves, particularly Great Britain and France, whose governmental attitudes towards the League were always cautious, often grudging and sometimes obstructive. The continued existence, long after the end of the war, of the Supreme Council, was a threat to the authority of the League. The Allies dealt in the Supreme Council, or in its subsidiary in Paris, the Conference of Ambassadors, with matters arising out of the peace treaties, matters which ought to have been referred to the League but which they found more expedient to keep to themselves. This angered other, smaller powers which might well be concerned in such issues and be affected by decisions taken in secret by the Supreme Council. As early as May, 1920, in Parliament, first Asquith, the former Prime Minister, and then Cecil, appealed to the Government for an early dissolution of the Supreme Council and the transference of its function to the League. The challenge represented by the Supreme Council was underlined by the decision to hold a meeting in Geneva in November, 1920, at exactly the same time as the Assembly of the League was to meet there for the first time. Lloyd George did try to mollify outraged feelings of League supporters by suggesting that the Allied leaders should take the opportunity, while in Geneva, to take part in the initial sessions at least of the Assembly, but the French would not agree.

The composition of the British delegation to the Assembly was also criticised as reflecting the Government's inadequate attitude towards the League. It was to be led by Balfour; Fisher, the Minister of Education, was to be the second Government delegate. The third, non-Government member was named as George Barnes. The absence of Lord Grey of Fallodon, the former Foreign Secretary, and a public supporter of the League idea from the earliest days, was particularly regretted, but it was Grey himself who had turned down an invitation to join the delegation because of failing eyesight. There were others in England who anticipated the first Assembly with anxiety for quite different reasons. Sir J. D. Rees, Conservative MP for Nottingham East, put a question to the Prime Minister in the Commons:

'May not the representatives of the great powers be outvoted by the representatives of the small powers? How can the Right Honourable Gentleman ensure that these gentlemen at Geneva will be endowed with sufficient grace, wisdom and understanding?'

'Nothing can be done,' Lloyd George assured him, 'except by the unanimous decision of the Council, and that means nothing can be done without the consent of the powers concerned.'

From the very beginning, there were members of the British Government on the look-out for any signs that the League was endangering the national interest or taking unto itself an authority which belonged to individual countries; they were also intent in keeping the Secretariat in its place. The minutes of the Cabinet meeting of January 14th, 1920, record the view that there were serious objections to the business of the League being conducted directly between the Secretary-General and the Dominions. 'If such a procedure were adopted it was inevitable that on controversial and doubtful issues different views would be communicated and sustained by different parts of the Empire, with the consequence that when a crisis arose they might well discover that they had drifted into divergent or even antagonistic attitudes. Such a result would damage the Empire in the eyes of foreign nations and have unfortunate reactions on the internal relations of the Commonwealth.' The Cabinet decided to ask the acting Colonial Secretary and the Secretary of State for India to get in touch with the self-governing Dominions and India, emphasising the importance of developing a common policy in regard to questions coming before the League and pointing out the 'dangers of separate and direct communication with the League.'

Later that same year, on October 18th, a conference of ministers met to consider a draft scheme, prepared by the commission set up by the League, for the Permannet Court of International Justice, a scheme which, it was generally agreed, 'was highly detrimental to our national interests and could not be accepted,' especially insofar as 'it would enable predominantly Land Powers to build up a code of international law which would fetter Britain's exercise of her sea-power.' In passing, the conference was reminded of the danger which might arise from the League of Nations propounding plans which no individual government would be prepared to endorse. 'The League of Nations Secretariat should be a post office between the League and the various governments, and should not of its own accord initiate action. Otherwise the governments might find that they were not masters in their own houses.'

Great Britain was not the only country to criticise the Secretariat for getting beyond itself. Throughout the history of the League, national delegations questioned the right or the wisdom of initiatives from the Secretariat. In fact, the strictly subordinate role of the Secretary-General could now be seen as one weakness which contributed to the League's ultimate failure. The first Secretary-General, Sir Eric Drummond, had been a senior Foreign Office man. He was appointed after Sir Maurice Hankey, the highly reputed Secretary of the British Cabinet and a major figure at the Peace Conference, had declined the job. The first Secretary-General had to be acceptable to the great powers—just as they were to insist that the appointments immediately below him should be filled by their nationals. Drummond had become well enough known and respected by the other delegations at Paris for his nomination to go through without argument. He was a good administrator, devoted to the ideal of the League, but he was not a strong man. He was not always strong enough even in dealing with his own staff. His intent was to create an international civil service, composed of men who would put the interests of the League, and therefore of the world, above those of their own countries. He recruited from many countries; many of the men were of remarkable calibre; they worked well and created an efficient machine: but some of them never managed to forget their national origins completely. This was partly, no doubt, because the idea of serving the international interest was a novel one and many served in the Secretariat only on secondment from their own country's civil service, partly because of the persistence within the Council and the Assembly of national interests, but partly, too, because of Drummond. He himself set a fine example of internationalism but he did not do enough to impose it successfully upon all his staff. Salvador de Madariaga recalls how at one time he even allowed an Italian member of the Secretariat to wear the Fascist emblem in his buttonhole. 'Drummond should have told him to pocket his emblem.'

The Secretariat went ahead of the delegations to Geneva. There were few regrets at leaving Sunderland House, the temporary headquarters in London, a large but uncongenial house at the corner of Piccadilly and Down Street. The new home in Geneva was much more to everyone's taste and comfort. At last, they were able to settle down with a sense of permanence; at last, the Assembly, the 'world parliament,' as some newspapers described it, was about to meet for the first time.

Although the Swiss Government had welcomed the proposal from the Paris Peace Conference that Geneva should be the home of the League, the city itself was far from prepared for the honour. (Geneva had been chosen despite strong advocacy, particularly by France and Belgium, of Brussels, but the Belgian capital was generally considered too associated with the war to be the home of an organisation dedicated to keeping the peace.) Geneva was a very modest place in those days, modest alike in its pretensions, its manners and its facilities. When its choice was first discussed, it was still assumed that the United States would be joining the League, and there were somewhat in-ebriated ideas about how much money would be spent on creating an appropriately lavish headquarters complex. By the time, nearly two years later, that the League went to work there, it was very much the morning after. Everyone was conscious of the need for economy and had to make do with whatever makeshift accommodation Geneva could offer. The Secretariat, for instance, took over the biggest hotel in Geneva, the National. It was a matter of improvising and there was some inevitable inconvenience, but the site was congenial enough, opposite the steamboat landing stage on the lakeside, looking towards Mont Blanc. It was here, too, that the Council held its meetings, in the glass-sided dining room, the representatives sitting around a big, circular table. On the other side of the lake stood the Salle de la Réformation, an old, austere, unbeautiful hall, fitting in its severity to commemorate Calvinism. It was here that the Assembly was to meet for the first time on November 15th, 1920.

As the day approached, the small town began to bulge and its streets babbled as more and more frock-coated and top-hatted diplomatists arrived. A large delegation came from Japan, accompanied by an enormous quantity of furniture and luggage and, it was reported, big cases reeking of dried fish. Hotels quickly filled up, prices soared. A German journalist reckoned that with 100 marks worth only about seven Swiss francs, it was costing him £35 a day to live in Geneva. Germany was not the only non-member country whose press was there to cover the Assembly; fourteen American newspapers and news agencies were represented. The American journalists came prepared to confirm the belief, firmly held at home, that the League was dead; but the corpse showed every sign of life. National flags fluttered from windows and rooftops, bunting hung in the streets, there were receptions and a gala performance. On the eve of the Assembly, special church services were held at which congregations invoked divine blessing for the League. Most members of the British and Dominions' delegations went to the Church of the Holy Family, where Lord Robert Cecil assisted in the reading of the lessons; then the delegates returned to the Hôtel Beau Rivage for a meeting together.

The next morning, under a blue sky and a sun of almost summer warmth, dense, animated crowds lined the street to watch members of the Swiss Government and city councillors process from the hôtel de ville, to the stately bridge of Mont Blanc, by which they crossed the River Rhône, and so on to the Salle de la Réformation, which was guarded by gendarmes in ceremonial long blue cloaks and cocked hats. Church bells rang throughout the canton of Geneva and a squadron of Swiss aeroplanes flew over the town. On the floor of the hall, desks were allotted to delegates according to alphabetical order (in French). In the front row were South Africa, Argentine, Australia and Belgium. The first delegation to take its place was the Japanese. Almost all delegates wore the customary black; one Chinese wore a khaki uniform with a row of medals, the only military decorations on show there; the representatives of New Zealand preferred light grey lounge suits—to emphasise their democratic outlook. Two galleries ran round three sides of the hall. The lower one, to the right and left of the presidential dais, was reserved for the press. Visitors were ushered to their places by huissiers, wearing robes of scarlet and yellow, the colours of the Geneva canton, and three-cornered hats with large gilt buckles. On the dais the chief attendant wore, not only a robe like the others, but also a snow-white cloak and a hat richly ornamented with gold lace.

By comparison with all this accompanying gaudy, the first session of the Assembly itself was marked by little ceremony. Paul Hymans, the Belgian Foreign Minister, elected President of the Assembly before the session began, tinkled his bell and Giuseppe Motta, the President of the Swiss Confederation, spoke for nearly half an hour, welcoming the delegates, and expressing 'a hope, or rather a keenly-felt desire, that America would before long take its rightful place in the League.'

The Assembly sat for five weeks, sometimes in full public session, sometimes splitting up into several committees to which were assigned special responsibilities; these committees, or commissions, met in private, despite impassioned advocacy of the virtues of open debate and publicity by, among others, Cecil. The first Assembly did much to establish the pattern of future ones. It saw it as its task—and privilege—to review the past year's work of the League, as well as receiving the recommendations of its commissions. The work of the League meant, particularly, the work of the Council, although it had never been the Council's intention to do more than submit a report on its activities for information. The Assembly, however, saw it as an opportunity also to examine the Council's work, and, where necessary, to offer its criticisms. The Assembly, in fact, was the one place where the small powers, who resented Anglo-French domination of the League, could claim equality with the big ones and they made the most of it, often making speeches of a length and intemperance which irritated the mighty, but which also chastened them with reminders of their obligations.

The issue which was characteristic of the Assembly was Armenia. Here was a people whose distress stirred the conscience and the compassion of delegates but their demands for action to save Armenia were not practical. Lord Robert Cecil, who had been persuaded by Smuts to go to Geneva as a representative of South Africa, pleaded for the League to intervene. He was one of a committee of six set up specially by the Assembly, and he called for a loan of £5 million to finance a military expedition.

Nansen, another member of the committee, said the League should raise and equip a force of 60,000 men. There was discussion of how it should be composed and who should command it and the estimated cost went up to £20 million. Both Nansen and Cecil won warm applause from their fellow-delegates. So did Arthur Balfour, but more perhaps as a display of respect for him than in appreciation of what he had to say. Balfour arrived a week after the start of the Assembly, having been ill. He spoke with gravity of the difficulties of helping Armenia, going again over the arguments which had persuaded the Council it should not take on any responsibility it had no chance of discharging.

But the Assembly was impatient. The Turks had crossed the border into Armenia and were ravaging the country: the League of Nations must act at once. When the Council, or at least the British and French, still dwelt on the obstacles to effective action, the Assembly took over. If noble language could have halted the invaders, Armenia would have been saved. But who would offer more than words? Would the Americans rush to the rescue? The appeal went out to Washington, and President Wilson, notwithstanding his defeat at the election or his illness, responded. In a telegram to the Assembly, full of solicitude for the Armenian people, Wilson regretted his inability to provide any military forces, but offered his personal mediation—'through a representative whom I may designate'—to end the hostilities and 'bring peace and accord to the contending parties, relying upon the Council of the League of Nations to suggest to me the avenue through which my offer should be conveyed, and the parties to whom it should be addressed.' The Spanish Government, too, held itself ready 'to contribute gladly to any action of a moral or diplomatic nature,' and the Brazilian Government was 'ready to contribute, alone or jointly with other Powers, to put an end to the situation of suffering in Armenia.'

Brave words, coming no doubt from brave hearts. In the evening of the same day that the Assembly heard them, December 1st, Balfour addressed a few fruity and encouraging words to the press on the nature of the League's achievements so far. Perhaps, he said, the League had fallen short of the extravagant expectations entertained by many, but the gentlemen of the press might come to the conclusion that it had nothing to be ashamed of. Those who regarded the League as a fantastic dream of 'sanguine speculators' should ask themselves whether such questions as Danzig or the International Court of Justice could ever have been dealt with successfully other than through the League. The same could be said on the matter of mandates, and there had been little success in dealing with the repatriation of war prisoners until the League had taken it up: he recognised the Council's good fortune in finding in Nansen the right man to handle it. Balfour had words of cheer even on the subject of Armenia. 'It is a wonderful thing when you come to think of it,' he said, 'that the League should be able to draw from North America, South America, and Europe, help for dealing with a difficulty in an obscure corner of the Black Sea.' He did add, however, his belief that the League would suffer more from those who sought to put too much upon it than from those who regarded it as impotent.

That was very much the attitude of Balfour's colleagues in London, when they came together the next day to consider an anxious telegram sent from Geneva by Fisher. Both Lord Robert Cecil and René Viviani, the former French Prime Minister, as members of the fifth commission, concerned with new members, were, according to Fisher, 'trying to rush Armenia into the League.' Fisher said that Balfour and he doubted the advisability of this but it was quite possible that when it came before the Assembly, Armenia's admission might be carried by nations which would not raise a finger to assist the cause of Armenia. It was an uncomfortable position for the British Government. There were strong objections to Armenia's entry into the League. Her boundaries had not yet been defined, an argument which had been used to deny admission to the Baltic States. Much more worrying was the fact that once Armenia was a member of the League, the obligation imposed upon fellow-members under Article 10 of the Covenant would take effect: 'to respect and preserve' Armenia's territorial integrity and political independence against external aggression. Echoing Balfour, the conference of British ministers in London deplored the undertaking by the League of obligations it could not fulfil, because it could only be weakened by it. But they had no wish to see

Britain standing out alone in opposition to Armenia's admission. Britain was spared such embarrassment and her attitude, harsh though it may have seemed at the time, was justified by events. Even while the Assembly was still considering the question of Armenia's admission, the news came that the independent republic of Armenia had already ceased to exist. Its government had been ousted by communists and the Red Army was occupying the country, which was now to become a new Soviet republic.

The Assembly was scarcely more successful in going to the aid of Poland in its fight against typhus, although no less passionate and moving appeals were made. One of these came from Prince Ranjitsinjhi, the Maharajah Jam Saheb of Nawanagar, the great cricketer, who brought to Geneva as his secretary another fine cricketer, C. B. Fry. 'Ranji,' as he was known throughout England, was something more than a cricketer; at home in India he took his responsibilities as ruler of Nawanagar seriously and carried out a programme of wide social reforms. His speech at Geneva was dramatic and challenging. 'It is up to the Assembly to act,' he said. But it had little material effect. Nor did telegraphic appeals sent to individual member-countries. Of the £2 million the Council had started asking for the previous May, only some £100,000 was raised.

One of the by-products of the Armenian issue was a revival of hope that the United States would, after all, enter the League. This was based, very tenuously, upon Wilson's offer to mediate. It took no account of the attitude of Harding who was to succeed him, nor of the mounting objections in America to entanglement in the affairs of Europe. The nations assembled at Geneva may have thought they had made a positive contribution towards persuading America to join, when the fifth commission came out with a declaration about the real meaning of Article 10 of the Covenant. Certainly, Article 10, which meant so much to Woodrow Wilson, offended many Americans, including good friends of the League, such as Elihu Root. Article 10 had seemed to imply that the League was pledged to maintain the political *status quo* throughout the world, for ever and ever, even against revolutionary or evolutionary movements within individual countries. That thought had caused a deal of anxiety elsewhere than in the United States. Now the fifth commission declared:

'It is not true that the League, under Article 10, guarantees the territorial integrity of any one of its members. The Covenant merely condemns any aggression directed from outside against the territorial integrity or political independence of members of the League, and in case of such aggression provides that the Council shall advise as to the means to be adopted for resisting such aggression.' That interpretation brought comfort to many, but it could not bring America into the League.

It was not only America's absence from Geneva which was lamented by observers and delegates alike. Germany and Russia were missing, too. As the Assembly began, the *Manchester Guardian* commented: 'The League, as it exists today, is a fragment, and a fragment which, unless enlarged and reinforced, cannot permanently fulfil its mission. What sort of League is that from which three of the greatest and most populous nations of the world are left out? It is a beginning, but it cannot be an end.'

When the Council had decided to invite ex-enemy states, including Germany and Austria, to the international financial conference held in Brussels in the early autumn, that had been regarded in some quarters as tantamount to inviting Germany to apply for membership of the League in the expectation of being accepted. Germany did not apply, but the need for her membership was proclaimed several times during the Assembly. Baron Hayashi, the Japanese Ambassador in London, and a member of the Japanese delegation at Geneva, said he deplored the fact that the time was not yet ripe for the inclusion of ex-enemy countries. 'For the League must be a world institution, and not merely represent a portion of humanity,' he said, 'even though that portion may be the majority.' Barnes, the third, non-Government member of the British delegation, speaking, as he claimed, in the name of the whole body of English Labour, said that former enemy states should be admitted, and he believed that view was shared by workers all over the world. Austria was admitted—as were Bulgaria, Finland, Albania, Costa Rica and Luxemburg—and in welcoming her, Motta expressed the hope that Germany might soon follow. Tommaso Tittoni, for Italy, said that all nations, without exception, should be members. But the fifth commission passed unanimously a resolution moved by Viviani, which effectively closed the door on both Germany and Russia. This resolution laid down that no new state would be admitted unless it had conformed to four rules:

1. The state must have fulfilled all its international obligations;
2. The state must have a responsible government capable of contracting engagements;
3. The state must possess an organisation which will warrant the League in believing that it can carry out all the obligations of the pact;
4. The state must have exact frontiers within the limits of which the populations constitute a nation.

The first of those conditions was directed against Germany, the others more or less against Russia. The declaration embodied France's determination not to allow Germany, in particular, into the League unless that country had paid for the war and had proved herself of good behaviour. But Fisher was the first to support the declaration, and, surprisingly, because he had insisted from the earliest days on the wisdom of admitting Germany, Cecil apparently raised no objection to the declaration.

Indirectly, Germany was the cause of the Argentine delegation quitting the Assembly long before it formally ended. Argentina put forward the suggestion that, instead of having to apply for membership of the League and having its qualifications vetted, a nation should choose whether to join or not. The proposal was worth discussing, but it was put forward, necessarily, in the form of an amendment to the Covenant, and a considerable one at that, and the Assembly had already agreed that, for the time being, the Covenant must be left as it was. The Argentine delegation left Geneva in a huff.*

Looking back twenty years later, Cecil described the first Assembly as 'disunited' and 'dispiriting,' until it came to deal with the issue of Armenia. That comment is reflective of the character of both Cecil himself and of the Assembly. If what they wanted the League to do over Armenia was undoubtedly impracticable, it was also indicative of what kind of League it should be and one day, perhaps, might be. It was not, as we have seen, the only issue on which the words spoken at the

* Although she never formally withdrew from the League, it was not until 1933 that Argentina came back to Geneva to take her place again as a member.

Assembly were greater than the deeds it could perform, but the delegates had no reason to be ashamed of what they did achieve. A lot of detailed work concerning the organisation and administration of the League itself was accomplished. The International Court was established, with the Assembly agreeing that its jurisdiction should be compulsory where both parties were willing to submit to it—a substantial change from the original draft and one which made it more palatable to the bigger powers. It took the first steps in setting up a number of specialised bodies under the League's auspices, and initiated action, for instance, to control opium and white-slave trafficking. It also made a start along the road towards limiting and reducing armaments, but no one then could know what a long and ultimately futile journey it was going to be.

Several of the delegates asserted their influence over the Assembly and excited the public galleries when they rose to speak. Cecil and Viviani, with his mellifluous tenor voice and his determination to have things the French way, were often in contest for domination of the Assembly. Balfour, tall, floppy, inelegant, could command the fullest respect when he could exert himself to do so. Nansen's magnificent stature and uncompromising idealism and Motta's firm common sense and realism also, in their wholly different ways, earned the admiration of the other delegates.

In view of what was to happen in later years, it is worth ending this sketch of the first Assembly with a speech made by Viscount Ishii, who was the Japanese Ambassador in Paris and Japan's representative on the League Council, a man of courtesy, intellect and sagacity. He left no doubt of his country's earnest good intentions towards the League and of its readiness to make the kind of generous gesture which would always be necessary if the nations were ever to work together successfully.

Ishii had tried to persuade the Assembly to meet in future every two years, but the decision had gone against him—there was to be an annual Assembly. Accepting it with good grace, he explained what it must mean for Japan. The sea voyage to and from Geneva took some four months. Added to that the month or more which the Assembly was likely to last and it meant that the Japanese delegates must be away for at least five months. With annual meetings, he said, the Japanese delegation would hardly have time to report on the activities of one Assembly before starting back to Europe for the next one. In future, Japan would have to choose delegates from among men who were already in Europe, or not too far away; that was one reason, he said, why the Japanese had brought such a large delegation this time: they wanted to educate as many young men as possible in the ways of the League, so that they could be called upon to serve in their delegation.

Then Viscount Ishii went on to a matter of profound concern to the Japanese. Japan had hoped, he said, when the Covenant was originally formulated, to declare her belief that equality before the law should be assured to all men irrespective of their nationality, race, or religion. 'It was to the poignant regret of the Japanese Government and people that the framers of the Covenant had found themselves unable to accept Japan's proposal in this matter.' (The truth was, as Ishii well knew, that in this respect there was no difference between Woodrow Wilson and William Morris Hughes: it would have been as embarrassing to America as to Australia to admit that yellow men and brown men and black men should enjoy the same rights and privileges as white men.) It had been Japan's intention, said Ishii to the Assembly, to raise the point again at the earliest opportunity. But, he concluded, 'in view of present circumstances, Japan is strongly persuaded that the League is as yet in a stage where the consolidation of its organisation and its actual working, based upon the present Covenant, should be accorded greater attention and deeper deliberation than questions relating to fundamental principle that might involve the revision of the Covenant. From that point of view Japan is refraining from making any concrete proposal at this Assembly as to the question of equal opportunity and treatment, and will patiently bide her time until the opportune moment presents itself.'

Ishii's syntax was tortuous, but his meaning was entirely clear. It was a handsome contribution by Japan to concord.

4

'Today the League has not failed us'

The League of Nations was never short of speakers to plead the cause of humanity; but not many of them—or the countries they represented—were prepared to contribute more than words. Nansen was a glorious exception. Not only did he come to Geneva to speak on behalf of the suffering; he also went to the suffering and worked with his own hands for their relief. He was by no means universally popular at Geneva. He had no taste for diplomatic euphemisms. He lashed the consciences of those who professed sympathy but gave nothing. So it was when he attended the second Assembly in September, 1921, and told of the famine which was threatening the lives of millions in Russia. He had been there himself on behalf of voluntary organisations; now he came to the League to call for aid on a scale which only governments could provide. He asked for £30 million. He met with excuses, evasions and even some outright hostility from those who suspected him of Bolshevik leanings, and who privately considered the famine a welcome intervention by an anti-Bolshevik divinity. The issue was shelved on the grounds that it was being examined by the Supreme Council of the Allies.

The British Government behaved as meanly as any other, and the recorded opinions of Cabinet ministers reflect poorly on all but Lloyd George and, unexpectedly, Curzon. The financial situation at home was tight, and our own unemployed were having a very rough time, but that could not justify the attitude taken up by Winston Churchill, for example. Curzon told the Cabinet on March 6th, 1922—by which time about a million Russians had died of starvation—of the work being done by the three British organisations, the Save the Children Fund, the Society of Friends, and the Russian Relief Fund. They were doing splendid work within their limited means, but the Government was being asked to make a grant of from £250,000 to £350,000 to match a similar sum subscribed by the public. With that money, hundreds of thousands of peasants could be kept alive until the next harvest in August. Churchill, who was Colonial Secretary, was strongly opposed to the proposal. Apart, he said, from the needs of our own people, such a grant would be deeply offensive to large numbers of Government supporters. The famine, Churchill declared, was 'mainly due to the inconceivable wickness of the Soviet Government, who could greatly mitigate its ravages if they diverted for that end money they were now spending on maintaining a huge Red Army, purchasing armaments and equipment, and organising propaganda against civilized states.' Churchill was only saying out loud what several of his colleagues probably also felt, although they prefaced their opposition with expressions of regret. The Prime Minister was unable to attend the meeting because he was ill, but he was in the chair again the next day. He had to accept that the Cabinet was against making a grant, but he 'deeply deplored' the decision which he reckoned would bring a good deal of discredit upon Britain. At least, his colleagues agreed with Lloyd George that a new gift of stores should be sent to Russia to replace a parcel which had been found to be 'rubbish.' But they refused a request from certain philanthropic organisations to allow Russian children into the country.

The League, as an organisation, failed to respond to Nansen's appeal. Individual countries, however, notably the United States, and individual organisations, did send massive aid and their help did much to prevent 1922 proving a repetition of the disaster of the year before.

In other respects, in the early years of its existence, the League could fairly claim a number of successes. Of these, the saving of Austria may be reckoned the most remarkable and some atonement, perhaps, for the failure over Russia. The disasters that

were to overtake Austria a few years later have obscured the
effective action taken by the League in 1922. The end of the war
saw the end of the dual Austria-Hungary monarchy, and its
disintegration into several different countries, Czechoslovakia,
Poland, Rumania, and Yugoslavia, as well as Austria and Hungary.
Austria became a republic, and in 1919, its assembly voted in
favour of becoming part of Germany. This might have been the
best thing that could have happened for both Germany and
Austria, but, not surprisingly, the Allied powers were determined
to keep them apart. What was denied by the peace treaties was
achieved by Hitler. From the start, the new Austria was riven by
violent political conflict and her people suffered harsh economic
distress. The great powers, particularly Great Britain and the
United States, poured money into Austria to try to keep her
from total collapse, but it was with an increasing sense of hopelessness. As early as December, 1920, the British Cabinet agreed
it was impossible to give Austria any more money. But ministers
were not entirely insensitive to the misery of Central Europe,
where millions were starving, and they agreed that '800,000
barrels of pickled herrings, which had been purchased by the
Government and were now in the hands of the English and
Scottish Fishery Departments, should be declared surplus and
transferred to the Disposal Board for export to the countries of
Central Europe so far as was found practicable.' And no doubt,
if the pickled herrings ever reached the hungry of Austria and her
neighbours they were duly grateful for them. The Austrian
question came up in Cabinet again later the same month where it
was reckoned there was every prospect of Austria breaking up
within the next few months and that 'there would be a general
scramble among the neighbouring states for her remains.'
Despite this pessimism, the Government went on trying, with
other countries, to raise funds to help Austria. At a Cabinet
meeting at the end of June, 1921, Balfour told his colleagues that
while most of the money had come from Britain and America
and France's contribution had been negligible, the French had
managed to give the impression that the money had come from
them.

A year later, on July 4th, 1922, the Cabinet was ready to give
up Austria for lost. Her condition was reported to be 'practically

hopeless.' The Governor of the Bank of England considered that the effects of a financial collapse in Austria would not be all that grave, chiefly because they had already taken measures to discount such a possibility. Now if the same thing happened in Germany, said the Governor, that would be a very serious matter. The Cabinet was convinced. There was general agreement 'that no useful purpose would be served by advancing further financial assistance to the Austrian Government merely with a view to postponing what appeared to be an inevitable financial catastrophe.' There was no doubt that Britain had done a good deal at a time when the demands upon her public purse, both from foreign countries and from her own people, were many and heavy. On August 14th, the Chancellor of the Exchequer, Sir Robert Horne, told his colleagues, with a strange imprecision, that, since the armistice, Britain had advanced to Austria between £10 million and £15 million 'without any satisfactory results.' Austria was in a very disturbed condition, he told them; wages were very high and the army was full of communists, whom he reckoned the chief cause of the unrest. Horne said he agreed with the Governor of the Bank of England that 'nothing possible remained to be done' and that Austria must be left to her fate. He was speaking a few hours before an inter-Allied conference decided to stop all further governmental loans to Austria and hand over the problem to the League.

What the Allied powers seemed to be doing—and probably thought they were doing—was washing their hands of Austria and leaving the League to take whatever opprobrium was going when the country broke up. Prudent voices advised the Council of the League to have nothing to do with it, because the certain failure to save Austria must harm the League. But the Council took it on. One of the curiosities of the history of the League of Nations is to observe how men like Balfour who, as a member of the British Cabinet, must be held responsible for the Government decision to abandon Austria, could strike a quite different attitude when representing his country in Geneva.

The Council set up an Austrian Committee, of which Balfour became chairman, and which included, apart from the French and Italian members of the Council, Eduard Benes, the Czech Foreign Minister, whose personal abilities and energies had given his newly independent country considerable influence in Europe and at Geneva, and Monsignor Seipel, the Austrian Chancellor. Delegates who had gathered in Geneva for the third Assembly of the League heard Seipel make a public appeal on behalf of his country to the Council. His manner was sober, restrained, but highly effective. The sympathy he attracted for his people was confirmed and strengthened the following day at the Assembly when successive speakers called upon the League to save Austria. It was another of those emotional demonstrations which so often passed as a substitute for action. On this occasion, however, the delegates were ready to translate their words into practical aid. In line with the proposals from the Austrian Committee a loan was floated in the world's great financial capitals. Several countries came together to support the loan with certain guarantees. The Austrians accepted the necessity for new taxes and rigorous measures to put her economy back into shape and to assure those subscribing to the loan that they need not fear for their money. A commissioner-general, appointed by the League, arrived in Vienna to oversee the whole operation. Austria had sunk so low she could not be rescued without much suffering. But rescued she was and although she was to endure intense political conflict her economy was stable—or as stable as it could be without union with Germany—until the world depression. It was a model example of collective international action. It justified Monsignor Seipel's statement at Geneva, 'Thank God we can say, today the League has not failed us.'

The Austrian issue was not the only occasion on which the League succeeded where the Allied powers had failed; Upper Silesia was another. By the summer of 1921, of all the new frontiers required by the peace treaties, the frontier between Poland and Germany in the rich industrial region of Upper Silesia was the only one which had not yet been drawn. As had happened elsewhere, a plebiscite had been held—in March that year—to find out what the people of the territory themselves wanted. It showed a majority in favour of belonging to Germany, but a substantial minority voted to be part of Poland. A solution to the problem was made all the more difficult because of the way in which the Polish and German peoples in Upper Silesia were intermingled; there was no simple territorial distinction to be made between them. The economic benefits of the industrial area were desired, understandably, by both Poland and Germany; but it was hard to see how there could be any physical separation of the factories and mines, the sources of power, and the means of transport and communication, which had developed a vital interdependence.

It was bad enough that Poland and Germany should be in bitter conflict over the future of Upper Silesia, with Germany claiming the lot, and Poland wanting all the industrial area and most of the rest. What was even more disturbing was the divisions it created among the Allies themselves. Britain and Italy sided with Germany, although they did not propose she should have the whole territory; France backed the Poles. The French accused the British of implicit encouragement to the German Government in its instigation of provocative action by German nationals in Upper Silesia; the British repudiated those accusations, citing evidence of the representations they had made in Berlin, and in turn expressed their alarm at the belligerent noises being made by France and at the hostile actions of the Poles. It reached the point at the end of July where the French were threatening to send in an additional division to reinforce their troops which, along with those from other Allied countries, were there to keep order. The French had not consulted the British or Italians on the need for another division; indeed, the British Cabinet was told that Briand had not consulted Marshal Foch or General Weygand, either. The French Prime Minister claimed that French forces in Upper Silesia were in peril and must be protected; the British attitude, he said, could lead directly to a 'rupture' of Franco-British relations. There was some discussion in Cabinet about the precise meaning of the French word 'conflit' used by Briand in his Note; but there was no doubt about his general intentions. The British saw his threatened independent action as primarily a political gesture, intended to intimidate Germany; they also took it as expressing the French view that the Alliance had served its purpose and could now be ended without undue concern.

Crisis meetings were held, the world waited for the break between Britain and France to be formally confirmed and for the explosions that were likely to follow as direct or indirect consequences. The break never came. The Supreme Council—that body whose continued existence was regarded by such as Cecil as obstructing the League's growth—decided to hand over the problem to the League Council and to abide by whatever solution might be proposed. This move was hailed, not only because of the immediate relief of tension it provided, but also as a significant enhancement of the League's authority. (Oddly enough Hughes, the Australian Prime Minister, had been among the first to urge the submission of the question to the League; one may safely assume, however, he did not do so for any better reason than to get shot of the whole business.)

Those who, as with Austria, forecast nothing but humiliation for the League had solid reason for their apprehensions. The problem was an ugly and intractable one, and the dangers of further violence—there had already been serious and protracted clashes between Poles and Germans resulting in numerous deaths—were real. But the League possessed a valuable quality denied to the Supreme Council: detachment. The Council set up a four-man committee, composed of the representatives of Belgium, Brazil, China and Spain; the committee called in outside experts from Czechoslovakia and Switzerland. Out of that committee came a brave solution. Upper Silesia was to be divided between Germany and Poland according to the clear preferences revealed by the plebiscite. The frontier would run through the heart of the industrial region but the two countries were to agree to conditions—that men and goods, for instance, should pass freely across the border—which would preserve its industrial and economic unity. There was to be a joint commission and a joint tribunal, both of them headed by neutrals, to hear complaints from either side of the frontier and to dispense judgements on questions of law. The arrangement was to last for an initial fifteen years.

That was the proposal the Council of the League put to the Supreme Council in October, some two months after it had first been asked to tackle the problem. The Supreme Council duly accepted it. In Germany the reaction was one of such outrage the League might have been suggesting that Upper Silesia should be handed over whole to Poland, whereas most of the territory and a majority of the population were to become part of

Germany. However, the Council had stipulated that the province would stay under Allied control until Poland and Germany had negotiated a treaty embodying the League's proposals and elaborating them in all the practical detail which would be necessary to implement them effectively. So, with continuing public shows of indignation, the Germans met the Poles. There was virulent ill-feeling between the two delegations, but they hammered out a comprehensive agreement—the Geneva Convention on Upper Silesia—and signed it on May 15th, 1922. It worked well, so far as the economic and industrial aspects were concerned. But the provisions which were supposed to guarantee the rights and security of the national minorities could not eradicate the historical animosities between the two peoples. Throughout the term of the Convention there were persistent complaints, from both sides of the frontier, of injustices and deprivations, which provided Hitler with just the kind of material he wanted to justify his demands and his aggressions. But no solution the Council could have devised could have prevented that.

In 1923, the Council, chiefly through the efforts of Lord Cecil of Chelwood (as Robert Cecil had now become), who, at Baldwin's invitation, had become Britain's representative there, reasserted its own authority and redeemed the good name of the League. Both had been in jeopardy because of the activities of the Saar Governing Commission and, in particular, the conduct of its chairman, the Frenchman, Victor Rault. Rault, a first-class administrator, dedicated to the wellbeing of the Saarlanders, had reacted to strike action by the Saar miners with measures of illiberal severity, issuing a decree restricting freedom of speech and curtailing that of the press. Acting, as he was, on behalf of the League of Nations, it was the League which could be accused of this attack on liberty. All five members of the commission were summoned before the Council at Geneva and examined, in public sessions, upon the way they had discharged their responsibilities. Rault had already withdrawn his decree before appearing before the Council in July, 1923, and the effect of those hearings was salutary both upon him and his colleagues and upon the press and spectators who attended them. The Council was seen to have exercised its ultimate power over the commission, but it had done so in a way which did not diminish that body or depreciate its members.

The League had had less reason to congratulate itself upon its handling of the Albania issue, although there, too, it could claim partial credit at least for the outcome. Albania—admitted to membership of the League at the first Assembly—was another of those countries which had to wait upon the decision of the Allied powers for the determination of her frontiers. This responsibility was delegated to the Ambassadors' Conference in Paris and the ambassadors seemed in no hurry to make up their minds. The League's performance was less than satisfactory because of the excessively patient way it waited for the decision, despite Albania's protests, while Greece, Italy and Yugoslavia made no secret of their designs upon Albanian territory. Troops from those countries, stationed in Albania—especially the Greeks and Yugoslavs—took up more and more menacing postures. Throughout 1920 and then deep into 1921 the ambassadors vacillated. The danger of war grew as eruptions of violence, with consequent casualties and refugees, multiplied. At last, in November, the ambassadors gave their verdict: the frontiers should be much as they had been in 1913, when Albania had become independent; only the Yugoslavs would make any gains and these would be very slight. But by now direct action by Yugoslavia had become an imminent possibility and, belatedly, chiefly as the result of Lloyd George hurling a threat of sanctions against the Yugoslavs, the League Council stepped in and insisted successfully upon the evacuation by foreign troops of Albanian soil. A League commission was there, on the spot, to see the Council's will enforced. Albania's freedom was brief, of course, for it was not long before Italy, acting as the agent of the Allies and concerned ostensibly to protect Albania's independence, attained economic domination over that country, followed eventually by the seizure of physical control of it as well.

Mussolini's successful grab in Albania was not to come until 1939. A much earlier adventure—involving Italian occupation of the island of Corfu—was seen by many contemporaries as a failure by the League to assert its authority over one of the great powers caught out in a flagrant breach of the Covenant. It is certainly impossible to record the incident as adding to the League's list of successes.

What happened was a consequence, in a sense, of the Albanian settlement, because it was while he was at work on Greek territory, marking the frontier between Greece and Albania, that the Italian general, Tellini, and four members of his staff, were murdered when their car was ambushed. The date was August 27th, 1923. Mussolini, who had come to power at the head of a Fascist government the previous autumn, reacted rashly and violently. He issued an ultimatum to Greece, demanding that an inquiry into the crime should be held, should be attended by an Italian representative, should be completed within five days, and that, irrespective of the result of the inquiry, Greece should pay Italy the equivalent of around £500,000. The Greeks showed themselves ready to go a long way to meet the Italian demands, but refused to pay compensation unless the inquiry proved the crime had been committed by Greeks. (The crime was never solved.)

Mussolini sent warships to Corfu, shelled the island, causing some deaths, and seized it. The invasion happened just as the fourth Assembly of the League was about to meet in Geneva, and on the very day when the Council was beginning its session. There was no doubt of the general outrage or of the almost unanimous acceptance of the Greek claim that the dispute had now reached a condition where, under the terms of the Covenant, it had become the League's responsibility. Greece declared herself ready to accept absolutely the League's decision. Mussolini's attitude was characterised by the kind of bombastic threats with which the world was soon to become familiar. The British Government's attitude, from the beginning to the end of the episode, was that Italy had failed to observe the conciliation procedures laid down in the Covenant and the 'authority and prestige of the League' must be maintained. That was the line taken in the Council by Cecil, in both private and public sessions.

The tension at Geneva mounted quickly. The small nations looked to the Council to act firmly to call Italy to heel, invoking, if necessary, the provisions in the Covenant by which member-nations could be called upon to join together in enforcing 'the maintenance of right and justice.' But, once again, the authority of the League was compromised by the dual loyalties of the Allied powers. Although Mussolini retreated before world opinion, he insisted that the dispute should be examined by the Conference of Ambassadors, the body which had appointed General Tellini as chairman of the commission entrusted with the task of determining the Albanian frontiers. The French saw it in their interest to play along with the Italian dictator. The British, through Cecil, worked to prevent the conflict between Italy and the League and between the Council and the Ambassadors' Conference from becoming so acute that it could do permanent damage to the League of Nations. The agreed compromise, however, was not a happy one. The Council did consider the dispute and put forward its views on how it should be resolved. But it put them to the Conference of Ambassadors, conceding, implicitly at least, that body's superior authority. Greece, too, said she would abide by the judgement of the Conference. The Conference accepted most but not all of what the Council of the League had proposed. In the end, although the commission of inquiry appointed by the Conference was unable to identify the murderers, Greece was forced to pay the 50 million lire (about £500,000) to Italy. That was the result of pressure exerted by Mussolini to which the other Allied powers submitted. He threatened to hang on to Corfu unless the Greeks paid up.

The settlement made a nasty smell. The Greeks were bitter; the Assembly felt it had been betrayed and that the League had been degraded. Mussolini appeared to have triumphed in his assertion that where a nation was powerful enough it was justified in using force to further its interests and the League had no right to interfere. But, in the face of obstructive tactics by the Italian representative, the Council reasserted its rights and responsibilities under the Covenant in a legal report which also repudiated the idea that a nation could be held responsible for crimes committed inside its borders. The Council, by calling for this report, had gone some way towards restoring its own standing and to healing the resentment in the Assembly. It was probably true, too, as Stanley Baldwin said, that if it had not been for the League the whole incident might have developed in a much more serious way. And although Mussolini had got his own way by bullying and while there is, at this distance, an inescapable temptation to draw a parallel with his successful aggression in Abyssinia, it could be said that he emerged from the episode with a greater respect for the weight of international opinion than he had felt before. That, at any rate, is what the optimists said at the time. The pessimists held that the League had been faced with its most important challenge and had been found wanting.

5

'The explosive temper of M. Poincaré'

On the agenda for the Cabinet meeting of October 20th, 1921, was the subject of the forthcoming visit to England of the wartime President of France, Raymond Poincaré. A number of public functions were to be held in his honour and that prompted a difficult question: which, if any, members of the Government ought to attend? There was a common hostility towards Poincaré. Ministers remembered strong criticisms he had made of the British Government; the embarrassment he had caused by publishing, without authority, a confidential letter written by the Prime Minister to Clemenceau. They reminded each other of his strong opposition to the current French Prime Minister and Foreign Minister, Aristide Briand. In the end, they agreed it would look too much like a deliberate snub if they all stayed away from the functions, but that there should not be any general attendance and certainly neither the Prime Minister nor the Foreign Secretary should be seen at any of them. Before long, Poincaré was to present the British Government with much more serious problems than those of etiquette and protocol, and whatever irritation he had caused Lloyd George in the past was trivial compared with what was to come. Poincaré was to embody French obduracy and his single-minded pursuit of what he regarded as legitimate and essential French interests was to attract an animosity which symbolised an astonishing deterioration in Anglo-French relations to the point where accusations of treachery were being hurled across the Channel and the

British Government was regarding French military strength as a threat.

Poincaré, the squat, inflexible lawyer from Lorraine, came back to the centre of the stage, succeeding Briand as Prime Minister in January, 1922, at a time when what Europe needed was a man of broad, generous vision in charge of French affairs. Instead, in Poincaré, it got a man in blinkers, obsessively legalistic in his interpretation of French rights, dedicated to the reduction of Germany to permanent impotence. Arthur Salter, who, as general secretary of the Reparations Commission, worked along-side Poincaré, its first president, has described him as a 'tireless, perfect machine, as efficient for the definite task, as unadaptable for any other, as cold and as inhuman.'* The machine applied itself to the enforcement of German obligations and French rights under the Treaty of Versailles with, as Salter says, no concern for what the effect might be elsewhere:

'The Treaty gave France the right to so many gold marks and these he would have . . . Impeccable in personal integrity, austere and unexacting in his own life, he was a patriot Shylock, exacting for his country the last ounce of flesh and blood, what-ever the consequences for his relations with his Allies or the ultimate future of Europe and the world.'†

The League of Nations was never involved directly in the question of reparations, but the story of Germany's ultimate admission to the League would be incomplete without a sketch, at least, of the dramatic events which preceded it; it is also necessary to trace the development of French policy towards Germany in the years immediately following the war and the conclusion of the Versailles Treaty.

First, and ever-present, were French fears for her security from yet another German invasion. These fears, above all other considerations, determined the behaviour of French governments between the two world wars. To understand them we have to go back, once more, to the failure of the United States to ratify the Treaty of Versailles and the Covenant. At the Peace Conference, Clemenceau, greatly to Poincaré's unease, had traded in French demands for a frontier on the Rhine for an Anglo-American guarantee against unprovoked aggression. When

* Op. cit. p. 196.   † Op. cit. p. 197.

Wilson lost the battle in the Senate, the 'guarantee' evaporated, leaving France exposed, yet again, to attack by Germany. That is why the British Cabinet returned, time after time, to the possibility of offering some sort of substitute assurance to France of military support in the event of invasion by Germany. It also explains why, when the lust for vengeance against Germany began to give way in other countries to a recognition that the restoration of German self-respect was as important to the whole world as it was to Germany, France continued to work for the subjection of her old enemy. That attitude was certainly not confined to Poincaré. Long before he returned to the premiership, the French Government had been threatening to occupy the Ruhr because of German failure to fulfil her commitments under the Treaty. In December, 1920, and the month following, for instance, the British Cabinet was seriously worried by 'Notes of a drastic character,' containing threats of action, which the French had sent to the German Government. The French had been provoked by what they regarded as the unsatisfactory progress of German disarmament as required by the Treaty and the existence of unauthorised military forces. The British Government took a much more tolerant view. It considered that the Germans had made good speed with their disarmament, particularly in handing over and destroying their artillery; they still had some machine-guns and rifles, but those represented no more than a technical violation of the Treaty. As for the unauthorised forces, which amounted to about a million in the whole of Germany, again the attitude taken by London was that they did not constitute any real danger and certainly could not be composed into an army capable of resisting an Allied advance. Those forces consisted of local formations, raised to support law and order, protect property and preserve constitutional government. They were about 300,000 strong in Bavaria, where memories of the temporarily successful Spartacist revolt were still very much alive and the population still extremely nervous. The British Government agreed that those forces should be reduced, but the Germans should be given reasonable time to do so. The Cabinet was unanimously opposed to any drastic steps, such as the French were proposing.

The French were no less assiduous in their insistence that

Germany should pay, according to the letter of the law, for the damage she had done during the war. It was understandable enough. Britain might adopt a more charitable attitude, but then Britain had not been invaded and the war had not been fought over her land. Industries, farms, livestock, houses, roads, railways had suffered terrible destruction or damage in France. It was reckoned by 1925, that a total of 80,000,000,000 francs had been spent on the work of reconstruction. In their determination to make Germany pay, the French were often isolated, their proposals for enforcement going ahead not only of what Britain considered justifiable, but also of Belgium and Italy; but, as she made clear, France was prepared to go it alone, if necessary, whether it be in the occupation of ports like Hamburg or Bremen, and the seizure of customs there, or in the occupation of the Ruhr and the taking over of administrative and financial control of occupied territories. As the years went by and the Allies failed to reach agreement with Germany on what the extent of the reparations should be, British irritation with the French Government intensified, while the French attitude towards Germany hardened. When the subject came up yet again in Cabinet, following another speech of a 'menacing character' by Poincaré, Balfour stressed the contradictory nature of French policy. Britain's misfortune, he said, was that we had an ally who, at one and the same time, wanted a Germany rich enough to pay indemnities and also a Germany that was ruined. Lloyd George said he was anxious to press the Germans to pay but in doing so he did not want to produce a disaster which would shake Europe. So far as possible French action was concerned, he pointed out that Britain had never refused, after consultation, to enforce sanctions on Germany. He instanced the occupations of Düsseldorf, Duisberg and Ruhrort in 1921. But now there was a threat of independent action by the French. A very serious situation would arise if the French advanced into the Ruhr, said the Prime Minister. It was true we could not actually declare war on France, but we could dissociate ourselves from her action.

That was on April 5th, 1922. That summer was one of chronic tension. On August 10th, ministers who had gone away on holiday were called back from all over the country to attend a Cabinet. Poincaré had put forward proposals of a most extreme kind, which would have bled Germany into a state of total collapse. Lloyd George was strongly antagonistic and saw no danger of Britain being out on her own if she refused to go along with France. The United States, he said, regarded France as 'imperialistic, militaristic and aggressive,' and if France were to march into the Ruhr he had no doubt whatever that the sentiment of the US would be behind Great Britain. In his view, Lloyd George added, there was evidence to indicate that France was endeavouring to re-establish the supremacy in Europe which she had exercised from time to time in history. If Poincaré were to deliver an ultimatum to Great Britain and British ministers were to accept it, the only interpretation to be placed upon their action would be that Britain had yielded up control of Europe, not to France, but to Poincaré and his chauvinistic friends. Then the Prime Minister made a comment which contrasted sharply with what he had said three years earlier during the Khaki Election. Then, he had thought it necessary to indulge the popular appetite for revenge: 'The Germans must pay to the uttermost farthing,' he had said, 'and we shall search their pockets for it.' Now, in Cabinet, he said that the British working man was definitely opposed to reparations. The only people in England, said Lloyd George, who supported the French point of view were those who had never ceased to fight against Germany since the armistice.

More remarkable than Lloyd George's change of attitude and, as he interpreted it, that of the British people, was the speed and extent of the decay in Anglo-French relations. This did not manifest itself only over Germany; indeed, it was French conduct during the Greco-Turkish war which provoked within the British Government the most vehement reactions. Britain's attempts to help Greece establish herself in Asia Minor nearly landed her in a war with Turkey, too, and contributed to Lloyd George's downfall. During this Near East crisis the Allies blatantly ignored suggestions that it should be referred to the League, although the British Government did make the right noises in response to moves at Geneva and was prepared to go to the League as a last resort. But the great powers preferred to work for a settlement at a limited, secret conference, calling in the League only to clear up the mess—the refugees, that is. But the road to that settlement was, from the British point of view, a most anxious one, and a major cause of British anxieties was the behaviour of the French. As Curzon said in Cabinet on November 1st, 1921, France appeared to be adopting an attitude 'definitely hostile' to British interests in the Near East, using underhand methods. The following March, the Foreign Secretary, pursuing the same theme, was recalling for his colleagues the 'consistent and almost treacherous attitude of the French.' Come September, members of the Cabinet were exchanging thoughts on the 'desertion' by the French of British troops when the Turkish leader, Mustapha Kemal, threatened the Allied forces guarding the approaches to the Dardanelles; this was described as 'a most formidable historical event.' When the British Government sent an ultimatum to the local Turkish commander, the French premier protested at Britain acting on her own, without consulting her allies. Curzon, whose own high-handed stubbornness could be a match for Poincaré's, went to Paris to try to reach agreement on the terms for peace with Turkey. In London, the Cabinet studied the texts of telegrams in which Curzon described his meetings with Poincaré. The first lasted three and a half hours and went on in an atmosphere of 'mounting tension,' until it reached the point where 'this provoked an exchange of somewhat pointed civilities between us, delivered in Monsieur Poincaré's case with that peculiar timbre of voice which he always affects in moments of exceptional emotion.' When Curzon returned home, he gave a verbal account of his dealings with the French Prime Minister, and described how at one stage Poincaré 'had lost his temper and had well earned M. Clemenceau's description of him as being both "weak and violent." '

On November 1st, 1922, after the Lloyd George coalition Government had fallen and had been succeeded by a wholly Conservative one, led by Bonar Law, Curzon, who was still Foreign Secretary, gave his new colleagues a summary of how difficulties had built up between Britain and France. 'These difficulties,' said Curzon, 'are not due merely to the explosive temper of M. Poincaré, but to the inherent perfidy and insincerity of French policy.' Poincaré, on this occasion, he described as 'a clever, hard, rigid, metallic lawyer.'

Distrustful of French intentions, the British were all the more anxious about the maintenance by France of powerful military forces. As early as December, 1921, when preparing for the forthcoming visit of the then French premier, Briand, to discuss war debts and reparations, the Cabinet heard the suggestion that if France was in financial trouble, it was her own fault. She had refused to economise, she was still maintaining a very expensive army, fleet and air force, and was engaging in costly adventures in the Near East. On March 15th, 1922, the Secretary of State for Air told the Cabinet of the new programme of aircraft construction which was designed to increase the number of French long-range bombing squadrons from sixty-two to one hundred and forty; Britain, he said, had just one bombing squadron in England. France was building 150 aircraft a month; Britain was building 23 a year. It was generally agreed, the Cabinet minute records, 'that French air development constitutes a formidable danger to this country.'

In September, 1922, when the frictions over the Near East situation were most acute, Poincaré sent a Note to the British Government, on the question of Inter-Allied debts and reparations, which cut deep. The tone of the second half was described as 'offensive' and it included a suggestion that France had been overcharged by Britain for consignments of foodstuffs and materials supplied during the war, by adding overhead charges and export duties. Some members of the Cabinet would have liked to pass over the allegations in silence, that being more in conformity with the dignity of the British Government. It was recognised, however, that to ignore the accusation might lead the USA to think there was something in them.* The Americans were now pressing their Allies to settle their wartime debts, and this was to engender further divisions and distrust between the nations which had fought side by side. (The American war debts, indeed, were to discolour relations between the United States and her former allies for many years to come.)

Throughout the second half of 1922, meeting after meeting was held to discuss war debts and reparations, none with any

* The Cabinet was told that it was possible one per cent had been charged in certain instances as out-of-pocket expenses; the same practice had been followed by the Americans. But no duties of any kind had been included. Furthermore, the accounts had already been agreed with the French authorities.

real success. So far as Germany was concerned, Poincaré refused to budge. Either she paid in full, or France would go into the Ruhr to claim her rights. In Germany, the mark had begun to slide. After the armistice, it had stood at six to the dollar. By July, 1922, it had fallen to five hundred to the dollar. At the end of that year, the rate was around ten thousand. It was then that Germany asked for a moratorium on reparations to save her economy. Yet another conference was held, first in London and then, after a break, in Paris. Bonar Law favoured temporary leniency towards Germany, but Poincaré regarded the British proposals as 'an abrogation of the Treaty of Versailles.' The French premier, who had rejected earlier suggestions from London that the issue should be referred to the League of Nations, now assembled his legal justifications—Germany had certainly defaulted on her reparations payments—and ordered the 'invasion' of the Ruhr. A team of engineers and managers, French, Belgian and Italian, with substantial military backing, took over the mines and factories. Poincaré's plan, for which he had the overwhelming support of the French Assembly and the French people, was to seize the production of the Ruhr industries. But the German Government organised passive resistance to the occupation. Work stopped. For nine months, the Germans held out, while the country was ravaged by a fantastic inflation which brought about the ruin and starvation of millions; the mark fell to a rate of more than four billion to the dollar. The rest of Europe was appalled and alarmed by the bitterness of this new conflict between France and Germany, but Poincaré blocked further attempts to involve the League of Nations by threatening, if necessary, to quit the League. The French and Belgians did manage to get the Ruhr industries going again, even in the face of German opposition and obstruction, which included sabotage, and they loaded trains with the 'productivity' which Poincaré had demanded. But by the time the German Government called off the strikes, admitting total defeat, there was considerable disenchantment within France about the whole operation. Poincaré himself showed no sign of repentance, but he had to submit to a demand that an international committee of experts should be set up to examine the whole question of German reparations. This committee, the Dawes Committee, at length produced a plan which, despite vehement opposition within Germany, was accepted by the German Government and approved by the Reichstag. The Dawes Plan committed Germany to heavy and regular payments, but it also stipulated that, if a default on Germany's part was established, sanctions could be imposed only upon the unanimous agreement of the Allied powers and in conjunction with the United States, which, while keeping its distance, had perceived the necessity of contributing to the settlement of an issue which had imperilled the peace of Europe once more. By the time that settlement had been achieved, Poincaré had fallen from power. But the consequences of his action were to show themselves in the years to come. The French economy was weakened—and he himself would be recalled to save it. The German economy had suffered total collapse and was rescued only by huge loans: it cost far more to put Germany back on her feet than she ever paid out in reparations. Worst of all, Poincaré's behaviour had nourished extremist forces in Germany and made the task of moderate leadership even more perilous than it was anyway bound to be. When all allowance has been made for French sufferings and French fears of Germany, it is hard to see Poincaré as other than the villain of the piece.

6

'Germany's empty chair'

The signing, in the summer of 1924, of the London agreements which formally settled the reparations question—for the moment, at least—and authorised a huge loan to Germany, cleared the way for the German comeback to the international stage. The man who had done most for his country to bring about that settlement was the same man who, at great political risk to himself, had called an end to passive resistance in the Ruhr, and who was to lead Germany into the League of Nations—Gustav Stresemann. Like Austen Chamberlain and Aristide Briand, the two men with whom he was to be so closely associated in that brief period when the sun seemed to be shining upon the League, Stresemann was to be subjected by contemporaries to extremes of adulation and abuse. Nearly fifty years later, a more dispassionate assessment can be made, and from it Stresemann emerges as one of the major figures of the twentieth century. It has been said that had he lived and had he been treated more generously by Germany's old enemies, particularly France, Hitler would never have come to power and Europe would have been spared the Second World War. To say that is almost certainly to exaggerate. Like all the fascinating ifs and buts of history it is impossible to say for sure whether Stresemann—the man who, as Chancellor, ordered the suppression of the 1923 Munich putsch and the arrest of its leaders, Ludendorf and Hitler—could have changed the course of events in any material way. Stresemann could not have changed the circumstances—above all, the world economic depression—

which Hitler was able to exploit to get control in Germany. But it is true that so long as he was Foreign Minister—his Chancellorship lasted a brief but critical hundred days—Germany pursued her interests peacefully, within the framework of international law and with a broad respect for her international obligations. Stresemann has been attacked by non-German critics for his two-facedness—for saying one thing at Geneva for world consumption and something quite other to his countrymen at home. In Germany, in his own time, he was called 'traitor' often enough (Chamberlain and Briand suffered the same kind of vilification from certain of their compatriots). The truth is that, of course, Stresemann worked first and last to further the interests of Germany, but he saw he must do this by licit means and he recognised that the creation of an effective international organisation was of as much value to Germany as to any other nation represented at Geneva. Like any other statesman, however, he could go only so far ahead of his own people and he was never free from the threats and pressures of the right-wing nationalists.

Stresemann would never have denied that he, too, was a nationalist, but Chamberlain's initial prejudice against him—fostered by Asquith—as a typical Junker was absurd. Stresemann was a middle-class Berliner. His father sold bottled beer and Stresemann's thesis for his doctorate was on the development of the bottled beer trade. He was a romantic, forever seeking pleasure and inspiration from Goethe; his devotion to his well-born Jewish wife lasted until his death. He was a square, chunky man, who enjoyed his food and drink and who, during those good days at Geneva, was often to be found at a restaurant table with a group of journalists around him. He suffered from kidney disease and a weak heart and was unfit for military service, but the man left behind when his contemporaries went off to the trenches had no doubts about the justice or prudence of the war and he shared the popular belief in a greater Germany. His views did not change much, and even where they did it was only gradually. But he was a realist and he had flexibility and he wanted a Germany which could live in peace alongside other great powers which recognised her equality. Stresemann, the outstanding political leader of the Weimar Republic, never really ceased to be a monarchist, but he would never have used violent means to bring about a constitutional change. His ultimate aims for Germany were a final solution to the reparations question, revision of her eastern frontiers—the recovery of Danzig and the Polish corridor and of Upper Silesia—a colonial empire and union with Austria. He would use every trick in the international negotiator's book to gain those ends, but he did not contemplate force. That does not mean he did not know of the secret deals concluded between the Russians and the German Army whereby the Germans, in defiance of the Versailles Treaty, should build aircraft and submarines and make weapons and poison gas on Russian territory. He, like other Germans, smarted under the sentence of the peace treaty limiting a German army to 100,000 men and insignificant arms, while France, in particular, did so little by way of achieving the general disarmament about which the delegates to the Paris Conference had talked so idealistically. The secret rearmament and training of troops and pilots was some solace to German pride; it made Germany a little less vulnerable; but it was never sufficient during Stresemann's lifetime either to endanger seriously the peace of Europe or to bring him under too much pressure from behind in the conduct of peaceful negotiations. The speeches Gustav Stresemann made at Geneva extolling peace and the community of nations were not, then, elaborate essays in duplicity. He deserved the Nobel Prize he was awarded in 1926 just as much—or just as little—as Briand with whom he shared it, and Chamberlain, who had shared one the year before with Charles Gates Dawes, the American Vice-President who had chaired the committee on reparations. The road from the Ruhr to Geneva had been a hard and skilful one.

From the earliest postwar days the British Government had favoured Germany's admission to the League. Even before the Allied delegates met at the Peace Conference, Lloyd George was advocating her entry, if for no better reason than that Germany might be less dangerous inside the League than outside. Thereafter, the question came up from time to time in Cabinet and, invariably, the general feeling was that Germany ought to be a member and that Britain would support her application, but perhaps the time was not yet quite ripe. It was not ripe because

France, as personified by Poincaré, was opposed to German membership. Attempts by Britain behind the scenes in Berlin to urge the Germans to apply for membership only encouraged Germany, which knew very well where the French stood, to play the reluctant maiden. Those who wanted to portray the League as nothing more than an exclusive victors' club were fortified in their arguments. When the British made a direct approach to Poincaré he rejected the idea contemptuously and the British, preferring discretion to valour, allowed him to get away with it.

The French attitude was entirely consistent. It was the direct product of America's failure to join the League and so to join with Britain in guaranteeing France against invasion by Germany. France's search for security was obsessive but scarcely surprising. She was also, as we have seen, determined—however disastrous the consequences—to make the Germans pay for their sins, and until Germany had done full penance she could not be considered cleansed and fit to mix with other nations. As often as the British Government pondered the possibility of Germany entering the League, so it also discussed the notion of offering France some sort of formal assurance that, in the event of an unprovoked aggression by Germany, the whole resources of the British Empire would be behind France. Such a guarantee, it was reckoned, would not only make France feel safer, but would also remove suspicions that Britain had turned her back on her ally in favour of Germany. Because of the strained relations which resulted from the French action in the Ruhr, this idea never got very far.

Coincident with the French quest for security went the moves within the League to achieve a reduction of armaments. The long, exhausting, frustrating, sometimes farcical, ultimately futile search for a disarmament formula which would satisfy the aims of Article 8 of the Covenant* will be dealt with in detail in a later chapter, but some mention of it must be made here because it is inseparable from the sequence of events which led to Germany's entry into the League.

To the 1923 Assembly, from the Temporary Mixed Commission—the special body set up by the first Assembly to plan the reduction of armaments—came proposals for a Treaty of Mutual

* See Appendix.

Assistance. The basis of the treaty was a belief that disarmament must go hand-in-hand with the promotion of security, because no nation would cut down its defences unless it could be sure of effective help and protection against aggression. The treaty was to be open to all countries, whether members of the League or not. Any nation which signed would assume an obligation to go to the aid of any other whose territory had been invaded. The Council of the League would decide whether aggression had taken place and, if so, by which country. It would have the power to tell each nation acceding to the treaty what economic sanctions it must impose on the aggressor and what financial, material and military help—the latter only inside its own continent—it must provide. The League would appoint a commander-in-chief under whom the multinational forces would serve. Lastly, only those nations which had accepted the Council's plans for cutting down armaments would be eligible for collective assistance under the treaty. Cecil was one of the most powerful influences in the shaping of the treaty; he held firmly to the view, throughout his life, that the provisions of the Covenant for the enforcement of sanctions against an aggressor were too generalised and would be inadequate when put to a major test. But it was precisely the unambiguous nature of the commitments envisaged in the proposed treaty which made it unacceptable to the British Government. If there was one line of thought which linked virtually all British Cabinets between the two world wars it was that they had no wish to extend Britain's international commitments beyond those prescribed by the Covenant—and there were times when they did their best to evade those as well. Even Ramsay MacDonald's first minority Labour Government, dedicated as it declared itself to be to the strengthening of the League, was no exception. It was this government which had to make the decision whether or not to support the Treaty of Mutual Assistance: it wanted nothing to do with it. Nor did the governments of the dominions. Nor did the United States, Russia or Germany. Italy was in favour on the whole, but disliked that part of the treaty which acknowledged the right of individual nations to make special defensive arrangements, tantamount to alliances, with any other nation or group of nations. Alone of the big powers, France, now under the premiership of Edouard Herriot, the radical-socialist leader, was fully in approval. The treaty was killed.

It would not be fair, however, to leave the impression of the MacDonald government as merely negative and destructive in its attitude towards the League. The British wariness about entering into comprehensive commitments was characteristic of the Foreign Office, where, as in the Quai d'Orsay and the Wilhelm-strasse, there was a professional distaste for open diplomacy and idealistic talk about a world parliament. No assessment can be made of MacDonald's reasons for any course of action without taking account of his colossal vanity. It was not enough for Ramsay MacDonald to be Prime Minister; he had to be his own Foreign Secretary as well. MacDonald was not simply opposed to the Treaty of Mutual Assistance; he had much greater ideas of his own which he wanted to expound at a world disarmament conference where he would be a leading figure. Yet MacDonald's internationalism was probably genuine enough in 1924 (the evidence of his decline in the Cabinet papers of the 1930s makes shameful reading); that of Arthur Henderson, who was to be Foreign Secretary in the second Labour Government, was certainly so. By leading a delegation to the fifth Assembly in 1924—the first Prime Minister to do so—MacDonald made a gesture which gave a significant boost to the prestige of the League. Herriot went to Geneva, too. The Anglo-French lead was followed by the smaller powers; in all, over twenty prime ministers or foreign ministers attended that Assembly. (MacDonald appointed, as British representative on the League Council and minister in charge of League affairs, Lord Parmoor, a politically inexperienced pacifist, whose younger son, Sir Stafford Cripps, was later to describe the League as 'an international burglars' union.')

MacDonald loved a great occasion. He particularly loved a great occasion at which he was the centre of attention. The atmosphere at the fifth Assembly in September, 1924, had everything he could have wished for. He was to initiate a debate on disarmament and security. The city of Geneva was overblown with delegates, journalists and visitors, who had been drawn there by the announcement that he, the British Prime Minister, and his French counterpart, were to speak. In the Salle de la

Réformation, which Vernon Bartlett described as 'the worst ventilated building put up in any modern city,' a most distinguished gathering of international statesmen and diplomatists took their seats in the hall. The heat was ferocious; before long people were fainting and had to be carried out. Unfortunately, MacDonald muffed his opportunity by showing himself insensitive to his audience, wholly misjudging the kind of speech expected of him, and thereby, incidentally, revealing his basic lack of sympathy for the League itself. However deficient in powers the Assembly might have been, the majority of the delegates did regard it as a world parliament and they conducted their debates in a parliamentary manner. But the Salle was not designed as a parliamentary chamber and when MacDonald went to the rostrum and looked ahead of him he saw not, as in the House of Commons, his fellow-parliamentarians, but the faces of visitors packed into the public gallery. The speech he made was the kind of speech he would make to a vast public meeting rhetorical, emotional, full of generalities: it was MacDonald showing off.

It would be easy to make too much, anyway, of MacDonald's respect for the League of Nations. At heart, he still believed, like Lloyd George, in the affairs of the world being settled by a few great men. True, his presence at Geneva did enhance the League, but that he was there at all probably owed more to Herriot than to any deliberate decision on his own part. It was Herriot who, after the British rejection of the Treaty of Mutual Assistance, initiated the discussions which were to lead, though accidentally, to Germany's admission to the League. He came to London in the summer of 1924, very soon after taking office. His main purpose was to talk about the forthcoming London Conference—which MacDonald was to chair with very considerable skill during July and August. (That was the conference which produced the agreements on reparations and a loan for Germany.) But he came also with ideas for a new formula for security. He found MacDonald in a receptive frame of mind, for the British premier was scratching around for some way of showing that, despite the killing of the mutual assistance treaty, he still wanted to strengthen the League. Out of their talks together, and following on the three-day debate which they led at Geneva, came the setting-up of a committee under the chairmanship of Eduard Benes, who was so often to be found assuming a major responsibility on behalf of the League. And from that committee came the Geneva Protocol.

The Protocol evolved logically out of the theme first deployed by Herriot: that security should still be linked to the limitation of armaments, but the backbone of the new treaty, or protocol, should be a system of arbitration. The Protocol also set out to remedy what was now seen as a weakness—or 'gap,' as it became known—in the Covenant. A nation still had the right to use war as a means of settling a dispute with another nation if, after it had submitted the issue to the Council, the Council had failed to reach a unanimous decision about how to solve it. The Covenant had also been criticised because the machinery it provided for examining an alleged aggression was too slow and cumbersome and could allow an aggressor to get away with his crime. All signatories to the Protocol would have to submit their disputes to arbitration, either by the League or some other body, and, where appropriate, to accept the compulsory jurisdiction of the International Court. Further, they must not mobilise their forces while a dispute was subject to arbitration and any nation which did go to war, whatever the circumstances, would be deemed automatically the aggressor. The arbitration decision was to be binding. The military obligations of the Protocol were somewhat less demanding than those of the Treaty of Mutual Assistance. It was for each member-nation to say what forces it would be prepared to use on behalf of the League and those forces would remain under national control. Those were the main provisions of the Protocol, which was seen as leading directly to a world disarmament conference to be held in Geneva in June, 1925.

On October 2nd, 1924, the Protocol of Geneva received the unanimous approval of the delegations attending the fifth Assembly. The Assembly recommended its acceptance to all member-governments. The Protocol was opened for signature at Geneva. Ten nations signed immediately, led by France. Britain's delegates, Parmoor and Henderson, could do no more than express their personal support: they had no authority to act on behalf of their government. The MacDonald government had been most insistent that the final decisions must rest with governments, not with the Assembly. Britain never did sign the Protocol. In Cecil's view, our failure contributed directly to the disasters of the 1930s. Not only was Britain seen as obstructing efforts within the League to reinforce the Covenant, but, by her default, giving positive encouragement to the aggressors to chance their arms. The blame for rejecting the Protocol is often laid wholly on the Baldwin government which succeeded Mac-Donald's in November, 1924. True, it was the Conservatives who swung the executioner's axe. But there is good evidence to believe that the Labour Government would probably have killed it, too. In his speech to the Assembly, MacDonald had declared his mellifluous faith in compulsory arbitration, but only in general terms; when it came to the binding commitments of the Protocol, that was quite another matter.

While the Protocol was still in the process of drafting, the Cabinet was expressing its anxieties about the new obligations which might be involved, and demanding the right to examine the proposals thoroughly before there could be any question of a British signature to the document. At its meeting of September 29th, the Cabinet heard the text of telegrams which had passed between the Prime Minister and Lord Parmoor. MacDonald's message of September 21st included this passage:

'. . . I also hope, as it is a thing that the French will never understand, that you are emphasizing at every point that all proposals *must be considered by Governments* and accepted by Parliament; and that while making this reservation we are just as sincere in our determination to come to an agreement as any of the countries which are trying to rush us.'

In his reply the next day, Parmoor said:

'We are all of the opinion that we are not committing HMG to anything outside the limits of your speech . . . We have emphasized at every point that all proposals *must be considered by Governments* and accepted by Parliament. There was a prolonged discussion on this point between British and French representatives in sub-committee. British delegate refused entirely to place Government under obligation until matter had been brought before it and proposal accepted by Parliament . . . Yesterday: Long meeting with British Dominions and full explanations that there was no committal of Governments at this stage of any kind. Dominions were in agreement and I think there is now no real difference between us. You may rest assured that we shall not go outside the above limitations.'

But not even those assurances completely satisfied the Cabinet at its meeting a week later and it authorised MacDonald (as Foreign Secretary) to send another telegram to Parmoor to the following effect:

'Cabinet has considered the Geneva position in view of confusing reports in papers regarding signing a protocol which might commit the Government in any way . . . You are urged to make clear that any signature you may give, if signatures are unavoidable, will carry no more meaning than that you are agreeing to make such a recommendation to your Government.'

Apart from opposition within his own Cabinet—and even granting, generously, that he himself would have accepted it— MacDonald, leading a minority Government, faced a largely hostile Conservative Party and suspicion in the country about the Protocol. The chief cause of disquiet among the people was the belief that if Britain signed the Protocol she would surrender control of the Royal Navy to the League of Nations. This misconception, repeated and exploited by Tory newspapers, fed that distrust of foreigners which never lies far beneath the surface of an Englishman, even one rationally dedicated to an international ideal. What is curious is that no steps were taken by the Government to squash it at the outset. MacDonald had assured his own colleagues on this point at a meeting on September 22nd. In the course of a progress report on the negotiations at Geneva, the Prime Minister said that the basis of the scheme was that any nation which refused arbitration would outlaw itself, and ['in that event the various nations would employ their forces as required. It had been made clear that acceptance of obligations of this kind would not in any way affect the principles of international law under which our Fleet would act in the event of the British Navy being at any time engaged after the British Government had decided to support the League of Nations against aggression or to assist a victim of aggression.] . . . The obligations assumed under this scheme did not exceed those incurred under the Covenant of the League of Nations, the extent of which did not appear at present to be fully realised.'*

In that final comment, MacDonald was voicing the argument, advanced by opponents of the Protocol, that there was no point in producing another document which said no more than the original Covenant. This was not a view, it need hardly be added, which was shared by such as Lord Cecil or Lord Grey, who believed the Protocol could make a member-nation's obligations more specific and action by the League more expeditious.

However, as we know, MacDonald did not have to declare his hand openly, for shortly after the Protocol had been opened for signatures, and after only nine months in office, he went to the country. The Conservatives swept back, helped no doubt by the tide of jingoism, with a majority of more than two hundred. As his Foreign Secretary, Baldwin appointed Austen Chamberlain, a man whose name was to be identified with those few years when it looked as though the League did mean something, and might mean so much more in the future. Chamberlain has had many detractors, including both opponents and supporters of the League, the latter on the ground that while he paid lip-service to the League, he continued to conduct British foreign policy as though the League of Nations did not exist. The truth is that Austen Chamberlain began his time at the Foreign Office very much as one of the old school, recognising, as he must, the necessity for Britain to do her bit at Geneva, but reserving always to the British Government the right to know what was best for Britain—and, perhaps, for the rest of the world—and the right to act on that assumption. It was not that he was opposed to the principle of a League but he would take a lot of convincing that it could do all it aspired to do. He expressed his reservations in a speech he made in his Birmingham constituency only a few weeks after the end of the war:†

* Minutes were taken of this meeting, as of a Cabinet, and they have been included in the documents now open for examination at the Public Record Office, but across the list of those present is scrawled the superscription: 'This was not a meeting of the Cabinet at all and no record should be made.' It bears the initials 'JRM.' Curiously, the passage enclosed in square brackets was crossed out on the original document and the word 'No' is written in the margin, apparently by the same hand.

† *Birmingham Daily Post*, December 13th, 1918.

'We want to establish among the nations some Council with authority to call before them disturbers of the peace, to have submitted to international judgement the alleged causes of a quarrel. To make this ideal effective there must be some international sanction behind it. There must be some force which that Council of Nations can employ in order to enforce its decrees. That involves, in the first place, the creation of a tribunal in which the different nations of the world have confidence. But if the tribunal is to have force behind it, it must be such a League as inspires such confidence in the different nations that, on the decree of that League, those nations will put their resources at the service of the League to execute its decrees. It means for ourselves, if such a League is to be brought to full perfection and fruition, that there should be some British force acting no longer on the orders of the British Government, but called into action, despatched here and there, at the demand of the League of Nations and its International Council. That is a tremendous demand to make on any nation, and probably such a League will only be the result of slow growth over long years.'

Austen Chamberlain's attitude towards the League never really changed in any fundamental way; he remained cautious and reserved when others wanted to enlarge its responsibilities. But he moved from a position of negative approval—an approval which never included Woodrow Wilson, whose speeches about the League he described as 'an orgy of rhetoric'—to one of positive promotion. He was, in so many respects, a most surprising man to carry the banner of internationalism. In appearance, he was the caricature of the English ruling class, tall, upright, his face of a heaviness that was almost brutish, monocle jammed in his eye, with a passion for—what else but gardening? The caricature was not entirely misleading. He was the eldest son of Joe Chamberlain, the Birmingham manufacturer who had broken with Gladstone over Irish home rule and later, as colonial secretary in Tory administrations, had become a zealous imperialist; Austen was devoted to his father's memory. He also had that high regard for personal honour and rectitude which foreigners are sometimes generous enough to associate with the caricature Englishman. Austen Chamberlain insisted on resigning from the India Office in 1917, when his department was held to bear some of the blame for the mistakes and horrors of the Mesopotamian campaign, showing an attachment to the concept of ministerial responsibility which has faded in British politics in more recent years. What the caricature conceals, but what his diaries and letters show,* is a sensitivity and capacity for warm emotion in personal relationships. Chamberlain was much more, after all, than a top hat, a frock coat, a monocle and a Union Jack could symbolise.

Austen Chamberlain's appointment brought little joy at Geneva, however, especially among members of the League Secretariat, who thought they could recognise an enemy when they saw one. Understandably, Chamberlain, who visited Geneva in December, 1924, almost immediately after taking office, seemed to them an opponent of all they respected and cared for. He distrusted not only rhetoric but logic, as applied to politics, as well, believing the relations between nations, as between individuals, too complex and too shifting to be confined within the barbed wire of a rule-book. They saw him as hostile to idealism. That was not altogether fair, but in politics he certainly put practicality first. Anyone working permanently for an international body wishes to see that body taking over more and more of the powers and prerogatives exercised by individual countries; very early in his time at the Foreign Office, Chamberlain made clear to the men at Geneva that Britain, under his guidance, was going to keep a tight watch on any attempts by the League to assert a supranational authority. At the Cabinet of December 3rd, 1924, for instance, he persuaded his colleagues to give him, as Foreign Secretary, a certain discretionary power when dealing with the League. If the League asked him to nominate British subjects to serve on League committees, he could 'require that the person nominated should act on instructions from HMG.' At that same meeting, he announced his intention of speaking to the Secretary-General of the League, Sir Eric Drummond, 'with a view to avoiding the possibility that British subjects might be asked to serve on committees without prior consultation with HMG.' Chamberlain intended,

* The Life and Letters of Sir Austen Chamberlain, Sir Charles Petrie (Cassell, 1940).

in other words, to see that neither the League nor its civil servants got above themselves.

There was little doubt that the new British Government would reject the Protocol, but it was duly considered, in formal fashion, both by the Cabinet and by the Committee of Imperial Defence, which came forward with the view, supported by opinion in the Dominions and in India, that the Protocol was 'open to grave objections and cannot be accepted.' The Cabinet recognised, however, that Britain must do the graveside honours decently. Balfour was given the job of helping Chamberlain to compose an appropriate elegy, the draft of which was approved by the Cabinet on March 4th, 1925:

'. . . As all the world is aware,' it ran, 'the League of Nations, in its present shape, is not the League designed by the framers of the Covenant. They no doubt contemplated, and, as far as they could, provided against, the difficulties that might arise from the non-inclusion of a certain number of states within the circle of League membership. But they never supposed that among these states would be found so many of the most powerful nations in the world, least of all did they foresee that one of them would be the United States of America.

'It is no doubt true that there are many points of view from which these unfortunate facts have not proved to be of vital importance. The work of the League goes on, beneficent and full of promise. Though the United States remains in friendly aloofness, individual Americans have freely helped both by sympathy and service, while the generosity of the American public has greatly aided some causes in which the League is deeply interested. Could, therefore, attention be confined to the present and the past, it might be said with truth that the problems which even a weakened League has had to face have never over-strained its machinery.

'The hope may be justified that this good fortune will continue. But surely it is most unwise to add to the liabilities already in-curred without taking stock of the degree to which the machinery of the Covenant has been already weakened by the non-membership of certain great states. For in truth the change, especially as regards the "economic sanctions," amounts to a transformation. The "economic sanction," if simultaneously directed by all the world against a state which is not itself economically self-sufficing, would be a weapon of incalculable power . . . But all this is changed by the mere existence of powerful economic communities outside the limits of the League. It might force trade into unaccustomed channels, but it could hardly stop it . . .'

That last paragraph gave a glimpse, at least, of one of the major reasons why Britain really rejected the Protocol. In trying to enforce economic sanctions against an aggressor, the League—as represented by the Royal Navy—might well find itself trying to interfere with American trade and shipping. The Americans themselves were stridently opposed to the Protocol—partly for that very same reason—as Chamberlain found out from a very confidential exchange with Frank B. Kellogg, who was retiring from the ambassadorship in London to become Coolidge's Secretary of State.

Eight days later, Chamberlain addressed a public session of the Council in Geneva and buried the Protocol.

'The Protocol,' he said, 'purports to be little more than a completion of the work begun, but not perfected, by the authors of the Covenant. But surely this is a very inadequate description of its effects. The additions which it makes to the original document do something quite different from merely clarifying obscurities and filling in omissions. They destroy its balance and alter its spirit. The fresh emphasis laid upon sanctions, the new occasions discovered for their employment, the elaboration of military procedure, insensibly suggest the idea that the vital business of the League is not so much to promote friendly co-operation and reasoned harmony in the management of international affairs as to preserve peace by organising war, and (it may be) war on the largest scale.

'Now, it is unhappily true that circumstances may be easily imagined in which war, conducted by members of the League, and with its collective assistance and approval, will become a tragic necessity. But such catastrophes belong to the pathology of international life, not to its normal conditions. It is not wholesome for the ordinary man to be always brooding over the possibility of some severe surgical operation, nor is it wise for societies to pursue a similar course. It is more likely to hasten the dreaded consummation than to hinder it.'

This, however indirectly, was another way in which Chamberlain was expressing his distaste for the legalism of the Protocol and the risk of unpredictable, indiscriminate future commitments. But, as a realist, Chamberlain had known from the moment he contemplated rejection of the Protocol that he must be prepared to offer some constructive alternative which, above all, would tranquillise France's obsessive insecurity. On this subject, Edouard Herriot seemed scarcely less demanding and uncompromising than Poincaré had been. Winston Churchill, then Chancellor of the Exchequer, reported briefly to the Cabinet on January 15th, 1925, of the anxiety he had found in Paris among leading statesmen about France's future, with Germany likely to revive in the next five to ten years. Chamberlain told of how Herriot had stepped wholly out of line with his Allies on the question of evacuating the occupation troops from the Cologne area. The French Prime Minister's attitude was that the evacuation should take place not, as had been agreed, when Germany had fulfilled the military conditions of the Versailles Treaty,* but only when the comprehensive question of European security had been solved.

Chamberlain toyed with the idea of a purely defensive pact with France, but not for long. He did not need to be told how unpopular that would be with the British people—who had reacted sharply and impatiently to French behaviour in the postwar years—and with his own party. It was now that the need to end Germany's exile became a matter of positive urgency, and, in Berlin, Stresemann, too, sensed that the situation might turn very sour again, unless a way was found of dispelling French fears. He took the initiative by proposing a four-sided pact of mutual security, by which Britain, France, Italy and Germany would guarantee the Franco-German frontier. There is no need to dwell on the hiccups caused in London and Paris by Stresemann's early attempts to deal separately and secretly with

* The French alleged that Germany had been secretly rearming (as she had, of course) and used that as justification for not withdrawing her troops as had been agreed between the Allies. Britain, though sharing some of the French disquiet over the revival of German militarism, did not consider this sufficient pretext for delaying evacuation. Stresemann mocked the notion of secret German rearmament.

Britain and France, nor with the manner in which the original proposition evolved. The memorandum which Stresemann sent to Chamberlain in January, 1925, set the major European powers on the road which led to the treaties signed at Locarno in October of the same year and ushered in what was seen at the time as a new era of peaceful negotiation and conciliation. What is relevant here is the way in which the construction of those treaties was linked to Germany's entry into the League of Nations.

In Chamberlain's view it was essential that Germany should join the League and that whatever security pacts were made should complement, not conflict with, the Covenant. Whatever the quality of his own regard for the League, there were solid political reasons for this attitude: he wanted Germany to do everything possible to dilute French suspicions about her intentions; and he had to show the opposition parties at home—and, not less important, the League of Nations Union, a most powerful pressure-group—that he was not trying to sidetrack the League, but to strengthen it. More than once during the summer months preceding the conference at Locarno, Chamberlain had to reassure his Cabinet colleagues, who were anxious about public opinion, that, generally speaking, the proposed pact could not be invoked until after the procedure of arbitration or conciliation provided by the Covenant had been exhausted. On the other hand, the British Foreign Secretary had to satisfy French doubts as well. Briand, while agreeing with Chamberlain that the pivotal idea of the pact should be recourse to the League whenever 'difficulties' arose, was worried lest the Germans might get away with aggression because some minor power represented on the Council, fearful of offending Germany, could block the vital decision. Chamberlain suggested that if any of the nations guaranteeing the Franco-German frontier was satisfied an aggression had taken place, it could take action to discharge its guarantee without necessarily waiting for a Council decision. But Chamberlain made it clear that the pact should not come into operation for any minor or technical breach of the peace.

Stresemann did not always make life any the easier for Chamberlain, either. Like his British counterpart (and like Briand, who had succeeded Herriot at the Quai d'Orsay after another upset in French politics), Stresemann had to pacify opinion at home. (He had little interference from Marshal von Hindenburg, who was elected President in 1925, despite the old man's detestation of the League; Hindenburg's election sent shivers down non-German spines, however.) Germany had made similar offers in the past of a security pact but they had always been spurned by France. The Germans had seen the British take diffident steps towards full reconciliation with Germany, including her entry into the League, only to retreat quickly again when rebuffed by France. If both the French and the British now wanted Germany, Stresemann was prepared to exploit the situation for all it was worth. There was a time immediately following the successful London Conference in 1924, when the League Assembly at Geneva waited expectantly for a German application for membership. The Germans made no move; Stresemann reckoned he needed more time to carry public opinion with him; before Germany would apply to enter the League she would want to know that her terms would be met. He gave some indication of what those were at a press conference on September 12th, at which he also inferred that if Germany were to apply to join she would be making a generous gesture, for, after all, what was the League but a cosy little club for victors?

'The constitution of the League of Nations was drawn up by the victors,' he said, 'without consulting Germany, and they desired to secure for themselves the preponderating influence. The intention of it was, after the Peace of Versailles, to establish the power of the Allies on the League of Nations, and it could not be regarded as applying to us; for it was wholly inspired by the spirit of the exclusion of Germany, just as the idea behind the Treaty of Versailles was to exclude Germany from the affairs of the world. If in the meantime the situation has altered, and if there is now talk of Germany's empty chair and the necessity for her presence, the entry of Germany into the League is only admissible if the intention is to treat her as a great power. . . .

'It is further stated,' Stresemann went on, 'that it is an honour to be elected as a member of the Council of the League. Such an election is merely temporary. Only the permanent membership of the League Council is the acknowledgement of the position of the states there represented as great powers, and I am firmly convinced that we shall never recover our position as a great power with equal rights if we do not insist on its recognition in this connection. An essential condition, therefore, is the acknowledgement of our equality by the other powers. If these conditions are met, then Germany is ready.'*

The reactions of those nations which were already either permanent or elected members of the Council suggested that there would be no difficulty in meeting Germany's demand. But Stresemann laid down other conditions. He insisted there must be no admission on Germany's part of responsibility for the war, such as she was forced to make in the Versailles Treaty—the 'war guilt' lie, as Stresemann called it. This demand was good for domestic consumption; but Stresemann himself did feel very strongly that losing the war was not synonymous with bearing the guilt for it. This condition raised no problems, either, for there was no intention of asking Germany to make any such confession before entering the League; the Allies merely wished Stresemann would not go on about it, though. The French took the view that the responsibility for the war had been settled once and for all in the Treaty of Versailles—to everyone's satisfaction except the Germans'—but it was never intended to regard war guilt as an eternal stain upon the reputation of Germany. The German Government persisted, however, even to the point of issuing what the British Cabinet agreed was an 'ill-timed, written declaration' of innocence on the eve of the Locarno Conference.

Stresemann further claimed the right for Germany to participate in the League's mandatory system, which meant, in effect acknowledging her right to colonies. This went through on the nod, with none of the colonial powers asking awkward questions about whose colonies or which mandated territories would be handed over to Germany.

It was his fourth condition which caused most trouble. Because Germany was disarmed, said Stresemann, her only defence lay in her neutrality, and she should not be asked to surrender this ultimate protection for her defenceless people, which would be the consequence of her accepting the obligations of Article 16 of the Covenant—to join in sanctions, economic and perhaps

* *Gustav Stresemann. Diaries, Letters and Papers.* Edited and translated by Eric Sutton. Macmillan, 1935. Vol. i, p. 449.

military, against an aggressor. Stresemann wrote in these terms on December 12th, 1924, to Sir Eric Drummond, the Secretary-General, asking whether the League would consider Germany's 'special difficulties.' Germany was asking to be allowed to maintain an even more rigid neutrality than Switzerland, which had recognised at least the obligation to take part in economic sanctions. Germany wanted nothing to do with sanctions of any kind and did not wish to agree even to the passage of troops, acting on behalf of the League, through her territory. The Allied powers on the Council, and indeed the other members, were anxious to do all they could to ease Germany's entry into the League, but to have released Germany from obligations which were common to all other members of the League would have been to discriminate in her favour in a way which could only damage the League. Drummond replied to Stresemann by telegram on March 14th, 1925, emphasising the obligations in the Covenant; but trying, without saying so directly, to assure Germany she would be treated with sympathy and understanding if and when it came to a question of meeting those obligations:

'The Council regard it as advisable to point out,' said Drummond, 'that the nature and measure of active participation by the member states in military operations that may be initiated by the League, on the basis of the Covenant, must necessarily differ in accordance with the military position of the various states. By the provisions of the Covenant, the Council is obliged to lay down the strength of the land, air and sea forces which the members of the League must contribute to enforce respect for the obligations of the League. It would be for Germany herself to say to what extent she would be in a position to accept the recommendations of the Council . . . Nonetheless, when action is to be taken on the basis of Article 16, the provisions of the Covenant do not permit every member state to decide on its own behalf whether it will take part. The Council feels bound to express its view that any reserve in this direction would be calculated to undermine the principle of the League, and that such a position would be incompatible with membership of the League.'

That passage itself illustrates the confusion which existed, throughout the life of the League, about the extent of the obligation. The Council was obliged to say what forces members must contribute, said Drummond. In the next sentence he is saying that it was up to Germany to determine whether she could accept the Council's instructions. And then a reiteration that member-states cannot decide for themselves. This ambiguity at the heart of the Covenant was its greatest weakness, a weakness which the Treaty of Mutual Assistance, with its emphasis on the compulsory nature of the obligations, would have remedied—on paper, at least.

Drummond, on behalf of the Council, went as far as he could at the formal level to show the League's sympathy for the German position. According to Stresemann's diary of the Locarno Conference, Chamberlain and Briand, in private, went a good deal further. This, according to Stresemann, is how Briand interpreted Article 16:

'He said that Article 16 had in fact no force, it merely constituted a moral obligation on those nations that participated. An attempt had been made to give a form and substance to the peace. This idea (he meant the Geneva Protocol, though he did not refer to it by name) had been defeated by the nationalism of other nations; at which Chamberlain grinned.'*

Chamberlain took much the same view as Briand, but in illustrating it he gave a clear indication of how decisively an awareness of British self-interest dictated his interpretation of his country's obligations:

'Briand was right in so far as Article 16 was in some measure both definite and indefinite. The obligation of the nations was solely moral. It lay with them to decide whether and how far they would interfere. If, for example, war broke out between two republics in South America, membership of the League would not impose upon England the duty of interference. But if a war broke out between France and Germany, she would then have to range herself with all her power on the side of the party attacked.'†

A few weeks after the Locarno Conference had ended, Stresemann told the press of Dresden: 'In the course of the negotiations at Locarno it was said that there would be much relief if even the majority of the League members complied with Article 16,

* Op. cit. Vol. 2, p. 174.   † Op. cit. Vol. 2, p. 175.

and the extent of that co-operation might well be nil.'* The other delegations had obviously done all they could to convince the German Foreign Minister that Germany's obligations as a member of the League would be minimal; it would be agreeable to censure them either for their cynicism or their irresponsibility, but, sadly, history was to vindicate their assessment of the reality, as opposed to the ideal, of the Covenant.

For all that Stresemann, in negotiation, may have exaggerated his difficulties at home there is no doubt he had always to be on guard against a political knife in the back. In the period immediately preceding Locarno, he had to offer his resignation when he found that colleagues in the coalition Cabinet, including the Chancellor himself, Hans Luther, were trying, in the face of public hostility, to plead ignorance of the memorandum which had first proposed the security pact and to leave Stresemann taking the entire blame for it. Stresemann's resignation threat was successful, but the campaign against him by the right-wing German National Party and intensely nationalist newspapers went on. He started a prosecution against one man, a major, who had called him a traitor, and forced a public apology.

Stresemann was fighting against suspicions and accusations that he was surrendering German territory to the enemy—he was freely renouncing any German claim to Alsace-Lorraine—and demeaning his country by making it a member of a League which had deprived Germany of her rights in Upper Silesia. Chamberlain, on the other hand, had to satisfy doubters and critics that he was neither entering into any new and dangerous commitments nor harming the League by negotiating a regional pact. In view of the subsequent facile depreciation of the Locarno treaties as worthless pieces of paper, it is worth asserting that Chamberlain himself, at any rate, whether illuded or not, believed that he had embarked upon a course of action of major significance to the peace of Europe. Chamberlain was not a man for hyperbole; he would rather say nothing or resign than defend himself by distorting facts or seeking refuge in rhetoric. When he addressed the House of Commons, then, on June 24th, 1925, expressing his conviction of the good faith of the Germans and paying tribute to them for their initiative, and when he

* Op. cit. Vol. 2, p. 199.

commended the projected pact, his words deserve to be taken at their own face value:

'These proposals offer a great and happy prospect of a better and more peaceful world. Initiated by Germany, and received in this friendly spirit by France, they will come to nothing unless this country will lend its co-operation. In view of suspicions and hatreds, too new as well as too old and too deeply rooted, such a mutual pact has no chance of ever being signed unless we take our part and give to each side the assurance that our co-operation will give, that that mutual pact will be observed not only in the letter but in the spirit which prompts its origination. I plead not for these proposals as a party measure, but as a national policy. I plead for them with all the earnestness that deep conviction gives, because I believe the peace of the whole world and the peace of our own land depend upon their coming to a successful fruition. Nations, like individuals, have responsibilities proportionate to their opportunities and their powers. Our nation can go to the bar of history and we can plead that we have a good record, and that our fathers were not slow to pay their tribute to the service of humanity. I plead now that we should in our day, for the sake of our children and for the sake of the generations yet unborn, show ourselves worthy of the great position we have inherited, and the great traditions of which we are proud.'

Chamberlain also had the role of middleman between France and Germany, making it his business to see that misunderstandings which could, and did, so easily arise between the two old enemies were not allowed to be dangerously blown up. Throughout the run-up to Locarno, Chamberlain conferred closely with Briand, a man who was much to his liking, and with whom he developed a friendship which was much more than a congenial professional relationship and which was to endure those inevitable phases of friction between their two countries.

Of the great trio of Geneva, Aristide Briand was perhaps the most remarkable; certainly the most colourful. Briand was a Breton, a dreamer who was almost as lazy as he pretended to be. He claimed—or boasted—that he regarded reading a book or, worse, a diplomatic despatch, as so much wasted time. He was excited by ideas for their own sake; as an orator he could be accused of a shameless attachment to the purple passage. But this man, who looked like a character out of a prewar Renoir film, with his hulking figure, his shaggy head and cigarette dripping from his mouth, was a man of great vision, never less than a patriotic Frenchman but incapable of translating patriotism in the narrow, shuttered manner of a Poincaré. He could not hate as Clemenceau could hate. He was every inch a French politician, the son of a small farmer, who started out as an extreme socialist and ended up an object of bourgeois reverence, eleven times his country's Prime Minister, a man who almost relished political crisis. But it was his flexibility, his generosity and his imagination which served Europe so well at Locarno and Geneva. Briand had less cause than Chamberlain and Stresemann to worry about public opinion as he headed for Locarno. The French were more than reconciled to the idea of Germany joining the League; so far as they were concerned it was one more means of guarding France against attack, and they could never have too many of those. Briand's troubles were to come later.

Chamberlain and Briand met in London in August and again in Geneva the next month at the Council. (Chamberlain set the example of attending all Council meetings in person, a lead which Briand and other foreign ministers followed: Cecil said the only reason Chamberlain attended the Council personally in the first place was because the League Secretariat protested so vigorously at his original intention to send a junior minister from the Foreign Office; if it had to be a minister of Cabinet rank, Chamberlain was determined to keep responsibility for League affairs firmly in his own hands.) Invitations were sent out for the conference which was to begin at Locarno on October 5th: Locarno had been chosen to suit Mussolini's convenience. Chamberlain and the British delegation travelled by the Simplon express, dining in Paris on the way. Briand made his way by car. The Germans left Berlin by special train, and at Locarno, according to *The Times*, 'a crowd of curious and silent towns-people lined the forecourt of the railway terminus' to watch them arrive. But Stresemann and Chancellor Luther had left the train at the little town of Bellinzona and came down the valley to Locarno by road. The Germans set up their headquarters on their own in an hotel about a mile from the town centre; all the other delegations were at the same hotel, overlooking Lake Maggiore. Stresemann made a statement to the two hundred-odd journalists that the choice of hotel had no symbolic significance: the Germans had no intention of pursuing a policy of isolation.

In many respects, it was Chamberlain's conference. He was asked to take the chair as a recognition of the part Britain had played in setting up the conference. He himself fussed over even the smallest details to make the negotiations a success. He tried, for instance, to get a big round table for the chief delegates so as to generate a sense of equality; he had to make do with a square one, which was created by having a long rectangular table sawn in two. His manifest personal goodwill contributed to the pervasive air of optimism. He had come to Locarno prepared to suppress his dislike for Stresemann. When he met him, his prejudice evaporated and, as with Briand, he formed a warm attachment to him.

Not even the efforts made by the Germans, from start to finish, to deny responsibility for the war and to secure an assurance that the Cologne zone would be evacuated by the time the pact was signed, could dampen the general euphoria. The question of war guilt was just shrugged off. As for the occupation of Cologne, the French and British refused to give any pledge, but assured the Germans they would make a real attempt to meet their wishes. The Germans were not satisfied, but were not prepared to scuttle the whole conference for the sake of that one issue.

The sun shone on the lake. On October 10th, to celebrate Mrs. Chamberlain's birthday—she was there with her husband— the French and Germans joined the Chamberlains aboard a steam yacht. It was rumoured on another occasion that Briand had been seen taking Stresemann for a trip in a rowing-boat, an unlikely but picturesque story. On October 16th, which was Chamberlain's own birthday, the talks ended in what was regarded on all sides as complete success. Mussolini had now arrived, just in time to join the others in posing for the photographers around the conference table. The ladies in the British party were allowed to see the room where the great men had talked, and then Mrs. Chamberlain suggested they should all go out for a cup of tea. As they walked to the teashop, they were escorted by pressmen and cheering onlookers. It was indeed Britain's day, and the British Foreign Secretary found it impossible not to yield, when he came that evening to the public ceremony at which the several treaties were initialled, to the mood:

'And then the closing scene and last words,' he wrote in a letter to England two days later. 'None of us who were there will ever forget them. You might think that it would have lost something for one who like me had helped to arrange it that morning. It was not so; it was too tense with emotion, too perfect in execution, too profoundly sincere and generous.'* A few, short, sanguine speeches, commending the significance of the work they had done together, were followed by what amounted to a vote of thanks to Chamberlain, proposed by Briand; Chancellor Luther led the applause. Briand, Luther and Chamberlain stood in an open window and showed themselves to the crowds below; someone picked up the pact and waved it in the air. Mrs. Chamberlain was waiting for her husband in a corridor, where Briand found her. He took both her hands in his, and with tears in his eyes, told her of all that Chamberlain had done. 'Without him,' said Briand, 'I should never have tried.' Then Mussolini, according to Chamberlain, 'the simplest and sincerest of men when he is not posing as the Dictator,' also took her hands in his and covered them with kisses. 'I have lived such days and celebrated such a brithday,' wrote Chamberlain, 'as it is given to no man to experience twice.'† To his Cabinet colleagues on his return, the Foreign Secretary gave a full report on the Locarno negotiations and told them of the tributes which other nations had paid to Britain's contribution and 'to the high position which this country occupies in Europe at the present time.'

The documents initialled by the statesmen at Locarno spelt out in detail the guarantees for the inviolability of the frontier between Germany and France and Belgium and the promises never to resort to war as a means of settling disputes between those three countries. The means of achieving a peaceful settlement, of arbitration or submission to the League Council, were detailed. Only where a guaranteeing power was satisfied that an unprovoked aggression had taken place would it go im-

* Op. cit. Vol. 2, p. 289.   † Op. cit. Vol. 2, p. 287.

mediately to the aid of the innocent party; even then, there was to be simultaneous reference to the Council and acceptance of its ruling. Other treaties were drawn up at Locarno, involving Germany's eastern frontiers. From the earliest soundings, Germany had refused to give any guarantee to Poland and Czechoslovakia compared to the one she was prepared to give to France and Belgium; similarly, Britain had determined to limit her commitments to the west. What Germany did agree with the Poles and the Czechs at Locarno was to submit any dispute between them to a similar system of arbitration as laid down between the western powers. France signed separate mutual aid pacts with Poland and Czechoslovakia, but they did little more than confirm their obligations to help each other, as members of the League upholding Article 16, if attacked by Germany. The French guarantee to the Poles and Czechs, then, was worth as much or as little as the commitment any member of the League made upon accepting membership. (As for the British, time and again in the years leading to the Second World War, they resisted all attempts to draw them into any commitments in eastern Europe beyond those of the Covenant, until their belated reversal of policy in March, 1939. Then, they guaranteed to fight to save Poland's independence; Czechoslovakia had already been swallowed up. Britain's negative attitude had offered implicit encouragement to German adventures in the east.)

If there had been anxieties at Geneva about the negotiations at Locarno, they were quickly relieved when it was seen that the treaties made there were so closely linked to the League. As Austen Chamberlain said in the subsequent debate in the Commons:

'... I would ask the House to observe ... that all the agreements initialled at Locarno conform strictly to the spirit of the Covenant and the spirit of the League of Nations, that they are placed under the guardianship of the League, that the League is the ultimate authority in regard to the issue which may be raised, and that what we have done is not to subtract from the power of the authority of the League, but to support and to underpin that authority and power for the settlement and reconciliation of conflicts between nations.'

At the Lord Mayor's banquet at the Guildhall in London in

November, Chamberlain said that 'Locarno is a beginning, not a conclusion. It is not merely the written treaty, it is the spirit of Locarno that the world needs.' Dr. Sthamer, the German Ambassador, had at first refused an invitation to that banquet but agreed to attend after being pressed by the Foreign Office and the Lord Mayor. As he walked to his place, all the guests rose to their feet and applauded him until he had sat down. Beside him sat Chamberlain, who raised the loving cup and drank to the German, expressing his feelings of 'respect and friendship' for Germany.

'Such a scene,' Stresemann recorded in his diary, 'is cabled all over the world; people read it in Capetown, in Rio, in Shanghai, and they say to themselves: "What is happening in Germany? The Germans must be becoming a great nation again if they are honoured in this fashion." '*

Later that month, Stresemann said in the Reichstag of the 'spirit of Locarno': 'I believe this spirit is best established when idealism and real interest combine to seek a common way out of the European imbroglio.'†

At the beginning of December, 1925, the Locarno Pact was signed in London. Not only did the way now seem clear for Germany's entry into the League, but the treaties she had signed made her entry that much more urgent and imperative.

* Op. cit. Vol. 2, p. 223.   † Op. cit. Vol. 2, p. 230.

7

'*We protest with the utmost energy ...*'

On Monday, October 19th, 1925, just three days after the pact had been initialled at Locarno, fighting broke out on the frontier between Greece and Bulgaria. At first, it seemed no more serious than a spasm, the kind of incident familiar to those nervous Balkan frontiers. The immediate accounts of what had happened were inevitably confused and contradictory. The trouble started in a mountainous region near a place called Demirkapu. According to the Bulgarians, a Greek soldier advanced into Bulgarian territory and fired several shots at the Bulgarian outpost sentry, who fired back in self-defence, killing the Greek. This provoked a general exchange of fire between the frontier troops and the fighting went on for several hours. According to the Greeks, the Bulgarians attacked Greek outposts, killing a sentry, and a Greek officer who advanced under a white flag to negotiate was also killed.

The Greek Government, headed by the obtuse dictator, General Pangalos, issued what was described at first as an ultimatum but later was held to be a 'demand for satisfaction with the briefest possible delay,' calling for an apology from the Bulgarians, the punishment of the officers responsible and payment of substantial compensation. The Bulgarians suggested an immediate inquiry and nominated its own delegates; Athens did not respond. On the Thursday, Greek forces invaded Bulgaria along nearly sixteen miles of frontier, attacking with rifles, artillery and bombs. The Bulgarian troops obeyed orders to retire from their posts and the authorities told the people living along the frontier to evacuate their homes. Between ten thousand and fifteen thousand people, from half-a-dozen villages and scattered houses, few of them bothering to take personal belongings or animals, began their trudge. Most of them were Macedonians, who had entered Bulgaria since the war; they knew already what it was like to be refugees and now they were being driven out of their homes once again. Behind them the Greek soldiers burned and pillaged, and their advance was accompanied by the usual rumours of atrocities. The Greek forces were considerably stronger than the Bulgarians, whose army had been limited to 20,000 men by the peace treaty signed at Neuilly in 1919, and incomparably better equipped. The Greeks advanced five miles into Bulgaria. Ahead of them lay the town of Petrić, which was subjected to a desultory bombardment, as the Greek army began to organise to attack it. Inside the town, the people started to dig trenches, and volunteers, with knives tied to long poles, joined the few hundred soldiers.

At 6 a.m. on the morning of Friday, October 23rd, the Secretariat at Geneva received a telegram from Sofia appealing to the League to intervene.

'. . . We protest with the utmost energy,' said the message, 'against this flagrant invasion of the territory of a country, which is well known to be disarmed, by the army of a country which is a member of the League of Nations, and which is acting in contravention of its fundamental obligations. In virtue of Articles 10 and 11 of the Covenant of the League, the Bulgarian Government requests you urgently to call together the Council of the League to take the necessary measures. Convinced that the Council will accomplish its duty, the Bulgarian Government is maintaining the order given to the Bulgarian troops to offer no resistance to the invader of the national soil.'

A few hours later, Austen Chamberlain was reporting to the Cabinet that a frontier incident between Greece and Bulgaria, which he had hoped would prove of no importance, had now flared into a dangerous situation. There was a real risk of war between the two countries; Article 11, cited by the Bulgarian Government, was concerned with 'any war or threat of war.' It was under that Article* that Drummond, the Secretary-

* See Appendix.

General, convoked an emergency meeting of the Council. He telephoned Briand, who was the current Council president, and by 11 a.m. the decision had been taken to summon members of the Council to meet in Paris on the following Monday. Briand sent telegrams to Sofia and Athens calling upon both countries to stop fighting and withdraw their troops behind their respective frontiers. That had the effect of causing the Athens government to order a halt, at least, to the invasion.

To Paris came Chamberlain from London, Hymans from Brussels, Scialoja from Rome, and Unden made the journey from Stockholm by 'plane, which was still a most unusual means of diplomatic travel. They were joined there by the two Latin-American representatives, Afranio de Mello Franco of Brazil and Alberto Guani of Uruguay; Ishii of Japan; and Quinones de Leon of Spain. Only the Czech member, Benes, was unable to make it. The Council met at the Quai d'Orsay and opened its extraordinary session at 6 p.m.—in public briefly, before going into private session for about an hour. When the members returned, Chamberlain, who was acting as rapporteur— or reporter—for the Council on this issue, said the Council was not satisfied that all hostilities had ended or the troops had been withdrawn as requested by Briand. It now asked both governments to inform the Council within twenty-four hours that unconditional orders had been issued to their troops to retire within their frontiers and, within sixty hours, that troops had actually been withdrawn, all hostilities had ceased and all troops warned that the resumption of firing would be severely punished. The governments of France, Britain and Italy were to send officers to report to the Council as soon as its request had been fulfilled. The Bulgarian representative, appearing before the Council to present his country's version of what had happened, found no difficulty in agreeing to the Council's resolution, for there were in fact no Bulgarian troops on the Greek side of the frontier and Bulgaria would be only too happy to see an end to all fighting. The Greek found it more difficult to speak with such assurance on behalf of Athens.

Chamberlain adopted a solemn and admonitory tone. This was a frontier incident, he said, of a kind which, more than once in the past, had had serious consequences when no machinery existed for the peaceful settlement of disputes. It would be an affront to civilisation, he declared, if now, with the machinery of the League at their disposal, the two governments concerned allowed such an incident to lead to warlike operations instead of submitting it to the Council, which would always have regard to their honour and security. The Council laid plans for the enforcement, if necessary, of its resolution. The British Cabinet was called to an urgent meeting in London on October 28th to give the Foreign Secretary the approval he sought for the line he proposed to take in the Council: he was intending to support firm sanctions against Greece, if she failed to obey the Council. The first warning was to be at the diplomatic level, with the immediate recall of chiefs of missions from Athens. That was to be followed, if the Greeks were still recalcitrant, by 'a naval demonstration at Piraeus.' The Cabinet went along with Chamberlain without misgiving, emphasising only that any 'demonstration' against Greece should be a joint one.

No such display of armed authority was needed. Although Briand's initial telegrams had not achieved an end to all fighting, they had certainly lowered the temperature. The Council's resolution did the rest. On Tuesday, the 27th, the Greek and Bulgarian representatives were called before the Council to state their cases. (When the Greek said his country's troops were acting only in defence of Greek territory, Chamberlain asked him, somewhat tartly, why, in order to defend a strip of land a mere fifty yards deep, his government had found it necessary to invade Bulgaria to a distance of five miles.) On Wednesday, the Council met again to hear reports of progress, and learned that some fighting was still going on; the Bulgarians said the Greeks had not withdrawn and the Greeks said the Bulgarians had fired first. On Thursday, however, the Council received a telegram from the British, French and Italian military attachés, who had been sent to the trouble-spot from Belgrade, that the Greek forces were withdrawing and had undertaken to complete the operation by eight o'clock that evening.

Peace returned to Demirkapu. The Council appointed a commission of five, headed by Sir Horace Rumbold, the British Ambassador in Madrid, to go there to conduct an inquiry. On Friday, October 30th, Austen Chamberlain went back to London, both Greece and Bulgaria having agreed to accept the commission's findings and its recommendations as to which side should pay compensation to the other. When the Council met in December, it had the commission's report before it. As might have been expected, it said that there was blame on both sides for the original frontier incident. Bulgaria should pay compensation for the death of the Greek officer who had been shot while carrying the white flag, but Greece must pay much more for the damage her troops had done when ordered to invade Bulgaria, in defiance of her League obligations. Greece had a bill for some £45,000.

As might also have been expected, neither country was content with the adjudication, but both accepted it. They also accepted the commission's proposal that two officers, drawn from the same neutral country, should be appointed to serve, one on each side of the frontier, to sort out any future quarrels on the spot, before they were able to grow into something more serious.

The Council had stopped what might have turned into a war, not just between Greece and Bulgaria, but one involving other countries as well. It had succeeded in imposing its authority on two member-nations. It had acted swiftly and effectively, using in exemplary fashion the machinery provided by the Covenant. Coming immediately after the giddy achievements of Locarno, it is small wonder the significance of the success was grossly magnified. What had really happened was that one small country, Greece, had been told by the great European powers, Britain, France and Italy, that if she did not do as she was told she would be made to do so. The warning was never expressed in explicit terms, but the Greeks understood very well what was meant. Yet it was a success, and the great powers had acted in the name of the League, according to the rules laid down in the Covenant, and it was indeed a model exercise which even Austen Chamberlain, normally so cautious about asking or expecting too much of the League, was to cite as an example of how, some day, the whole world might be kept in order.

*   *   *

Vilna, Albania, Upper Silesia, Mosul: all these were territories whose postwar frontiers or status were the source of contention and the League had the responsibility of finding a formula for settlement. The dispute over the ownership of Mosul generated one of the more dangerous situations with which the League had to deal and exposed once again Britain's alarming uncertainty of touch when handling Middle Eastern and Near Eastern affairs.

The Turks were never able to reconcile themselves to the loss of the provinces of Basra, Baghdad and Mosul, which had been part of the Ottoman Empire. They had been taken from the Turks by British forces and after the war had been brought together to constitute modern Iraq; the responsibility for helping Iraq to full independence was given to Britain by a mandate in 1920. Turkey resented most of all the loss of Mosul, the rugged, mountainous area which forms a natural barrier between Turkey and Iraq, and which was soon to be proved rich in oil. When the Turks and the Allies met at Lausanne, after the Greco-Turkish war, to negotiate a fresh peace treaty, Mustafa Kemal, the creator of the new Turkey, demanded that Mosul should again be Turkish. Britain refused to agree. The Lausanne treaty was signed with the fate of Mosul still undecided. Britain and Turkey were given nine months to try to settle it between themselves. They failed and, as previously determined, the dispute was handed over to the Council of the League.

That was in August, 1924. Both nations argued their cases at Geneva. The Council decided, as it so often did, to send a special commission to investigate the situation on the spot and to find out what the local population, most of them Kurds, felt should happen. Britain and a more reluctant Turkey—which was not a member of the League—promised to honour any solution the Council might propose and, meanwhile, to maintain the *status quo*. But, as soon became apparent, the two sides had different ideas about just what the *status quo* was and where the dividing line ran between Turkey and Iraq. Given that kind of confusion and the already high degree of tension it was not surprising that there should have been an eruption of violence. Briefly, it threatened once again to send Turkey and Britain to war.

So far as the British Government was concerned, all the blame lay with Turkey. On September 29th, 1924, the Cabinet was told that 'difficulties had arisen in Iraq owing to the ill-treatment by the Turks of certain Assyrians . . . who had fled, with the Turks in pursuit, across the boundary of the territory now being delimited by the League of Nations. The presence of the Turks across the frontier was calculated to cause great trouble in Iraq, and it had been necessary to bomb some Turkish forces.' The Prime Minister, MacDonald, told his colleagues he had called in the Turkish minister in London and made it clear that Britain could not allow Turkish troops to enter territory which was under consideration by the League. Britain did offer not to send her aeroplanes beyond a certain line, however, provided the Turks withdrew their troops. The situation appeared to be easier for the moment, said the Prime Minister, but he had warned the Turks that Britain would not be rushed into anything while the League was investigating.

A few days later, the Turkish troops were still there, and Britain issued an ultimatum giving them just forty-eight hours to get out or face military retaliation. Turkey appealed to the Council to say where the line between the opposing forces ought to be drawn. The Council held an emergency meeting in Brussels and settled on a demarcation line which the two disputing nations again pledged not to violate.

The situation quietened down and the commission appointed by the Council went to work. But the Turks tried to make sure of a satisfactory outcome without waiting for the Council's decision. As Chamberlain told the Cabinet in a memorandum the following April, Turkey had made several attempts to get a direct settlement with Britain, proposing a deal whereby Britain would hand over Mosul in return for economic and commercial advantages. These overtures had been repeatedly rejected, said the Foreign Secretary, and he himself had told the Turkish minister in January that it was unthinkable for the British Government to bargain away the rights of Iraq, of which it was the trustee, to profit British businessmen. Despite that, Turkey had now come forward with formal proposals for just such an agreement. The Cabinet agreed that Chamberlain should give the Turks a polite but firm refusal, reiterating the necessity of waiting for the result of the commission's inquiry.

When the commission did report its recommendations gave little joy to Turkey, Britain or Iraq. According to the commission, the people of Mosul had no wish to be part of either Turkey or Iraq. If they had to choose one or the other, they would prefer to come under the Iraqis, but only on condition that the British mandate continued for another twenty-five years. The commission recommended that, if that condition were accepted, then the frontier between Turkey and Iraq should be drawn along the same line which had been fixed by the Council at Brussels; that meant, in effect, that Iraq would get all but a thin slice of the Mosul province. If the condition were not accepted, said the commission, virtually the whole of Mosul should pass into Turkish control.

The idea of continuing under British mandate for another twenty-five years was grossly repugnant to the Iraqis. Right from the start, they had resented the necessity of the mandate, and Emir Feisal who, having been expelled from Syria by the French, had been invited by the British to become King of Iraq, had tried hard to persuade Britain formally to abrogate the mandate. He had also pressed for Iraq to have its own separate representation abroad, instead of being represented, according to terms of the mandate, by Britain. That was a prospect which filled the then Foreign Secretary, Curzon—in April, 1922—with some alarm. He sent a letter to the Prime Minister opposing the idea. 'Once Feisal attains his representation,' he wrote, 'he will not have much more to say to the Colonial Office and will cause us an amount of diplomatic trouble which I regard with the gravest apprehension and dismay. Mr. Churchill [who was Colonial Secretary] has been good enough to relieve me of Feisal. The last thing I want is to have him back again.' Britain placated Feisal by substituting a treaty relationship for the mandatory one, although still retaining the responsibilities conferred by the mandate. It was also understood that Britain would help Iraq to progress rapidly towards full self-government and to sponsor her admission to the League as soon as possible. The British had honoured their promises to the full and Iraq was looking forward to the ending of the dependent relationship when the League commission made its recommendation about Mosul. There was never really any question of Iraq refusing to accept the condition and allowing Mosul to return to Turkey. But her acceptance was made slightly less bitter when it was agreed that she would be free to apply for membership of the League within the twenty-five years, and if she was admitted the mandate would lapse.

The Council accepted its commission's recommendations but, before they could be implemented, the Turks raised a fundamental objection, questioning the Council's authority to make a decision unless both Britain and Turkey agreed, or to support any resolution unless all were in favour. Rather than take the risk of overstepping its authority, the Council decided to seek a ruling from the Permanent Court of International Justice. The Court did not take so long as many people feared. It ruled that the Council must be unanimous in reaching a decision, but it did not matter whether Britain and Turkey agreed or not; the decision must be accepted. The Turks protested but without effect. The Council went ahead and reached the expected decision in line with the commission's recommendations. That was on December 16th, 1925. For a few days before and after that decision, the British Cabinet held anxious meetings to discuss what ought to be done if, as was rumoured, the Turks took aggressive action to frustrate the fulfilment of the Council resolution. It was agreed that British warships should not enter the Dardanelles and the Sea of Marmora, unless the Turks had actually first attacked in the Mosul area, and even at the end of January, 1926, the Committee of Imperial Defence had before it a report on 'Possible action by the League of Nations to bring economic pressure to bear on Turkey.' Any such action proved to be quite unnecessary, just as Lord Cecil, back from Geneva, had assured the Cabinet on December 16th. He said that General Laidoner, who was chairman of the commission of inquiry and had just returned from the demarcation line, had gained not the slightest impression that the Turks intended to attack Mosul.

In June, 1926, Turkey, along with Britain and Iraq, signed the treaty embodying the Council's decision about the frontier. But it was still a Turkey yielding, under protest, to the inevitable. The British Government, having won the day, began to show rather more sensitivity to Turkish interests. According to the report of the Iraq policy committee:

'The main object of Turkey is to obtain a sense of real security within her own borders. This cannot be done by a guarantee to assist Turkey if attacked . . . but it could be pointed out to her that, in addition to the guarantee which we should be ready to give regarding the Turco-Iraq frontier only, she could obtain a great measure of security on her other frontiers if she came into the League. Her present distrust of the League could be met by the same arguments as were used in the case of Germany, namely, that the more Turkey is dissatisfied with the League, the greater the reason for her to seize the opportunity of obtaining a voice in the League's proceedings. But the suggestion might be approached upon much wider grounds. The Turkish Government is anxious to qualify in all respects as an up-to-date Western Power. It could therefore be represented to them with great force that membership of the League of Nations is the hall-mark of Western civilisation . . .'

But Turkey, which, before the Mosul affair, had seemed on the brink of applying for membership of the League, did not join until 1932, the same year as Iraq was admitted and Britain's mandate ended. Insofar as Britain had helped Iraq to fashion her administration, to develop her economy, and to establish parliamentary government, she had discharged her mandatory responsibilities to a high degree of success. But the assurances both Britain and Iraq gave to the League, in advance of Iraq's entry, about the protection of minorities were to be betrayed within twelve months when the Iraqi Army massacred several hundred Assyrians. It was the only episode of its kind, and the army had been provoked, but it was bound to bring accusations that Britain had been in too much of a hurry to give up her mandate.

8

'No more blood ... no more machine-guns'

Even after Locarno, Germany still hesitated before making her formal approach for membership of the League, despite the fact that the Locarno treaties could not come into force until she was a member. In the months that followed the initialling and the signing of the pact, and while the world waited upon Germany's pleasure, new problems arose which were to complicate her admission and might well have dealt the League a mortal blow there and then.

The trouble sprang from Germany's demand to become a permanent member of the League Council, thus demonstrating her status as a great power and her equality with her former enemies, Britain, France, Italy and Japan. That demand had been freely granted and there was an enthusiastic readiness within the League to accept Germany on to the Council. But now other nations claimed that they, too, were worthy of permanent seats in the Council and argued that if the Council could be enlarged to make room for Germany then why not for them, too? Spain, Brazil and Poland all pressed their claims, and other members of the League, including the great powers, began to take sides.

Chamberlain has been much criticised for his part in the whole messy business, both for not standing firm, in the first place, upon the principle that permanent seats must be reserved only for the great powers, and, later, for trying to find a solution by secret meetings of the Locarno countries instead of allowing the Council and Assembly to deal with the issue out in the open. Chamberlain, who was now Sir Austen, having been made a Knight of the Garter, met strong opposition both in the country and in the Cabinet for the line he took and Cecil, his close colleague at Geneva, threatened to resign.

Germany did not apply for membership until February 8th, 1926, but three months before that, on November 11th, the British Foreign Secretary was alerting the Cabinet to the difficulties which were likely to arise when three other countries staked their claim to permanent seats alongside Germany: Chamberlain said he had already undertaken to support Spain.* By the time the Cabinet met for a long discussion on the subject on February 17th, he seemed to have come a long way towards backing Poland's claim, too. But he must have found a lukewarm response to the arguments he produced to support his policy, for when he had finished speaking, he had to listen to one objection after another. The Council might well be diminished in authority, not increased, if it were made bigger. The basis on which permanent membership had been fixed at the Paris Peace Conference had been to limit it to powers whose interests were so worldwide that they could be regarded as concerned in the settlement of every serious international dispute. The Foreign Secretary's suggestion that because she was in a condition of 'acute controversy' with Germany, Poland ought to be granted permanent membership of the Council was seen as a curious argument and one which, if adopted, would provide a dangerous precedent. Chamberlain was also told that the great success of his policy up to that time had been the result of treating Germany as an equal for the first time; to support Polish membership of the Council would tend to weaken the popularity of his policy both at home and in the Dominions.

A week later, the Cabinet again discussed the question and Chamberlain again advocated a permanent Council seat for

---

* That great Spaniard, Salvador de Madariaga, tells of his retort to King Alfonso, who felt that Spain ought to have a permanent Council seat. 'But won't being *elected*,' said Madariaga, 'mean a greater honour?'

Spain, advancing yet another justification. He said that Drummond, the Secretary-General, had drawn his attention to the fact that, in 1921, it had been proposed that Spain and Brazil should become permanent members and that when the proposal was rejected, Lord Balfour had proposed that Spain alone should be added to the Council; Balfour had argued the case for Spain 'with great cogency and had almost carried it,' the proposal being defeated only by the opposition of Brazil. The policy of supporting Spain's claim, said Chamberlain, which he had put to the Cabinet in November, was therefore no new policy.

It was true enough that the Council had met in secret in 1921 to discuss the Spanish and Brazilian claims; what is surprising is the clear inference that Drummond was providing Chamberlain with ammunition in 1926, for Drummond of all men was aware of the constitutional principles involved, as well as the strong feelings of Germany. The Secretary-General had gone to Berlin, where he was warmly received, after Germany applied for membership of the League. Stresemann argued that her permanent membership of the Council would be devalued if others were given permanent seats at the same time. Knowing this, and knowing the destructive nature of the issue, it seems most unlikely that Drummond would have done anything to nourish it. Either Drummond was playing a foolish game, or Chamberlain was using his name to bolster his own case.

On March 3rd, the Cabinet returned to the subject to agree on the line to be taken at the special Assembly which was due to start in Geneva on the 8th. While giving Chamberlain and Cecil the discretion to do the best they could depending on the circumstances, the Cabinet laid down the principles upon which they were to act:

'No change in the Council can be admitted which would have the effect of preventing or delaying the entry of Germany. It would be best that Germany should, as a member of the Council, have full responsibility for any further change in the Council beyond her own admission;

'The rule that only great powers should be permanent members of the Council should in principle be maintained. Spain is in a special position and may require exceptional treatment;

'Neither Poland nor Brazil should be made permanent

members at present. But Poland should be given a non-permanent seat as soon as possible.'

The world's press had been following the growing controversy and adding fuel to it with nationalistic editorials, all of which Chamberlain deplored as unhelpful. At Geneva the delegations were arriving, aware that the League was in the middle of another crisis, but most of them still optimistic that before they packed their bags and left for home again they would have taken part in an historic moment, the entry of Germany. The Germans themselves were not deterred by the complications surrounding their admission. They could have taken the huff and stayed in Berlin until everything had been sorted out. Instead, Luther and Stresemann led what looked very like a triumphal procession. They were accompanied by a vast official retinue plus an even stronger contingent of German journalists sent to cover the once-only story of Germany's formal reinstatement as a great power.

In the French Chamber, just before the Assembly was due to meet, Aristide Briand, speaking of his first meeting with the German Foreign Minister, said, 'Stresemann and I then talked a new language, the language of Europe.' But it was an old language that they and the other Locarno powers, whipped in by Chamberlain, talked at Geneva, the language of secret diplomacy. Chamberlain genuinely believed that the way they had done things at Locarno, which was the way British Foreign Secretaries had always been accustomed to doing things, would be the most effective way of tackling the problems, and they would come out of hiding to present a grateful Council and Assembly with a ready-made solution. Day after day the men of Locarno came together for their secret discussions, Chamberlain, Stresemann, Briand, Scialoja for Italy, Vandervelde the Belgian, Benes and Count Skrzynski, the Polish Foreign Minister, who had a reputation for eccentricity and had refused to shake Stresemann's hand at the end of the Locarno negotiations. (Stresemann was assured later that there must have been a terrible misunderstanding which might be accounted for by Skrzynski's notorious absent-mindedness.)

The other delegations, which had come prepared for significant work in the Assembly, waited for more than a week while the secret talks went on, with mounting anger at their frustration and seeming impotence. Cecil felt himself at times almost as much in the dark as the others, and he left Chamberlain in no doubt of his view that the attempt to by-pass the Council and the Assembly was wrong, both in principle and as an effective practice, and damaging to the League.

All the comings and goings, the secret hagglings in hotel rooms, and the generous offer to stand down by Sweden and Czechoslovakia to resign their seats, failed in the end. Mello Franco, the Brazilian delegate, acting on inflexible instructions from Rio, refused to accept any solution which did not give Brazil a permanent seat in the Council at the same time as Germany. In the face of that attitude, the choice before the Council was simple: put the question to the vote, see it vetoed by Brazil, and risk a public snub to Germany which might force her to leave Geneva for ever; or adjourn the whole issue until the regular session of the Assembly in September. The Germans themselves had no doubt that an adjournment was preferable to what would be regarded at home as a public humiliation. After more arguments in the Council about the tactics to be employed, it was agreed that Chamberlain, as reporter, should speak first, explain why no solution had been found which would facilitate Germany's admission to the League, and voice his own disappointment, but also his confidence that the September meeting would see an end to the difficulties. Then Briand was to follow, expressing the Assembly's regrets and hopes for September in a formal resolution, a gesture which, it was felt, would at least soften the blow to Germany's pride.

Even after this had been agreed by the Council, there was what looked like another, last-minute hitch. Chamberlain was told that if he laid the blame for the failure upon Brazil's threatened use of the veto, then Mello Franco would follow him to the tribune and deny that his country had blocked German entry. Chamberlain heard that, late at night, after dinner. He arranged for the Council to meet yet again the next morning, before the Assembly, to hammer things out with the Brazilian delegate. Even later that same night, when he returned to his hotel, he was confronted by a threat of immediate resignation by Cecil.

But Cecil did not resign, and, the next day, before Chamberlain spoke, the little Brazilian, his face drained of colour, reluctantly but loyally carrying out his country's orders, told the Assembly that an additional permanent seat on the Council should not be given to another European country unless one were given at the same time to one from the American continent, to Brazil, in other words. Mello Franco said this, as instructed, despite not only personal appeals by Briand and Chamberlain to Rio, but also similar ones by the representatives at Geneva of the other South American countries. Mello Franco also criticised the way in which the Locarno powers had handled the issue, a view which found plenty of sympathy in the Assembly. When Briand spoke, it was with warm praise for the way the Germans had behaved in the face of a grievous frustration and he reaffirmed Germany's right to take her place in the League and in the Council.

There was no doubt that when the special Assembly ended, there was an overwhelming feeling that the League had been seriously damaged by what had happened, and the smaller powers were vehement in their criticism of the way the Locarno powers had tried to stage-manage the whole affair, thus depreciating the authority of the Council and the Assembly. Cecil, although persuaded to withdraw his resignation, wondered afterwards whether he should not have gone through with it. 'I never doubted,' he wrote in 1941, 'that our only hope of lasting peace was in the maintenance of a strong and effective League of Nations, or that a clear and courageous lead by this country was essential to the achievement of that object. The kind of fumbling that went on over the admission of Germany should have showed me that the Cabinet did not really agree with me.'* However justified his censure of the Locarno diplomacy, it is extremely doubtful whether, even if Britain had given the firm lead he wanted, and even if the whole issue had been exposed in public debate, the result could have been any different. The attitude of Brazil, determined by the dictatorial president, Arturo Bernades, was impervious alike to persuasion or criticism.

Austen Chamberlain, for his part, considered there was room, within his disappointment, for a degree of self-congratulation. No-one could have worked harder to find a successful formula;

* _A Great Experiment_, Jonathan Cape, 1941. p. 178.

an open conflict in the Council had been averted; most important of all, the unity of the Locarno powers had been preserved. He would have regarded a split among them—which was always possible—as nothing less than a disaster, a disaster, as he said himself, 'of unequalled magnitude.' Beside that, the sense of anti-climax and the pessimism which followed the failure at Geneva; the sneers now directed at the League by its enemies; and the fears among its friends of its imminent collapse seemed to him no more than a cause for real but measured regret.

The right-wing nationalists in Germany quickly exploited the situation, portraying it as one of humiliation and defeat for Germany. But, in defending to the Reichstag the decision of himself and the Chancellor to stay at Geneva, Stresemann was wholly justified in saying that the idea of a German defeat was held only in Germany and nowhere else in the world.

'Dispatches reached us by the dozen,' said Stresemann, 'telling us to come home. We should, I believe, have won ourselves very cheap laurels by doing so . . . We should have provided those very people who wanted to formulate a further charge of guilt against Germany with the material for doing so, if we had gone away at such a juncture.'*

There were many reasons for regretting the failure of the negotiations at Geneva, said the German Foreign Minister, but the chief mourner was the League itself.

'Different views may be taken of the League,' he told the German parliament. 'One—I may call it the idealistic view—sees in it the union of the nations for the sole purpose of the maintenance of peace and the furtherance of all humanitarian ideals. Those who are disposed to this view will be sorely shaken by such a meeting as this in which it was clearly shown how powerfully individual interest could make itself felt against just those general aims of humanity. The other sees in the League merely a new diplomatic method of international representation, and sees it from a strongly realistic standpoint. But from both standpoints,' Stresemann declared, 'its reputation has suffered. No matter which view of it is the right one, if the League has an aim, it must be the aim of universality.'†

Germany's request for admission was a step towards the

* Op. cit. Vol. 2, p. 523.　　† Op. cit. Vol. 2, p. 522.

achievement of this aim of universality, said Stresemann, and everything else, all other interests, should have been subordinated to it. But Germany's demand for a permanent seat in an un-modified Council did not mean that Germany was saying the Council should not be enlarged or that she was denying the rights of other powers to assert their claims later to a seat.

'Though we were not in a position at that meeting to support the Brazilian claim . . . we had no sort of intention of thereby expressing the view that the League was for us a European affair, in which the European powers claimed sovereignty over the nations of the rest of the world. The League in its true character must be a world League, and the claim of great conti-nents to be represented on it for effectual collaboration in what-ever form will be least of all disputed by Germany, whether it be Asia or America or any other continent that may come into question.'*

While not surrendering an iota of principle so far as the German demand was concerned, that speech, delivered as it was to his own parliament and his own electorate, immediately after what many of this countrymen were interpreting as a rebuff and an insult to Germany, must be regarded not only as a brave one but as much more than the kind of lip-service a statesmen might be expected to pay to the ideal of internationalism when addressing, say, a gathering of foreign journalists in Geneva.

But for all that, and for all their understanding and reasonable-ness during the abortive talks at Geneva, it was a matter of only five weeks before the Germans were to sign the Berlin Treaty with the Russians, an act which tested the nerves and the trust of many who had seen Locarno as evidence of a completely new departure in German foreign policy. The event, and the timing of it, was uncomfortably reminiscent of the pact signed between Germany and Russia at Rapallo almost exactly four years earlier. But the circumstances in which the two treaties were signed were very different, and, as Chamberlain assured his Cabinet colleagues, so was the German motivation and the manner in which Germany had entered into negotiations with the Russians.

The signing of the Rapallo Treaty in April, 1922, effectively shattered what might have been the grandest of Lloyd George's

* Op. cit. Vol. 2, p. 514.

many grand designs. It was he who had fathered the idea of a great conference, to be held at Genoa, which would 'remedy the paralysis of the European system,' and plan the way ahead for massive reconstruction. Economically, Europe was a shuffling cripple; vast numbers of people were hungry to the point of starvation; in even the more fortunate countries, like Britain, unemployment ran into millions. Politically, the wounds left by the war were healing slowly; frontiers were still unstable, governments were elected only to be quickly kicked out again; two great powers, Russia and Germany, were still treated as pariahs. Lloyd George proposed to change all that with a meeting of the mightiest men in Europe, who would make far-reaching decisions in which, he hoped, the United States would want to participate: it was indeed a vision to excite Britain's wartime leader. It was also a vision which betrayed Lloyd George into revealing his true attitude towards the League. When the idea of a conference was first mooted, supporters of the League, and certainly its Secretary-General, feared that one outcome might be the creation of new European institutions, agencies, and understandings, which would jeopardise the League itself and diminish its status, if not actually contravene the Covenant itself. When Eduard Benes, that loyal and industrious defender of the League, came to London to see Lloyd George in February, 1922, the Czech premier not only offered his mediation in trying to arrange an informal meeting between Lloyd George and Poincaré, who had just taken over from Briand as Prime Minister and Foreign Minister, but also pleaded for the League to be associated as closely as possible with the proceedings at Genoa.

Lloyd George said, accurately, that if the conference was placed entirely in the hands of the League, neither Germany nor Russia, as non-members, would be able to take part. The Russians, said Lloyd George, 'had an idea that Poland ran the League of Nations,' and they were very suspicious of the Poles. He added that the United States Government had been elected by opposing the League and consequently would be unable to participate in any international business undertaken by the League. In fact, Benes was asking only that the League should be allowed to handle particular, secondary questions. Lloyd George said he could not see any harm in that; he also agreed with Benes that, first, Germany and then Russia should be admitted to the League, if France would agree—which he knew very well she would not.

But it was when Carlo Schanzer—one of Italy's leading representatives to the League during its early years—came to Downing Street towards the end of March that Lloyd George removed the seventh veil. Schanzer had come to discuss the arrangements for Genoa and the British Prime Minister told him he was in favour of limiting the representation on the various committees at the conference. Schanzer said he feared it would produce a bad effect if the small powers were ruled out of the committees. The small states, he argued, would make adverse comparisons between the Genoa Conference and the League of Nations; at the League they were all represented. That, said Lloyd George, was one of the reasons why the League of Nations had not accomplished more.

The Genoa Conference opened on 10th April, 1922, and in terms of the men who gathered there on behalf of their countries, Lloyd George could hardly have wished for more. Never was the League to attract so mighty and glittering an assembly. All but a few of the nations of Europe were represented by their prime ministers, backed up by top ministers and the inevitable teams of experts and officials. From Moscow came the Soviet Commissar for Foreign Affairs, Chicherin, and Maxim Litvinov, the man who was later to succeed him and to represent Russia with such distinction at Geneva; with them was Leonid Krassin, who, in 1921, in London, had signed the Anglo-Soviet agreement which constituted *de facto* recognition of the Soviet Government. Only France, as an act of deliberate policy by Poincaré—it had been Briand who had committed France to taking part—tried to play down the importance of the conference by sending just one minister, Louis Barthou, and his brief was to be obstructive.

Lloyd George could not be blamed personally for the failure at Genoa. He laboured hard, using all his charm and negotiating skills, commanding the centre of the stage. But, apart from the French attitude, destructive forces had been at work even before the conference began. The Russian team went to Berlin before Genoa and put pressure on the Germans to make a separate deal with them before entering into any international negotiations with the western powers. These two countries, 'outsiders' so far as League membership was concerned, had already made their secret military agreement; now Russia wanted to return to a full diplomatic and consular relationship and to foster much closer economic and trading ties. The Germans did not yield at Berlin, but there were strong domestic pressures upon the Government. The leaders of heavy industry were anxious to get back their traditional and valuable markets in Russia and their interests coincided with a powerful faction inside the German Foreign Office, which favoured a positive eastern policy. Lloyd George was clearly unaware of the danger and, in fact, inadvertently exacerbated it. In the first few days of the Genoa Conference he appeared to be courting the Russians, inviting them to private meetings with him, and ignoring the Germans. The reality was that their discussions with the British Prime Minister, chiefly concerned with financial claims and counter-claims arising out of the war, were giving the Russians little satisfaction, and when they decided to try for a treaty with Germany there and then, they found the Germans in a receptive mood. The two delegations met some twenty miles along the coast from Genoa at the beautiful resort of Rapallo and, within a matter of hours, reached agreement along the lines already discussed in Berlin. That was on April 16th. Lloyd George kept the conference going until May 19th, but the spirit of hope with which it had opened had been broken by the Rapallo Pact. Its achievements were negligible.

The effect of the pact at Rapallo was to give Germany a reputation in Allied eyes for treachery. It confirmed all France's suspicions and shocked and antagonised opinion in Britain, much of which had been leaning towards Germany, especially at a time when feelings about Poincaré were running so high; it was some time before the more charitable and the more perceptive were able to appreciate why the Germans should have felt the need to forge closer links with Russia.

The relationship between the two countries was a curious one. On the one hand, there was the secret rearmament and the mutually beneficial trade between them; on the other, there was political warfare of the deadliest kind. In October, 1923, when, after the French invasion of the Ruhr and the destruction of the mark, German fortunes were at their lowest, Moscow ordered communist leaders in Germany to rise and carry out what was intended to be a revolution. It failed completely. Where it did not fizzle out, it was crushed by the German Army. After that the relationship between Germany and Russia could not be as it had been, but the links were maintained and they continued to be of value to both sides. When Stresemann began to feel his way towards a reconciliation with France and Britain, it was always with an insistence that, in doing so, he was not at the same time cutting Germany off from Russia to join an anti-Russian alliance. Some of Stresemann's reservations on this score were consciously exaggerated; he knew the value of the German ties with Moscow as a bargaining counter in dealing with the western powers, and he exploited it skilfully. At the same time, he felt genuine inhibitions, and it was the need to accommodate these which additionally complicated the question of Germany's admission to the League.

By the beginning of 1925, the diplomatic and commercial boycott of Russia was virtually at an end, for one country after another had formally recognised the Soviet Government. Of the great powers, only the United States still refused to enter into official relations. But Russia continued to suffer from a sense of isolation and insecurity. She was obsessed by fears of British intentions. She lived with a neurotic anticipation of an Anglo-Polish attack. Any movement towards a Franco-German reconciliation intensified Russian anxieties. Apart from any fears of his own about possible Soviet exposure of the secret military deal, Stresemann saw no profit to Germany in a rapprochement with the western powers which was bought at the cost of a breach with Russia. Germany and Russia had common needs. As he speculated upon the possibility of Britain sponsoring Germany's admission to the League, Stresemann saw how desirable it was that Russia should also become a member. 'From the German point of view,' he wrote in February, 1924, 'it is of immense importance that, if and when this question becomes urgent, it shall be raised by England not merely on behalf of Germany but of Russia, too, the English government having made considerable progress towards the recognition of that country. Our relation with Russia will be of the greatest importance to us on both political and economic grounds. Any action of the League directed against Russia and involving this country would lay a heavier obligation upon us than on any other country. For us the League would be a quite different instrument if all great nations were really represented in it.'*

That was written, of course, when the first Labour Government was in power in Britain and before the scare of the Zinoviev Letter—the alleged call from Zinoviev, a prominent figure in the Third International, to the British Communist Party to promote armed insurrection—during the general election the following October. Relations between Moscow and the Tory Government quickly deteriorated. Any prospect of British advocacy of Russia's admission to the League receded. But that only increased Stresemann's concern to protect Germany's relations with the Soviet Government.

The Russians watched the Germans move towards Locarno with the most acute apprehension. When Litvinov came to Berlin in June, 1925, Stresemann tried hard to reassure him that Germany's entry into the League would not mean an inevitable rupture with the USSR; nor, above all, would it mean Germany siding with Britain in aggressive anti-Russian policies. Somewhat optimistically, Stresemann wrote, 'I fancy that . . . Russia understands our position, and that when we come to enter the League it may be possible to find a modus vivendi that may relieve us from applying any coercive military measures against Russia. Our entire campaign against Article 16 has been carried on for this reason, and it has actually been made a matter of reproach to us by the opposition that, out of favour to Russia, we have impeded what would otherwise have been a quite straightforward understanding with the western powers.'†
Stresemann wrote that before seeing Litvinov. The Germans never succeeded wholly in quieting Russian fears and suspicions. The understanding Stresemann managed to win from Briand and Chamberlain over Germany's obligations under Article 16 in the event of League action against Russia was not enough to reassure Chicherin and Litvinov. The Berlin Treaty of April, 1926, was Germany's reaffirmation of her Rapallo policy, her formal guarantee to Russia that by joining the League she was not joining an 'imperialist conspiracy' against Russia. The treaty provided that 'should one of the contracting parties, despite its

* Op. cit. Vol. 1, p. 293. † Op. cit. Vol. 2, p. 473.

peaceful attitude, be attacked by one or more third powers, the other contracting party shall observe neutrality for the whole duration of the conflict.' In the event of a coalition being formed with the intention of imposing a financial or economic boycott on either of the two countries, the other undertook not to have any part in it. Stresemann also pledged the German Government to stand out against any anti-Russian activities within the League and make up its own mind, if the question arose, whether or not Russia was an aggressor and how far, if at all, Germany should join in applying sanctions.

Considering those terms, it is not difficult to understand why the signing of the treaty revived scepticism about the credibility of Germany's professed readiness to assume the full responsibilities of League membership. In Poland, Czechoslovakia, and in the Quai d'Orsay, the treaty was certainly seen as inconsistent with Locarno and with the requirements of the Covenant. But Chamberlain persuaded the Cabinet and then Briand there was nothing to worry about. Unlike at the time of Rapallo the Germans had told Britain and France in advance of their intention to conclude the Berlin Treaty. Furthermore, the German Government had resisted strong pressure from Moscow not to take part in the Locarno negotiations or to go to Geneva; but it did attach political importance to maintaining some sort of relations with Russia. As described by Stresemann to the British Ambassador in Berlin the treaty, said Chamberlain, would be 'innocuous.' He himself saw nothing in it he regarded as incompatible with Germany's pledges at Locarno or her obligations as a member of the League. The Foreign Secretary pronounced himself satisfied that Germany intended to remain loyal to the new orientation of policy implicit in her acceptance of the Locarno Treaty and that 'this had been confirmed by the rejection of Herr Adenauer for the post of Chancellor, on the ground that he was not sound on the Locarno policy, to which he had previously declared himself opposed.' The Cabinet was glad to hear that the treaty was innocuous, but some ministers were worried about how relations between Germany and Russia might develop if Germany were to be humiliated at Geneva, by her application for entry being rejected. They heard that the Foreign Secretary was going to see what could be done to bring diplomatic pressure on Brazil by other South American states, and how Brazil could be immediately removed from the Council in September if she remained obstructive.

At Geneva, the special committee set up to look into the whole question of Council membership met for the first time on May 10th. Britain's representative was Lord Cecil. His instructions were to make it clear that, so far as Britain was concerned, the committee was starting from scratch. What had happened in March had created an entirely new situation and Cecil had no firm commitments other than support for Germany's claim to a permanent seat. Chamberlain gave the Spanish Ambassador much the same message. When King Alfonso came to London at the end of June, the British Government's delicate task was to explain to him how difficult it was to secure unanimity at Geneva for the proposal of a permanent seat for Spain and at the same time persuade him that Spain ought to stay in the League. There was some talk of soothing Spanish resentment by supporting Spain's desire for a mandate over Tangier; Chamberlain told Alfonso Britain had no objection, although the Cabinet agreed the terms of the mandate would have to be scrutinised very carefully indeed. When Alfonso left England again, he left behind him the impression that, even if Spain stayed in the League, she would probably take no further part in the Council.

The work of finding a way of reorganising the Council so that Germany, and Germany alone, could get a permanent seat, went well. After his criticism of Chamberlain's secret diplomacy, Cecil insisted that the committee of inquiry should meet always in public; he shared Woodrow Wilson's faith in doing business out in the open; it was a faith he never lost, and when League affairs were discussed behind closed doors and things went wrong, he was not slow to point the lesson. On this occasion, certainly, he seemed to be justified, although the success of the committee could not be considered more than partial.

The final plan which the committee took to the Assembly for approval was pretty much along the lines of the brief Cecil took with him from London. There were to be four more seats on the Council, bringing the total up to fourteen. Only one of those additional seats was to be a permanent one and that should go to Germany. The nine elected members were to sit for three years and three of them could be re-elected time after time—giving them the status of semi-permanent seats—if the Assembly voted in favour with a two-thirds majority. The immediate and practical intention was these semi-permanent seats should be taken by Poland, Spain and Brazil, the three countries which had been staking claims to permanent seats along with Germany. The plan ought to have worked, but, so far as Spain and Brazil were concerned, it failed. Neither found the compromise acceptable; their pride remained unsatisfied.

The proposals came before the Council in June. Spain made clear they were unacceptable, and her departure from the League seemed likely. But her attitude was not destructive. Before the new plan could be put into effect, it was necessary to give the Assembly the power to regulate all future elections to the Council. That could happen only after an amendment to the Covenant, approved by the 1921 Assembly, had been ratified by all the then members of the Council. Spain alone had yet to ratify; she now promised to do so, thus making it possible for the League to proceed with its necessary compromise for Germany's sake.

None of the behind-the-scenes pressure on Brazil—which included exploitation of the fact that she wanted to negotiate a loan with Rothschild's—was effective. Mello Franco told the June Council meeting that Brazil was resigning her Council seat forthwith, to be followed by her withdrawal from the League. Both Spain and Brazil gave formal notice of resignation. Their notices could not become effective for two years. Before the end of that period Spain had returned, although her demand for a mandate over Tangier had not been granted. Brazil never came back, although, after the election of a new president, she maintained close relations with the League and its institutions. The sacrifices had been made; Germany could come again to Geneva, sure this time that there would be no snags.

Even so, there was a last spasm of anxiety when the Assembly met on the morning of September 8th, 1926, exactly twelve years after the first battle of the Marne in which the German advance on Paris was halted when within sight of the Eiffel Tower. There was a brief phase of protest in the Assembly, not against Germany's admission but about the way the resolutions which would make it possible were presented. The Assembly was asked to vote twice. The first vote was for admitting Germany to the League. The second was on a resolution which combined approval for the allocation of a permanent Council seat to Germany with acceptance of an increase in the number of non-permanent seats from six to nine. There was strong feeling in the Assembly against making the Council any bigger, and a sense of affront at being forced either to accept the increase or, by voting against the resolution, to deny Germany her seat on the Council.

Motta, who was reporting to the Assembly on behalf of the Council, had the task of justifying the procedure. He did it, as always, with great tact and good humour, apologising to the Assembly for what he knew was an unpopular proposal. In its defence, he pointed out that the increased size of the Council would allow a fairer representation of the different continents and would facilitate the principle of rotation. But the real justification for what the Council was proposing lay in his argument that the crisis had got to be settled, that this was the only possible compromise which could be accepted and that if the question of a permanent seat for Germany were not taken at the same time as the increase in number of seats there would no longer be unanimity in the Council. And that, all the delegates knew, would mean another and certainly disastrous crisis. But they were determined not to let the occasion pass without a demonstration of their feelings.

First, Jonkheer Loudon of Holland attacked the procedure because it amounted to forcing the Assembly's hand. Holland had opposed the 1922 decision to increase the Council by two seats and maintained all its previous objections now. The increase, said Loudon, jeopardised the balance which ought to exist between the Assembly and the Council and serious difficulties might arise if the Council had to take a sudden decision in some crucial emergency. He was absolutely right and most of the delegates to the Assembly, including those whose countries had contributed to the compromise proposals, must have known it.

Nansen, rising once again to defend the rights of the Assembly and especially of the smaller nations, was less restrained in his language. He declared the procedure unconstitutional. The first

time most members had heard officially of the proposal to
increase the number of Council seats had been that very morning.
Only fifteen of them, he said, had had any opportunity of
expressing their opinions on it. The rest were being asked to
accept it without any serious consideration. Nansen regarded
the manœuvre as one which infringed the liberty of the Assembly;
as a precedent it might prove a serious menace to the working of
the League. Löfgren, the Swedish delegate, took up a similar
line. Each of the speeches of protest was received with emphatic
applause by the Assembly.

Although each delegate knew what he must do for the sake of
the League, the Assembly experienced a few more tense minutes
as the President, Nintchitch, a Serb, called for the vote. The
head of each delegation had to answer yes or no as the roll was
read in alphabetical order. Heads craned over the galleries as the
vote was taken on the first resolution. At the end of it, the
President, speaking in slow, sombre tones, announced: 'The
number of votes was 48. All states have voted "Yes." I therefore
proclaim the admission of Germany into the League of Nations
by a unanimous vote.' The whole of the hall, including the
galleries—where Mrs. Woodrow Wilson, among other distinguished American political figures, was watching—burst into
prolonged applause. When, at last, it died down, Nintchitch
continued, 'We have succeeded in bringing to a successful
conclusion one of the most important, one of the most delicate,
one of the most necessary tasks for the future of the League of
Nations, and I feel sure I shall be voicing the unanimous feelings
of the Assembly in expressing my joy, in proclaiming my
legitimate satisfaction at the action taken by the Assembly, as
well as expressing the hope of seeing the new member take her
seat among us at the earliest possible moment.'

After the second vote, which was also unanimous, a member
of the Secretariat slipped through the curtains behind the platform
to send an official telegram bearing the news to Berlin. That
afternoon, Chamberlain summed up the achievement to journalists in a cautiously euphoric manner. 'Today has justified the
optimists,' he said, 'in their belief in the power of the League and
its usefulness to humanity. The greatest danger to the League,'
he added, settling into a familiar groove, 'is to regard it as some-

thing perfect and less human than it is. Public opinion must realise its defects and human failings, but at the same time the League is capable of still greater services in the future.' Then he spoke of that which, politically, was even closer to his heart.

'As to Locarno,' said Chamberlain, 'was there anybody that Saturday morning after the treaties were initialled who was bold enough to believe that they would survive the fortnight we passed through in March? I, with all my confidence in Locarno, would have hesitated at the time to say that confronted with the failure to see the entry of Germany, Locarno would have survived. The most remarkable thing in March was that the parties interested reasserted their fidelity to the agreement they had signed.'

After the events of March and despite the last-minute tensions, the news came, inevitably, as something of an anti-climax in Germany; the delay had been too long and it had taken the edge off the pleasure. The credentials of the chief German delegates, Stresemann, von Schubert, the permanent under-secretary at the Wilhelmstrasse, and Friedrich Gaus, their legal expert, were signed by President von Hindenburg, holidaying in Bavaria, and brought to Berlin. The party left by train for Geneva late on the afternoon of the 8th.

As they made their way to the Salle de la Réformation on the morning of the 10th, to take their places in the Assembly, the German delegates were cheered on by crowds lining the streets, and their reception in the hall itself may have been all the warmer for the frustrations which had been experienced and for the relief which all felt that the fact of entry was at last accomplished.

When the session began at 10.30, the seats reserved for the Germans were empty—the only ones in the entire hall which were. All had to be done according to due form. Nintchitch called upon de Bethancourt, who was president of the commission responsible for ratifying credentials; the credentials of the German delegates had been examined, said the Cuban, and found in order. 'I invite the German delegates to take their places,' said Nintchitch. There was a shuffling among the officials thronging the entrance to the hall before Stresemann appeared, smiling. His colleagues followed and they made their way to their seats, accompanied all the way by clapping. They were made welcome by the President. He had an easy task, he said. It was simply to voice the unanimous feeling of the Assembly, which had waited long and eagerly for this moment. His speech was brief, warm, graceful. As he finished, he called upon Stresemann.

There was long, extended cheering as the bulky figure of the German Foreign Minister slowly mounted the steps to the rostrum. It was evident that Stresemann found the occasion an emotional one. At first, it seemed as though he had difficulty in getting his breath; his speech was broken up into short, sharp bursts. Soon, however, he regained his full command, and he read his address in a measured voice. He pitched his message at a lofty, philosophical level, somewhat rococo in its style, but that was Stresemann's way; nothing less would have satisfied him, and probably nothing less was expected of him. He was wholly conscious of the historic role he had been called upon to fulfil, and he bestowed upon it his own slightly pot-bellied dignity and a visionary sense of the occasion's significance.

Stresemann said the fact that nations which had fought each other in the Great War were now leagued together for permanent and pacific co-operation was the best proof that the world could develop in new directions. The nations were animated by different ideals, he said. Some were so obsessed by the idea of national unity they rejected the idea of international co-operation.

'I hold,' Stresemann declared, 'that no country which belongs to the League of Nations need surrender its national individuality. The Divine Architect of the Universe has not fashioned humanity as a uniform whole. He gave to the nations different blood-streams. He gave them their mother tongues as the sanctuary of their souls. . . . But it surely cannot have been His purpose that they should direct their national energies against one another. The greatest benefactor of humanity is he who, rooted in his own people, develops what is in his soul and mind to its utmost significance, and thus, reaching out beyond the frontiers of his own people, has something to confer upon humanity as a whole, as the great ones whose names are written down in the history of humanity have done. Thus, nation and humanity are united in the sphere of the spirit, thus also may they be united in the work of politics.' It was a moral obligation, said Stresemann, to collaborate peacefully in solving the great moral problems of humanity, and no other law should be applied to them than that of justice. He stressed the word 'justice.'

The League was in many respects the heir and executor of the treaties of 1919, declared Stresemann. In the past, Germany and the League had had differences about those treaties. He hoped now that her participation in the League would make things easier. Mutual confidence was a great creative force. It was on a basis of mutual confidence that Germany wanted to co-operate.

'Of all the nations here assembled,' said the German leader, 'we belong to the race that is striving from darkness into light. May the work of the League be accomplished on the foundation of the great ideas of Freedom, Peace and Unity: thus we shall approach the objectives for which we all strive. And to labour to this end is Germany's steadfast will.'

Stresemann was applauded enthusiastically from the floor, the galleries, from the platform, as he went back to his seat. Because he had spoken in German, the next half-hour or so was taken up by translations into French and English. The only other speaker was Briand, a symbolic choice, to mark the reconciliation of the two great continental powers, and a wise one, for Briand possessed an appropriate gift of oratory. His speech was preceded by a thunderous ovation.

The contrast between the styles of the two men was marked. Stresemann had read his address, in the manner of a lecturer. Briand had what his countrymen called a 'golden' voice, marvellously supple in range and inflexion. He was an actor, unafraid of the large bold gesture and the theatrical pause.

Briand started solemnly, stressing the remarkable nature of the circumstances which had brought him, a Frenchman, to follow a German to the rostrum of the League of Nations. What would the scoffers, the detractors of the League, say today? he asked rhetorically. If there had been no League of Nations would this event ever have been possible? What was its meaning? It meant that the long series of wars between the two countries which had stained the pages of history was now at last ended. Henceforth, like two private individuals taking their disputes before a magistrate, they would settle their quarrels by peaceful methods. There would be no more trials of strength and heroism. Then, reaching out deliberately for the emotive images which stirred the whole Assembly to applause, Briand said, 'No more blood, no more cannon, no more machine-guns.' He turned towards the German delegation. 'Herr Stresemann and I have laboured for many months at a common task,' he said. 'I have kept my confidence and so has he. The fact that you and I can communicate easily in this Assembly does not mean that all our difficulties disappear. But if we each represent the true feelings of our countries and face our difficulties with the determination to settle them peacefully, there need be no strife.' With Briand, humour was never repressed for long, and even on so sober an occasion he could not resist a sly dig at Stresemann's high-blown references to 'the Divine Architect.' If it had really been the Creator's plan that nations should not fight one another, he said, then nobody had taken much notice of it so far, but he hoped now they might help to put it into operation.

'If you are here simply as a German,' he said to Stresemann, 'and I am here simply as a Frenchman, agreement will not be easy. But if, without departing from the standpoint of our respective countries, we can regard ourselves as fellow-workers in the cause of the League, then everything can be settled.' He told Stresemann there were two ways of coming to Geneva—in an impartial spirit or in a militant, partisan one. If delegates came there regarded by their compatriots as national champions, who had got to achieve victory at any price, then they were bound to fail.

'I swear, gentlemen,' Briand declared, 'that I shall do my best not to come here in that spirit, and I count on the intelligence and pacific temper of the German delegate to make the same effort . . . Let our countries sacrifice their *amour propre* for the sake of the peace of the world.'

Briand's speech was at once exemplary of his own great talent, of his established assurance and reputation in the Assembly, and also of the peculiar intimacy which the makeshift hall conferred upon the 'world parliament.' The applause which Briand received at the end of his speech was both a mighty tribute to the man himself and a collective recognition that an historic occasion had been celebrated in a manner wholly worthy of it. At Chamberlain's suggestion, it was decided that the two speeches should be published verbatim in the Assembly's official journal. A large part of the world joined in agreeing that Geneva had enjoyed a great day. Among the exceptions was the newspaper *Izvestia*, official organ of the Soviet Government. Its leading article emphasised how often the Government and press of Russia had warned Germany against this 'false step,' and prophesied disappointment for the Germans in 'this wasp's nest of international intrigue, where political sharpers and thieving diplomatists cheat with marked cards, strangle weak nations, and organise war against the USSR.'

9

'When Great Britain stops, the League stops'

If it had been within the capacity of any two men to settle all the issues which stood in the way of a full reconciliation between France and Germany, Briand and Stresemann would have done it. They failed, but not for want of their trying. One of their efforts, at least, although it did not achieve what they thought it had achieved, remains a picturesque, almost romantic incident. It was in 1926, not long after Germany's entry to the League, and immediately following the end of the November Council meeting in Geneva, that the two Foreign Ministers agreed upon a secret rendezvous. Stresemann crossed the Lake by motor-boat. On the other side, he took a car to a small inn at Thoiry. In the dining room there, he and Briand talked in the most friendly way for several hours. They worked out, in broad outline, what they thought was a practicable agreement between their two countries, which would include the total evacuation by the Allies of occupied territory in Germany in return for some financial payment by Germany, and also the settling of the Saar question. It was, in Stresemann's view, a 'comprehensive solution.' But when their financial experts came to look at their proposals, they did not share the statesmen's optimism about their practicality. Nor did their countrymen share their readiness for such a brisk burial of differences. Briand was hissed at the Gare de Lyon upon his return from Geneva, and attacked in the

French press. Although he had done so much to guide French opinion into a more conciliatory and more imaginative attitude towards Germany, and had established a wide popularity, Briand had now run ahead of public opinion too far and too fast. Stresemann, predictably, was accused by German nationalists of being prepared to make costly concessions to the French.

Both men tried to justify themselves to their own people. They denied that because they had eaten and drunk together with such evident mutual sympathy they supposed they had solved every-thing. 'A talk between two ministers in the dining-room of an inn,' said Briand in the French Chamber, 'cannot at one blow alter the position of France and Germany and wipe out the bloodstained past.' But he did not overdo his apology. 'It has been accounted to me as an infamy,' he said, 'that at Geneva I admitted a certain greatness and nobility in our former foe. If that is a blunder, then I regard myself as honoured by having committed it. I firmly intend to do my utmost to prevent another clash between the nations, though in so doing I never lose sight of my anxiety for the security of France. When the Allied control of Germany is replaced by a League control, the security of France will not thereby be diminished, but even enhanced.' But Briand's task was not made easier by the fact that Poincaré had returned to the premiership during the summer of 1926. Govern-ments had been coming and going, and Briand himself had become Prime Minister again for a few months, but now Poincaré was called back to rescue the franc. He did it—by imposing drastic financial austerities—so rapidly and so successfully that he was to stay in power for three whole years until ill-health forced him to retire. Although even Poincaré had relaxed somewhat his former intransigence towards Germany, he still represented the most narrow concept of French national interests, and he was always there to act as a brake upon Briand's generosity.

Sir Austen Chamberlain betrayed just a hint of satisfaction when he reported to the Cabinet on the disappointing outcome of the Thoiry meeting. Dr. Stresemann, he told his colleagues, had 'lately realised that conversations with M. Briand alone were not likely to lead to results, and was anxious to get back to conversations comparable to those at Locarno, at which Great Britain, and perhaps Italy and Belgium also, would be represented.' Chamberlain certainly had no objection to secret meetings, but he probably felt they were more likely to be successful when he was one of those taking part in them. He was therefore happy with the pattern which developed at Geneva after Germany took her seat, when the monthly meetings of the Council were a convenient excuse for separate, private meetings of the Locarno powers. There was even a tentative proposal for another full-scale conference along the lines of Locarno, but Chamberlain rightly sensed that the moment was not opportune, and he considered that if anything useful was to come out of such a conference the ground must be well prepared.

The personal relations between Stresemann, Briand and Chamberlain had developed in the period following Locarno, despite the anxieties and tensions accompanying Germany's entry into the League. But the famous pact which brought the three statesmen their Nobel Prizes had not borne the fruit they had expected. Even now, there was still no final agreement about reparations: and, even now, there were Allied troops occupying the Rhineland; in March, 1927, Stresemann put their strength at 75,000, the bulk of them French. At Locarno, the Allies had resisted all attempts by the Germans to link the security pact with the withdrawal of the occupation forces. But Briand had given Stresemann every reason to believe that, even if there was no immediate and total evacuation, there would be steady and substantial reductions. But such cuts as were made were minimal. Briand pleaded difficulties inside the French Cabinet. In exchanges with the British Government, the French still argued the need for keeping the troops in Germany to safeguard their country's security. Stresemann saw the consequences as an encouragement to nationalist movements in both Germany and France; he accused Britain of indifference. Chamberlain admitted to a bad conscience; he recognised the damage being done by keeping the troops in Germany. He did try to bring pressure on Briand, but he argued that if Britain were to take away her few thousand troops, without getting French agreement to big cuts, then the only result would be to weaken Britain's influence.

At Geneva, however, the spirit which had made Locarno possible persisted. The Big Three met there regularly and their presence enhanced the prestige of the League. A superficial observer visiting Geneva at that time might well have gained the impression that the League of Nations had really begun to work as its founders had intended. There was an intimacy about the monthly Council meetings, held in what had been a hotel dining room, with the delegates jammed together round the table and the press almost leaning over their shoulders, which was not only physical. There was also a manifest willingness to give and take, genuinely to listen and to try to understand. It was this attitude which made it possible for the Council to chew over seemingly intractable problems in public and for a formula or a solution to emerge from its free discussions. In those days there were no interpreters, hidden away in cubicles, feeding simultaneous translation into delegates' headphones. Most speeches were delivered in either English or French—the two official languages—and then translated. If a delegate chose to speak in any other language he had to bring his own interpreter with him.* While a speech was being translated, delegates who had understood the original would pop out for a drink or go for a stroll. This was one more factor contributing to the valuable informality of the Council. Then there was the atmosphere of Geneva itself. Working there for the League, or reporting its activities, was like belonging to a small university town, where everyone knew everyone else, where delegates, officials and journalists lived in the same hotels and shared the same social pleasures. It was an hotel and café society, in some ways narrow, gossipy and introverted as it was bound to be, but also genuinely excited by the cause that had brought them all together there. Of course, it was easy enough to find cynics in Geneva, but it was not a place of cynicism.

Both Briand and Stresemann relished their visits to Geneva. Stresemann, in particular, was a gregarious man, who loved talking the hours away, and he was often to be found holding

* Count Albert Apponyi, the Hungarian delegate, whose public argument before the Council with Titulescu, the mercurial Rumanian, in a dispute over minorities, provided one of the more remarkable episodes of this period, was known to exploit this situation from time to time. Apponyi would declare his intention of acting as his own interpreter. Then he would speak first in German, following with an entirely different speech in French, and then yet another in English. Although he was still straight-backed and extraordinarily robust, he was also very old, with a long white beard, and no-one cared to accuse him of breaking the rules.

court to a huddle of journalists around his table at, say, the famous Bavaria restaurant (where the great days of the League are still recalled in its collection of caricatures). Chamberlain had much less taste for the social round and if he were ever found in the company of newspapermen it was strictly in the line of duty. Austen Chamberlain had the highest and most honourable regard for what he saw as his duty. He was also very conscious of the dignity of the British Foreign Secretary and, as Anthony Eden has described it, the manner of Sir Austen's progress from London to Geneva was nothing less than stately:

'The top-hatted stationmaster and the Foreign Office representatives at Victoria, the harbourmaster at Dover bowing us on to the ship, the préfet and the mayor at Calais, then a drive across Paris and dinner at the Embassy, the night train at the Gare de Lyon, where probably M. Briand and some other of Sir Austen's colleagues were also embarking for Geneva. Finally, the arrival at Geneva, about 7.30 in the morning, when the whole staff was paraded to meet their chief at the station, a barbaric and totally unnecessary custom which I was finally able to suppress when I became Foreign Secretary myself some years later.'*

Eden first went to Geneva, as parliamentary private secretary to Chamberlain, in 1927, when Britain's reputation was high and her Foreign Secretary was much in demand, liable to be buttonholed in the lobbies or corridors and cornered at diplomatic receptions by those seeking to enlist his influence. Although it exhausted him and he sometimes found it distasteful, Chamberlain put up with it all conscientiously. He was quoted once as saying, 'It is my job to shake the hands that my King must not shake.'

The appearances at Geneva, then, were of the great powers participating seriously in the business of the League and actively promoting its role in ordering the affairs of the world. The reality was that the celebrated trio devalued the League. Each could point to the record and show how he had striven and continued to strive to commend the League to his fellow-countrymen. Stresemann, in particular, countered the sceptics and those who assailed him for sitting down at the same table with Germany's former enemies. Less than a month after taking his seat at Geneva, he told a rally at Cologne of his party, the

* *Facing the Dictators*, Cassell, 1962. pp. 8-9.

German People's Party: 'In Geneva an international forum has been created, which already possesses a powerful influence through the mere existence of such a permanently available apparatus . . . For me,' he said, 'the League of Nations is not merely a means contrived from opportunist considerations for the furtherance of the individual aims of our foreign policy . . . the League of Nations embodies the idea on the realisation of which depends the political future of Europe; and that is the idea of a policy of reasonable understanding.'*

Stresemann's conduct at Geneva was always compatible with that statement of faith. Sometimes, though, he was less credible. In December, 1926, for instance, in Hamburg, he said, 'Perhaps the most valuable result arising out of Geneva lies in the fact that the method of open discussion, for which the League of Nations provides such excellent scope, has again been completely vindicated.'† But a private note he made early in October the following year was a truer reflection of what he really felt: He considered it impossible, he wrote, 'that negotiations regarding the prospect of avoiding possible conflicts could be carried on in public as foreseen by the statutes of the League . . . If 200 journalists are to be present, if the whole world is to be informed two hours afterwards when any unguarded word is spoken, confidential discussions are out of the question, and we shall all have to read out formal declarations.'‡

That was certainly a view shared by Chamberlain and Briand, and whenever the Council had any delicate business to handle, especially any business directly involving any of the great powers, it was done behind closed doors. But what gave much more offence and detracted from the League much more seriously was the way in which the representatives of the Locarno powers got together in secret meetings in Geneva. They were not technically in breach of any requirement in the Covenant, for there was nothing to stop any group of nations meeting to discuss matters of common interest. But the matters discussed at these so-called 'Locarno tea-parties' were as often as not matters due to be discussed at the Council, and those members of the Council who were not also signatories of the Locarno treaties naturally resented

* Op. cit. Vol. 3, p. 36.   † Op. cit. Vol. 3, p. 81.
‡ Op. cit. Vol. 3, p. 227.

it when they found themselves being presented with ready-made solutions, emanating from gatherings which excluded them.

Not for the first time, the smaller powers represented at Geneva felt they were being used merely to provide an audience and to give their assent to settlements arranged in advance, in secret, by the big powers. Their resentment and anxieties boiled up at the eighth Assembly held in September, 1927, a year after Germany's entry. Briand and Stresemann managed to convince the Assembly of their devotion to the League and their innocence of any intention to bypass it or diminish its authority. Stresemann was particularly successful, praising the Assembly itself as a demonstration of the strenuous independence of the smaller powers and of the democratic idea in practice. He also quoted with approval the opinion of Giuseppe Motta, the Swiss Foreign Minister, who had said the League could survive although great countries remained outside it, but it could not survive the abstention of the neutrals and the 'so-called smaller nations.' Stresemann's speech was an admirable display of political tact, which won much goodwill for his country. It was impossible to say the same for Austen Chamberlain, who engaged the Assembly head-on. He did not say anything which amounted to a retraction of his support for the League, but he made it clear that the smaller powers ought to think themselves lucky that Great Britain accepted her obligations under the Covenant and that her Foreign Secretary honoured the Assembly with his presence. Chamberlain, like the British Government he represented, was determined not to be drawn into any new obligations, and he expressed his own fears lest Britain's loyalty to the League should damage her relations with the countries of the British Commonwealth. It was a tough, honest speech but one which, as Stresemann noted, did damage to Britain's reputation at Geneva.

Despite the antagonism they attracted, the 'tea-parties' did have some value. Above all, they provided the opportunity for regular, private talks between the Big Three which, even if they failed to end the causes of dispute between Germany and France, prevented an extension of conflict through misunderstanding. Stresemann had good reason to value them, too, when, for instance, Poland put forward a proposal to extend the Locarno treaties to Eastern Europe—something which the German delegation at Locarno itself had opposed from beginning to end. In a letter from Geneva, dated 21st September, 1927, Stresemann wrote to Chancellor Marx: 'In this business our personal relations with Chamberlain and Briand stood the test admirably. Chamberlain told me in advance that he would not admit any proposal that placed him and myself in opposing camps, and that to him the collaboration of the Locarno Powers was of more value than all the resolutions of the League . . . The proposal of the Poles for an Eastern Locarno is rejected. The collaboration between the great Locarno Powers has proved steady and secure . . .'*

Whatever they might say publicly about their belief in the League and their wish to strengthen its authority the Big Three really turned to the League only as an instrument of last resort. They kept from it issues of serious significance, where the League might have seemed the proper agent of conciliation. Britain's influence was often the most decisive in keeping the League out of things.

During 1926 and much of 1927, for instance, the great powers with concessions in China—Germany surrendered hers to Japan under the Versailles Treaty—were much concerned by developments in that country. The Government at Peking lived on only in name, although it still had a seat in the Council of the League. Large areas were effectively under the domination of rival war-lords, until the Nationalist armies, commanded by Chiang Kai-shek, advanced north from Canton, establishing some semblance of unified authority as they did so. Of the western powers, Britain was well aware of the importance of these events and, through Chamberlain, showed a positive sympathy for the aspirations of the Nationalists. The British Foreign Secretary respected the slogan of 'China for the Chinese' and was anxious for the day when he could recommend formal recognition of a Nationalist Government as the effective and legitimate government of China. In the early months of 1927, however, these hopes were submerged by concern, as incidents of mob-violence and what looked like a deliberately fostered xenophobia multiplied and spread. There were attacks on people and property in the international settlement of Shanghai, in Canton, Hankow and

* Op. cit. Vol. 3, p. 209.

Nanking. The British had much the worst of it, and they had little success in persuading either the Americans, the Japanese or the French to join them in reinforcing their troops there. The Japanese, who had so often been the chief target for attack and boycott in the past, while genuinely anxious to co-operate with Britain, wanted to do nothing which would invite retaliation by the Chinese. The French annoyed Chamberlain by their luke-warm attitude, which, in reporting to a sympathetic Cabinet, he contrasted with Britain's helpfulness over Locarno. The French wanted to protect their nationals in China but they did not want to risk an open conflict with Chinese troops. The French, indeed, did suggest referring the trouble to the League. This, too, irritated the British Foreign Secretary, who thought he had already explained why recourse to the League was an inappro-priate and unwise way of dealing with a threat to western interests in Asia: the League, he said in effect, should confine itself to European affairs, certainly so far as the great powers were concerned. He felt obliged, however, to send a letter to the League, outlining the nature of British policy towards China, disavowing any imperialist pretensions, and defending the dispatch there of British reinforcements as essentially protective; but he did not ask the League to help or consider any form of intervention.

Chamberlain was entirely genuine in declaring his wish to see a united, independent China, where foreigners could trade in peace, his one justifiable fear being that Russian plotting and influence would ensure the supremacy of communist elements in the new Chinese Government. He was no less determined than the French, either, to avoid any risk of British troops finding themselves fighting the Nationalists in what could be portrayed as an act of British aggression; indeed, he faced some criticism at home for his alleged pusillanimity. Yet Chamberlain was still essentially in the tradition of pre-war Foreign Secretaries, adapting his policies to changed circumstances, but seeking the defence of British interests, not through the machinery of inter-national conciliation and co-operation, but by trying to concert the actions of all those countries with interests in China and, if necessary, finally going it alone. There is no doubt that, in the event, the League would have been powerless to intervene, but that was not the mainspring of Chamberlain's behaviour. He started from the assumption that it was no business of the League to get mixed up in such matters, anyway.

The incidents in China reached a climax when Nanking fell to the Nationalists and the murder of foreigners, including British and Americans, brought a grave threat of a clash between the Chinese forces and the foreign powers. The British Government saw these latest outrages as part of a pattern of aggression which would soon affect other powers as seriously as Britain. A telegram, sent from the Foreign Office on April 1st, 1927, instructed the British Ambassador in Tokyo, Sir John Tilley, to make this view known to the Japanese Government:

'Recent events on the Yangtse have convinced His Majesty's Government that what is happening there amounts in fact to the triumph of the Communistic system of subversive and anti-foreign propaganda and agitation which has developed for the last few years in China . . . Unless this wave of mob rule is speedily checked, His Majesty's Government fear that it will soon burst all bounds and extend so as to dominate the whole of China. Hitherto it has directed its energy mainly against British interests which have accordingly suffered more than those of other foreign nations. But it is quite obvious that this is only the first stage of those communist activities which so soon as they have undermined the British position in China will turn their energies against all other foreigners. The turn of the Japanese will most certainly follow . . .'

But the Japanese still preferred discretion. So did the Americans, who Chamberlain felt sure would be provoked into a show of strength by the Nanking killings. But the Americans were not looking for more trouble, either, and although the other foreign powers with interests in China all expressed their friendship, Chamberlain realised that Britain had been left in the uncomfortable position whereby, if she wished to get tough with the Chinese, she would have to do it on her own. Fortunately, Chiang Kai-shek, under challenge from his communist allies, took ruthless and drastic action to assert his own authority and to restore order. Chamberlain was able to retreat with dignity, and a telegram sent from the Foreign Office on August 4th, 1927, to Sir Miles Lampson, the British Minister to China, shows

Chamberlain acknowledging the new international realities with a certain melancholy:

'. . . It is true that your US and Japanese colleagues have at times led us to believe that their governments might be induced to accept their own views in regard to the practicability and efficacy of a show of force for political purposes in China. But your US colleague has had frankly to avow that his government do not accept his recommendations, and the Japanese Minister is clearly equally out of touch with the views held by the government in Tokyo. It is therefore fairly clear that HMG could not count on the support of these governments, in whose countries any policy of an active or aggressive nature would be most unpopular. As members of the League of Nations, however, HMG must themselves take into careful consideration their own obligations and responsibilities to the League, as well as the general growing tendency in the rest of the world to condemn the exercise of methods of violence in international relationships.

'From the above it will appear that however justifiable and even sound may be in principle a policy involving threat or use of force in China in certain circumstances outside the elemental necessity of protecting British life there, it is becoming more and more clear that in practice such a policy must be discarded as a practicable and effective means of defending British Treaty rights and established interests in that country, or of bringing the Chinese to see reason . . .'

Chiang Kai-shek's triumph in 1927 also meant the total failure of Russia's hopes to bring China under her domination. That same year saw the British Government cut off diplomatic relations with the USSR and end a trading agreement between the two countries, accusing the Russians of espionage and subversive propaganda activities. However dubious the justification for the British action, the rupture between the two countries was an event of high political importance, whose shock-waves were felt internationally. But the situation was never formally considered at Geneva. The British Government did not see that it had anything to do with the League. The USSR was not a member and while, behind the scenes, there were hints of a new attitude evolving in Moscow, Chicherin's denunciations of the League made it inconceivable that Russia would have been prepared at that time to submit itself to any form of arbitration by the League.

Much the most blatant instance of the Locarno powers acting together in disregard of their clear obligations to the League occurred early in 1927. The ostensible cause of concern once more* was Albania. According to the Italians, whose hold over Albania was by now an accomplished fact, the Yugoslavs were getting ready to invade their neighbour. If this were true, it represented a threat to the peace demanding immediate investigation by the Council of the League. In support of the charge, Italy had alleged that Yugoslav forces were massing on the Albanian frontier. Whether they were or they were not should have been easy enough to establish: the League could have sent a military commission there to find out and report back. That is precisely what Yugoslavia, denying the Italian accusation, proposed the Council should do. The hostility and suspicion between Italy and Yugoslavia was a potential danger to Balkan peace. The Yugoslavs were resentful of the way the Italians, with the tacit connivance of the Allies, had advanced their so-called 'special interest' in Albania. Mussolini, for his part, had no intention of making any concessions, and was trying to mask his own activities by smearing the Yugoslavs as would-be aggressors. The issue was certainly discussed at Geneva—but not in the Council. Despite the Yugoslav proposal, it never reached the Council agenda. It got as far as being raised at private meetings of the Locarno powers and Italian influence there was strong enough to ensure that it went no further. Chamberlain, who would have supported a formal investigation by the Council, bowed to the wishes of his Italian and French colleagues and Stresemann went along with him. The British Foreign Secretary, harking back once again to the success of the Council in the Greco-Bulgarian dispute, did propose, with Cabinet approval, that British, French and German military officers should make an investigation on both sides of the Yugoslav-Albanian frontier. Their report could then be considered, not by the Council in public session, but in the privacy of a Locarno tea-party. But even this cosy arrangement was repugnant to Mussolini, and so Chamberlain, ever ready to believe the best of the Italian dictator, whom he found 'a strong

* See Chapter 4.

man of singular charm,'* a man whose word was to be trusted,
let the suggestion lapse. Yugoslav resentment continued to
simmer and relations between Italy and Yugoslavia festered, but
Mussolini had got his way. Their motives for meeting his wishes
had varied, but the essential fact was that the Foreign Ministers
of Britain, France and Germany, had all placed the harmony of
the Locarno powers above the reputation of the League.

Throughout the period of Chamberlain's tenure at the Foreign
Office the Conservative Government was sufficiently respectful
of the existence and influence of the League of Nations to do its
damnedest to make sure that certain issues, of vital and peculiar
concern to Britain, were not raised at Geneva. Foremost among
these was Egypt, and in particular Egypt's desire to apply for
membership of the League. That Egypt was declared independent
in 1922, yet did not become a member of the League until
fifteen years later, is to state the bald facts of a most curious story.

At the end of the war, the Egyptians had been misled by
Wilsonian rhetoric about self-determination and by Anglo-
French promises of independence for peoples 'long oppressed by
the Turks' into imagining that the day of their national freedom
was just around the corner. Instead, the Versailles Treaty merely
confirmed the British protectorate over Egypt—proclaimed by
Britain in 1914, following her declaration of war on Turkey.
After a lamentable phase of savage colonial-style repression,
however, Britain yielded to nationalist agitation and rioting so
far as to recognise Egypt's sovereign independence, in name at
least. It was, in fact, very much a qualified independence, with
the British presence still much in evidence and British influence
a major element in determining Egyptian policy. In proclaiming
the independence of Egypt, the British Government had reserved
four points, which she regarded as vital to British interests, for
inclusion in a subsequent treaty: the right to safeguard communications with and between countries of the British Empire—in
other words, to defend the Canal Zone; to defend Egypt; to
protect foreign and minority interests in the country; to continue
the Anglo-Egyptian condominium in the Sudan with British
responsibility for its defence. Britain insisted in the years following
Egyptian independence that there could be no permanent settle-

* Op. cit. Vol. 2, p. 295.

ment and therefore no question of Egypt's admission to the League until these reserved points were safely embodied in a treaty. In 1926, for instance, the Cabinet was still talking of Parliament's ratification four years earlier of the proclamation of Egyptian independence as 'a provisional settlement.' Britain's official representative in Egypt was still a high commissioner, suggesting either that Egypt was a member of the British Commonwealth or a British dependency. At the Cabinet of July 30th, 1926, it was agreed that it must be made clear to the Egyptians that HMG 'could not allow them to join the League of Nations until after the settlement of the four reserved points, with a view, if possible, to preventing the question being raised at Geneva.' At that same meeting there was talk of the British 'placing ourselves in a position to carry out our obligations for the good government of Egypt and for protection of foreign communities in that country . . .' A strange sort of independence. Nearly two years later, at the Cabinet of May 23rd, 1928, Chamberlain was given authority 'openly to oppose any application from Egypt for membership of the League of Nations on the ground that Egypt was not qualified until the reserved points had been settled.' He was to have the discretion, if necessary, to announce that Britain could not take part in any discussions at the League with the Egyptian Government, a position which Chamberlain reiterated at the Cabinet on January 21st of the following year. British policy was successful in preventing Egyptian membership until, with the signing of the treaty of alliance in 1936, providing for a British garrison for the next twenty years and recognition of Britain's special interest in the Canal zone, the way was quickly cleared.

But there were occasions when Chamberlain had to remind his colleagues—especially Leo Amery, the Colonial Secretary— that there were some things even Britain could not get away with. In the latter part of 1928, there was a dispute with Persia about the extent of Britain's rights and dispositions in the Persian Gulf, including a Persian claim to Bahrain, which Britain had rejected. At the Cabinet of November 5th, Amery—in Chamberlain's absence—put forward a paper advancing the view that in no circumstances should Britain submit any of the points at issue to the League and that the Government might have to announce publicly that 'we regard the Persian Gulf as an area where interference with our supremacy or with our established rights will be resisted as a direct act of aggression against ourselves.' That paper came up again at Cabinet on January 21st, 1929, when the Foreign Secretary reminded the bellicose Amery that Persia no less than Great Britain was a member of the League. Chamberlain pointed out Britain's obligations under the Covenant: she could not refuse to discuss the Persian Gulf if the question was brought up by Persia or by a friendly nation. 'We would be forced to plead our case before the Assembly or the Council and we were pledged not to resort to warlike operations without having exhausted methods of conciliation laid down by the Covenant, if we could not accept arbitration.' The stand Chamberlain took in the Cabinet on this issue is worth underlining because he has often been accused of being, if not an opponent of the League, then paying as little attention to it as he could. It is true, as we have seen, that he resisted all attempts to extend British obligations under the Covenant, but he was not prepared to disregard those which already existed or to go along with those of his colleagues who advocated the high and mighty line. Whether his motivation was ultimately idealistic or wholly practical, Chamberlain knew there were certain things Britain must not do and he told the Cabinet in grave terms the reasons why.

Even if we had any grounds for refusing to submit the Persian Gulf issue to the League, we could not afford to do so, he said. 'At home, any Government that failed to carry out our engagements under the Covenant would be regarded as one which was not fit to be entrusted with the conduct of affairs. In Europe, a policy which could be interpreted as one of hostility to the League would set public opinion against us, and deprive us of the valuable position we at present hold as a recognised force for conciliation and the preservation of peace.' In the event, Britain was spared the embarrassment of defending herself at Geneva.

Some serious issues, however—not involving directly any of the great powers—did find their way on to the Council agenda. In the autumn of 1927, the always animose relationship between Poland and Lithuania looked like erupting once again.* Lithuania had maintained a technical state of war with Poland, determined

* See Chapter 3, pp. 61–63.

173

that there should be no dealings between them until Vilna was restored to her. Each side had horror stories to tell of the persecution of minorities, but there had been no flare-up between them on any scale to concern the rest of Europe. The build-up of mutual accusations and hostility in 1927 looked more ominous, and when the Lithuanian dictatorship claimed to have knowledge of Polish attempts to connive at a coup in Lithuania another outbreak of fighting between the two countries seemed imminent. The Lithuanians clearly believed the threat to their regime was a real one, but chose to meet it by appealing to the League. Chamberlain took it seriously, too, and he told the Cabinet that, because Lithuania had insisted on continuing a state of war with Poland, he feared what action Marshal Pilsudski might take. From what he said when he came to Geneva, it seems that the Polish leader had been tempted to dramatic action, but had contented himself, temporarily at least, with torrential abuse of his enemy. As had happened before, when the two representatives of the nations in dispute appeared before the Council—Augustinas Voldemaras for Lithuania and Auguste Zaleski for Poland—it seemed impossible that they should be reconciled. But the initial recriminations were followed by long hours of negotiation by which they were brought to such a degree of conciliation that they agreed to end the state of war between them and there were exchanges of promises of good intent for the future which they hoped to translate into practical effect at a formal conference. Pilsudski shook hands in public with Voldemaras, the same man who had shaken hands with Paderewski, creating a moment of rich theatrical optimism, seven years before. As on the previous occasion, the hopes were not fulfilled. Negotiations between the two countries led to little positive improvement in their relations; but at least a dangerous deterioration had been averted. Reporting to the Cabinet on what then seemed to be the Council's success, Chamberlain paid tribute to Stresemann's efforts and also to those of Maxim Litvinov, who was in Geneva for the first time, heading a Soviet delegation to the Preparatory Commission which was supposed to be paving the way to a general disarmament conference; Litvinov's value, said Chamberlain, had been to put pressure on Voldemaras to end the state of war with Poland.

A warning against the League biting off more than it could chew, and against any attempt to extend Britain's obligations, was never far from Sir Austen Chamberlain's lips. He sounded it again during meetings of the League Council at Lugano in December, 1928, when reports came in of an outbreak of fighting between Bolivian and Paraguayan forces in the Chaco, a vast area lying between their two countries. The Chaco was almost wholly uninhabited and undeveloped, but both Bolivia and Paraguay had for long years nurtured ambitions to possess it and, sometime, somehow, to people it and exploit it. To that end both nations had established military outposts and occasionally the troops manning them came into conflict with each other. In this instance, it appeared that a local Paraguayan commander had won himself a brief slice of glory by taking a Bolivian outpost; a local Bolivian commander was preparing his counterattack. Bolivia had broken off diplomatic relations. It was the stuff of which superior jokes were made in the clubs of imperial London and it is not surprising that the British Foreign Secretary wanted nothing to do with it. Understandably, Sir Austen dismissed the thought that British troops, under any conceivable circumstances, should be pitched into a wilderness in the heart of South America. But he was not successful in persuading the Council to ignore it altogether. As he reported to the Cabinet on his return from Lugano, the delegates of other South American countries had said that the League must intervene. If the League, they said, was going to treat disputes between nations on the American continent differently from those in the rest of the world then it would be the end of the League so far as South America was concerned.

They argued their case with the strength behind them of a statement made by the Council only a few months before on the meaning of the reference to the Monroe doctrine in Article 21 of the Covenant: 'Nothing in this Covenant shall be deemed to affect the validity of international engagements, such as treaties of arbitration or regional understandings like the Monroe doctrine, for securing the maintenance of peace.' This clause, a last-minute demand by Woodrow Wilson to buy off opposition at home, was resisted strongly even at the time the Covenant was being drafted, because it was feared it might be used to deny the right of non-American states, acting according to their obligations as members of the League, to intervene on the American continent, and might even be cited by the United States as an excuse for not intervening in European disputes. Even though the United States was not a member of the League, the great powers represented on the Council were still unwilling, in 1928, to give offence to the Americans by questioning the propriety of the Monroe doctrine, or of saying how and when it should or could be applied. But the South American countries on the Council—Colombia, Chile and Cuba—expressing the resentment of US pretensions to continental hegemony, had insisted upon a clear statement of what Article 21 meant in relation to America. The Council had then said, in effect, that whatever significance the Monroe Doctrine might have for the United States the reference to it in the Covenant could do nothing to qualify the rights and responsibilities common to all members of the League. In other words, if there was trouble in South America it was just as much the business of the League as trouble in Upper Silesia.

Now there was trouble between Bolivia and Paraguay. Both countries were members of the League, but neither of them had thought of submitting their dispute to it. So, despite Chamberlain preaching caution, the Council decided it could not afford to close its eyes to the fighting. Briand, the current President of the Council, accepted the challenge cast down by the South American delegates and asserted with much vigour and eloquence the duty and authority of the League. Long telegrams were sent to the governments of Bolivia and Paraguay, recalling them to their obligations as League members, and alerting all other member-countries to the threat to peace. When he returned to London, Chamberlain asked the President tof the Board of Trade what the consequences to Britain would be if she was required—under Article 16—to apply economic pressure on either or both of the nations in dispute. The uncomfortable reply was that, if Britain applied sanctions, she would lose the concessions she enjoyed in those countries and they would probably go instead to the United States.

Fortunately, Bolivia and Paraguay agreed to accept the help of a body meeting at that time in Washington—the Pan-American Arbitration Conference—and the trouble died down.

Just how serious it might have been was to be demonstrated a few years later when it blew up again. In 1928, the Council's action was certainly one factor which contributed to pacification. The telegrams not only gave the two countries chiefly concerned a salutary reminder of their responsibilities to the League, which helped to bring them back to their senses, but also gave the rest of South America a most important assurance that the League belonged to them just as much as to Europe. As Chamberlain said to his Cabinet colleagues, 'It would certainly be a misfortune if South America were divorced from the League. The prospect of the Pan-American union on one side of the Atlantic and on the other side the League of Nations embracing only European and Asiatic nations was not a pleasant one.'

South America was one thing, however; Africa was quite another. The British Government, with its vast colonial interests in that continent, never quite accepted the idea that the League ought to be concerned with what happened there. Nor, in 1926, had it quite accepted that Abyssinia was just as much a member of the League as any other country. Britain, with some support, had been most reluctant to admit Abyssinia to membership, because of the slavery and slave-trading that went on there. She had withdrawn her opposition, in face of strong advocacy by France and Italy, and Abyssinia, making a pledge to work for the abolition of slavery, had been admitted at the 1923 Assembly. Despite the efforts of the Regent, Ras Tafari—later to become the Emperor Haile Selassie—slavery continued in Abyssinia; Britain also continued to treat Abyssinia as being in a somewhat different category from other League members. Just how different was disclosed in a way which caused the British Government no little embarrassment and brought forth a disingenuous protestation of the purity of its intentions towards Abyssinia. The cause of discomfiture was an agreement between Britain and Italy, made in December, 1925, which amounted to something resembling an economic carve-up of Abyssinia. Britain wanted to dam the waters of the Blue Nile, which was so important to irrigation in the Sudan and Egypt; the dam was to be built on Lake Tsana, near the source of the Blue Nile in the tablelands of Abyssinia. Britain also wanted to run a motor-road from the lake to the Sudanese frontier. Italian ambitions were less modest.

Mussolini wanted to send a railway the length of Abyssinia to link his two colonies, Eritrea in the north and Somalia in the south. The British and Italian governments agreed to act together, respecting each other's particular interests—which, in Italy's case, embraced a comprehensive and exclusive economic exploitation of Abyssinia—and to back each other in demanding these concessions from the Abyssinian Regent.

Their agreement was a secret one and they did not tell Ras Tafari anything about it for some six months. When they did tell him what they had agreed and what they wanted him to agree to, he was, not unnaturally, a little upset. He protested to the League, questioning the propriety of the Anglo-Italian demands upon another member-nation and whether they were tantamount to an infringement of, or disregard for, Abyssinia's independent status. The questions had only to be asked to achieve the Regent's purpose. Before the possibility could arise of any formal discussion by the Council, the British and Italian governments ran for cover, assuring the world, through notes sent to the Secretary-General, that they had been misunderstood, that the last thing they intended was to subject Abyssinia to anything which could be described as pressure—which is what Ras Tafari had called it. Their agreement was designed merely to eliminate any harmful conflict of interests between their own two countries.

Ras Tafari had used Abyssinia's membership of the League in a most effective manner to protect his country. But relations between Britain and Abyssinia remained uneasy. They were, said Chamberlain some eighteen months later, among the 'least satisfactory.' No progress had been made, he told the Cabinet, towards an agreement about building the dam on Lake Tsana, and there had been a diplomatic tiff with the Regent provoked by a tactless remark by a member of the British Legation at a dinner party: slaves, the gentleman had said, could still be bought in Abyssinia. The offender had been sent on leave, but it looked for a while as though the Regent intended to send him to a diplomatic Coventry when he returned to Addis Ababa, the capital. The British Foreign Secretary sought and received his colleagues' approval to take a strong line. The British Minister in Addis was to tell the Empress that if there was any such snub to a member of the British mission, Britain might feel impelled to justify his remarks before the League and ask whether Abyssinia had fulfilled her obligations to suppress slavery.

Ironically, in view of the tragic events of the next decade, it was with Italy that Ras Tafari signed a Friendship Pact in 1928. When that treaty was cynically discarded by Mussolini, it was Britain, with whatever initial doubts and subsequent betrayal, which led the League in resistance to the Italian invasion. But even then, the agreement Britain had made with Italy ten years earlier tarnished the purity of the British attitude, and Ras Tafari was to find that his appeal to the League for help was ultimately in vain.

In trying to assess the value of Britain's contribution to the development of the League during the second half of the 1920s, one is confronted by a paradox. Undoubtedly, the regular presence of her Foreign Secretary at Geneva did much to raise respect for the League. British participation was vital to the League in all its activities. Robert Cecil quotes Madariaga as saying, 'When Great Britain stops, the League stops; when Great Britain goes forward, the League goes forward, too.'* But it did not go forward very far or very fast while Sir Austen Chamberlain represented Britain at Geneva; and, as Cecil had discovered, Chamberlain's attitude was entirely consistent with that of his senior colleagues in the Baldwin government. The authority and power Chamberlain was willing to cede to the League was always strictly qualified. He delivered a characteristic appreciation of the League's virtues and its necessary limitations early in 1930, some eight months after the change of government which resulted in his loss of office:

'To assert that peace can only be secured by the common surrender of their sovereign independence by all nations is to pose as essential a condition which no nation has ever yet admitted, or is ever likely to accept unless under compulsion and as the consequence of defeat. It can only distract our attention from the practical methods which are open to us to avert the danger of war and, by destroying our belief in the possibility of securing peace, lessen the effectiveness of our efforts to maintain it. It is to the League of Nations that we must look to find the solution

* Op. cit. p. 197.

of the problem, but to a League in which the nations co-operate as equals, not to a super-State of which all are subject provinces.'*

Chamberlain had been no less than honest when he had told Stresemann he placed a higher value on making Locarno work than on subscribing to high-flown aspirations as embodied in resolutions of the League Assembly. The League was potentially a useful instrument for building better international relationships, and it was one which a British Foreign Secretary should help to develop and be ready to employ, but never, never, asking it to do what it was not designed to do:

'To help the continuation and development . . . to maintain old friendships whilst cultivating new ones; to act loyally with the Council; to promise no more than we can perform; to strive to keep a reasonable balance between conflicting interests and from our semi-detached position to exercise a moderating and harmonizing influence; above all to preserve union among the great powers and to prevent Europe settling down again in two great camps—this, as it seems to me, should still be in the twentieth century the aim of British statesmanship, as it was a hundred years ago the policy of Castlereagh.'†

Britain's concern to confine the activities of the League within what the Government considered proper boundaries was reflected in critical opposition to proposed increases in the League's budget. On one occasion, Britain attacked the proposal for an extra £60,000 a year of which her share would be £6,000. In 1928, Britain and Italy joined in attempts to cut back the League's budget to a round £1 million a year and to hold it there.

Yet it was a time of optimism at Geneva. There was a long way to go, there were still big problems to be solved—including disarmament, the biggest of all—but there was a general acceptance that the League, if falling short of the ideal, had now established itself. A world without it was unthinkable: the League would go on growing and getting stronger and soon all nations, as a matter of course, would see conciliation and arbitration as the only way of settling disputes between them. The world was not without incidents and developments which caused serious concern, but none assumed the proportions of an international crisis to shatter the illusion that man was turning to reason in the conduct

* Op. cit. Vol. 2, p, 376.　　　† Op. cit. Vol. 2, pp. 376–7.

of his affairs. Symbolic of this confidence in the future was the laying—in September, 1929, a full five years after the project had been approved—of the foundation stone of the Palace which was to be the League's permanent and appropriately magnificent home.

Despite the harm which they did to the League by locking it out of some of their most important discussions, the regular presence of Chamberlain, Briand and Stresemann provided a solid assurance of continuity; but each of those three men suffered severely from the strains imposed by his responsibilities. This meant, very occasionally, their missing a Council meeting; more often, they turned up and took their seats when they ought to have been in bed.

Of the three, Stresemann suffered the most grievously. From the beginning of his career as an international figure, he had been warned against over-exertion, but he consistently ignored medical advice, continuing to work even when, ostensibly, he was convalescing at some health resort, like Baden-Baden. Relentlessly, he went on dredging his body of strength, until, in 1928, the last two years of his life, it began to be obvious to all who saw him that he was steadily and certainly killing himself. He worked on in chronic risk of total physical collapse, his face drawn and pallid, short of breath, mopping the sweat from his forehead. He could not and would not take the long rest from work which was his only chance of recovery. He was still engaged in bitter political conflicts at home, and, for all he had done to win back international respect and prosperity for his country, he had still not achieved all he had set his heart on doing. The last months of his life were acted out at a level of physical and moral heroism and, even now, despite the catastrophe that was to overtake Germany, they can be seen as a major triumph on behalf of his country.

Stresemann had hoped that the signing of the Locarno treaties would be followed quickly by the withdrawal of Allied troops from the Rhineland. What justification could there be for the presence of foreign forces on the soil of a friendly neighbour? What reason could the French now have for feeling insecure? What had been the worth of those professions of good intent by Briand at Locarno when, three years later, the French Army was still there occupying the territory of the defeated enemy? Locarno was in ruins, said Stresemann; he had been deceived. The continuing occupation was driving Germany into the arms of the nationalists. But the political realist knew that the only way he would get rid of those foreign troops was to negotiate a final settlement of the reparations problem.

The German Foreign Minister was pursued by accusations, particularly from the French, that the Germans, although meeting their current commitments, could well afford to pay more by way of reparations. While he, on the one hand, pleaded poverty, his words were mocked by the gross demonstrations of extravagance by the German states and municipalities, of which Cologne, where Konrad Adenauer was lord mayor, was a conspicuous example with its construction of an exhibition building containing the largest organ in the world. Apart from lavish spending on public culture, bureaucrats were given massive increases in pay and they multiplied their kind wantonly. Stresemann tried to argue that these were but superficial flamboyances and that, underneath, Germany was still poor and the German people still dedicated, not to hedonism, but to honest toil. He knew his case was weak. As he wrote to the mayor of Duisberg: 'Will you please have the kindness to tell me what answer I am to make to the representatives of foreign powers when they tell me that all these things give the impression that Germany did not lose but won the war?'*

In the summer of 1929, a conference was held at The Hague with the aim of settling reparations once and for all—or, to be precise, for the next fifty-nine years, for that is what the Young Plan, so named after an American financier, Owen D. Young, specified. It lasted a whole month, a month of haggling day and night, a month of tension, disappointments, recriminations and, more than once, the near-certainty, as it seemed, of failure. Stresemann's associates were appalled by his condition, but he drove himself on, making essential concessions but coming out at the end with the prize he most desired—the guaranteed evacuation of the Rhineland the following year, five years ahead of the date set at Versailles.

On the other issues which deeply concerned him—and the

* Op. cit. Vol. 3, p. 283.

German people—he was unable to claim similar success. Although, during the latter part of his life, he might have indulged moments of hope about a general disarmament* he could be seen ultimately to have been participating in an exercise in futility. He earnestly wished for the day when former German territories would come under government from Berlin once more, but the Saar was administered by a League of Nations commission and, although there was no evidence of any significant discontent, the Saarlanders, according to the timetable laid down at Versailles, must wait until 1935 to decide whether they wanted to continue to be governed by the League, or return to Germany, or be transferred to France. Stresemann resolutely refused to acknowledge explicitly or otherwise the permanent loss of Germany's eastern territories. In his championship of the rights of the German minorities there he was in tune with the nationalists who were his political enemies in Germany. Like the nationalists, he believed the day must come when the Germans in the east would be part of Germany. They were the cause of his more explosive contributions to Council debates. Minorities in general were a source of persistent concern to the Council, whose sub-committees handled a stream of complaints of injustice and maltreatment. Probably none was more vociferous than the German minority living in that part of Upper Silesia given to Poland under the 1922 settlement. The Germans gave articulate and cohesive expression to their grievances and their protests through a German national association. Not surprisingly, their activities and almost professional discontent irritated the Poles. Zaleski, the Polish Foreign Minister, gave free rein to this annoyance at a public session of the December, 1928, Council, which was being held at Lugano, rather than Geneva, because of Stresemann's ill-health. No doubt the German's condition contributed to the shortness of his temper, which flared up into a mordant counter-attack upon Zaleski, defending his countrymen's determination to speak out for their rights, and accusing Poland of discrimination and a betrayal of her obligations: where the Poles were concerned, Stresemann found it hard to keep his balance.

Stresemann made his last speech before the League Assembly

* See Chapter 10.

on September 9th, 1929, a speech twice postponed by heart attacks. His mind was still concerned with those same issues which had preoccupied him from the day he had led the German delegation to their seats three years earlier—still emphasising the supreme importance of disarmament; the natural affinities between the Saarlanders and the fatherland; the precious responsibilities of the League to safeguard the rights of national minorities. But Stresemann's mood was philosophic and visionary, ridiculing the material barriers which divided the nations of Europe and rebuking the reactionaries who believed that mankind must continue to live as it had always lived, committing the same follies, harnessing the idealism of youth to war.

But when Gustav Stresemann went back to Berlin, after a uselessly brief holiday, he found himself facing a direct challenge from the men who were so soon to canalise and corrupt that youthful idealism, and to exploit and pervert that national pride which he had epitomised and had done so much to restore. They would deal with the problem of Poland and Germany's eastern frontiers in a way Stresemann would never have contemplated. Two men dedicated to the overthrow of the Weimar Republic and the repudiation of the Versailles Treaty, Alfred Hugenberg, a wealthy, influential industrialist, owner of a vast propaganda machine, joined forces with Adolf Hitler. They formed a committee and campaigned against the Hague settlement, branding Stresemann as a traitor for having laid upon the German people obligations whose acceptance was tantamount to a recognition of German war guilt. Stresemann and his supporters fought back and defeated the challenge. It was his last victory. He died on October 3rd, 1929, after suffering two more strokes.

10

'This curious combination of irresponsibility with idealism'

Nothing could characterise more aptly the hopes and the illusions of the late 1920s than the Kellogg-Briand Pact, which had brought Stresemann to Paris only a few days after suffering a slight stroke. Crowds lined the Paris streets, crying out, 'Long live peace,' and 'Long live Stresemann.' The German Foreign Minister was considered too ill even to meet the press, but his doctor allowed him brief meetings with Briand and the French Prime Minister Poincaré. It was Briand once again who adorned what everyone took to be an historic occasion, the signing of the pact in the famous Clock Room of the Quai d'Orsay on August 27th, 1928. 'Can the civilised world,' he asked, 'present a nobler lesson than the spectacle of this gathering, where Germany appears for the signature of a pact against war, of her own free will and without reserve, among all the other signatories, her former enemies?'

The pact which, as Briand remarked, saw the welcoming, for the first time for more than a century, of a German Foreign Minister on French soil, renounced war. As, on the one hand, it contained no provisions for deterring an aggressor but was, nevertheless, something Washington had set its heart on, other nations were only too happy to put their signatures to it. It meant no new obligations and cost nothing but a promise of good behaviour. Yet at the time it seemed very much more than a moral fashion show. Coming at the time it did, after years of disappointment over disarmament, it revived hopes that the world would find a way of living permanently at peace and that one day perhaps the Americans, whose defection had crippled the League at the outset and had been directly the cause of another decade of European insecurity, might take their place at the Council table at Geneva.

But in reality the pact brought the world not a single step nearer to the fulfilment of Article 8 of the Covenant, the article which enshrined some of the most fervent aspirations of its draftsmen. The first clause of that article reads:

'The Members of the League recognise that the maintenance of peace requires the reduction of national armaments to the lowest point consistent with national safety and the enforcement by common action of international obligations.'

It was not just the ordinary people, but also the statesmen, who believed that if there had not been an arms race between the great powers there would never have been a world war. Armaments were seen as an unmitigated evil. So the popular demand was for general and, if possible, total disarmament. Yet almost as strong was the concept of united action to defend the peace, to deter and, if necessary, to fight an aggressor nation. Throughout the years between the two wars there was an extraordinary failure to recognise that collective security could not be maintained or enforced without arms and armies: the advocates of total disarmament could talk in the same breath of collective security without sensing the contradiction. But too many commentators have laid this charge indiscriminately against a whole generation of politicians as though they were all lacking in a perception of political realities so obvious to their successors. Some, certainly, were victims of this delusion. But others, including those most intimately concerned with trying to achieve disarmament, just as certainly were not. Lord Robert Cecil, for instance, who served for several years in the abortive disarmament commissions set up by the League, was fully aware that disarmament was impracticable without the assurance given by collective security.

The French have often been portrayed as putting up the most obstructions to disarmament. Perhaps they did, but only because they knew that no nation could really agree to disarm itself until it was sure it was not thereby exposing itself to attack, a fear which France understood better than most countries. But they were not merely negative about it. Even when the Covenant was being drafted, the French proposed that the League should have a military general staff, with forces at its disposal, and that this staff should be given the authority to carry out inspections in every country to check on military establishments and armaments. But neither Britain nor the United States would agree and so, in the years that followed, the French went on repeating—varying the form but never the substance—that they were not prepared to abandon the security of their country upon the receipt of mere protestations of good faith by other nations. The frustrations of the interminable commissions, committees and subcommittees, set up at Geneva to prepare the ground for the ultimate disarmament conference, have led to a cynicism about the original intentions of the founders of the League, particularly of the French and the British. Their leaders, it is said, merely subscribed a few fine phrases to the cause of disarmament, never seriously intending to do other than strip Germany of her military power and to keep her impotent.

It would be truer to say that, after the first flush of optimism had faded, the political leaders of the great powers usually found it much easier to give all the reasons why they should not disarm than to promote constructive proposals to bring about a cut in armaments. But that should not prevent us from taking at their face value the sentiments expressed at the time of the Peace Conference, even by such a relentlessly realistic man as Clemenceau. 'The Allied and Associated Powers wish to make it clear,' he said, 'that their requirements in regard to German armaments were not made solely with the object of rendering it impossible for her to resume her policy of military aggression. They are also the first step towards that general reduction and limitation of armaments which they seek to bring about as one of the most fruitful preventatives of war and which it will be one of the first duties of the League of Nations to promote.' But once the Americans had deserted Europe, the French put first things first, and the first thing so far as they were concerned was to make their country secure against the Germans.

According to Article 8 of the Covenant, it was the Council's responsibility to formulate plans for the reduction of armaments, but its attitude might be described as doing as little as it was forced to do—an attitude which was a direct response to French indifference or positive resistance. But elbowed on by an impatient Assembly—many of whose members, being virtually without arms themselves, could campaign wholeheartedly for the disarming of their stronger brethren—the Council established machinery to study the facts and submit proposals. The first of these bodies was called the Temporary Mixed Commission for the Reduction of Armaments. That lasted for some five years and could be credited with the treaties of Mutual Guarantee and of Mutual Assistance and of the Geneva Protocol, none of which ever got anywhere;* in an evolutionary sense, the commission could also be said to have contributed to Locarno.

By the time Germany entered the League, however, no matter how high her expectations or those of other countries, no effective advance had been made towards the ideal of disarmament. Of course, there had been some cutting of armaments and armed forces, but not in accordance with any plan for a balanced reduction. The only advance in this field was the Washington Conference held during the winter of 1921–22, and to describe that as a success would be a distortion. It was called by President Harding; Lloyd George had been planning to stage one himself in London, but, under pressure from the Dominions, gave in with bad grace to Harding. The purpose of the conference was to achieve agreements on disarmament between the five main maritime powers (America, Britain, France, Italy and Japan) and on Far Eastern affairs. The American interest was to establish her right to naval parity with Britain and to loosen the British association with Japan, to which Lloyd George was much attached. The treaty which the five powers signed was a limited one, even in naval terms, and it ignored military and air strengths. It prescribed a so-called 'holiday' for ten years in the building of capital ships and fixed limits to the individual tonnages of battleships, battle-cruisers and aircraft-carriers, and to the size of their guns. There was no agreement about smaller warships, including submarines. But the American demands were satisfied

* See Chapter 6.

by the fixing of a ratio for capital ships between Britain, USA and Japan, of 5 : 5 : 3. Britain also agreed to allow her alliance with Japan to lapse. In return, to meet the Japanese demand for security, Britain and America agreed not to increase or strengthen their naval bases in the Pacific islands, a bargain which they were later to regret. Another treaty was signed pledging the Pacific powers to respect each other's possessions and to combine together to repel any other country which tried to gatecrash; and one to which Portugal, Belgium, Holland and China put their signatures emphasising Chinese independence and asserted again the Open Door principle, guaranteeing equal opportunity in China for the trading nations.

In terms of disarmament, the achievement was little enough, but that was more than was ever to be achieved again in the period between the two world wars. At least, the naval limitations were accepted by the powers which mattered at that time. Those who suffered the agonies of negotiation at Geneva never had as much to show for their work and their lack of progress was a continuing source of European tension. A great world disarmament conference was always just round the corner, but year after year more good reasons were found for postponing it. In December, 1925, the Council set up a new body, called the Preparatory Commission for the Disarmament Conference, whose specific task, as its name suggests, was to prepare the ground for a general conference. Its membership was not confined to members of the League; the United States and, later, Soviet Russia, were among the outside powers represented on it. The commission met for the first time the following May. Its progress was so slow that even the British Government was worried. To speed things up, there was talk at a meeting of the Cabinet on June 9th, 1926, of sending a member of the Government out to Geneva to head the British delegation. This was in direct response to a plea from Cecil, who, as Chancellor of the Duchy of Lancaster, was Britain's permanent representative on the commission and, like his colleagues, was frustrated by the slow pace. Before any minister could be sent to Geneva, the commission adjourned.

The commission had been briefed by the Council to concentrate on the technical aspects of disarmament. That in itself revealed either just how far away the great powers were from understanding the essential problem of disarmament or how far they were prepared to deceive their peoples. The reality was that there were no technical aspects of disarmament, only political aspects. The failure to make progress in cutting down armaments was not because of arguments over how many bombers a particular nation should possess or what size guns a cruiser should carry, but because of an absence of political agreement. Disarmament was, and is, from first to last a political question.* That anything at all had been achieved at the Washington Conference was the consequence of the political will among the nations taking part to come to some sort of agreement. Despite the pledge given by the Locarno signatories to further the cause of disarmament taken up by the League, that political will was missing in 1926 when the Preparatory Commission set about its task.

For the Council to call for a report on the technical aspects of disarmament was diversionary, but it was a diversion which absorbed the energies of scores of politicians, diplomatists and high-ranking military men for several months, particularly the latter, who had the job of drawing up a report which could be studied by the commission as a whole. When they produced it, in November, 1926, none could deny it was a remarkable piece of work, covering as it did every conceivable aspect of the problem of disarmament and trying, as the Council had asked the commission to do, to answer complicated and sometimes unanswerable questions. What was the distinction, for instance, between offensive and defensive weapons? Should civil aircraft be counted as potential instruments of war? What consideration should be given to a country's industrial and financial strength when determining how far it should reduce its arms? How could an effective and acceptable means of international inspection be devised? It would have been impossible to expect a body of men with vested interests in their country's armed services, and always conscious of the need to refer back on policy questions,

* This was a truth which Salvador de Madariaga, from 1922–27 Director of the disarmament section of the League Secretariat, tried to propagate. When he recognised he had failed, he resigned and took up a professorship at Oxford.

to achieve unanimity, and all the report's conclusions were hedged about by qualifications or positively contested by counter-arguments.

The situation was no better when the full commission met again in March, 1927. For week after week the delegations wrestled in public, displaying for all the world to see the disagreements between them—not least between the British and the French. If there was such discord within the Preparatory Commission, what hopes were there for a full-scale disarmament conference? The people waited and waited but the men at Geneva did not possess the power to work miracles—and a miracle would have been needed to achieve a meeting of minds on disarmament at that time.

The Germans waited with increasing impatience. At Locarno, Stresemann had insisted on general disarmament and an end to Germany's military inequality. Even before Locarno, Emile Vandervelde, Belgium's socialist Foreign Minister, had warned his allies against the danger and folly of keeping Germany disarmed, while France was still heavily armed. As we now know, Germany, long before Locarno, had sought secret means of building up her armaments, but there is no reason to doubt that when the Germans entered the League they—as personified by Stresemann—were ready enough to comply with any international system of inspection and control. What they could not endure indefinitely was a condition of military inferiority. It was not only a betrayal of the spirit—as well as the letter—of Locarno; it also rendered Stresemann and all those Germans who believed in negotiation and international conciliation vulnerable to the forces in Germany which were ever ready to denigrate the League and the infant democracy of Weimar. So it was to the end of Stresemann's life. None knew better than he did the frailty of the republican system of which he was the international symbol. He needed generous concessions from the other Locarno powers, above all France, to prop him up. The reward would certainly not have been a pliant obsequious Germany; Stresemann never ceased to be a nationalist, seeking to restore the greatness of his country; but Hitler, and those he led, would have been deprived of a major weapon. The concessions were never made.

So long as the contentious, sometimes acrimonious, discussions went on within the Preparatory Commission, there remained the remote prospect of something concrete and practical emerging which would form the basis of a world conference. Then came another diversion, which offered a new hope of progress. It began with informal approaches to Cecil from John Foster Dulles, then one of the American representatives on the commission (some thirty years later the intransigent US Secretary of State during the Cold War), proposing negotiations to take the Washington Treaty a stage further with additional cuts in naval strengths. At first, the British Government held the view that there could be no conference unless France and Italy took part, but those two countries believed the only result of such a conference could be a confirmation of their relative naval inferiority, not only in capital ships, but in the smaller warships, and that was something they saw as wholly against their interests.

So there was a conference of just three powers, America, Britain and Japan. It was not until a year after the first feelers that it was convened, but it soon became obvious that, for all the exchanges which had taken place in advance, there was no ground for any comprehensive agreement. The longer it went on—it lasted some six weeks in all, ending early in August, 1927—the sharper and more damaging became the differences between Britain and the United States. Each side accused the other of obstinacy and their misunderstandings were relayed to and exploited by the press on both sides of the Atlantic at virtually every stage. Japan showed herself willing to make concessions, and tried to devise ways of saving some partial agreement, at least, from what threatened to be a total disaster. The comings and goings of telegrams and of members of the British team between London and Geneva—the conference was held in the League building, with the help of League officials, although formally dissociated from the League—took on a more and more agitated and exasperated air. The Cabinet was summoned time and again to urgent meetings to consider the latest shifts in negotiations.

Only the most diligent naval historian would wish to pursue the detail of the conference manoeuvres, although at this distance their tragi-comic flavour does command a certain fascination.* The major technical disagreement between the British and the Americans was over the size of cruisers, how many of them each should build, and what guns they should carry—six-inch (as the British proposed) or eight-inch (which the Americans wanted), or perhaps of a calibre somewhere between six-inch and 7.5 inch, a compromise the British were at one time prepared to consider. Beside those arguments, any dispute between Britain and Japan about submarines seemed insubstantial. But the technical gap between the two great naval powers was merely a symptom of the gulf of political understanding which separated them. Each went to the conference with quite different, and opposing, aims. Britain believed the Empire had special needs, which America would not recognise. The Americans believed the British were determined to hold on to a position of privilege. Extracts from a long telegram, sent by Chamberlain to the British Ambassador in Washington, Sir Esmé Howard, as the conference neared breakdown, indicates—for those who can master the sometimes tortuous syntax—the extent of the differences and the bad feeling they had generated:

'Proposal to adjourn will not deceive anyone or affect US building programme. I therefore see no object in proposing it, but if US put it forward we could accept it after our delegation had had fair opportunity of explaining our proposals as a whole and reasons why we cannot accept the terms which US delegation sought to dictate to Japanese and ourselves. We have tried to compromise repeatedly. No response from US. . . . Where has there been through whole conference *any* recognition by American delegation of special position and special needs of British Empire clearly stated by Mr. French? American argument (as far as they have consented to argue) seems to be:—To claim equal tonnage with you . . .

'. . . If America claims to build equal numbers in face of admittedly unequal needs we have no intention or need to quarrel with her and we have been prepared to make an agreement up

* The world was spared an agonising debate about the use of torpedoes from aircraft, an issue which had been discussed at the Preparatory Commission and seen to be, as the British Cabinet agreed, 'rather complicated' and best left outside the Three-Power Conference's terms of reference.

to 1936 which would leave her full liberty to do so though we are not prepared to admit as an immutable principle that parity of numbers where the needs of dangers to be met are quite unequal can result in real equality of sea power . . .

'. . . Restrictions of total tonnage without restriction of types and classes is meaningless . . . We proposed limits in each class as surest way of restricting both armaments and cost. Americans insisted on higher limits in every class. Up to present they have refused to discuss further limitation of size and gun of capital ships, they have refused to limit use of 8 inch guns. In provisional agreement on minor classes flotilla leaders, destroyers and submarines they have insisted in every case on higher individual limit than we had proposed.

'. . . You must realise the strength of our position and the repeated efforts that we have made at conciliation whilst the American delegation has not made any advance and every one of its proposals has meant greater armaments and more expense. A mistake to suppose that HMG recalled the British delegation for consultation because we thought them too unyielding. Our anxiety was of quite a different kind.

'*Confidential.* If the Conference breaks down, as now seems certain owing to American intransigence, I do not anticipate any early change in our present programme of construction whatever the future may have in store for us.'

The conference did break down. It had revealed no recognition in London or Washington that common interests might make compromise acceptable. Their blinkered pursuit of traditional objectives made failure of the conference an inevitability, but the consequences of their conflict were not limited to them alone. One major by-product was a weakening of the moderates, the 'peace party' in Japan, which was to have its issue in the Manchurian episode. Nor did the futility of the Three-Power Conference represent merely a negative phase in the progress towards disarmament: it was a most definite step backward in both practical and psychological terms.

Five months after the collapse of the naval conference, the Preparatory Commission met again. Attempts behind the scenes, in direct negotiations between the powers, to arrive at some sort of agreed convention, had been barren; their meeting in public now could demonstrate only that the ideal of disarmament was as remote from fulfilment as ever. Yet the commission's debates did contain an invigorating new element in the person of Maxim Litvinov, Soviet Russia's Deputy Commissar for Foreign Affairs, as head of a Soviet delegation. Litvinov was an attractive figure, a bulky, round-faced man, with a revolutionary background every bit as valid as that of other Soviet leaders, but one which made him more attuned to western ways. His origins were in the Jewish middle-class, a promising young businessman before he joined the secret brotherhood. That brought him a spell in prison, but he escaped abroad to continue his work for the revolution, smuggling arms into Russia. In 1908, he was arrested at the Gare du Nord in Paris, and deported. He went to London, where he married an English-woman, Ivy Low, and worked as a clerk; that was a cover for his activities as an agent. After the October revolution in 1917, he was made the official representative of the Soviet Government in England, but he was arrested by the British as a reprisal for the arrest in Moscow of Sir Robert Bruce Lockhart. The two men were exchanged and Litvinov went back to Moscow to serve under Chicherin, who himself had been imprisoned in Brixton and exchanged for Sir George Buchanan in January, 1918. Litvinov was quick-thinking, with a corrosive wit and an utter disregard for the status or reputation of his adversaries. He was formidable in debate, speaking in eloquent but sometimes unintelligible English, so thick was his accent. On one occasion, Briand, having listened in his sleepy way to a fiery speech from Litvinov, called for a *traduction anglaise.*

In later years, when Russia had entered the League and Litvinov, as his country's Foreign Minister, came to Geneva as a respected and familiar figure, he was less aggressive and abrasive. But when he first went there, to the Disarmament Commission, he discomfited his colleagues both by his manner and by the content of his contributions to their debates.

Soon after his arrival, Litvinov proposed to the commission an alarmingly simple solution to the problem of disarmament. He proposed the abolition of all armed forces, whether on land, sea or in the air, the destruction of all existing armaments, an end to military training, and the scrapping of ministries of defence, general staffs and military budgets. The plan was to apply throughout the world and was to be carried out so that within one year the only weapons left would be those used by police and customs officers. Litvinov said he had full powers to sign an agreement along these lines and called upon the capitalist imperialist nations to show there and then whether all their past talk about disarmament had been sincere or mere rhetoric. It was a triumphant piece of public relations for the Soviet Government. The Russians had absolutely nothing to lose. There was not the slightest prospect of their suggestion being accepted, anyway, but—to play with the hypothesis for a moment—even if it had been accepted and had been implemented, the Russians could have faced with equanimity the prospect of a return to wars fought with fists and clubs and slings. Litvinov knew as well as any of the other delegates that what he had proposed was wholly impracticable in political terms. He was blithely ignoring the central problem; how to create that security which was the essential condition for any controlled reduction of arms. But for anyone else to say so could only serve to enhance still further the image of Litvinov, in the eyes of the world, as a man whose idealism shone forth, unblurred by the kind of considerations which led other men into shabby compromise and cynicism. If it was not true to say, as Litvinov did back in Moscow, that his proposal was received 'as a sacrilege, as an attack on the very foundations of the League of Nations, as a breach of all the proprieties,' there is no doubt that the Soviet delegation* had made a disturbing impact.

Even before Litvinov put forward his proposal, the British

* It was not the first Russian delegation to go to Geneva. Earlier that same year, the Soviet Government had agreed to take part in the general economic conference organised by the League. The Russians, although not yet prepared to seek membership of the League, did now see the possibility of political dividends as a result of co-operating with it. An important obstacle to their participation had been removed when, at last, a settlement was signed between the Russian and Swiss Governments, formally ending the ill-feeling which had existed between the two countries since the murder, at Lausanne in May, 1923, of the Russian envoy, Vorovsky. Apart from exploiting any obvious opportunity to advance Russian interests, Litvinov did make genuine efforts to be constructive, as, for instance, in the dispute between Poland and Lithuania (see Chapter 9).

Government had been sensitive to accusations of obstructing the progress of disarmament. At home, it had come under political attack for the failure of the naval conference. That had been the breaking-point for Cecil, whose frustration had been growing, and now he resigned. In his letter to Baldwin, the Prime Minister, Cecil analysed the cumulative sins of the Government he had represented at Geneva:

'I look back on the refusal to accept the Treaty of Mutual Assistance, the unconditional rejection of the Protocol, the Ministerial declaration against compulsory arbitration, the partial failure of the Preparatory Commission, and now the breakdown of the Three-Power Conference. An advance in the direction first of security, then of arbitration, lastly of disarmament itself, has been tried, and in each case has made little progress. In each case the policy advocated has been more or less completely overruled. As it has been in the past so it will be in the future. The same causes will produce similar effects. For the truth is, however unwilling I am to recognise it, that in these matters my colleagues do not agree with me.*

The Cabinet was, therefore, the more particularly anxious that, when the Preparatory Commission met, the British representatives should not create an impression of being purely negative and destructive. They should endeavour, the Cabinet agreed, 'to avoid using language of an absolute and final character when opposing disarmament proposals which today were impracticable but which at some future date HMG might find easier of acceptance in their present or in some modified shape.'

A Cabinet committee came out against the adherence by Britain to any scheme at Geneva for limits to be fixed to military budgets. But a warning against this line came from an unlikely quarter. It was the Chief of the Imperial General Staff who pointed out to the Cabinet in a memorandum that:

'Our representative at Geneva will . . . be placed in a very difficult position if, after taking a strong line on the limitation of trained reserves, he is compelled to admit that we have no proposals of any kind for limiting material for land armaments. We shall be open to the accusation that we are ready to press a

* Op. cit. p. 363.

form of disarmament upon others from which we ourselves are immune, whereas we refuse to accept any limitation at all where our own interests are concerned. It is at least possible that we may be faced at Geneva with a unanimous demand for a limitation of budgets. In that event the Cabinet will be faced with the possibility of a breakdown of the conference owing to our attitude, or of an eleventh-hour surrender entailing an inevitable loss of prestige and the probablity of considerable odium . . .'

Having heard Litvinov's suggestion, however, the Preparatory Commission decided, with the Russian's acquiescence, to adjourn for another three months until March, 1928. The purpose of that break was to allow the major powers to have further private discussions in the hope of presenting the commission with some constructive plan. But they made so little headway that the British Government was looking for methods of protecting itself against unpopularity. On February 17th, it was agreed that:

'If the breakdown of the conference appears inevitable, our representatives should endeavour to secure that the breakdown occurs on the refusal of the French Government to consent to the limitation of military reserves.'

On March 13th, instructions were telegraphed from the Foreign Office to Lord Cushendun, who had taken over from Cecil, about the policy he should pursue in the Preparatory Commission:

'. . . With regard to Russian proposals, M. Briand's suggestion approved, viz., that proposals should be subjected at outset to searching question, such as are they calculated to prevent not only war between nations but also civil war the instigation of which has hitherto been the avowed object of Soviet Government. In supporting French attitude we leave a great deal to your discretion but in regard to these questions you will of course be careful to avoid using any language which might be construed into implying HMG was obstructing reduction in arms so as to be able to suppress legitimate Labour movement . . . Adjournment of Preparatory Commission is desirable, but British responsibility for seeking such adjournment should if possible be avoided. Interval between adjournment and next meeting of Preparatory Commission should be utilised to forward the compromise between France and ourselves in regard to land

and sea armaments as outlined in conversation between Sir Austen Chamberlain and M. Briand . . .'

A few days later, on March 21st, Chamberlain drew the attention of his colleagues to the speech Cushendun had made at Geneva on the Russian proposal for total disarmament,

'in which, after his foreign colleagues had confined their remarks to generalities, Lord Cushendun had exposed the said proposals to a searching criticism, thus repeating the experience (so common in Geneva) that it was left to the British representatives to utter what most of those present felt.'

The Cabinet authorised the Foreign Secretary to send Cushendun a letter of congratulation and support, but there was little enough being achieved in the way of disarmament to please anyone else, least of all the Germans. On June 13th, 1928, Chamberlain placed a memorandum before the Cabinet telling of a conversation he had had with von Schubert, of the German Foreign Office, in which

'after disclaiming any idea of using language in the nature of a threat, Herr von Schubert had said that failure to make some advance in disarmament shortly would make it impossible for the German Government to resist the conviction which was forming in Germany that the whole pretence of disarmament was a sham, and that the opening words of the Treaty of Versailles which imposed disarmament on Germany meant nothing and that the basis of restrictions imposed on Germany was gone.'

The British and French did manage to make a deal, but it was not one which was welcomed by the rest of the world. In return for Britain going along with the French view that there must be no limit placed on the numbers of trained reserves any nation might have, the French made important concessions to the British line on naval questions, a line which had been rejected by the Americans at the Geneva Naval Conference. The negotiations had proceeded in secret, and the Americans, the Italians and the Japanese, all of whom were vitally concerned with any maritime agreement, learned of the deal between London and Paris only through a leak to an American newspaper. Such was the suspicion generated about what the British and the French had been up to behind everyone's backs and so loud were the cries of outrage that the agreement had to be abandoned.

The episode was seen at Geneva as another let-down for the League, another example of the way the big powers could bypass the League and do their international business together in the old-fashioned way favoured by their Foreign Offices. But the despondency engendered by the Anglo-French compromise of July, 1928, was mitigated by the signing of the Kellogg-Briand Pact in Paris a month later.

The idea for such a pact had originated in the United States, but it had been Briand who picked it up and took the initiative of proposing to the American Secretary of State, Frank B. Kellogg, a joint renunciation of war; Kellogg responded by suggesting a general renunciation. The British Cabinet discussed it first in April, 1928, and without much enthusiasm. Sir Austen Chamberlain doubted whether such a treaty could be consistent with British obligations under other treaties, such as Locarno, and under the Covenant itself. There were many questions Chamberlain wanted answering, some by the legal advisers to the British and French Foreign Offices, and some by the American Government about the effect their proposed renunciation of war would have upon their traditional attitude towards the Monroe Doctrine, for instance. Chamberlain expressed the view to his colleagues that 'the only practical result of M. Briand's rather indiscreet initiative had been to revive controversy between France and the USA and make things worse.' He saw the need to handle the whole business with great tact and care, and, when he discussed it with the American Ambassador in London, Chamberlain thought it wise to send a record of the conversation to the British Ambassador in Washington with an explanatory note:

'The Ambassador might think that I was unduly under the impression of my experiences at Geneva, perhaps I was, but it had been my not uncommon fate there, to be confronted with large, and generous propositions or engagements proposed, and sometimes accepted, by men [who], if you examined those proposals quietly with them, admitted that they either did not mean what they said, or that they were incapable of execution. I was, I repeated, most anxious to take full advantage of the proposals which had come from Mr. Kellogg, but I wanted to be sure that, if we signed the Treaty, we all meant the same thing and that we should not be exposed to subsequent accusations of bad faith because years afterwards we discovered that we had used language with different meanings. Above all did I feel the necessity of caution in this respect as between ourselves and the USA, for Mr. Houghton knew as well as I did what charges of ill-faith had been spread against us in the US in respect of the Washington Treaty of Naval Disarmament, even though the US Secretary of the Navy had borne testimony to our loyal observance of our obligations.'

Chamberlain had good grounds for wariness over the proposed treaty, which has been described as expressing the dominant characteristics of American foreign policy at that time—'this curious combination of irresponsibility with idealism.' Signatories to the treaty were required to 'condemn recourse to war for the solution of international controversies, and renounce it as an instrument of national policy in their relations with one another.' Did that mean that members of the League acting together against an aggressor under Article 16 would be in breach of the Kellogg Pact? The British and French advisers, Sir Cecil Hurst and M. Fromageot, considered that the terms of the proposed treaty did not cover their countries' obligations under the Covenant and under the Versailles Treaty. But their German counterpart, Friedrich Gaus, reckoned that Germany could accept the proposal without any breach of existing obligations.

Whichever interpretation might be legally more correct, the tide was running so strongly in favour of acceptance that Britain saw no point in resisting it. France had already joined Germany in deciding to sign the treaty. Chamberlain considered that 'the French and Germans have skated over the thin ice of whether the Treaty is in conflict with the Covenant,' but he told his colleagues he was sure it would be 'a mistake for us to enter into an elaborate argument on a subject which other Powers have treated so lightly.' To do so, he said, 'would make it appear that we were far harder to please than the Germans or even the French.'

So the British fell into line and agreed to sign a treaty of whose value the Foreign Secretary still felt substantial scepticism. He expressed it when he handed over the British reply to the American chargé d'affaires, but he also had the diplomatic good sense to allow the Americans the benefit of the doubt.

He welcomed the proposal, he said, 'first, because he was always glad to co-operate with the USA in any matter, and, second, because he was specially glad to observe the renewed interest of the USA in maintaining the peace of the world.' He had further pointed out, he told the Cabinet, reporting his conversation, 'that the result would depend on what the USA did in the event of some nation breaking the Treaty. If they merely adopted an attitude of reproof towards the aggressor, not much progress would have been made; but if they refused to give any sort of aid to an aggressor then, in his view, Mr. Kellogg would have made a great contribution to the peace of the world.'

The Americans refused to commit themselves to any generalised pledge, so that, by the time the statesmen gathered in Paris for the signing ceremony, no-one was any the wiser about how the United States Government would interpret its obligations under the treaty in the event of some nation taking military action without first having tried to settle its dispute peacefully. But then, by the time the signatories met in Paris, the pact had been the subject of so many different interpretations that its utility, as providing binding criteria for international behaviour, had been seriously damaged. The pact was supposed to be a renunciation of war, but both Britain and the United States, for instance, reserved to themselves the right to make war, nevertheless, where war was deemed necessary to the defence, not only of their homelands and colonial possessions, but also of other parts of the world where they might feel their interests in jeopardy. Kalinin, the titular head of Soviet Russia, described the pact as 'a huge smokescreen.' But Litvinov signed it, and the Russians were the first to ratify it.

As seen from Geneva, and from many European capitals, the importance of the pact lay not in its value as an instrument for peace, but in the role America had played in promoting it. This bred the hope that, more and more, the Americans would offer their wealth and their strength to the creation of a stable, law-abiding world. The new President, Herbert Hoover, who, although a Republican, had done much good work under Wilson's leadership during and immediately following the war in administering American relief in Europe, now threw himself with enthusiasm behind the efforts to translate the ideals of the Kellogg Pact into reality, and he wanted to end the bitterness in Anglo-American relations which had followed the collapse of the Geneva Naval Conference. His Secretary of State, Henry L. Stimson, Kellogg's successor, was a man who deeply regretted his country's retreat from international responsibility; he also recognised the danger of the rift between Britain and the United States and the folly of a naval armaments race in which America was engaged largely for reasons of prestige.

When the American Senate ratified the Kellogg Pact in January, 1929, it seemed to supporters of the League a clear sign that it was only a matter of time before the Americans came out from behind their high walls to join with the rest of the world at Geneva in working for peace. It was the Senate, after all, which had repudiated Woodrow Wilson and the Covenant. In Paris in August, 1928, and in Washington in January, 1929, it was possible for men to dare to hope, despite all the disappoint-ments and set-backs of the past ten years, despite the fact that all the talk about disarmament had led to nothing, that better days were ahead of them.

PART TWO

The Fall

11

'Bearing in mind that this would offend the Japanese Government . . .'

The hope that accompanied the signing and ratification of the Pact of Paris was soon to be snuffed out. The month of October, 1929, not only deprived Germany of Gustav Stresemann; it was also the month of the great crash on Wall Street, the beginning of the economic catastrophe which was to engulf the world and whose ultimate consequence was the second world war. It is impossible to say how different the shape of history would have been if the depression had never happened; Mussolini, after all, was already firmly in power in Italy; Hitler and right-wing nationalism had presented a chronic threat to the Weimar regime and to Stresemann throughout his time as Foreign Minister; and although they presented little real threat during the 1920s, no Japanese Government could ever forget or ignore the militarists and anti-democratic forces. But as the effects of the Depression spread, impoverishing and wasting the lives of hundreds of millons of people, so the spirit of mankind withered. Before, even if some of them had been merely mouthing, the leaders of the great powers had talked of deterring and punishing aggression; now they turned their backs and surrendered the field to the bully-boys. In Britain, as the crisis in Europe deepened, there came as champions of the cause of peace the likes of John Simon, mockingly nicknamed 'Battling Jack Simon'; Samuel Hoare, who was happily sacrified by his own colleagues to save, not Abyssinia, but themselves; and Neville Chamberlain, who reckoned the betrayal of a small, 'far-away country' a small price to pay for a good night's sleep in his own bed. And in France, which had proved so stubborn in the search for security, the spirit of Clemenceau, of Briand, and no less of Poincaré, degenerated into Pierre Laval, the epitome of dishonour. These were men not suited to their times but fashioned by them. It was not that the leaders of Britain and France during the 1930s did not see the dangers; some of them, at least, knew also what they ought to do; but they had neither the collective will, nor the individual courage, nor the means to do it. Their moral and material capacity to react to the challenge had been steadily eaten away. So, too, the League of Nations. In the decade that led to the 1939–45 war, the League would still have achievements to its credit, some nations at any rate would continue to make their genuflections of respect to Geneva, but fewer and fewer people would be able to delude themselves that a new, effective system for international conciliation and peace enforcement was in the making. The League of Nations was to provide the stage for many dramatic episodes but they were sequences in a relentless theme of tragedy. And throughout it all, the American people remained as spectators, withdrawing further and further into themselves, their Presidents, first Hoover and then Franklin Roosevelt, and their Secretaries of State, first Stimson and then the self-righteous Cordell Hull, conscious of their irresponsibility, but corrupted by fear of the mighty electorate.

The long slide into world war began at Mukden, a city in South Manchuria, on the night of September 18th, 1931. Many years later, it was to become obvious that the so-called Manchurian Incident had been engineered by the local Japanese army, without the knowledge of, and indeed in defiance of, the expressed wishes of the liberal government in Tokyo, of Emperor Hirohito himself, and even without the authority of the army command. But all that was known at the time was that fighting had broken out between the Japanese and Chinese. The Japanese alleged that the Chinese had blown up part of the railway track near Mukden and then opened fire on the Japanese railway guards. The Japanese army overcame the Chinese garrison at Mukden, occupied the city and was advancing elsewhere. The rest of the world had no means of knowing either the real cause of the incident or just how serious it was, but the news was bad enough to sound an alert in Washington, London, Moscow, and Geneva.

Manchuria offered a fertile potential as a source of trouble in the Far East. It had been part of the Chinese Empire and was theoretically subject to the Nationalist Government, but it was ruled almost independently by a Manchurian warlord; at the same time it was a sphere of important economic interest for the Japanese. Their victory in the Russo-Japanese war of 1904–5 had gained them the lease of Port Arthur and the administration of the South Manchurian railway. With administration of the railway went its protection by Japanese troops: hence the presence of a Japanese army. Where the railway went, so, too, went Japanese settlers and Japanese enterprises, and by 1931 Japan regarded the territory as one of direct and vital concern to her, not least for the promise it held out, in raw materials and developing trade, for the future. But the Chinese were intent on claiming back what they had been forced to cede under duress, just as they were determined to resist Russian ambitions to spread into Northern Manchuria, where a conflict of interests had led to a dangerous flare-up in 1929. Then there was also the continuing friction and suspicion between Russia and Japan, for which Manchuria provided a stage and a possible prize.

Nevertheless, when the trouble erupted at Mukden there was some sense of shock in other countries. This shock was in part a tribute to the way in which Japan had conducted herself during the previous decade. The Japanese had pursued a policy of conciliation in foreign relations and had sought to expand their commercial markets by wholly peaceable methods. At Geneva, Japan had been a conscientious and often valuable member of the League, working for constructive solutions, her detachment from many of the issues enabling her to play the honest broker. She had showed herself at her most co-operative at the London naval conference of 1930, when she had accepted an agreement on tonnages which determined her inferiority to Britain and the United States. Even in 1931, her foreign minister, Baron Shidehara, was actively seeking a pacific solution to the differences between China and Japan. But the Depression hit Japan especially hard and generated an unrest and discontent which could be exploited by those who wanted to oust the men of moderation. The military felt humiliated and betrayed by the London naval treaty and the plotting and secret planning flourished. The assassination in 1930 of the Prime Minister, Yuko Hamaguchi, heralded the violence of the years ahead, the years which were to see the betrayal of the League idea and to issue in the horrors of Hiroshima and Nagasaki.

At Geneva, the incident at Mukden was very quickly under discussion. The Council—which had just been newly elected and included China for the first time—was anyway due to meet the following day; when it did so it asked the Japanese and Chinese representatives to find out from their governments more about what had happened. The Japanese delegate, Kenkichi Yoshizawa, said he was certain his government would do everything possible to settle the matter; he referred to the clash as 'a local incident.' The Chinese delegate, Dr. Alfred Sze, said he was greatly disturbed and his information showed that the incident had not been provoked in any way by the Chinese. The *Manchester Guardian*'s correspondent commented, 'This is the first time a menace of war between two great powers has been dealt with by the Council, and it is early yet to say that the last has been heard of the dispute.'

The Council had very little hard information to go on at first and the world had other preoccupations. Just three days after the fighting started in Manchuria, Britain went off the gold standard, a decision which rocked the world and lent an unhealthy excitement to the proceedings of the League Assembly, then in session. But September 21st was also the day when Dr. Sze told the Secretary-General of the League that he had now received information about the Mukden incident which disclosed a 'situation of greater gravity' than the earliest reports had indicated. China appealed to the League under Article 11 and requested an immediate meeting of the Council. The British representative on the Council, Lord Cecil, asked the Government for instructions. The Cabinet approved Cecil's own approach, which was to aim for a withdrawal of troops behind a certain line, and to send observers, probably military attachés, to see for themselves on the spot what was happening. This was by now an established practice of the League and it had demonstrated its usefulness more than once. In the light of later criticisms by the Americans of non-co-operation and back-pedalling by the British, it is important to note that Cecil was making this proposal and the Cabinet approving it within four days of the first news from Manchuria. The British Government wanted American support for it and the Foreign Secretary, Lord Reading, had immediately informed both Washington and Tokyo of the line Britain was taking.

It has sometimes been said that what happened in Manchuria seemed important only in retrospect and that because it happened thousands of miles away, Europe did not concern itself overmuch. That is not borne out by contemporary records. At Geneva, there was immediate recognition of the test of authority with which the League might be confronted. The British Government and Parliament, the leader-writers and public opinion—as represented by the powerful League of Nations Union—all responded in a way that showed full awareness of the dangers implicit in the situation.

When the Council met on September 22nd, the atmosphere was taut and nervous. In the morning session, Dr. Sze told his colleagues that hundreds of men, women and children in Manchuria had been killed by the Japanese troops and the massacre was continuing. By the time the Council met again in the late afternoon, and after two postponements, the tension had risen. Yoshizawa, who spoke English in a slow, faltering manner which made him hard to understand, said again that Japan would observe her obligations under the Covenant, but he felt bound to refer to the enormous Japanese interests in Manchuria—including one million nationals and investments amounting to two million yen—which had been constantly jeopardised by incidents of one kind or another. This was a theme to be pursued by Japan with more and more emphasis and obduracy as time went on: the importance of her Manchurian interests and the justification of her military actions as retaliatory ones and taken solely as measures of self-defence. Sze's reply to Yoshizawa was to snatch up a pile of telegrams and wave them. Those telegrams had reached him that day, he said; they reported 'revolting acts' and proved that the situation was getting worse and worse. At last, the Spanish president of the Council put forward three proposals. There was to be an urgent appeal to both sides to stop any further aggression; the Japanese Government should arrange for the withdrawal of its troops and the United States should be kept informed.

At this stage, there was no assumption of Japanese guilt. The Japanese Government itself was obviously trying to regain control and sent repeated assurances to Geneva that its troops would pull back. The Council was ready to give Tokyo time to sort things out and for the Japanese to deal directly with the Chinese, if this could bring about a quick and acceptable solution. But the dispatch without delay of a team of experienced observers, directly responsible to the Council, could have acted as a powerful aid to the Japanese Government, much as it might have argued against it. As it was the Americans dragged their feet, Stimson making no secret of his view that the Council should stand aside, while the two powers in dispute tried to come to an agreement between themselves. The Japanese Government, in a difficult position with the army and with its own people—who generally applauded the action in Manchuria—saw no reason for any show of repentance. At Geneva, Yoshizawa took the attitude that the Japanese soldiers had been more sinned against than sinning, that they were only defending legitimate national interests, and that they were innocent of any territorial ambitions. Both Chinese and Japanese representatives expressed their countries' desire for peace; Sze said China would be glad to negotiate with Japan as soon as Japanese troops were withdrawn from the places they had occupied: Yoshizawa said most of them had already gone and the rest would do so as soon as the threats to Japanese people and property were removed.

A resolution, embodying expressions of restraint and good intent on both sides, was adopted by the Council on September 30th. The tension at Geneva relaxed as members of the Council—and of the Assembly, which had been impatient for effective action—sat back to wait for things to get better. Even then, it was still probably the genuine wish of the Japanese Government to end the conflict peaceably, though without seeming to have betrayed its country's interests in Manchuria. But the military, not having been checked, set about extending its success in

Manchuria. The local army commander at Mukden issued a statement saying that Japanese recognition of the regime of the Manchurian warlord, Chang Hsueh-liang, was at an end and struck at Chinchow, in the south of the province, sending eleven aircraft to bomb the town, where Chang was still in command. The Japanese Government denounced these freelance activities of the army, but continued blatantly to play for time in its exchanges with the Chinese and in the conditions it laid down as necessary preliminaries to a withdrawal of forces. It still denied any breach of either the Kellogg Pact or the Covenant. This was where the damage done by America's initial policy was to be seen. The Japanese had interpreted the American attitude as one of weakness, assuring them that the United States had no wish to get involved in a private row between China and Japan. The Tokyo Government bowed to the stronger pressures and its attempts to reassert its authority over the military in Manchuria slackened to the point where it was hard to distinguish between what was its ineffectuality and what might be its active complicity.

The Japanese bombed Chinchow on October 8th. At Nanking, on October 12th, Chiang Kai-shek, the Chinese generalissimo, voiced the impatience of his people in the kind of speech which seems destined, if not designed for, the history books. 'China,' he said, 'respects the Covenant and the Kellogg Pact, but, if the League and the Kellogg Pact signatories fail to uphold their sacred duties, China will not hesitate to make the supreme sacrifice of bankrupting the country for half a century to go to war in order to uphold the dignity and sacred rights of international agreements and to safeguard world peace.'

When the Council met again, on October 13th, its earlier optimism had evaporated. Even the Americans seemed to be moving towards a stronger line and Stimson, even before the Chinchow bombing, had sent a message to the Secretary-General, exhorting the League not to relax its vigilance and he held out what appeared to be a significant promise to back up independently any action taken by the League. This encouraged the Council to invite the United States to join it temporarily to help decide what action could be taken under the Covenant and the Kellogg Pact. The Japanese did not like the idea but the invitation was sent, anyway, the Americans accepted, and the

United States consul in Geneva, Prentiss Gilbert, sat down under Briand's chairmanship. But the reaction to his presence there at the Council table worried Stimson into rapid retreat. In Europe, and particularly in Geneva, the Secretary of State's acceptance of the Council's invitation had been acclaimed, not merely as a potentially valuable contribution to solving the Manchurian dispute, but also as one more step towards the day when the Americans would take their place in the Council as of right. In the United States, the isolationists clamoured for Stimson's head. The vehemence of those attacks, plus the strength of the Japanese objection, were more than enough. The Americans were ready to offer the League what amounted to all help short of actual assistance. Those were the instructions Gilbert took to the Council: advice, yes; moral support, yes; but, in the unlikely event of the Council deciding to bring any positive pressures to bear, perhaps even some form of sanction, then the most to be expected from the United States was a rallying of public opinion. By the time the Council broke up again on October 24th, the one plain message Gilbert had managed to convey was just how little the Americans were prepared to do in co-operating with the League.

Even without that disappointment the October meeting of the Council would have been depressing. The Japanese delegate was full of reassurances, as usual, but rejected adamantly a proposal for a fixed time-limit for the withdrawal of troops. And when the Council considered a resolution incorporating a provision that the withdrawal should be completed within three weeks— by which time the Council was due to meet again—Yoshizawa voted against it. That, so far as action under Article 11 was concerned, amounted to a veto. There is no doubt that the other members of the Council, had they wished, could have found a way round the veto to make compliance with the resolution obligatory upon Japan. But there was no will to do so. Stimson had made known American opposition to the resolution, because he did not think Japan could possibly meet the demand. The British Government was critical of it—although Britain voted for it—because the League had no means of making the three weeks' notice to quit effective, so the Council separated, seemingly having submitted to the Japanese veto, thus providing one more encouragement to the Japanese army in Manchuria and to all those immoderate elements in Japan which were gaining ground, step by step, over the liberal democrats. The Japanese people, suffering genuine hardship from the world slump, anxious, frustrated, resentful, identified Manchuria with national pride and prosperity and the emotional build-up began which was to culminate in mass military fanaticism. In the past, the Japanese had pooh-poohed suggestions of their aggression in Manchuria, referring to the mere handfuls of troops stationed here and there in the province. However picturesque an under-statement that might have been, and however unauthorised the action at Mukden had been, the army command now set about the serious business of expanding the occupation. Powerful reinforcements were sent to Manchuria and the Japanese made fast advances, moving into central and Northern Manchuria as well as the south, establishing as they went a puppet adminis-tration.

At the next meeting of the Council, in Paris, Britain was represented by the new Foreign Secretary, Sir John Simon. The Cabinet did discuss Manchuria before he left, but throughout the early months of the dispute the Cabinet was concerned, almost exclusively, with the financial crisis and the consideration of possible economies, such as the reimposition of an admission fee of one penny on schoolchildren visiting Kew Gardens. When it came to discussing international affairs, the first concern of ministers was to avoid adopting any policies which might cause trouble and, above all, which might affect trade. Simon was particularly worried about the difficult situation which would arise, if the Chinese delegate chose to switch his appeal to the League from Article 11 to Article 16. Article 16 had much more serious implications, for, as Simon reminded his colleagues, it provided that:

'Should any Member of the League resort to war in disregard of its covenants under Articles 12, 13 or 15, it shall *ipso facto* be deemed to have committed an act of war against all other Members of the League, which hereby undertake immediately to subject it to the severance of all trade or financial relations, the prohibition of all intercourse between their nationals and the nationals of the covenant-breaking State, and the prevention of all financial, commercial or personal intercourse between the nationals of the covenant-breaking State and the nationals of any other State, whether a Member of the League or not . . .'

As had been shown at the time of the Corfu incident, went the argument in Cabinet, 'it was not practicable policy in a case of this kind to impose the sanctions provided for in Article 16, which would involve the imposition of very drastic restrictions on trade . . .' The Corfu incident had proved nothing of the kind. The lesson of Corfu was that when the Council showed itself unwilling to act as it had the power to act—in that instance, largely because France was trying to buy Mussolini's backing against Germany—the aggressor was encouraged to hang on to what he had taken by force. Robert Cecil had certainly not taken that line in 1923 and he was not taking it in 1931. But Cecil's known disposition to call aggression aggression, and to argue for the strict application of the Covenant, was not endearing him to many members of the Government. Simon made quite clear that, although Cecil was to attend the next Council meeting, he himself, the Foreign Secretary, intended to act as spokesman for Britain. And the line he suggested he should take and which the Cabinet generally approved, was 'one of conciliation, with an avoidance of implied threats':

'The League of Nations should be upheld. The Cabinet recognised, however, *inter se*, that the sanctions provided for in Article 16 of the Covenant were not suitable and could not in practice be applied in the present case. In the interests of the League itself, therefore, every effort must be made to avoid the Chinese appeal being shifted from Article 11 to Article 16. If necessary, it must be impressed on the Chinese delegate that he must assist the League and not throw the responsibility on the other members of the Council. . . . The Secretary of State was also asked to bear in mind the importance of not giving the Japanese hostile press any excuse to place the odium for the initiative on this country as had already been done for com- merical reasons. . .'

In that minute of the Cabinet meeting of November 11th, 1931—Armistice Day of all days—the British Cabinet enunciated a novel interpretation of the responsibility of a country which feels itself the victim of aggression: its delegate 'must assist the

League and not throw the responsibility on the other members of the Council.' It is so easy in retrospect to forget or ignore the harassing circumstances in which the men of November 1931, arrived at that conclusion; but it is even harder to forget or ignore the tragic and humiliating consequences of applying that very interpretation, time after time, in the years from 1931 onwards.

The French Government was no less anxious than the British to avoid any risk of sanctions against Japan, and joined in persuading the Chinese delegate, when the Council met again on November 16th, not to switch the basis of his appeal. But, if the Council was not prepared to stiffen the pressure on Japan, and if the Japanese were not prepared to withdraw except at their own convenience—if at all—what was to be done? It was the Japanese delegate himself, Yoshizawa, who came up with a proposal, which, though it must mean waiting and doing nothing for several months, was eventually accepted by the Council, and by China as well as Japan. The proposal was for the League to send out to Manchuria a commission of inquiry. It took the Council another three weeks even to agree the commission's terms of reference, and when it had done so it was seen that Japan had again had it all her own way. The commission would have no power to recommend any solution for the Manchurian dispute, nor to interfere in the military dispositions. Its purpose was confined to examining the causes of international friction between Japan and China. Japan continued to assert that the army operation in Manchuria was not the concern of the Council or the Kellogg Pact: it was a defensive operation against bandits.

Even Sir John Simon did not pretend that the Council had performed a great deed. While negotiations within the Council upon the terms of the resolution were still going on, he put a memorandum before the Cabinet in which he pointed out the shortcomings of the commission of inquiry. It would not be able to report for eight or nine months. 'Meanwhile,' said the Foreign Secretary, 'there was no assurance that the Japanese would evacuate the territory which they had occupied and which they had been asked to evacuate.'

'The Council, therefore,' the memorandum went on, 'would have failed in its immediate object of putting an end to the

Japanese occupation of Chinese territory, and would have to look on while its own summons was ignored. It would have to realise that it had failed to enforce the fundamental principle that a State may not, without prior recourse to the recognised means of peaceful settlement, take the law into its own hands.'

Simon advocated that, even if the resolution setting up the commission were adopted, the Council should issue a statement reaffirming the fundamental principle which it had failed to enforce. Any declaration to this effect, he said, would come best from the president of the Council, at that time Briand. But, if Briand was not prepared to make a strong enough declaration, the question, said Simon, was whether the British delegate should take the lead in doing so, 'bearing in mind that this would offend the Japanese Government.'

The Cabinet knew the answer to that one:

'The Cabinet, while favouring a statement by the president on behalf of the Council, indicating the principles of the League, and regretting that in the present Manchurian controversy those principles had not been more completely complied with, was opposed to the British representative taking up a special and separate attitude, and preferred that he should do his utmost, in association with other members of the Council, to press privately for a statement to this effect, on behalf of the whole Council, from the president.'

Briand did make a statement reaffirming the principles of the Covenant, when the resolution agreeing to the dispatch of a commission was passed on December 10th. But it was, for the most part, a frustrated and shamefaced Council which adopted the resolution, and American support for it was small consolation. Simon did not try to present it as a success. British public opinion—or that influential part of it represented by the League of Nations Union—had been dismayed by the events at Geneva. In the last fortnight of November there had been no fewer than six hundred and twenty meetings of the Union all over Britain and letters and resolutions had been showering on the executive and its chairman, Professor Gilbert Murray. The *Manchester Guardian*, in those days the militant voice of League supporters, was merciless:

'The League Covenant,' it said in a leader on December 8th,

'can apparently be ignored with impunity. Japan has ignored it by invading Manchuria; the nations represented on the League Council have ignored it by refusing to insist on the withdrawal of Japanese troops as a condition precedent to direct negotiations with China or to the dispatch of a Commission of Inquiry. The Covenant has failed to save China from aggression as completely as a signed and ratified treaty failed to save Belgium from German aggression in 1914, and the Great Powers, despite all their fine pacifist gestures, have to their great shame not even seriously protested against, let alone resisted, such a state of affairs.'

When Briand, just before Christmas, gave the foreign affairs committee of the French Chamber an account of the proceedings of the Council he was severely cross-examined, especially on the question of why the Manchurian dispute was being dealt with only under Article 11 of the Covenant. He replied, stating something less than the whole truth, that it was because China had requested it to be dealt with under that Article. Briand ended by congratulating the Council on having stopped war in Asia.

It was sad to see the great Aristide Briand descending to such a posture, but the truth was that Briand had been desperately ill throughout the Manchurian crisis, falling asleep for long stretches of Council meetings, presiding over them in name only. When the Council met again in public at Geneva in January, it began with a tribute to Briand, who was absent for the first time in six years. Paul-Boncour, deputising for him, said that Briand would soon be back among them. But within a few weeks of his retiring to his country estate he was dead. Neither Briand nor Europe had ever been able to recapture the euphoria which had accompanied the signing of the Locarno Treaty, but, almost to the end of his life, he displayed that imagination and generosity of vision which had done much to foster the illusion of constructive peacemaking and progress at Geneva for just a few years. In 1929, he had put forward an ambitious proposal for a European federal union and the following year saw the Assembly set up a commission to inquire into the possibility for creating such a union. But if the death of Stresemann, an enthusiastic supporter of the idea, followed by the rise of German nationalism, had not quite killed it, the depression would certainly have finished it off. The world was entering a phase which must either have brought a man like Briand to total despair or else have brought him down to the level of the others around him; it was not going to be the kind of world he could enjoy.

Just how completely he was fooling himself, or trying to fool the French Chamber, in praising the Council for having stopped war in Asia, was soon to be demonstrated. Within days of his making the statement, the Japanese forces in Manchuria were advancing again; indeed, it is doubtful whether they had ever stopped. It was not until the beginning of February that members of the commission of inquiry, under the chairmanship of Lord Lytton, left for Manchuria, and so roundabout was their route that they did not arrive there until April. By that time the Japanese army had effectively occupied the whole of Manchuria and on March 9th, 1932, Japan—whose moderate government had been displaced in December by one sympathetic to a 'positive' policy in Manchuria—had proclaimed to the world that, henceforth, Manchuria was to be known as the independent state of Manchukuo, administered by governors chosen and installed by the Japanese, and ruled by their puppet emperor, Pu Yi, who had reigned briefly, in his boyhood, as the last Emperor of China.

At Geneva, the Chinese and Japanese delegates exchanged familiar charges of aggression. When the Council met on January 25th at his request, Dr. Yen said that about 200,000 square miles of Chinese territory, with a population of more than twenty million, had been seized and occupied by Japan by military force, and, since the Council had adjourned six weeks earlier, the aggression had continued relentlessly. Mr. Naotuke Sato said it would be impossible for a mere 25,000 Japanese troops to occupy 200,000 square miles. Japan wanted nothing more than an assurance of peace and order in Manchuria; the troops could not be withdrawn until they had completed the task of eliminating banditry. Dr. Yen said that banditry existed in European and American cities, but he trusted the time was not coming when it would be necessary for foreign troops to invade those cities to suppress the bandits. Mr. Sato retorted that what had incensed the Japanese people to a dangerous degree was a caption to a picture in a Shanghai newspaper dealing with an attempt to blow up Emperor Hirohito with a bomb. The caption read: 'Unfortunately another carriage was hit.'

It was in Shanghai that Japan was to strike one more blow at China, a move which, because it was a direct threat to western interests in China, provoked a show of action from Geneva and evidence of distinct concern from Washington. The American State Department had already made a significant departure from the role of passive bystander—in the sense of making known its moral condemnation of Japanese aggression, at any rate. Stimson's hopes for the policy of conciliation towards Japan steadily faded during the autumn of 1931; when Japanese troops occupied Chinchow in the far south of Manchuria, near the Chinese border, they disappeared completely. He determined to make plain to the Japanese that the United States would not condone any settlement between China and Japan which was the consequence of military aggression, and that he held Japan to have betrayed her treaty obligations and to be threatening American rights and interests in China. He also wanted to assure the Chinese, in whose development the Americans had played such a leading part, that, while it might be impossible to stop the Japanese, the United States would not cynically shake hands with the aggressors.

He did this by means of a note addressed to both China and Japan on January 7th, 1932, which declared that the American Government would not admit the legality of any fruits of aggression. This was Stimson's enunciation of what became known as the doctrine of non-recognition, the application to Japan of a moral sanction. Stimson had hoped that other nations which had signed the Nine-Power Treaty in 1922—guaranteeing the independence and integrity of China and reaffirming the 'Open Door' principle of equal rights for trading and investment in China— would follow the American lead. He hoped, particularly, that Britain would so so, but Simon was still pursuing a policy of doing nothing that would unnecessarily offend Japan. So far as British interests in China were concerned, Simon was content to rely upon Japanese assurances about the Open Door. The Foreign Office issued a statement which amounted to a slap in the face for Stimson: 'His Majesty's Government,' it ran, 'have not considered it necessary to address any formal note to the Japanese

Government on the lines of the American Government's note, but the Japanese ambassador in London has been requested to obtain confirmation of these assurances from his Government.' That was one request Tokyo was only too pleased to meet. The British statement had said nothing about Japan's breach of her treaty obligations, or of the doctrine of non-recognition. If Britain saw no need to send a note to Japan, nor did the other signatories to the Nine-Power agreement. Stimson was out on his own. The Japanese exploited the opportunity skilfully and with evident relish, sending a reply to Washington which was a model of diplomatic effrontery. They thanked the Americans for supporting them in their efforts to defend the sanctity of treaties. Japan had been given, and had seized, one more encouragement to continue with her aggression.

For all the tension that it created at Geneva and in the foreign offices of the major powers, it was possible for ordinary newspaper readers to forget Manchuria. There were the reports from the League Council or Assembly, but little first-hand news from Manchuria itself. Shanghai was different. The fighting there could threaten the lives of westerners living in the International Settlement; it could jeopardise trade and financial investment; it could be seen and reported by journalists.

In Manchuria, the Chinese had offered little military resistance. The one way they had been able to retaliate was by organising a successful boycott of the Japanese in Shanghai, cutting deeply into their trade. There were incidents of physical attacks on Japanese citizens. The Japanese response came on the evening of January 28th, 1932, when the commander of Japanese forces in the International Settlement, Admiral Shiozawa, sent marines into Chinese territory. Unlike in Manchuria, the Chinese fought back hard, and the behaviour of the infantry of the Nineteenth Route Army was to attract more active sympathy to China's cause than had ever been aroused by Manchuria. The Japanese admiral ensured further hostility for his country by ordering the indiscriminate bombing of civilians in the Chapei area. Whereas, only three weeks earlier, Stimson had found himself isolated, all the powers that mattered were now as one in opposing the Japanese action, and, though the form that opposition took was frail and cautious, the ultimate result of collective action was to get the Japanese troops out of Chinese territory and back into the International Settlement. Before that was achieved, there were many more tense, emotional passages at Geneva.

China herself took the initiative to force the Council into some sort of response. This time there was no persuading her to hold back. The day after the Japanese attack in Shanghai, the Chinese sent a note to Drummond, the League's Secretary-General, invoking Article 15 of the Covenant, which committed him to a full investigation of the dispute. The Japanese delegate, Sato, in angry and minatory tones, tried to muster juridical arguments against the application of Article 15, but he failed. He could do nothing more to impede an investigation by the League which could lead to a decision to impose sanctions upon the guilty party. But that, it soon became clear, was never more than a theoretical possibility. For all that he wanted to put pressure on Japan, Stimson was limited to moral condemnation, the mobilisation of world opinion. Whatever his own inclinations might have been, his President, Hoover, was inflexibly against any proposal for sanctions or military action in Asia. So was the British Cabinet, which reacted with irritation and embarrassment when Cecil, at that moment Britain's representative at the Council, favoured a more forceful policy by the League towards Japan. And, although Britain and the United States did work closely together, there were still occasions when they fell out of step. Stimson, for instance, pressed the British Government to associate itself with a 'strong indictment' of Japan drawn up by him. He was told that Britain considered an appeal to Japan from the League Council, posed in measured terms, was preferable. Small wonder that once again Chinese patience gave out.

On February 9th, the Council met at the urgent request of the Chinese delegate, Dr. Yen. The previous week, he said, Britain and America had acted to end the Shanghai fighting, but it had made no difference. Chinese cities were being bombed and bombarded, thousands of lives were being lost, there were tens of thousands of refugees, and damage to property was enormous; despite Britain and America, despite the League Council, the end was not in sight. It was true. The Japanese had expanded their operations, their destroyers had bombarded Chinese forts on the Yangtse, and reports reaching London talked of more Japanese troops being moved into China. But Dr. Yen spoke in vain. The Council meeting came to an end leaving things much as they were before, and Sir John Simon made a short, characteristic speech which he ended by taking note, with satisfaction, of the Japanese delegate's reassurances, expressing the hope that hostilities would cease as quickly as possible, and declaring that the British Government viewed the situation with the gravest concern and anxiety and placed all its influence at the service of the Council. According to one report, when the session ended, Dr. Yen staggered from the Council chamber, almost in tears. In the crowded corridor he was accosted by a fellow-Chinese, who violently denounced him for his passive attitude, and told him he should have withdrawn from the meeting.

A week later, the Council—excluding China and Japan—appealed to the Japanese Government. The wording of the appeal was placatory and went as far as was tolerable—some of the smaller nations thought the Council went much too far—to woo the Japanese back into lawful behaviour.

'The twelve members of the Council,' said the appeal, 'are far from disregarding grievances advanced by Japan and throughout all these months have given her the full confidence which they owed to an associate of long standing, who had ever been punctilious in fulfilment of all her obligations and duties as a member of the community of nations.' But the appeal did manage to regret that Japan had not used the methods of peaceful settlement provided by the Covenant and appeared to have ignored her solemn undertaking in the Kellogg Pact never to solve international disputes by other than peaceful means. The Council contrasted the attitude of China in agreeing, from the start, to accept any proposals put forward by the League for a peaceful solution, and the Council now repeated Stimson's refusal to recognise any territorial change or change in political status, which came about as the result of aggression from outside.

The appeal was ineffective, so much so that the Japanese Government's official reply to it was described at the time as one of the most severe snubs ever administered to the League. It did nothing to halt the fighting. The Japanese issued an ultimatum demanding the withdrawal of Chinese troops at various points to a distance of $12\frac{1}{2}$ miles and the dismantling of their forts on the Yangtse. The Chinese rejected the ultimatum and once again China requested a special meeting of the League Council. It started only hours before the midnight deadline for the ultimatum. Once more, Dr. Yen, whose simple modesty and personal charm had done much to help his country at Geneva, spoke for China at a moment when the atmosphere was brittle and emotional.

'We are on the eve of a big battle,' said Dr. Yen, 'in which hundreds of thousands of men with modern armaments and with 40 Japanese warships will be engaged.'

Sato, who was an old hand at Geneva and had conducted himself throughout with a cool correctness, now made a long speech in French, speaking so quietly he could scarcely be heard, restating the whole Japanese case, denying the relevance of the Covenant to the situation in China.

'The Covenant,' he said, 'applies only to organised States, not to anarchies like the Chinese. There is no such thing as a responsible Chinese Government—if there had been we would have acted differently. . . . The Covenant does not fit the realities of the Far East. Japan cannot see in the League an effective safeguard of her rights. She cannot abandon Shanghai and entrust her rights to the Chinese or to anyone.' The two delegates were at each other's throat once more.

'Is Japan,' asked the Chinese, 'with her army and navy running amuck, an organised country? She makes a promise one day and breaks it the next. Is that a test of organisation? And if China is an anarchy with which there can be no negotiations, why has Japan negotiated with it?'

The Japanese reply to the Council's appeal, written by Yoshizawa who was now Foreign Minister in Tokyo, had an exquisite impertinence about it:

'I would ask you to express to your colleagues who collaborated in its composition my very real and sincere appreciation of the extremely courteous and sympathetic terms in which it is couched: terms which are flattering to the legitimate pride taken by the Japanese people in the record of their country as a devoted friend of peace. No one can read their statement without being profoundly impressed by their keen realisation of the perils and difficulties of the situation and by the generous anxiety which is apparent on their part to leave no avenue unexplored by which the unhappy state of affairs, now unfortunately prevailing in the neighbourhood of Shanghai, might be remedied. I cannot but feel, however, that they have addressed their moving appeal to a quarter where it is not necessary. They are "forcing an open door." It lies in the hands of the Chinese leaders to bring about the discontinuance of the armed conflicts which Japan would never have begun, and which she intensely deplores and dislikes.'

China decided to take her appeal beyond the Council to the Assembly. This was a move Britain had been trying to prevent. There were rumours in Geneva that Britain had done some sort of a deal with Japan in return for Japanese acceptance of the London Naval Treaty. It was also being said that the British had tried to hold back the Council and the Cabinet saw what it fancied was a campaign to saddle Britain with any failure by the League. Certainly Sir John Simon resented the criticism by smaller powers of weakness on the part of the Council. He told the Cabinet that 'the strongest clamour for action against Japan came from quarters which could render little or no assistance to the League in the event of serious reactions in the Far East.'*

Meanwhile, despite an appeal from the Council to delay the expiry of their ultimatum, the Japanese had launched a major attack. This coincided with the publication of Tokyo's reply to the Council. Public opinion in the United States was impassioned and Stimson took the opportunity of issuing what became known as the Borah Letter. In this letter to Senator Borah, the American Secretary of State insisted upon the maintenance of China's independence and territorial integrity, upon the obligations of those nations which had signed the Nine-Power Treaty—Japan was one of them—and offered to the world the doctrine of non-recognition as the one means available to it of countering and condemning aggression. The British Government showed itself possessed of an infinite capacity for pusillanimity. Anthony Eden,

---

* When Madariaga, the Spanish representative on the Council, pressed Simon for Britain to take more positive action, the Foreign Secretary asked, 'And will the Spanish Navy sail with the British Navy?' 'Sir John,' said Madariaga, 'the Spanish Navy will sail with the British Navy whenever Britain is defending the League of Nations.'

then Parliamentary Under-Secretary at the Foreign Office, gave in the Commons the official response to the Borah Letter: 'We should certainly not agree,' he said, 'to seeing the terms of the Nine Power Treaty flouted, but in face of the assurance given by the Japanese Government I can see no justification for our assuming that anything of the kind is likely to take place.'

That statement was made on February 29th, at a time when truce talks between the commanders and representatives of Japanese and Chinese forces in the Shanghai area were being held on board the British flagship, HMS *Kent*, in the presence of the British C.-in-C., Admiral Sir Howard Kelly, and the British Government was hopeful of ending the fighting without ever having to say which country was to blame for it. Simon also hoped, as he left for Geneva and the special Assembly, to keep the Manchurian question out of any resolution that might be proposed, on the grounds that the League should wait for the Lytton Commission—which was still on its way—to report. On March 2nd, the day before the Assembly was due to begin, the Secretary of State for India, Sir Samuel Hoare, in London, spoke to Simon in Geneva. The Foreign Secretary 'was naturally anxious about what would happen at the meeting of the Assembly on the morrow,' Hoare told the Cabinet, 'but he considered that British prestige at Geneva was high at the moment.'

Simon's purpose at the Assembly, agreed with the Cabinet, was to try to limit any resolution to a reaffirmation of the principles of the Covenant; he 'should do his best to avoid aggravation of Japan and should not go beyond some such expression as "strong regrets." ' By those lights, Simon succeeded admirably.

The Assembly had a somewhat sluggish, unreal air about it when it began. The opening speech by the president, the Frenchman, Paul-Boncour, was passionate in manner but shallow in content, full of florid gestures, a bombastic appreciation of the work done by the League in the Far Eastern dispute. It was wholly inappropriate, recognising neither the failure of the League nor the nature of the crisis now facing it. Not even the angry exchanges between the Chinese and Japanese delegates could quite shake the Assembly out of its torpor, although the reception accorded to the two men by the public galleries—

defying the regulations with applause for Yen, hearing the Japanese, Matsudaira, in absolute silence—showed the emotions that were waiting to be released.

It was not until the fourth day of the Assembly that delegates made the kinds of plain speech the occasion demanded, and those speeches came from the representatives of the smaller powers.

'If the League does not succeed in securing peace and justice, then the whole system by which right was meant to replace might will collapse,' said the Norwegian.

'The League has been considering the Far Eastern conflict for six months but it has been a voice crying in the desert. Not even moral force has been exercised. The default of the League will have the most serious effect on international relations,' said the Dutch delegate.

'Is the League a reality or not?' asked the Finn. 'Is it a debating club, or, at the best, merely an instrument of mediation? Nothing has been done for fear of doing too much. It would be much better to recognise the inadequacy of the League than to pretend that the Covenant can do what it cannot do.'

Those were the voices of nations which feared that, if the League could fail China, it could also fail them in their turn, and they hoped desperately that the Assembly would disprove their fears.

Simon took the initiative in promoting a resolution embodying Stimson's doctrine of non-recognition. It was a strong assertion of the principle of peaceful settlement of international disputes and insisted that the Covenant was applicable to the Sino-Japanese dispute. *The Times* welcomed it in a way which might have perturbed supporters of the League. 'Its language is moderate and its general tenor shows recognition of the League's limitations without any recantation of principle,' said its editorial on March 11th. 'No phrases are used which could be interpreted as a direct condemnation of or an affront to either party to the dispute; and still less is combined punitive action, in the sense of Article 16 of the Covenant, recommended. That this folly should have been avoided seems to have been largely due to the influence of the British Foreign Secretary, who was guided, no doubt, by the prudent warnings of His Majesty's Ambassador in Tokyo . . .'

Yet there was a firmness about the Assembly's resolution which had been absent from the Council meetings, and the force of the collective moral will did succeed in checking the Japanese at Shanghai—but did not manage to discomfit Naotuke Sato. The Japanese delegate, courteous as ever, now almost cordial, expressed the fundamental agreement of his government with the resolution. In view of the disregard the Chinese had always shown for treaties, he said, he was glad the resolution reaffirmed the sanctity of treaties.

When Sir John Simon returned to London the Cabinet congratulated him on the 'remarkable success' he had achieved at Geneva.

It took two months to agree the terms of the armistice at Shanghai, but, by the end of May, the Japanese had withdrawn their troops from all areas outside the International Settlement, and their Foreign Office issued a statement admitting that the withdrawal was aimed at ending the 'world-wide odium' which the action at Shanghai had brought upon Japan.

In the British Cabinet, among other places, there was an exaggerated self-satisfaction about the Shanghai achievement and the means which had been employed. Henry Stimson was less optimistic. The American Secretary of State had regarded his doctrine of non-recognition as the least of the deterrents which ought to be applied to aggression; Hoover considered it the maximum desirable sanction. So, it seemed, did many of Europe's leading figures, whom Stimson met when he visited Geneva soon after the special Assembly. He was apprehensive for the future.

Geneva saw again at that time a famous figure from the past, when Sir Austen Chamberlain went there at Simon's request upon some piece of League business.

'It was delightful to be received with such genuine pleasure and cordiality by all old friends,' wrote Chamberlain, 'but sad to find them all so dejected, the Assembly a dead thing, the Council without confidence in itself or authority elsewhere, and people as little given to hysterics or high-falutin as Benes saying, "I tell them they are too frightened. We are not going to have war now; we have five years before us, perhaps six. We must make the most of them." '*

By the early autumn of 1932, the Lytton Commission had

* Op. cit. Vol. 2, pp. 397–8.

finished its investigation and had written its report. By the time it had been translated and printed, more than a year had passed since the Japanese attack at Mukden. If that delay could be excused, then the report of the commission was everything the League could have expected, a model of its kind,* combining a historical survey and a detailed study of the events leading up to the proclamation of an independent state, objective in its assembly and collating of the evidence, admitting shortcomings in the Chinese administration of Manchuria and some legitimate causes of Japanese grievance; but its conclusions amounted to a decisive condemnation of Japan. Manchuria, said the Lytton report, was an integral part of China; the military action by the Japanese could not be justified as self-defence; there was no spontaneous movement to gain independence for the province and the creation of Manchukuo was the work of the Japanese. The commission had not been asked to suggest the shape of a settlement, but it did make a positive recommendation that all Japanese troops should be evacuated from all positions outside the railway zone and a genuinely Chinese regime should be re-established in Manchuria.

That report was to be the basis of the League's attitude towards the settling of the Manchurian conflict; it also had the full support of the American State Department. It was the cause of clash after clash between Japan and China at Geneva, the first of which happened when the Council met on November 21st, 1932, to consider the Lytton report. This time Japan was represented by Yosuke Matsuoka, a passionate nationalist with a profound conviction of Japan's civilising role in Asia. In his initial appearance at the Council he challenged the findings of the report with familiar arguments about the chaotic condition of China and the provocations in Manchuria, but he had little effect. He was more successful in his references to the Kellogg Pact, at least in producing some embarrassment in Washington and London. Matsuoka quoted Stimson's Note of June 28th, 1928, in which he said that the pact did not restrict the right of self-defence and that each nation was alone qualified to decide

* At a dinner given in honour of Lord Lytton by the League of Nations Union, Lord Cecil described the report as 'one of the greatest State papers of our time,' showing the rarest of all political qualities—courage.

whether the circumstances justified its resorting to war for legitimate defence. The Japanese delegate also quoted Chamberlain's letters of May 19th and July 18th, 1928, in which the Foreign Secretary put forward Britain's reservations about the pact, claiming the right to defend British imperial interests if they were threatened. Matsuoka's interpretation of the British and American positions was a distortion, but the fact that he was able to make it at all—with Simon listening to him, silent—proved what some had realised at the time of its creation, that the Kellogg Pact was virtually worthless.

China's reply came from Wellington Koo, a highly cultivated, extremely able representative of his people, whose speech took up the whole of the afternoon sitting of the Council. After saying that the Lytton report could not be too highly praised, Koo launched into a long analysis of Japanese history, going back to the sixteenth century, to show the continuous link between the aggressive attitude of old Japan and 'the spirit and policy of modern Japan.' He was caustic and florid in his characterisation of Japan's so-called 'Continental' policy.

'The double-armed Continental policy of expansion, which is the crystallisation of several centuries of teaching by Japanese warriors,' Koo declared, 'is aimed at China as the first stage of the conquest of Asia, and to be carried out from the north and from the south, just as a virulent scorpion attacking its victims by its foreclaws and its tail.' He voiced yet one more Chinese appeal. 'The time has come now for prompt and effective action by the League. Further hesitation will not only entail more bloodshed and suffering to the 30 million Chinese people in Manchuria, but will perhaps irretrievably shake the general confidence in the efficacy of this great institution of peace.'

If Wellington Koo could have attended the meeting of the British Cabinet two days later, he would have heard little to reassure him that the League would take 'prompt and effective action': that, in the British view, was something to be avoided. The Cabinet had before it a memorandum from Simon, examining the Lytton report and outlining possible ways of handling it. The League was likely to find it very difficult, wrote the Foreign Secretary, not to pronounce what would amount to a condemnation of Japan. That, however, might produce embarrassing and dangerous results, including the possibility of Japan leaving the League. His conclusions were set out in the last paragraph of his memorandum:

'In these difficult circumstances it seems to me that British policy must keep in mind the following *desiderata*; though it will be difficult to pursue them all at the same time. We ought to act as a loyal member of the League and avoid, as far as possible, bringing down on ourselves the condemnation which would attach to isolated or prominent individual action. It is impossible to abandon loyalty to the League and its principles merely because Japan would prefer this: we must explain to Japan that the course we take is *pro* League and not *anti* Japan. Even if other considerations did not compel this course, we have to remember the serious consequences to our trade of antagonising China. In fact, we must strive to be fair to both sides. But we must not involve ourselves in trouble with Japan.'

According to the Cabinet minute, 'the view was expressed that the last sentence of the above paragraph was the most important, but it was generally recognised that the matter was a delicate one which must on no account be mentioned publicly or talked about.

'The Cabinet appreciated the difficulty the Secretary of State for Foreign Affairs would have in carrying out his conclusion as quoted above . . .' But as the next weeks and months were to show no-one could say that Simon did not try.

The Council spent two more days considering the Lytton report, with further exchanges between the Chinese and Japanese delegates. The Council decided, as expected, and despite Japanese objections, to refer the report to the Special Assembly of the League. Simon reported in person to the Cabinet before returning to Geneva for the Assembly: he was still looking for ways of minimising any condemnation of Japan. The Foreign Secretary told his colleagues he proposed to do his utmost to avoid having to take a lead. He thought it probable the Assembly would approve the first eight chapters of the Lytton report, dealing with questions of history and fact; he could see no other course. But it was possible the Assembly might want to go further and either adopt some action on behalf of the League or pass a resolution unacceptable to Japan. Sir John Simon was not too pessimistic, however. He had noticed, he said, that the Lytton Commission did not recommend the League to do anything in particular; most of their recommendations were addressed to China or Japan: he thought he might be able to make some use of that point. He promised the Cabinet that if a resolution not to recognise Manchukuo was moved he would do his best to oppose it. So much for his erstwhile support of Stimson's doctrine of non-recognition. Simon justified his attitude by reminding the Cabinet that recognition was given, not for the benefit of the state being recognised, but for the convenience of the country giving the recognition. He was already being pressed by commercial people to recognise Manchukuo, and he said how inconvenient it would be if a British subject were kidnapped in the territory and we had no diplomatic representation there. All of which was consistent with the traditional Foreign Office attitude towards recognition, but it failed totally to appreciate that, if the Assembly agreed upon the non-recognition of Manchukuo, it would be in order to impose a moral sanction upon Japan as the aggressor—which, considering the prescriptions in the Covenant, was surely the very least it could do. But the first concern of the British Foreign Secretary—and the British Government as a whole—was not the upholding of the principles of the Covenant but keeping in with the Japanese.

By that criterion alone, Simon's speech to the special Assembly, which opened on December 6th, 1932, was a remarkable accomplishment; by any other it was a disaster. So selective was he in his interpretation of the Lytton report, he almost succeeded in giving the impression that it was largely sympathetic to the Japanese cause and critical of China. What he said was pleasing to some ears. An editorial in *The Times*, for instance, struck that note of 'realism' which was to be heard more and more emphatically under Geoffrey Dawson's lamentable editorship in the years preceding the Second World War. Simon's speech, said *The Times*, 'was a useful corrective to some of the minatory utterances which have been heard during the last two days.' Matsuoka was more lavish in his tribute. Sir John Simon, said the Japanese delegate, had managed to say in half an hour in a few well-chosen phrases what he himself had been trying to say in his bad English for the past ten days. The Americans were less enthusiastic. In particular, they resented the air of rectitude in which Simon wrapped up his policy and his impertinence in quoting Abraham Lincoln in support of it. Representatives of the smaller powers, who had been calling for effective action against Japan, were both angered and dismayed by Britain's advocacy of caution and continued conciliation. Nor was the British Foreign Secretary on his own in taking that line. Both von Neurath, for Germany, and Aloisi, for Italy, spoke as though any positive recommendations for action by the Assembly were unthinkable.

Even Simon was somewhat taken aback, though, by the reaction to his speech. He saw both Matsuoka and the Chinese representative, Quo Tai-chai, and urged them to be moderate. Instead, Matsuoka, no doubt encouraged in his defiance by what the spokesmen of the great powers had said, made a speech full of arrogance and fanatical nationalism, remarkable in its deployment of irony, outrageous in its analogies. It lasted nearly an hour and a half. He said that while many people in Japan were disgusted and exasperated by the failure of the League to understand the Japanese position and wanted their country to withdraw from the League, the majority still believed in it. He did not think that public opinion of the whole world was against Japan, and, even if it were, public opinion might well be wrong: it might change, said Matsuoka, as it had before when Christ was crucified. 'There is a desire today in some quarters to crucify Japan,' he said. 'Well, we are ready to be crucified.'

The effect of his speech was dramatic and striking, and it undermined the efforts of those, like Simon, who had been calling for conciliation. It also fortified the scepticism with which Matsuoka's own appeals, to give Japan more time to put forward proposals for an agreed settlement with China, were received. However, the special Assembly did avoid an immediate vote on a resolution by some of the smaller powers for non-recognition of Manchukuo. The Committee of 19, which had been appointed to deal with the Manchurian dispute, was asked to study the Lytton report, the observations of the parties concerned and the opinions and suggestions expressed in the Assembly; to draw up proposals for settling the dispute and to submit them to the Assembly at the earliest possible moment. But it was obvious that the crisis in the League's affairs, created by the conflict and by Japan's attitude towards it, had been only postponed: the possibility of an agreed settlement, acceptable to both China and Japan, and to the League, was too remote to be imagined. And so it proved.

The Committee of 19, strongly influenced by Simon, set up a group to pursue the possibilities of conciliation, and went so far as to bow to Japanese objections to Soviet Russia and the United States being invited to join it. But the Japanese soon showed they had no intention of making any concessions that would really mean anything. All that was left to do was for the committee to prepare its report to the special Assembly; even Sir John Simon recognised that could not be avoided. But Simon rarely failed to find sources of comfort. On January 19th, 1933, when he flew back from Geneva for a Cabinet, he was able to give an account of a conversation he had had with a Chinese delegate, which he had found somewhat reassuring. The reason: the Chinese did not seem to expect very much from the League of Nations; they were now more and more inclined to rely on their own forces and strength. Moreover, the Foreign Secretary stressed that the important new factor in the situation was that 'nearly every responsible person now realised that the application of sanctions to this dispute was not feasible.'

Unfortunately, for Sir John's peace of mind, the Chinese turned out not to be such reasonable people, after all. He had to tell the Cabinet on February 8th that false rumours were being spread in China about British policy at Geneva. One story had it that Britain had struck a bargain with Japan whereby, in return for a free hand to the Japanese in Manchuria, Britain should be given a free hand in Tibet. There was absolutely no truth in such rumours, said Simon, and he was doing his best, with the help of Reuters, to correct the false impressions. But according to Sir Miles Lampson, the British Minister to China, the Chinese were getting somewhat hysterical and there was a risk of a boycott of British goods.

This helped Simon to realise that, if serious trouble in China was to be avoided, he must go along with what now appeared to be the general trend of opinion at Geneva: that Japan had broken the Covenant and that no recognition of Manchukuo could be contemplated. The Japanese, he thought, could hardly object to our adopting that line, for he had always warned their delegation at Geneva that, if conciliation failed, Britain would have to act as a good member of the League. Even so, Simon could not resist a qualification. If circumstances made it necessary, he added, there was nothing to stop Britain from recognising Manchukuo, but she would first have to consult members of the League and signatories of the Nine-Power Treaty. At the same time he dismissed, as out of the question, Chinese wishes to see Article 16 of the Covenant—involving the imposition of sanctions—applied. A fortnight later, when he asked the Cabinet for a definite decision about sanctions, there was a general agreement that, whatever the pressure from the smaller powers, Britain must dissociate herself from any such proposal.

Meanwhile, on February 17th, the Committee of 19 had published its report and distributed it throughout the world by means of the League's new wireless station at Geneva. The committee's statement substantially recapitulated the findings and recommendations of the Lytton report. It declared that members of the League should not recognise Manchukuo either *de jure* or *de facto* and called upon both parties to the dispute to negotiate a settlement based upon the restoration of a largely autonomous regime in Manchuria within the context of Chinese sovereignty. Simultaneously with the publication of that report by the committee, came a further deterioration of the situation in Manchuria. The Japanese threatened now to invade the province of Jehol—formerly known as Eastern Inner Mongolia—and add it to Manchukuo; the Japanese war minister, General Araki, stated that Jehol was no concern of the League. The Japanese Cabinet decided to reject the recommendations of the Committee of 19, and to instruct its delegation at Geneva to vote against the report and then withdraw to London or Paris to await further developments. General Araki had something to say, too, about this withdrawal from the League: 'Better to have a short, heavy shower followed by sunshine than many days of continuous drizzle.'

The Japanese persisted with their attempts to justify both what they had done in Manchuria in the past eighteen months and what they had started to do in Jehol. To the League's

Secretary-General, the Japanese delegation sent a defence of the military operation in Jehol, which lacked nothing in audacity. According to Japan, since the foundation of Manchukuo, Jehol had been part of that state. The cause of the military operations was the concentration of 'hostile' Chinese troops in Jehol; they presented a serious danger to Manchukuo. The delegation's statement promised that Japanese forces would not advance south of the Great Wall into the Peking and Tientsin districts of China unless troop movements compelled them to do so; even if that happened, it would not be an invasion of Chinese soil, nor a Japanese action against China, but simply an action in defence of Manchukuo territory in co-operation with the forces of that state. Up to the last moment, the Japanese Government tried to persuade the League not to go through with a resolution adopting the committee's report. On February 21st, three days before the special Assembly was due to meet again, Tokyo issued a detailed reply to the report, couched in conciliatory tones and ending with an appeal to the Assembly to 'think twice' before making any decision.

The special Assembly was to be held on February 24th in one of the halls of the Disarmament Conference building. There was not overmuch room for the public and people started queueing at eight o'clock in the morning to get in, two and a half hours before the meeting was to begin; when Paul Hymans, of Belgium, took the presidential chair, every part of the hall was crowded. No-one needed to be told that he was about to participate in a memorable day in the history of the League and therefore of the world, a day when, for the first time, a nation found guilty of an international crime was to be arraigned and solemnly condemned by the assembled representatives of the other nations. Matsuoka had already marked it with one of his picturesque analogies. In a statement before the Assembly began, he said, 'I am speaking as a Christian. The affair between Japan and China is like the parable of Christ and the woman who had sinned. Christ said "Let him that is without sin among you cast the first stone." Japan is perhaps in the position of the woman. Let, then, the Great Powers be asked which among them is without sin and whether they could cast stones.'

No stones were cast at the Assembly; there was no more

debate; but the committee's report was adopted by forty-two votes to one. China voted in favour; Siam abstained; Japan voted against. Immediately after the vote, Matsuoka said his government found itself compelled to conclude that Japan and other members of the League entertained different views of the manner to achieve peace in the Far East, and were obliged to feel that they had now reached the limit of their endeavours to co-operate with the League in regard to Sino-Japanese differences. They would, however, make the utmost efforts for peace in the Far East and for the maintenance and strengthening of good and cordial relations with other powers. With that, Matsuoka walked out of the hall, followed by the rest of his delegation, presenting an image of collective self-possession. It was to be Matsuoka's last dramatic gesture at Geneva and one which was received by a tense and silent Assembly. On March 27th, 1933, just four weeks later, Japan announced her formal withdrawal from the League.

The Assembly set up another committee with the optimistic purpose of helping China and Japan to carry out the recommended settlement of their dispute. Both America and Soviet Russia were asked to join this advisory committee. Stimson had sent a message to the League the day after the special Assembly, associating the United States Government with the League's decision. Now Stimson was going out of office. His successor, Cordell Hull, supported by the new President, Franklin Roosevelt, followed the precedent set by Stimson. He agreed that the American Minister to Switzerland, Hugh R. Wilson, should join the committee, but without the right to vote. Hull considered that was as far as he could go in view of the strength of isolationist sentiment in America. The Russians rejected the invitation, but did so in terms which indicated a significantly less intransigent attitude towards the League. Not surprisingly, the committee did little and got nowhere.

As Japanese troops rapidly carried through the occupation of Jehol and threatened to move south beyond the Great Wall, the British Government pondered earnestly the possibility of an arms embargo. The discussions in Cabinet revealed an agonising conflict. Ministers recognised the course of action which had the most moral strength—and one for which there would be considerable backing in the country—was to ban the sale of arms to Japan but allow China to continue to buy them. But the objection to that was even more persuasive: Japan would almost certainly retaliate, and might even well blockade China or intercept foreign ships: that would entail a grave risk of extending the war. So the argument was about whether to go on selling arms to both sides or to ban their sale to both China and Japan. The armament manufacturers were big employers, and to deny them orders at a time of heavy unemployment was an extremely serious step to take. Yet there was also a strong body of feeling in Britain which found repugnant the making of money out of instruments of war. The Cabinet was very conscious that, if it acted alone in imposing an embargo, other nations would happily take on the orders which would have come to Britain. But it did place an embargo on the sale of arms to both sides, a ban which was to affect any orders received after February 27th but not those received before that date. Foreign governments were asked whether they were in favour of an embargo. The replies were not hopeful. Some would go along with an embargo if it was universal; Stimson told Simon that no action was possible until a special session of Congress, and there was potent opposition in Congress.

Announcing the British embargo to the House of Commons on February 27th, Sir John Simon had said that 'any efforts and any sacrifices are worth making which will reduce the risk of a widening of the field of conflict.' On March 13th, the Cabinet had a telegram from Simon in Geneva, saying that enquiries there had made it plain that no international agreement was realisable: Britain lifted the two-week-old embargo.

At the end of May, with the Japanese in full control of Jehol and endangering Peking itself, Chiang Kai-Shek agreed to an armistice; the Far East returned to something like peace, however uneasy a peace.

At Geneva, no-one who cared about the League and believed it to represent the one hope for establishing a new system of international relations and peace enforcement could hide from himself the fact of failure. The League had been put to the test and had failed. There were reasons enough for failure. The test had come in a part of the world remote from the vital, immediate interests of the most important members of the League. It had come at a time of European crisis and world depression. But there had never been, in those countries which alone had the power to act, any serious consideration of sanctions. Britain's concern, from the first to last, had been to do as little damage as possible to her relations with Japan. There was, in the early days at least, a considerable public sympathy with Japan and a willingness to acknowledge that the Japanese had a special interest in Manchuria, as well as a need to expand. Even after the Japanese withdrawal from the League, Simon continued in public utterances, to concede this 'special interest' and to regret the rupture of the Anglo-Japanese alliance at the Washington Conference just after the war. The British Foreign Secretary took pride in having steered a 'middle course' throughout the Manchurian crisis. Stimson recognised later that the United States had been as much to blame as any other country, although the fathering of the doctrine of non-recognition showed that the American people were clear enough about the moral principles involved. It was those principles which informed the special Assembly's condemnation of Japan and allowed the Chinese delegate, Dr. Yen, to praise the 'League's courageous verdict' and to conclude, with more generosity than truth, that 'the League has emerged stronger and revitalised.'

The men who came to that special Assembly did their best to comfort each other and persuade themselves the League had done its duty. Hymans, the Assembly's president, spoke for them when, after the Japanese delegation had walked out, he wound up the proceedings. 'The League of Nations is working, and will continue to work,' said Hymans, 'in the midst of the conflict of passions, carrying out the work assigned to it by the authors of the Covenant—that is to say, the bringing about in a world sharply divided by so many disputes, prejudices and misunderstandings, of an international order in which concord and justice will bring the peoples together and ensure the peace of the world.'

Brave words: braver words than the situation justified. There were those at the time who considered that the Manchurian affair had been an exceptional challenge to the League and should not be seen as a guide to future behaviour. There have been those since who have held that Manchuria aroused little interest at the time and has achieved significance only in retrospect. The reality is that the statesmen at Geneva knew very well that the League was on trial, and that, after Manchuria, the world's expectations of the League, and particularly those of the smaller powers, had been grievously diminished. Japan had smarted under the massive condemnation, and there is no doubt that she quit the League with very real reluctance and regret. But what really mattered for the future of the League, and therefore of the whole world, was that Japan had committed blatant aggression and she had got away with it.

12

'I earnestly besought them'

Another war was going on at the same time as the Manchurian conflict, a war which, although it lasted longer, was every bit as savage and killed more men, is little remembered today—in Europe, at any rate. It was a war which showed it was not only the big powers which, during the 1930s, blatantly betrayed their obligations under the Covenant and it was not only belligerent nations which obstructed the League in its efforts to enforce peace. The scene of the fighting was South America, a continent which prided itself upon fidelity to the League. By excluding the League from early efforts to achieve a settlement, the Latin-Americans—much encouraged and abetted by the United States—made it that much more difficult for the League to intervene effectively when eventually its authority was recognised and its help sought.

The cause of the trouble was, once more, the Chaco,* but, this time, the fighting between Bolivian and Paraguayan forces had a more serious and determined quality about it than in 1928. In both countries nationalistic passions were whipped up in support of their warring armies. To the rest of the world the war seemed an outstanding demonstration of madness in international affairs. Here were two poor countries, which could neither feed their people nor clothe most of their soldiers in uniforms, bringing still deeper suffering upon themselves, bleeding their treasuries

* See Chapter 9.

and slaughtering their men—and for what? For a vast tract of wasteland, about twice the size of England, which lay between them, stark, barren territory of scrub and savannah, much of it uninhabited. For the best part of a century they had disputed its possession and where the border should run. Reasonable men in other countries could not see any difference between Bolivia and Paraguay about the Chaco which could not be solved by negotiation or arbitration, and, even if a solution were hard to find, they could see no possible justification for war. But the Bolivians and Paraguayans had gone beyond the point of reason. Bolivia claimed the right to a port on the River Paraguay which would give her access to the Atlantic; Paraguay held that development of the Chaco was vital to her economy. In addition to such material arguments, there was, on both sides, a heavy investment of national pride.

The war started in the summer of 1932 with the kinds of clashes between rival patrols which had provoked Briand, as president of the Council, to send those long telegrams to the two governments in 1928. This time, however, the skirmishes were the fuse which would set off a much bigger explosion of violence. This time, both countries possessed the weapons, old-fashioned though many of them were, to conduct full-scale operations; Bolivia even had an air force of sorts. The armaments makers of the world had been pleased to do business with them, and, somehow or other, Bolivia and Paraguay borrowed the money to pay their bills. Bolivia had a German veteran of trench warfare, General Hans Kundt, to train and command her army; the Paraguayans, by good fortune, had José Felix Estigarribia, a man of exceptional military skill and personal authority; both had been preparing for war.

During the early months of the fighting, Bolivia and Paraguay sent protests to the League's Secretary-General about the other's hostile actions, but neither honoured its obligations under the Covenant by submitting the issue between them to the Council. The war lasted three years. It was not until almost the end of the first year that the Council was able to take the first step towards stopping the fighting and starting the process of conciliation. Until then, the League had been kept out, not only by the failure of the two members to submit to the Council, but also by the desire of other South American countries to prove they could keep the peace inside their own continent without the help of outsiders. This, certainly, was not because of any sympathy with the Monroe Doctrine or the paternalistic pretensions of Washington. But the flare-up between Bolivia and Paraguay in 1928 had ultimately been stopped—though not settled—by the intervention of a body called the Neutral Commission, which, with League approval, had been appointed to the task by the Conference of American States. The commission was composed of representatives in Washington of Mexico, Cuba, Colombia and Uruguay, plus a chairman from the State Department. Now the same body, meeting in Washington, took upon itself the responsibility for bringing back peace to the Chaco. It held up to Bolivia and Paraguay, in an eloquent appeal, the exemplary tradition of their continent for settling disputes over borders in a peaceable manner. It also affirmed the Stimson doctrine of non-recognition, first enunciated a few months earlier during the Manchurian conflict: any territory won by war would be regarded as an illegal gain. It sounded impressive enough, but the two countries to whom it was primarily addressed were not listening. The Neutral Commission was not discouraged. Nor was the State Department, which continued to insist that the Washington negotiations between the commission and the representatives of the belligerents were going well and there was no need for the League to do anything. Nor did the League Council get anywhere with its advice to the commission to send a mission to the Chaco to investigate what was really happening.

The Neutral Commission failed to persuade Bolivia and Paraguay to accept its proposals for a settlement, but, even then, was not ready to let the League take over. Instead, at the end of 1932, after six months of fighting, it asked the countries neighbouring the belligerents—Brazil, Peru, Chile and Argentina—to take up the challenge on its behalf. The new team was, if anything, less likely than the commission to be successful. Bolivia had a justifiable suspicion of Argentina's impartiality, for Paraguay had received very substantial financial assistance in the past from Argentina in the colonising and development of a strip at the southern end of the Chaco. But the chief difficulty in seeking an acceptable formula for ending the war was, from the start to the finish, the fact that both countries had wanted the war. There was never a moment when one or the other did not think it was winning and therefore disinterested in 'fair' proposals for peace. At first, it was the Bolivians who seemed to be winning, as they forced the Paraguayan forces to retreat: the Bolivian Army of a quarter of a million was almost twice the strength of Paraguay's. But, the further the Bolivians advanced, the more exposed and vulnerable they became. The point was reached where a major Bolivian offensive failed and the Paraguayans were seen to have the advantage, which they showed every intention of exploiting to the full.

The one potentially useful action by the League during that first year lapsed, because of the refusal of the United States Senate to go along with it. France and Britain took the lead in the Council in proposing that all members of the League should ban the sale of arms to the belligerents. That was in February, 1933, when Hull was about to take over from Stimson in the State Department. Both men supported the idea and a Presidential request went to Congress for powers to impose a similar embargo in the United States. The Senate turned it down. No other nation was prepared to give up its trade in arms only to see it taken up by the Americans: the proposal was dropped.

In May, 1933, the four neighbours of Bolivia and Paraguay admitted that they had failed to bring the two sides to a settlement, and the Neutral Commission, too, felt there was nothing more it could do. So, at last, the League could act. The Council now determined to do what the Washington peacemakers had thought was unnecessary: send out a commission to make an on-the-spot investigation on behalf of the League. The Council secured the easy agreement of Paraguay to the dispatch of a commission and, less easily, that of Bolivia, which, at that moment, was very much on top in the war. It was impossible to get agreement on conditions for a ceasefire; nevertheless, arrangements went ahead to send out a commission. It was with a considerable sense of frustration and impatience that the Council received a request from Bolivia and Paraguay for the League to allow their neighbours to try once more to achieve a settlement. That was in July, when the commission was ready to set off. Another two months went by while the four South American nations took a further look at the situation, only to conclude that there was nothing more they could do.

It was November by the time the League commission, headed by the Spaniard, Alvarez del Vayo, reached Paraguay, where it began its inquiries and observations. The following month, it moved on to Bolivia. That coincided with news of a major success in the war for the Paraguayans, who thereupon suggested to the commission there should be an armistice and peace talks. Bolivia fell quickly into line and agreed to a meeting at Montevideo, the capital of Uruguay, where the seventh Pan American Conference was meeting and where, so late in the day, all the countries taking part, including the United States, proclaimed themselves ready to co-operate with the League in applying the provisions of the Covenant.

Once again, however, Bolivia and Paraguay were to reject the terms for a settlement drawn up by the League commission. The Paraguayans, like the Bolivians at an earlier stage, wanted to capitalise upon their military success. It was towards the end of February, 1934, that the talks broke up and the commission went back to Geneva. The Chaco commission gave the Council its appreciation of the causes of the war, its military prognosis and its recommendations for settling the dispute. It suggested, as an immediate step, an embargo on arms to both sides.

Once more, the Council, with Britain's representative, Anthony Eden, especially vigorous in support, called for a universal ban. The British Government had preceded this appeal from the League—which went out on May 19th, 1934—by suspending the issue of any new licences for the export of arms and war material to Bolivia and Paraguay, in the hope that all other arms-producing countries would follow suit. Switzerland and Denmark, did so, and so too did the United States, even before the Council's formal appeal reached Washington. Congressional opposition had completely evaporated. The American embargo was on sales, not shipments, and this caused some anxiety in the British Cabinet, lest a third nation should order munitions in the United States and then transfer them to one of the belligerents, thus defeating the embargo; but it was recognised that the same thing could happen just as easily in Britain. The Russians joined in the ban and so, too, did Germany and Japan in their own reluctant ways. The Italians were among the most difficult to persuade but, when they also agreed, objections in other capitals collapsed and the international embargo became effective.

The embargo offered one of those rare examples during the lifetime of the League when all nations perceived a common interest and agreed upon a common action, an action which called for a greater or lesser degree of material sacrifice. It was not in itself enough to stop the war but, at least, members of the League were no longer actively, and for their own profit, feeding it.

The international embargo was imposed at a time when the Bolivian Army was on its knees. Bolivia now invoked Article 15 of the Covenant. In doing so, it requested, as it was entitled to do under that Article, that the Assembly should take over the dispute from the Council. In a last attempt to conciliate, the Assembly set up a committee, composed wholly of South American countries; it invited the United States and Brazil, as non-members, to join the committee, but both refused. Out of that committee came a draft treaty, embodying in comprehensive detail its proposals for an end to the war, the withdrawal of forces, and the future of the Chaco.

The Assembly, meeting in November, 1934, adopted the treaty and presented it to Bolivia and Paraguay for acceptance. The machinery of the League was working according to the manual. A neutral military commission, consisting solely of American states, was set up to supervise a zone in the Chaco, which was to be evacuated of Bolivian and Paraguayan forces; both the United States and Brazil agreed to serve on it. Paraguay refused to accept the treaty as it stood; Bolivia agreed to it. Paraguay was held to be defying the League. The committee, which had framed the treaty, proposed that the arms embargo should be kept only against Paraguay. The American President was not empowered by Congress to act against one country, to the favour of another, and there was no attempt to ask Congress for the authority to do so. The United States continued the embargo on sales to both countries.

Paraguay protested against the proposal. She did not see herself as the aggressor, who should be blamed for the war. Her present attitude was no different in kind from that adopted by Bolivia, when she was on top in the war. The Paraguayan Government gave formal notice of its intention to leave the League. The war went on with the Paraguayans largely victorious, but lacking the strength to press their success to a decisive conclusion. Nor did Bolivia possess the resilience or the resources to return yet again to the attack. Both sides, at last, were ready for an end to the fighting and their representatives were brought to the same table at Buenos Aires in May, 1935, by other American states, led by their neighbours, Chile and Argentina. The next month, the fighting ended, although it was three more years before the formal signing of a peace treaty, a treaty which awarded most of the disputed territory to Paraguay and left Bolivia without the port she had wanted. The cost of the war in terms of life was appalling. Bolivia, whose population was three million, counted 57,000 dead; Paraguay, with a million people, estimated 36,000 dead. The cost, in terms of money, ran into many millions of pounds and devastated the economies of both countries.

The League might have been able to bring the war to an end more quickly had it been able to act much sooner. It was not able to do so because of the determination on the part of the American states to settle their own problem. Certain members of the Council, such as Britain and France, also had an exaggerated concern not to offend the Unites States by appearing to offend against the Monroe Doctrine and intervene in the American continent. Among the least palatable aspect of the whole affair was the retrospective self-satisfaction expressed by Cordell Hull, the American Secretary of State. He believed the American states offered a model of behaviour for the rest of the world to follow, that the decisions reached by the Pan American Conference at Montevideo, and the principles they embraced there, ought to commend themselves to all mankind.

'Throughout 1934 and into 1935,' he wrote,[*] 'I seldom lost an opportunity, in my conversations with the ambassadors of the major countries in Europe and Asia, to point to the example of Pan America. I assured them that the principles we were laying down and the agreements we were reaching were not exclusive. We should be more than delighted to share them with

* *The Memoirs of Cordell Hull*, Hodder and Stoughton, 1948. p. 349.

the nations of the rest of the world. I earnestly besought them to urge their Governments to observe the same tenets of non-intervention, peaceful settlement of disputes, and liberal non-discriminatory commerce . . .

'Had their Governments heeded our words the remainder of the world might have avoided the tragedy of arms that was to come five years later.'

There were powerful domestic political reasons why successive Presidents and Secretaries of State failed to bring to the League, and therefore the world, the moral and material help which was their clear responsibility. Henry Stimson recognised that, whatever the excuses and explanations, he, like other statesmen in the western democracies, had failed, and he regretted he had not been able to do more. Cordell Hull actually dared to deliver sermons about how right he had been.

Even Hull, however, was able to realise that the high-handed, unilateral actions of the United States in dealing with countries to the south must stop, and it is only fair to record that at the time of another South American dispute—between Peru and Colombia—the State Department after trying, at first, to negotiate a settlement in Washington, decided to give the League its full backing. It was not done without much agonised heart-searching by Roosevelt and Hull, who had been in office only two weeks. If they were to acknowledge implicitly the League's right to intervene in the heart of the western hemisphere, could that set a dangerous precedent infringing the Monroe Doctrine? They decided to take the chance, and accepted—as did Brazil—the Council's invitation to join an advisory committee to help to end the dispute.

It was a dispute which had flared up quite unexpectedly into a near-war situation between Colombia and Peru. The cause of the conflict, Leticia, was once again a large wedge of border territory, wholly without industry and a population to be counted in hundreds. But it mattered to Colombia, to whom Peru had ceded it in a recent treaty, because it gave her an outlet to the Amazon. There was little in the way of a Colombian presence at Leticia, and, when a band of freelance Peruvian conquerors from the province of Loreto attacked it, they had no difficulty in taking it over. That happened in September, 1932. The Peruvian

Government gave no support to the adventure, and it seemed likely that the whole thing would blow over quickly without the rest of the world ever being bothered by it, even if the news of the raid had been recorded. But, when a Colombian military expedition was already on its way to re-occupy the settlement, the official Peruvian attitude changed and the Colombians were warned that, if they tried to take back Leticia, they would be resisted with force. It was learned later that the decision had been that of the Peruvian President, Cerro, who had a taste for one-man rule. At the same time, though, all that the Colombians could know was that the Peruvians had dishonoured their treaty and were rejecting all attempts by friendly neighbours to clear up the affair peacefully; indeed, Leticia was now occupied and defended by the Peruvian Army itself.

Sean Lester, the representative on the League Council of the Irish Free State—who, along with Madariaga, had borne the burden of the League's efforts to end the Chaco war—sent telegrams to both countries, emphasising their obligations under the Covenant. The Colombian and Peruvian delegates came before the Council to justify their respective positions. But it was February before Brazil and Washington gave up their separate efforts at conciliation and left the way open for the Council, and, in the five months which had passed from the initial incident, tension had built up, war passions had been inflamed, both countries had employed conscription to strengthen their armies and open war seemed imminent. Colombia called upon the Council to deal with the crisis under Article 15, as China had done, a short time before, over Manchuria. The Council, as required, tried to find a solution which both parties could accept, but failed, Peru proving intransigent, as she had throughout. The Council wasted no time in deciding what must be done. On March 13th, it said that Peruvian troops must quit Leticia and evacuate those Peruvians who had invaded Colombian territory. The Council was unanimous. It was then that the Council set up its advisory committee, on which the United States agreed to be represented, to see what could be done to ensure that the Council's recommendations were implemented.

In the next six weeks, the Peruvian Government showed every intention of defying the Council, thus laying itself open to whatever sanctions, under Article 16, might be decided upon. Peruvian forts shelled Colombian ships in the Putumayo River, which marked the frontier between the two countries, and Peruvian aircraft bombed them. Here and there the Colombians struck back. Most serious of all was the news that four Peruvian warships were heading into the Atlantic with the aim of steaming up the Amazon to strengthen Peruvian forces within striking distance of Leticia and to oppose any Colombian attempt to execute the Council's recommendations by retaking Leticia. Despite a call from the Council's advisory committee, for member-nations of the League to refuse the Peruvian cruiser and sub-marines the fuel and provisions they would need, the warships called at Curacao and Trinidad, took on board what they wanted, and sailed on towards the mouth of the Amazon. A major naval battle and full-scale war between Colombia and Peru became more and more likely. It was not the League, nor indeed Brazil, which might have had its own ideas about letting those warships steam through Brazilian territory to make war, which saved the day. That was done, on April 30th, 1933, by an assassin, who shot and killed President Cerro. It was not long before the new President agreed to accept the Council's report, and the Colombian and Peruvian delegates signed their agreement at the Council on May 25th. The following month, a League commission went to Leticia and received its surrender from the Peruvian commander, thus carrying out the solution which the Council had proposed when it first came to deal with the dispute, and which Peru had then turned down. A League flag, a white rectangle bearing the words, in dark blue letters, 'League of Nations Commission, Leticia,' flew for the first time in the western hemisphere. The commission, whose membership included Americans, Brazilians and Spaniards, stayed at Leticia for a year, administering it while negotiations went on between Colombia and Peru. At the end of that time, the Colombians took over the territory once more and the commission went home, having participated in an important way in one of the few stories of the League during the 1930s which had a happy ending.

The coming together at the Council table of the Colombian and Peruvian representatives might almost be seen as a farewell present to the League's Secretary-General, Sir Eric Drummond, whose resignation took effect shortly afterwards, in June, 1933. Drummond had served the League extremely well within his limits, which were those of the British civil servant. With the integrity and conscientiousness of his breed went a professional inclination for staying out of the picture. This allowed him a comfortable ride with men like Austen Chamberlain, who would have quickly reminded Drummond of his proper station had he ever attempted to magnify and over-personalise the role of the Secretary-General. Yet, more positive assertion on his part at crucial moments of the obligations member-nations owed the League by their acceptance of the Covenant might occasionally have stiffened a backbone or two. Although he himself set a good example, he never really modelled a wholly international civil service. That was not entirely his fault, for the insistence of the permanent members of the Council upon perpetuating their representation in the hierarchy of the Secretariat meant that nationalism and national loyalties were bound to persist among its ranks. Whatever his weaknesses—of which gullibility was one, as he was to show when he became British Ambassador at Rome— they were trivial compared to those of his successor, Joseph Avenol, a Frenchman, who had served well enough for ten years as Drummond's deputy, but simply did not have the qualities required for the top job, especially at the time he succeeded to it. He was an intelligent administrator, but hopelessly inadequate before the challenges and disasters which were to befall the League. He was never more than a French civil servant, and, unlike Drummond, he never really tried to lose his national identity as the job demanded.

13

'Like the unfolding of a great Greek tragedy'

The early 1930s saw the failure of two world conferences, one which was called to beat the great Depression, and the other which was intended to bring about disarmament. Both carried a heavy investment of hope, and their failure deepened the despair which was to characterise the decade.

Although the economic conference of June, 1933, was held under its auspices, the League had never had the authority in economic matters to do much more than offer good advice. It was excluded from discussions of vital concern to the world politically, such as German reparations and Europe's war debts to America. It did seem at one time, however, that the League might be the means of bringing more sense into the economic relations between countries just as it aspired to do in their political relations. The first world economic conference, held in 1927, did seem to point the way to the clearing of obstacles to trade and perhaps even a lowering of tariffs. But when it came to putting its proposals into practice, the enthusiasm of governments, as contrasted with that of the experts who had comprised the conference, withered. A serious attempt, by the 1929 Assembly, to refloat those ideas in the form of a coherent and comprehensive plan, foundered, like so many brave aspirations, in the slump. In the same way in which it brought about the collapse of liberal governments and nurtured political nationalism, so the Depression fortified the already powerful tendencies to economic nationalism. It was irrational, it was suicidal, but the warnings of such bodies as the League's financial committee went unheeded. The economic policies of individual nations became more and more restrictive and introverted.

There were phases of reason amid the madness. As the world crisis deepened, Germany, foremost among the major European countries, faced economic collapse. It was then, in 1931, that President Hoover proposed a moratorium on the payment of inter-governmental debts, a move which he hoped would not only bring immediate relief to Germany but would also stimulate a revival of world trade. A year later, in June, 1932, at Lausanne, the victorious Allied powers, under the leadership of Ramsay MacDonald and, with conspicuous political courage, of Edouard Herriot, at last recognised how unrealistic were their demands upon Germany for colossal reparations. They wiped out all previous proposals, by which Germany was expected to go on paying forever and a day, and agreed on so substantial a cut in her obligations as virtually to cancel them altogether. At Lausanne, they made to von Papen the concession they had refused to Stresemann, but by that time it was too late to bring any effective aid to the forces of moderation in Germany.

Belated though it was, the agreement was welcome. The European statesmen who made it suffered, however, from a serious delusion. They supposed that their gesture to Germany would be matched by a comparable gesture from the United States to write off Europe's war debts. That, indeed, is what Stimson would have liked to see, but his President was not thinking that way at all. Hoover insisted that the 'holiday' he had proclaimed was for one year only; that year was over and the United States now expected the debtor-nations to resume their payments. His successor, Roosevelt, showed no sign of disowning that policy. The consequence was a profound embittering of relations between the Americans and their former allies in Europe. If the Germans had considered reparations a major injustice and the prime cause of their economic strife, so countries like Britain and France resented American demands, believing wartime debts to belong in a special category. The United States was cast in a Shylock role. Britain did pay up in full, on the dot, in December,

1932, but only after much anxious debate in Cabinet. At one point, there was a suggestion that the ten million dollars' instalment should be paid in silver—Britain had gone off the gold standard the year before—but the majority of ministers did not like the Judas association. Some other nations followed Britain's lead, but not the French, who led the defaulters, although Herriot—trying to promote international concord—stood out for payment against massive and impassioned opposition: he was kicked out of office.

The question of war debts was still festering, when delegations assembled in London in June, 1933, for a world monetary and economic conference. Such a conference had been called for at the annual conference of the International Labour Organisation the year before, as one of the ways of tackling world unemployment. The statesmen at Lausanne had also perceived the necessity for coherent international action and their decision was confirmed by the Council and League Assembly in the months following. The League was given the job of organising it. The United States and Soviet Russia were among the sixty-four countries which agreed to send delegations.

There was little enough cause for hoping that the conference would achieve anything positive and worthwhile. The political background—with the coming to power of the Nazis in Germany in March, the same month in which Japan announced she was quitting the League after the Manchurian resolution—was darkening. The economic scene was scarcely more cheerful. The question of war debts apart, the United States had also gone off the gold standard, and the protectionists were dominant in every part of the globe. A month before the conference was due to start, President Roosevelt made an appeal to other world leaders to ensure that neither the economic conference nor the disarmament conference—which was meeting in Geneva at the same time—should break down in failure. Yet the leader of the American delegation, Cordell Hull, arrived at the conference knowing that he possessed none of the authority necessary for effective negotiations. Above all, he had no power to make any trade agreements involving cuts in tariffs without their being submitted to the Senate for approval by a two-thirds majority. The other delegations came to the conference, therefore, with their spirits limp, not only from the hardships and troubles in their own countries but from the foreknowledge that the representative of the world's greatest capitalist power would be unable to offer any deal worth the taking. Cordell Hull has described the effect upon the conference and the atmosphere in which it met:

'Never in my life have I witnessed such bewildering movements and utterances containing the most surprising changes of opinion without a moment's notice to anyone. There was never so much milling around and tugging and pulling as characterised this conference. It seemed to be moving and operating most of the time in a dense fog. Here the demagogue, the agitator, the perverse person, and the chronic critic could keep thoroughly busy. . . .

'We moved in vicious circles. I wanted tariff reductions but could offer nothing satisfactory myself. France and gold-bloc countries wanted currency stabilisation before they would consider tariff reductions, but I could not talk about it. Britain and others wanted debt settlement, but I could not discuss it. A Secretary of State at the head of a delegation to a great world conference is under a heavy handicap if his hands are thus bound . . .'*

According to Hull, the bitterest recriminations came from the Americans, the British and the French. And 'the dictator nations occupied first-row seats at a spectacular battle.'* It was a battle which was lost, by all, before it began. The conference achieved nothing which could be measured against the crisis which afflicted all taking part in it. Its failure merely gave further ammunition to the advocates of a narrow economic self-interest and to those who were preparing for military aggression.

*   *   *

At the time when the row between America and her European allies over war debts was at its height, President Hoover delivered himself of the tart opinion that, instead of running out on their legal and moral obligations, the debtors ought to do something about cutting their armaments. However unwelcome his comments, Hoover was no doubt expressing the view of many of his

* Op. cit. pp. 254, 257, 268.

countrymen, not only on the question of paying back the loans, but also about disarmament.

In July, 1929, the Prime Minister, Ramsay MacDonald, wrote to the American Ambassador, General Dawes, with whom he had been talking about limiting the size of their navies. 'I feel,' the letter ended, 'that time is precious and should not be lost. People are expecting much from us and I am sure we can satisfy them.' Following the collapse of the Geneva talks two years earlier, the United States had embarked upon a heavy building programme to bring their cruiser strength up to that of the Royal Navy, and this had been accompanied by mounting anti-British sentiment. President Hoover, who had put all his energy behind the Kellogg Pact, determined to end the wasteful and dangerous competition between America and Britain. He found in MacDonald, then a man of driving optimism and outstanding political skill, another leader resolved to bestow the gift of disarmament upon his people. In the autumn of 1929, the Prime Minister went to America and scored a personal triumph, great enough even for his appetite. In practical terms, the outcome was the London Naval Treaty of April, 1930, by which the British, the Americans and the Japanese agreed on the relative sizes of their navies. The treaty was short-lived, effectively buried, indeed, even before its formal expiry at the end of 1936. When it was signed, however, it was acclaimed by the optimists; it also ended the animosities between America and Britain. But it seemed no more than a peep at that heaven of general disarmament for which the world had been waiting, year after year after year.

The first specific date named by the League Assembly for the holding of a disarmament conference had been June 15th, 1925. That was just one of the dates on which it was not held. The conference was forever—or so it must have seemed—in the process of gestation. The preparatory commission for the conference was set up in December, 1925. It was five years before it produced its draft of a disarmament convention for the conference to work on. They had been five years of recurrent and repetitive argument, misunderstanding and disappointment. The conflicts were not just between countries; they were going on within countries as well. Ranged against those campaigning for disarmament on political and economic grounds were the military men, fighting old wars and preparing for new ones and defending with the utmost tenacity the integrity of their own establishments. Exchanges within the British Cabinet could probably be reproduced in the records of other governments. Just before the London naval conference opened, for instance, the Chancellor of the Exchequer, Philip Snowden, who was out of the country, wrote to Ramsay MacDonald, making the most stringent criticisms of the British proposals, which, he said, 'entirely fail to achieve the primary purpose of the conference, namely, an all-round reduction of the fighting forces of the powers . . .' They were framed, said Snowden, without any consideration of the financial implications and offered no relief to the taxpayer. Snowden told MacDonald he was 'seriously disturbed about the probable results of the conference.'

'Your visit to America had aroused great expectations of naval reductions, and when the public realise that our own proposals to the conference involve millions a year of increase in naval estimates the reaction will be terrific. Lloyd George, I know, is feverishly waiting for just this opportunity, and our own people will be driven into revolt . . .'

But disarmament itself could cause distress in those areas where making munitions meant work for the local people, and, more than once, principle gave way to bread and butter politics, as in the selling of arms to other countries. At the end of September, 1930, after hearing from the First Lord of the Admiralty about how other countries were cashing in—especially Italy, which was said to be doing big business in building and selling warships on long-term credits—the British Cabinet agreed to reverse a previous decision forbidding the sale of Government-owned arms to foreign countries.

The chiefs of Britain's armed services, particularly the army and the RAF, were understandably alarmed by some of the suggestions emanating from Geneva. There was a Dutch proposal, for example, for much more information about national armaments to be made public. The brasshats were appalled at the thought of revealing British weaknesses; for the same reason they also opposed any provision for international inspection of armaments, as well as arguing that some nations would build up their strength secretly. The Secretary of State for Air underlined the embarrassing reality of Britain's position in a memorandum to the Cabinet in December, 1931. When she came to the Disarmament Conference, he pointed out, she was bound to claim 'full theoretical parity' with the world's strongest air power, but the fact was that Britain's front-line air force ranked only fifth in the world and was outnumbered by three to one in Europe by the French.

The draft convention which eventually emerged from the preparatory commission was a highly generalised affair; the hard bargaining had yet to be done at the conference. For all the impassioned efforts of the British Foreign Secretary, Arthur Henderson, and the selfless labours of men like Cecil, whom MacDonald had brought back to represent Britain at Geneva, the commission had produced only a mouse.

Yet another year was to go by before the first meeting of the Disarmament Conference on February 2nd, 1932. During that year, the economic situation worsened, Japan invaded Manchuria, and, always hovering in the background, was the menace of German nationalism. One small note of cheer was struck by an Assembly resolution by which all governments agreed not to increase their armaments for one year from November 1st, 1931. It had been proposed by Dino Grandi, Mussolini's mouthpiece at Geneva, and it was fine, supposing every country kept its word.

There was no sign, however, of any change of attitude in France, and, without that, as events were to prove, there could be no substantial progress towards disarmament. The French would never cut down the strength of their armed forces, until they received the kind of guarantee they had been seeking ever since the Americans had repudiated Woodrow Wilson and the League. In 1931, they tried again. Pierre Laval asked President Hoover for a promise that, if there were a breach of the Kellogg Pact, America would 'consult' with France. That, and nothing more. Laval told Hoover and Stimson that such a gesture would have a big influence upon French policy on disarmament. But Laval got the same answer Briand had received: it was 'a political impossibility,' said the President. And so once again the Americans had failed to make the concession which might even have saved Europe.

In Britain, the second Labour Government resigned and gave way to a National Government, a coalition of which Mac-

Donald remained Prime Minister. A general election confirmed the new government in power. During the latter half of 1931, the British Government had had too many other things on its mind to worry overmuch about a distant conference on disarmament and, indeed, no ministerial decisions relating to it had been taken between July 16th and November 18th, 1931. That did not inhibit the Government, however, for the King's Speech to the opening of the new Parliament on November 10th contained these words:

'My Government intend to pursue the policy of promoting peace and goodwill and to continue their active interest in the work of the League of Nations. Particularly, they are giving close attention to the preparations for the approaching Disarmament Conference, the successful result of which would, I am convinced, produce great and universal benefit . . .'

It was not until December 15th that the Cabinet—whose meeting was interrupted while several ministers went to a special service at St. Paul's Cathedral for the Disarmament Conference— got down to the formidable task of trying to determine what British policy should be. The problem facing Britain was the same as that facing every other nation which hoped to make the conference a success: how to reconcile the French demands for 'security' with the German demands for 'equality.' Both the French and the Germans became more insistent and less disposed to compromise as the conference approached. The rest of the world looked to Britain to bring them to a settlement, without which all talk of general disarmament must be futile.

In one respect, at least, the stance adopted by the British Government of 1931 was consistent with that of Sir Austen Chamberlain throughout his time at the Foreign Office: if it was to prove itself firm in little else, it resolved not to enter into any new commitments. The report of a Cabinet committee posed the questions: 'What is the British answer to the French claim for security? Are we prepared to pay the price which may be the only means of bringing about a reduction in French armament, e.g. some form of guarantee over and above Locarno?' The answer, as recorded in the minutes of that meeting, is emphatically clear:

'. . . the Cabinet are not prepared to enter into some form of guarantee over and above Locarno under which, in conceivable circumstances, British forces might be engaged in a war on the Continent of Europe, even in respect of the Eastern frontier of Germany. . .'

Nor did the Cabinet look any more favourably upon an alternative proposal 'of a somewhat shadowy kind,' which came to the forefront of French thinking from time to time, for the creation of a standing international police force, at the disposal of the League Council. It is hard to see how any system for the keeping and enforcing of world peace could be effective without such a force, but the Cabinet wanted nothing to do with it. The farthest they would go that day was to agree that the idea of 'a Mediterranean Locarno' was worth exploring, that and nothing more. The Cabinet ended with the dilemma unresolved:

'. . . it should be borne in mind, on the one hand, that Germany has a strong moral backing for her claim to the principle of equality; but, on the other hand, that it is necessary to avoid a decision on that claim of such a character as would outrage French public opinion. The solution must lie between these two positions.' An accurate analysis of the problem, if not exactly illuminating the answer.

The next day, the Cabinet also took note of another possible embarrassment. One of the products of Geneva, which had caused a deal of dyspepsia in the Admiralty, the War Office and the Air Ministry, was the Model Treaty to Strengthen the Means of Preventing War. The Chiefs of Staff recommended to the Cabinet that Britain should have nothing to do with the model treaty, which, among other objectionable features, contained that provision which might lead to international inspection of HM Dockyards. The model treaty, said Britain's top military brains, 'might result in the imposition of unacceptable and harmful conditions and might interfere with and impede the execution of legitimate action for the purpose of maintaining peace and safeguarding British interests.' The likely embarrassment arose from the fact that both Germany and France were expected to sign the model treaty before the disarmament conference; the new Foreign Secretary, Sir John Simon, was also uncomfortably aware that the previous government had been the treaty's main supporter. What to do about it now was one more decision the Cabinet left to another day and, early in the New Year, despite

Simon's arguments, it was agreed that Britain should not sign the model treaty until and if a general disarmament convention had come into force.

But the Prime Minister rode above it all, dismissing doubts and pessimism. He told the Cabinet on January 14th, 1932, that he did not share the view—expressed the day before—that the British case at the Disarmanent Conference was going to be ineffective.

'It might be lacking in new proposals, but the sentiment and the intention behind were excellent. The Delegation ought to emphasise the fact that we had not waited for the Disarmament Conference to begin disarming, and to describe the situation which had been reached as the result of our efforts. In this respect we had a magnificent case. Whether other nations believed us or not was not very material provided that the whole case were put and reached our own public.' Some might describe that as an example of MacDonald embracing a position of weakness and converting it into one of strength. Others might prefer to see it as a demonstration of his fatuity and ultimate irresponsibility.

A Cabinet committee expressed its view that failure of the conference would be 'a disaster.' That was the way millions of people throughout the world felt, as they showed by the petitions which flooded into Geneva, a massive reminder to the delegates of the precious responsibility with which they had been entrusted. The man they had elected as president—Arthur Henderson—was one to remind them of that responsibility when they fell to bickering and trivialities. Henderson, among the parliamentary pioneers of the Labour Party, had lost his seat in the general election which had followed the formation of the National Government. With MacDonald leading the coalition, Henderson was elected leader of his routed party, although he was outside the Commons. Henderson had shown remarkable loyalty to MacDonald over the years and, even now, refrained from the kind of vehement denunciation of the Prime Minister in which many of his Labour colleagues, believing MacDonald to have betrayed his party, indulged. But there were major differences between the two men, and between Henderson and members of the new Government. These did not deter other delegates from choosing him as their president, for while he had been at Geneva as Britain's Foreign Secretary, he had impressed them by his prudence, his conscientiousness and his dedication to the ideal of the League, and especially to the cause of disarmament. The man who had started his working life as an apprentice moulder had certain disabilities for the office of conference president, chief of which was his lack of understanding of French, the language used much of the time for debate; he had to wait for the translation, a fact which added to the physical strain of the work. But the positive qualities he brought to it far outweighed any short-comings.

At first, although the draft convention, the product of five years' work by the preparatory commission, was quickly pushed to one side, and despite the fact that, as the other great powers saw it, France was being awkward again, Geneva began to allow itself to hope that, after all the waiting and all the disappoint-ments, the conference might really be on its way to a worthwhile agreement. The French had put forward a detailed and ambitious scheme for collective security, whose strength would lie in compulsory arbitration, the identifying of an aggressor and an effective system of sanctions, plus a permanent League police force, assured of reinforcements, when necessary, from members' own armed forces. The leader of the French delegation, André Tardieu, soon to become his country's Prime Minister, included certain provisions for disarmament in his proposals, but the emphasis, as so often before, was on security, and new guarantees of security were a precondition of disarmament. It made magnifi-cent sense as the ideal foundation for world government, and, had the plan been put into practice, must have appeased France's chronic apprehensions about Germany. Some of the smaller nations responded to it, but there was never a hope of it succeed-ing in the international political climate of the time, and it certainly was not the sort of thing the Germans had come to hear.

Other ideas, however, took over and seemed to be making some headway. From Britain and America came the concept of qualitative disarmament, which proposed the total abolition or the cutting-down of offensive—as opposed to defensive—weapons. From Italy came a suggestion for getting rid of all the most destructive ones. That went a long way towards meeting the Russian argument for total abolition of all means of warfare. The

Germans were behaving with moderation, calling yet again for equality by a general scaling down to the level of German armaments. The conference was developing an impetus to agreement which made it possible to believe that, for all the old and familiar obstacles still standing in the way, success was in sight.

Then came inevitable distractions: the special Assembly, following closely upon the Japanese adventure at Shanghai; a general election in France and a presidential election in Germany. The main disarmament conference—and its principal delegates—went into recess, and left their experts behind them to do the work of defining which weapons were offensive and which defensive, and to explore the possibilities of imposing disarmament by limiting armament budgets. And now, once again, big, bold ideas were lost in the enveloping fog of technicalities. What were the characteristics of an 'offensive' weapon? Did it not often depend on when it was used, and how, and by what country? That, surely, was true of submarines, and no less so of tanks and even the biggest artillery? When the conference met again, the Americans put forward a formula which offered a way out, but that was blocked by the French, insisting uncompromisingly upon a more effective system of security before they would accept any proposals for cutting down armaments.

Now the American Secretary of State, Henry Stimson, came to Europe. Ramsay MacDonald, for whom Stimson had a remarkably high regard, joined him in Geneva. So did the German Chancellor, Heinrich Brüning, bringing with him proposals which, while affirming Germany's equality of status, were restrained and constructive enough to be acceptable by all the major powers. Or so it seemed to the three statesmen talking in secret. Certainly, the Americans and the British were ready to take them as the groundplan for agreement. So were the Italians, when they had had a chance to study them. But Tardieu would not leave his election campaign even to discuss them. Another chance had been dropped. We shall never know for sure whether the acceptance of his plan and a breakthrough on disarmament at Geneva could have saved Brüning. What is certain is that his failure made his fall inevitable. At the end of May, President Hindenburg removed Brüning from office. In his place as Chancellor he appointed Franz von Papen.

Germany had taken one more step towards ultimate self-destruction, confirming Stimson's perception of the world situation, which he had described to Brüning, when they were together in Geneva, as 'like the unfolding of a great Greek tragedy, where we could see the march of events and know what ought to be done, but to be powerless to prevent its marching to its grim conclusion.'*

During May and June, Stanley Baldwin, then Lord President of the Council, was expounding in Cabinet his audacious suggestion to scrap all military and naval aircraft. On May 11th, he pointed out just how close were the links between one kind of disarmament and another. For example, says the record of the meeting,

'the size of capital ships depended to a great extent on the necessity for protecting them against submarines and air bombers. The Italians refused to abolish submarines unless capital ships were also abolished. If, therefore, it was possible, by abolishing military and naval aircraft, to make an offer greatly to reduce the size of capital ships in return for the abolition of submarines, great results might be achieved. A reduction in the size of the capital ship would affect coast defences and the size of new docks, and if submarines were abolished he gathered that the abolition of the laying of contact mines in the open sea would also be acceptable to the Navy. His proposal opened up prospects of great economies at a time when the world could not afford their existing expenditure, and he thought the time was not far distant when the nations might be willing to listen to such proposals . . .'

The Secretary of State for Air, Lord Londonderry, defending the interests of his department, tried more than once to discourage Cabinet sympathy with Baldwin's ideas. Large proposals of that kind were not likely to contribute to progress at Geneva, he said; he was anxious to get the conference down to the practical aspects of disarmament. Londonderry put his weight behind a recommendation from the Committee of Imperial Defence that military aircraft should not be allowed to weigh more, unloaded, than 11,000 pounds. This, as the Committee had pointed out, would not involve Britain in any great sacrifice, for the RAF had only five 'planes of that size.

* On Active Service in Peace and War. By Henry L. Stimson and McGeorge Bundy. Hutchinson, 1949. p. 112.

On June 7th, the Viceroy of India, Lord Willingdon, came out against Baldwin on different grounds. He pointed out how essential it was, for police purposes, to have aircraft to control the tribesmen on the north-west frontier. Who, he asked, could contemplate a return to pre-war methods of controlling them? It was an argument which was to be heard again, much to the embarrassment of Britain's representatives at Geneva.

What was recognised in the Cabinet is that the British Government—'the foremost exponent of disarmament'—was being criticised and reproached for failing to give the conference a decisive lead. It agreed that the Prime Minister and his colleagues should enter into private and informal conversations with Herriot—who had replaced Tardieu as French premier—and Grandi, Mussolini's most able Foreign Minister, to try to find the basis for a settlement. The conference at Lausanne on reparations enabled them all to get together, with much coming and going from there to Geneva, where the American, Hugh Gibson, was to be found, and where the president of the conference, Henderson, waited, almost helplessly, in the hope that something would come out of conversations of which he had no part. Simon, the Foreign Secretary, found little to encourage him. On June 20th, 1932, he wrote a private and personal letter to Sir Robert Vansittart, the permanent head of the Foreign Office. It started, 'My dear Van,' and first of all praised the courage and resource of the Prime Minister at Lausanne, 'which makes us all proud of him.' The latter half of the letter dealt with the disarmament talks:

'Passing from Lausanne to Geneva (and at present I am doing this journey in the early morning and late at night daily), Henderson has in fact declared a suspension of his operations to see whether private conversations offer more prospect of practical and quick achievement. The Home Secretary has been good enough to come over to help at Geneva. Londonderry, he and I have had two or three days of pretty continuous labour, first seeing the Americans and now in a tripartite discussion including the French. We also had Grandi to lunch today: Nadolny [leader of the German delegation] tomorrow. Our object is to find out what can be done in the course of the next month, and, while we none of us despair, it becomes increasingly obvious that on every point of substance there are mountains of difficulty to be overcome. Indeed, it is questionable whether the French (who thoroughly realise that their ambitious plan for turning the League of Nations into a super State and forming an international force is doomed) are really contemplating any serious agreement. We can only afford a few days for these informal discussions for they are in no sense a substitute for Henderson's authorised machinery. If, after a few more days, this does not produce agreements of value, we contemplate trying to frame a British proposal covering land, sea and air on wide lines such as we think ought to be the results of the Conference and to bring it forward publicly in a week or two in order to "give a lead"—whether the lead is followed or not. Of course, we cannot formulate this programme without first deciding on its terms and secondly getting full authority for putting it forward. And it is an appalling job.'

The British were beaten to it by the Americans, who announced, just two days after Simon had written his letter, and with a minimum of notice to their colleagues, comprehensive and detailed new proposals for cuts in land, sea and aerial armaments. At the request of the Americans, Henderson called a general meeting of the conference to hear Gibson spell out the plan which Hoover was at the same time announcing in Washington. The general response at Geneva was one of warm, sometimes excited, approval. The Italians and the Russians accepted them in full. So, naturally, did Germany, for here at last, it seemed, was the kind of package which could fulfil her demand for equality. But the French were still asking awkward questions. They wanted to know what help from the Americans a nation could expect which, having conscientiously disarmed according to the Hoover proposals, was then attacked. Washington could give no satisfactory answer; France shrugged shoulders at what she regarded as one more empty and impracticable plan. Japan wanted nothing to do with it.

The British, though making polite noises in public, were scarcely more enthusiastic than the French. Certainly they were not ready to accept the proposals without a lot of modifications. The Americans had made much of the huge cuts they would have to make in their own armaments. But the British Government—or at any rate the First Lord of the Admiralty, Sir Bolton

Eyres-Monsell—reckoned that the Empire would have to do most of the sacrificing.

'The ten capital ships and 30 cruisers that would remain to the USA and British Empire under the Hoover proposals, while being more than ample for the purposes of the USA,' said the First Lord, 'would render our Navy incapable of guaranteeing the security of the British Empire or the arrival of the food upon which this country depends.

'Under the Hoover proposals,' he continued, 'the sacrifice of the British Empire, in addition to that already accepted under the London Naval Treaty, is approximately double that required by the USA for the British Empire would have to scrap 289,576 tons and the USA only 149,600 tons.

'Under the Hoover proposals, the British Empire would be called upon to scrap 74,625 tons of its inadequate cruiser tonnage, while the USA could build 33,750 tons.'

Eyres-Monsell was expressing a resentment felt by other members of the Cabinet, not only at the detail of the American proposals, but at the 'somewhat theatrical procedure' by which they had been launched upon the world. The Government had gone ahead with the publishing of a declaration of British disarmament policy, but it had been done with more consideration for American feelings than some ministers had wanted to see; MacDonald had been a powerful voice in preventing an open affront to the Americans. The declaration had not been sufficient, however, to cool the pressure and propaganda in Britain in favour of Hoover's proposals—from the League of Nations Union and in some newspapers.

Soon, there was much larger cause for concern. The mood among the delegations to the Disarmament Conference was one of frustration and intense irritation at the delays and the goings-on behind the scenes among the big powers. But even the critics felt it was better to adjourn until the autumn, rather than hang around indefinitely and ineffectually. The conference agreed that a resolution should be drawn up, recording the progress to date. The text of that resolution could only reflect the failure to give practical application to the principles upon which virtually all delegations were agreed. More significantly, there was no mention of equal status for Germany. On July 22nd, the leader of the German delegation, Nadolny, expressed the justifiable impatience of his country. It was Germany's resolve, he said, to bring her claim to equality of treatment to the forefront. The next day, the conference voted on the resolution. Russia voted against it, Litvinov reiterating his frequent criticisms of the behaviour of the other major powers. Several countries—including Italy, whose policy had taken a sharp turn for the worse—abstained. Germany voted against the resolution and Nadolny announced that the German delegation would not be back to take part in the work of the conference until and if their claim to equality had been formally acknowledged.

Thirteen years after it had been signed, the Treaty of Versailles could claim responsibility for one more international crisis. The Germans posed as innocents, who had carried out their part of the Treaty in good faith, prejudicing their own security by denying themselves those armaments forbidden them at Versailles, only to be cheated of their reward, the disarmament of the other major powers. It was a performance which won them a good deal of sympathy and even those who, with good reason, were suspicious of just how far Germany had gone with her rearmament, had to admit that she had a just grievance.

The British Government had no doubts about just how serious a situation had been created by the German decision to quit the Disarmanent Conference. At one Cabinet meeting after another, discussion turned on the necessity of getting Germany back. To that end the Government was ready to make several concessions to the Germans: recognition of the principle of equality; a short-service militia (one of the things Brüning had proposed); and 'samples' of those weapons she was not allowed to possess. This last provision brought forth from the Chancellor of the Exchequer, Neville Chamberlain, the comment that it did not matter very much whether Germany was allowed specimens of the forbidden weapons or not, since she probably already possessed them. Time and again in Cabinet, Chamberlain showed a thoroughgoing scepticism about German pretensions and a distrust of their intentions, which makes his later behaviour, as Prime Minister, all the more disreputable. During a particularly long Cabinet discussion of disarmament on October 31st, 1932, he said he understood it was now being suggested Germany must make a declaration that she would not upset the territorial settlement of Europe during the lifetime of any disarmament convention. That, said Chamberlain, was an undertaking Germany could easily give, because in any event she would not be able to take aggressive action before 1938—that was the time when the dangerous period would begin. Simon, the Foreign Secretary, said that, if Germany would not give such an assurance, she would prejudice her position in the eyes of the world, especially as she had signed the Kellogg Pact and the Locarno Treaties. To which Lord Hailsham, the Secretary of State for War, retorted that he thought the Germans probably would give the assurance, but they would not have the least intention of keeping it. Hailsham was a consistent pessimist about Germany. He reckoned her aim was to put herself in a position to redress her grievances on her eastern frontier and later, perhaps, in the west. He doubted, he said, whether she cared at all about the mobilisation of world opinion; after all, other nations, Italy over Corfu, Japan in Manchuria, had successfully flouted world opinion in the past.

Nevertheless, Hailsham, like his colleagues, recognised the need to give Germany what she wanted by way of a disarmament convention based on her equality of status. The British Government was acutely conscious of the way in which other nations looked to Britain for a lead and feared to be laden with the blame if the conference were to fail. There were occasions when British resentment over what they considered the 'unreality' of much that went on in Geneva boiled over. On November 16th, for instance, the Cabinet had before it a Foreign Office memorandum about chemical warfare. The bureau of the Disarmament Conference had been discussing methods of banning it, but Britain was unwilling to agree to a total denial of the right to retaliate, if attacked with poison gas, unless the most effective supervision existed to make sure no country was preparing for chemical warfare and also there were such effective sanctions against any offender that retaliation would be superfluous. The Cabinet minute sums up the discussion which followed:

'The proposals from Geneva provide a typical example of the unreality of much of the proceedings at the Disarmament Conference. It is inconceivable that the Governments represented at the Disarmament Conference can possibly intend to allow their nationals, whether soldiers or civilians, to be gassed by an enemy and in no circumstances to resort to retaliation. Neither is it conceivable that they would entrust the safety of their nationals to the vague and uncertain sanctions contemplated at Geneva. As usual, however, other delegations have shirked the true issues and have left it to the representatives of this country to state the realities and to incur the odium of rejecting impracticable proposals.'

But the Foreign Secretary was asked by the Cabinet 'to do all in his power to avoid the United Kingdom or the British Commonwealth of Nations being placed in a minority of one.'

The pressure of the Government, in the months following Germany's withdrawal from the conference, mounted to an intense level. Petitions and addresses, bearing the names of many distinguished in public life, poured in on the Prime Minister, who also had the task of trying to pacify anxious delegations and assure them that his government was doing all it could to save the conference. MacDonald knew that the consequences of failure at Geneva would not only be grave for the future of international peace: they would be disastrous for the National Government. He decided to go to Geneva himself to try to find the means of persuading Germany to return to the conference. Herriot, the French premier, went there, too, and they joined in talks with Konstantin von Neurath, who had become the German Foreign Minister and was attending the League Council; Baron Aloisi, Mussolini's representative, and Norman Davis, head of the American delegation. The British Prime Minister later passed on his general impressions of Geneva. The United Kingdom, he said, 'was very weak there.' That was because some other nations had permanent delegates, who did a lot of work, circulating memoranda, holding informal meetings, even when nothing much was happening at the Disarmament Conference itself. The result was that 'when UK Ministers arrived they found a great deal had been settled behind their backs.' Not that MacDonald was deterred. As he told his colleagues upon his return from Geneva, 'he had been on the verge of securing agreement in the afternoon of his first day in Geneva. At that moment, however, the American representative had intervened in an unfortunate manner which had seriously delayed matters...'

The talks did succeed, however, insofar as the statesmen did agree a form of words which enshrined Germany's demand for equality and France's quest for security, although the major work of translating the principles into a practical convention had still to be done. On December 14th, 1932, the German delegation was back in its place at the Disarmament Conference. That was the day MacDonald, back in London, asked his Foreign Secretary also to return from Geneva immediately, because the French Government had fallen yet again. The conference adjourned until the New Year.

Whatever hopes were aroused by Germany's return quickly evaporated. Simon placed a memorandum before the Cabinet on January 19th, 1933, in which he said that '. . . unless a new direction and an effective lead could be given to the Conference now, the impetus which it had received from the return of Germany would quickly die away and the Conference would reach a complete standstill.' So it proved. The conference reconvened on January 31st and within a short time seemed to be dying. The delegates were meeting in an atmosphere of deep foreboding. One did not need to be a seer to recognise the inevitability of Japan's resignation from the League. The National Socialists had become a major force in Germany and Hindenburg was soon to appoint Hitler as Chancellor. The European air was nervous, as the men of aggression began to strut upon the stage.

On March 1st, the Foreign Secretary warned the Cabinet that 'the international situation in Europe was deteriorating very fast . . . In Germany the immediate situation was particularly critical. He had news from Geneva that there was a real danger that the Disarmament Conference might break down within the next ten days or a fortnight.' The initiative that was needed came, not from within the Cabinet, but from Anthony Eden, the Parliamentary Under-Secretary at the Foreign Office, who was leading the British delegation to the conference. He and his team produced a draft convention which, unlike previous proposals of a similar kind, was bold enough to make detailed, numerical suggestions about the limits to the armaments any nation could possess. It brought together and tried to combine in one package all those elements which, during past negotiations, had either been demanded by this nation or that or had represented a point of agreement. The German insistence upon equality was recognised from the outset; the target would be achieved at the end of five years of phased disarmament by the other great powers.

The Cabinet studied the draft with some caution. Few ministers liked committing Britain to specifics. But they accepted that the situation at Geneva must not be allowed to degenerate still further and, after making some amendments, gave provisional approval to the draft. Next, the Prime Minister and Foreign Secretary determined to go to Geneva themselves to try to save the conference. MacDonald refused to postpone his journey when he learned that there would be virtually no other representatives of rank to meet him in Geneva. The Nazi Government had just taken power in Germany and was too preoccupied with internal affairs to concern itself with Geneva. Mussolini would certainly not be there. The French took the view that it was no good expecting anything from the Germans at that time.

The British Prime Minister still thought he ought to go. He felt it was all the more important, he told the Cabinet, for the United Kingdom to let the world know that we would leave no stone unturned to establish peace in Europe. His colleagues agreed, and one even suggested that, if European countries behaved badly by not responding to the proposal for a meeting of heads of delegations at Geneva, 'they might be brought to their bearings by a hint that we should withdraw ourselves from European politics.'

MacDonald and Simon found the situation at Geneva every bit as bad as they had feared. The Foreign Secretary sent a telegram to Baldwin, which the Cabinet read at its meeting on March 13th:

'. . . The Prime Minister and I, as a result of many interviews yesterday and today, entirely confirm Mr Eden's view that the Disarmament Conference is in a most serious condition and adjournment with nothing more done would be equivalent to veritable downfall. The committees now sitting have been marking time and are in a state of deadlock. Consequently the choice is between letting the Conference fade away without anything material being achieved and making promptly a new effort along some fresh lines. Consequences of a breakdown are so serious that we are bound to examine the alternative, unattractive and doubtful of acceptance as it may be, with close attention.'

The unattractive alternative was for MacDonald to put before the conference the draft convention, as amended by the Cabinet. As Simon said in his telegram, they recognised that the convention might not produce agreement and that Germany might even 'run out' of the conference. But the British initiative would stand them in good stead with world opinion and 'the Prime Minister can neither stay here nor go away with nothing attempted.'

But MacDonald and Simon were worried about what the draft convention had to say about tanks. They reckoned that if they had to propose—as in the amended draft convention—that a nation could have an unlimited number of tanks so long as they did not weigh more than 16 tons each, then Germany would obviously have to be given the same freedom. 'We would earnestly ask,' said the telegram, 'that the Secretary of State for War and the Cabinet should consider whether in view of all that is at stake in other directions proposal on this head cannot be modified.'

Hailsham refused to budge and he was supported by all his colleagues in Cabinet, including Neville Chamberlain. Baldwin replied to Simon:

'Your telegram No. 180 L.N. was discussed at a meeting of the Cabinet this morning. Lord Hailsham summarised the highly secret statement he had made to the Ministerial Committee on Disarmament on March 7th showing that tanks are the pivot of our post-war army and that a holiday in tank construction for five years, such as you suggest, would render our army almost impotent to conduct any kind of war . . . In the White Paper of the 17th November it was pointed out that the admission of equal treatment would make it impossible to deny in principle to Germany the right to possess a limited number of tanks.

'While recognising and sharing your anxieties, and anxious to assist you in every possible way, the Cabinet felt that it would not be justifiable to risk undermining our whole scheme of military defence on the chance of a possible, though as we gather not very probable, success at Geneva. In reaching this conclusion the Cabinet were not unmindful of your own caution to the Ministerial committee that any statement today is liable to be quoted against us on future occasions. We suggest that if you put forward a scheme it should be on the previously agreed basis, and that if later on the proposals as to tanks prove a stumbling-block, the question should be re-examined to see if any modification is possible. The Secretary of State for War would gladly come to Geneva if you think it is desirable, but on this subject he had nothing to add to the statement he made to the Ministerial committee.'

The Prime Minister and Foreign Secretary did not think they needed Lord Hailsham's company in Geneva, but two days later, on March 15th, they tried again to get the Cabinet to change its mind. Another telegram from Simon to Baldwin told the Cabinet that MacDonald was contemplating making a statement to the Disarmament Conference, outlining the draft convention and stressing the cardinal importance of reducing the political tension, without which no scheme of disarmament could be generally acceptable. The Prime Minister and the Foreign Secretary pointed out that the convention would provide for the creation of a permanent disarmament commission, and 'invited the Cabinet to authorise the suggestion that one of the functions of the commission should be to advise upon the number of tanks, if any, not exceeding 16 tons weight to be retained by each party, with a view to their reduction to the lowest number consistent with its national safety and obligations.'

Baldwin replied:

'Your telegram No. 185 L.N. was discussed by the Cabinet this morning. I ought to mention that some members of the Cabinet are rather apprehensive as to the expediency of tabling a draft convention in present circumstances, lest it should give the Germans a pretext for leaving the Conference and casting the blame on us. The risk of this would of course be greatly increased if the tables of figures contained in the original draft were included, but the Cabinet presume that this is not your intention. It is however impossible here in London to appreciate the situation at Geneva with its complexities and anxieties, and the Cabinet were unanimous in leaving to you the decision, which will have their confident support.

'The Cabinet felt that it was impossible to accept your suggestion as to tanks. It would in practice compel us to justify the numbers of tanks we require for Imperial Defence (including the defence of India) before the permanent disarmament commission on which presumably Russia would be represented . . .

'In stressing the danger of Germany starting to build unlimited tanks you will of course not overlook that tanks are very expensive and that Germany has many other immediate requirements, including aircraft . . .

'If you decide to table a draft Convention Cabinet hope you will agree to base any reference to tanks on previous decisions, which have been several times reaffirmed.'

As the Prime Minister was to tell the Cabinet when he was back home, it became obvious to him and the Foreign Secretary that the British had to do something to end the stalemate at Geneva. MacDonald himself produced the British rabbit out of his hat, with a deal of theatricality; he also gave the conference some specific figures to bite on. The conference showed mild appreciation of Britain's initiative, but its effect fell short of Simon's description of it to his colleagues. The Prime Minister, he told them in his fulsome way, had made 'a tremendous impression and had raised British prestige to the highest point.'

But both Prime Minister and Foreign Secretary were even more rapturous in telling the Cabinet of their visit to Rome. They had gone there just two days after MacDonald had presented the draft convention at Geneva; Mussolini's invitation had come while they were at the conference and they, with the Cabinet's blessing, had hastened to accept. They found the Italian dictator full of his great idea for a pact between the four major European powers, who would work together to secure the peace for at least ten years, which meant in effect imposing their will upon smaller nations who might disagree with them. As another purpose of the pact was to revise the Versailles Treaty—within the context of the League, of course, said Mussolini—this could only mean concessions to Germany over her eastern frontiers: in other words, some enforced sacrifice by her eastern neighbours, probably Poland, in particular. Mussolini told his British visitors he was strongly opposed to German rearmament, a statement which ran contrary to article 3 of the Italian proposal, which set out the method by which, if the Disarmament Conference were to fail, Germany should make a phased advance to parity in armaments.

But the Prime Minister and Foreign Secretary lapped it all up. MacDonald loved to see himself cast in an heroic role in the political drama. He had no real understanding of the League of Nations, for all that, as Labour leader, he had certainly shown positive support for it, and despite the fact that, in Rome, he stressed to Mussolini the necessity of consulting with any other countries which might be affected by treaty revision. But Mussolini had won the admiration of one more British statesman. On his return to London on March 22nd. MacDonald gave the Cabinet 'a number of illustrations of the extraordinary regeneration of Italy under the Fascist regime—a regeneration which affected not only the efficiency of the whole administration and system of government but had resulted in a widespread spiritual development among the Italian people.'

The Prime Minister agreed with his Foreign Secretary that Mussolini's proposed pact had saved Europe from dividing into two camps; one of the problems which faced Britain now was how to avoid the isolation of France. MacDonald and Simon had stopped over in Paris on their way back from Rome to discuss the Italian proposals which had been sent to the French and German governments. According to the Cabinet minute, MacDonald said he had 'tried to bring home to M. Daladier (whom he had found exceptionally pleasant to deal with) the realities of the situation and the importance of France coming into line with the other Great Powers.' The French Government had been told plainly that the present position could not be held for ever. MacDonald quoted Mussolini: 'All treaties are holy, but no treaty is eternal.' The Prime Minister 'felt that the situation was full of danger. We might make some move at Geneva which would result in isolating France; or, by sticking too closely to France, we might run into an opposite danger. The greatest service we could render to France at the moment was to get her to realise what was going on in Europe outside her own country.' The Prime Minister and Foreign Secretary received the warm congratulations of the Cabinet upon the results of their visit.

It was more than possible that the French had a much sharper perception of what was going on outside their own country than the British, who were full of such gratuitous advice. However ready MacDonald and his ministers might have been to delude themselves about Mussolini's purposes, they had no excuse for mistaking Hitler's intentions. Within weeks of the Nazis taking power, the British Cabinet heard of a despatch from the British Ambassador in Berlin about persecution of the Jews in Germany. That was on April 12th. In the weeks that followed, Eden was reporting upon a deteriorating situation at Geneva and confessing his own anxiety at the way in which German demands were changing and mounting. The Prime Minister said in Cabinet on May 10th he feared it might be necessary for the Foreign Secretary, who had been ill, 'to go to Geneva and make one of those speeches in which he was unequalled, setting out the whole position in order that the facts might be on the records of the Conference.' That was just one more occasion when MacDonald seemed almost more concerned to demonstrate Britain's virtue than to achieve anything at Geneva.

Simon sent a message to Hitler:

'At this critical juncture in the life of the Disarmament Conference and on the eve of the World Economic Conference, it is clearly in the interests of the whole world, and not least of Germany herself, that international tranquillity and confidence in Europe should be preserved and, if possible, increased. Unfortunately, the recent change of regime in Germany has produced the opposite effect—a fact which His Majesty's Government deeply deplore. We trust, therefore, that during the difficult time ahead of us all we may hope that the German Government will not merely abstain from doing or saying anything which may increase the already existing nervousness in the public opinion of Europe, but that it will go further and within the framework and in the spirit of the Covenant of the League of Nations, collaborate in the common task of establishing that confidence which is necessary to the success of the Disarmament Conference, which is the aim of the Four-Power Pact negotiations, and which is essential to the success of the World Economic Conference.'

European apprehensions crossed the Atlantic and on May 16th, 1933, President Roosevelt appealed to all the other nations taking part in the disarmament and economic conferences not to let them fail. He put forward his own formula for disarmament. Its chief ingredients were that every country should abolish offensive weapons; accept the draft convention presented by MacDonald;

sign a treaty of non-aggression; pledge itself not to send armed forces across frontiers into the territory of another country. If any of the major powers were to reject his plan, the world, said Roosevelt, would know where the responsibility for failure lay.

When the Cabinet considered the President's statement the next day, the response was one of very modified enthusiasm. The Foreign Secretary pointed out that, if the proposal about not crossing frontiers were strictly interpreted, a fleet would never be able to leave territorial waters and the presence of British and American troops in Shanghai would represent a breach of the agreement. Simon also criticised another suggestion from Roosevelt, 'that no nation shall increase its existing armaments over and above the limitations of treaty obligations,' as unlikely to please Germany and other ex-enemy states, because they were bound by treaty obligations, whereas other nations were not.

It seemed for a moment, however, as though Roosevelt's appeal had influenced Hitler to a more conciliatory attitude: that, at any rate, is how Cordell Hull interpreted the speech Hitler made the following day, a speech directed to the outside world, offering hope that, after all, Germany would pursue her aims within the framework of international negotiation and arbitration. It was the first of those effective bromides Hitler administered so generously at intervals during the 1930s. Greatly encouraged by the speech and by the German backing at Geneva for the MacDonald plan, Hull sent Norman Davis authority to announce to the Disarmament Conference the further steps the American President was willing to take to save the conference. On condition that international agreement were reached to bring about a substantial cut in armaments, then the United States would be ready to consult with other nations, whenever peace was threatened; to help in devising means of 'effective, automatic and continuous supervision' of national armaments; and not take any action which would defeat collective action against an aggressor. This last offer meant that the Americans would be abandoning the concept of freedom of the seas, by cutting off trade with any nation that had been found guilty by the League and subjected to sanctions. In retrospect, it might seem that Roosevelt's gesture towards the League was, for the most part, a negative one, yet Cordell Hull was right to see it at the time as a major departure in American foreign policy. Unfortunately, its impact was somewhat muffled when the Senate refused to approve legislation designed to give the President the right to embargo arms shipments to a nation convicted of aggression.

The British Government was more immediately concerned with Mussolini's idea for a four-power pact. The French were being contrary as usual. The secret negotiations between the four European capitals were a secret no more; the press had splashed the story and the reaction of other nations was, generally, one of intense resentment that the big powers were again ignoring them and the League, while France's allies in the Little Entente—Czechoslovakia, Rumania and Yugoslavia—and Poland, the countries most likely to suffer from any treaty revision, were angry at what they saw as a betrayal by France. The French set about changing Mussolini's plan, linking it much more firmly to the League, inserting a reference to Article 16 and sanctions. Italy and Germany agreed reluctantly to go along with France's amendments, but the British were most unhappy about that mention of Article 16 and talk of 'method and procedures' to put it into effect. There was a nasty suspicion of new obligations. As Simon told the House of Commons on May 26th, 'The obligations we have entered into we shall strive to perform, but our friends on the Continent well understand, and it cannot be too clearly understood, that it is no part of the policy of Great Britain to assume further obligations of this character. We take our existing responsibilities too seriously to be willing light-heartedly to enlarge them.' Britain managed to get the wording of the pact watered down. The end-product, after drastic French amendments and British qualifications, bore slender resemblance to Mussolini's original. Just before it was signed in Rome on June 8th, 1933, Simon assured the Cabinet the pact was now 'less contentious and more anodyne.' Yet it appeared to satisfy all four signatories, and the changes made by the French had gone a long way towards soothing the anxieties of Germany's neighbours—Poland excepted. Whether it was of any practical value was quite another matter: that was never to be put to the test.

At Geneva, the situation had developed into what the Foreign Secretary, basing his assessment upon telegrams received from Anthony Eden, described as 'exceedingly critical.' As he told the

Cabinet on May 31st, immediate decisions were required on matters of high political importance, not the least of which was the question of supervision of national armaments. The French, who were now deeply disturbed by the rate at which they believed Germany was rearming, were placing their main emphasis on the need for inspection rather than 'security.' The British service chiefs were strongly opposed to any routine inspection of armaments, which would expose to the world 'our grave shortage of war supplies.' In talks in Paris with the British and the Americans, the French Prime Minister, Daladier, insisted that 'no supervision could be too rigorous.' At the Disarmament Conference France suggested numerous amendments to strengthen the clauses about supervision in MacDonald's draft convention. Interpreting the French attitude, Eden told the Cabinet the French considered their evidence of German rearmament was so strong—it included reports of concrete emplacements being built in the Black Forest —that, when it came to light, nobody would be able to ask France to do very much in the way of disarmament. Daladier was also demanding automatic sanctions against any nation found to be violating the disarmament convention.

Eden's task at Geneva was often an embarrassing one, for, while the basis of discussion at the conference was the Mac-Donald plan, which meant that Britain was supposed to be leading the way, there were a number of issues where she seemed to be dragging her feet. Supervision was one; another was bombing. It was generally agreed that bombing was to be forbidden, but Britain wanted to make an exception for 'police bombing,' for which the Viceroy of India had argued so strongly the previous summer. Eden has told of his difficulties in trying to defend the British case at Geneva:

'I urged that the Government should reconsider their attitude towards questions where their view was at variance with that of most other members of the Conference, for example in the matter of "police bombing." This was a claim to be allowed to use bombing in "outlying regions" to restore order. Such areas as the frontiers of the Aden Protectorate were given as examples for the exception. The provision had proved indefensible in international debate and raised such unanswerable questions as "outlying from where" and "what parts of the world are to have the privilege of being bombed by the British?" Exceptional cases make bad law.'*

It was not only foreigners who found the British argument indigestible. The Prime Minister had received a large number of letters containing resolutions opposing the Government's policy on police-bombing, and in a debate in the House of Commons on July 5th, no less a person than Sir Austen Chamberlain, still a figure of immense influence, made a powerful speech against the retention of police-bombing. Eden, in his reply to Chamberlain, said, 'I can assure him that I should feel as strongly as he the terrible responsibility of any breakdown of the Conference upon such an issue.' Some of Eden's senior colleagues—he was only a parliamentary under-secretary, and not a member of the Cabinet —questioned whether his statement was consistent with the Cabinet decision in favour of maintaining the right of bombing in outlying areas.

When it became evident at Geneva that the conference was bogged down again, it was agreed—despite the danger of a violent reaction from Germany—that it would be better to adjourn and try again in October. In the meantime, the president, Arthur Henderson, took on the formidable job of trying to narrow the differences between the discordant powers, especially between the French and Germans. Before he set off on his journeys, Henderson had a private talk with Eden.† Henderson warned him that certain questions were bound to arise in his conversations in Berlin, Paris and Rome, such as police-bombing, the definition of 'aggression,' and the proposal to extend to the whole world the declaration of 'no-resort-to-force.' As Mac-Donald said when he heard this in Cabinet, these were precisely the points the British Government did not want to discuss.

During the adjournment, the British Government found itself presented once again with a situation in which principle was in conflict with material interest. The Germans wanted to buy British civil aircraft for 'police purposes,' a use which was forbidden by the Paris Air Agreement of 1926. The Cabinet's

* Op. cit. p. 42.

† Anthony Eden paid a warm tribute to Henderson in his memoirs: 'I always found him a completely loyal president of the Conference and I valued the friendship he showed to me, though half his age and a member of another party.' (Facing the Dictators, p. 40).

impulse was to ban the sale, but then there were the familiar, and no doubt justified, arguments about the trade merely going to some less principled country. A compromise was agreed, whereby the British manufacturers could go ahead with negotiations, but British envoys would try to persuade other governments to agree that no aircraft or aero-engines should be sold to the Germans, unless the Nazi Government gave a categorical written assurance that they would not be used for any purpose proscribed by the Paris Agreement.

Much more serious was the news from Austria, which was being subjected to a sustained barrage of German propaganda, the obvious prelude to an eventual Nazi takeover of the country; the Germans were also busy fomenting sedition and sabotage there. The Austrians asked the British, French and Italian governments to give them official and public support. The Cabinet asked itself whether it mattered to Britain that Austria should retain her independence, decided it probably did, and then wondered what Britain could do about it. There was the Four-Power Pact, of course; there was also the League, but the thought of the League brought up the possibility of economic sanctions against Germany: that was more than enough to make the Cabinet take the view that 'we should not be drawn in the direction of referring the question to the League of Nations.' Ministers also agreed that, really, Italy was the key to the whole situation: it was her reaction which would determine any collective policy towards Germany. The first thing they ought to do, said MacDonald, was to try 'to get arm in arm with Signor Mussolini.'

Arthur Henderson had no success in his European journeyings. Far from bringing the nations closer to a formula acceptable to all, he saw the gap between them widening still farther. The French were more and more convinced that the Germans were bent on war again. They insisted upon a major change in the MacDonald plan, a change which, surprisingly, was accepted by the British, Italians and Americans: surprisingly, because it was unthinkable that the Germans should agree to it. The original plan had been for a phased disarmament by the other big powers to bring them down to equality with Germany by the end of five years. The French proposal was to stretch this period to eight years and for there to be no disarmament at all for the first four years. During that time the Germans would be, in effect, on probation, and would have to submit, along with other countries, to inspection by the Disarmament Commission. If, at the end of the four years, Germany had proved she could be trusted, and if the Commission had shown that effective supervision was possible, then the French would start cutting down their forces.

In Geneva, towards the end of September, talks began between the representatives of Britain, France, Italy and the United States on the one hand, and Germany on the other, to try to reconcile their differences. The Germans left the others in no doubt about their attitude: they had accepted the MacDonald plan, subject to a few changes; they rejected the idea of a 'trial' period; they demanded immediate and substantial disarmament by the big powers. It was all done without threats, however, and this may help to account for the surprise and sense of shock expressed throughout the world at the German behaviour on October 14th. Even Goebbels, the Nazi propaganda minister, who was in Geneva as a member of the German delegation to the League Assembly, was wholly pacific in his public utterances. At the end of September, at a reception for the foreign press, while complaining bitterly of the way in which National Socialism was mistrusted and misunderstood, he was mild in word and manner. Goebbels expounded a theme of the Nazi contribution to world peace, and lamented the slanderous accusations made against the German Government's domestic regime. The picture he drew was of a benevolent paternalism. There were concentration camps, yes, but they were really very pleasant places, fully open to inspection, where the critics of Naziism were re-educated to become worthy citizens.

On the morning of Saturday, October 14th, Sir John Simon, with the full backing of the French, the Americans and the Italians, was to report publicly to the bureau of the conference on the results of the conversations during the recess and to explain how the British draft convention might have to be amended, if it were to be acceptable. The day before, Hitler held a long Cabinet meeting in Berlin; President Hindenburg was brought specially from East Prussia.

Simon's speech was in many ways a skilful one, minimising the concessions to the French, and certainly not couched in terms which the Germans could construe as 'take it or leave it.' The German representative, Baron von Rheinbaben, made an extremely brief reply, merely reiterating the two main claims of his government, that the heavily armed powers should start a real disarmament and there should be immediate application of an equality of status; the question of the quantities upon which that equality could be based, said the baron, was open to negotiation. The German gave no suggestion that even he knew what was about to happen.

The delegates went off to lunch. There was to be a public meeting of the League Council that same afternoon and the full Disarmament Conference was to meet again the following Monday morning to debate Simon's report. The Foreign Secretary talked to the press, never for a moment giving the impression that the situation was hopeless; rather, he implied that all Germany's demands had been met and now it was just a question of her accepting the revised timetable for disarmament. During lunchtime, delegates and journalists heard the news that brought them rushing back: Henderson had received a telegram from von Neurath, the German Foreign Minister, telling him that the German delegation was quitting the conference. Henderson, with a somewhat wan smile, described the situation as 'a bit awkward.' At three o'clock that afternoon, the text of the German telegram was published. It stated that the 'failure of the conference was due solely to the unwillingness on the part of the highly armed states to carry out their contractual obligation to disarm.' Neurath described the probationary period as 'defamatory,' an 'insulting slander' on the German Government. When the League Council assembled for its afternoon meeting, Simon, Paul-Boncour and other members took their places and proceeded to examine, as the agenda required, questions concerning Liberia and the Assyrians with a professional display of calm. But the seat usually occupied by the German delegate, von Keller, who, ironically, had become one of the popular figures of the Assembly, remained vacant. He had sent word that he was 'prevented' from being present. None of the German delegation was to be seen and its headquarters refused to make any comment, beyond the fact that the German representatives were packing their bags and soon they would have left Geneva for good.

The decision was announced to the German people in two manifestoes and in a forty-minute broadcast by Hitler, who had a lot to say about honour and the humiliation of the German nation, which had been treated as a second-class nation without rights. Germany intended not only to withdraw from the Disarmament Conference, but also to leave the League. Hitler declared his willingness to negotiate with individual countries 'elsewhere' than Geneva.

The reactions in the world's capitals were a compound of shock, astonishment, outrage and alarm. It was obvious that not even Mussolini, who had been urging the necessity for granting Germany's demands for immediate equality, had been warned of what Hitler intended to do. The British Foreign Office heard the news early that Saturday afternoon and at once telephoned the Prime Minister who was weekending, as usual, at Chequers. MacDonald talked on the 'phone to Simon. The following day he returned to Downing Street in the late afternoon and conferred with Baldwin, who came in from Number 11. They spoke again to Simon, who briefed them on the latest developments in Geneva. The Foreign Secretary, along with Norman Davis, Paul-Boncour, the Italian, Soragna, Benes, and the Greek vice-president of the disarmament meeting, Politis, had attended talks which lasted seven hours at Henderson's hotel. There was little hope among them that the conference could now be rescued from total collapse.

Elsewhere in the city, however, the voices were to be heard of those who denied that Germany's action must paralyse all other nations. At a crowded demonstration in favour of disarmament, Lord Cecil of Chelwood stated an inescapable truth, that, if the conference failed, the world would be nearer to war. The conference must continue; a treaty fair to everyone must be drafted, and should be presented to the German Government for its acceptance or rejection. A treaty fair to everyone, and one acceptable to the Germans, was, of course, precisely what so many men—including Cecil himself—over so many years had been trying to achieve. Germany had quit at the very moment when, according to *The Times*, only 'comparatively slight differences' remained. It is difficult at a distance to accept that interpretation, but it was undoubtedly one shared by Allied statesmen and by other British newspapers, including, significantly, because of its consistently sympathetic attitude towards the German claim for equality, the *Manchester Guardian*.

On Monday, October 16th, Henderson received a deputation led by Cecil, who presented the resolution passed at the meeting the previous evening. Henderson had a brave reply for them.

'My message to you,' he said, 'is that the struggle for disarmament must go on and that the Covenant will not be treated as a scrap of paper. It cost ten million dead and twenty million wounded to bring the League of Nations into being. We will not break faith with the dead, who fell that there should be no more war . . . To you who represent public opinion I would say—nail your flag to the mast of the League. Make the will to peace stronger and more steadfast than the will to war.'

A little later in the day, Henderson presided over the scheduled meeting of the Disarmament Conference. He replied to Neurath's telegram, a short, dignified reply, moderate in tone, expressing his regret and declaring that the 'grave decision' had been taken for 'reasons which I am unable to accept as valid.' He pointed out that Germany had taken the decisive step 'at the very moment that the bureau have decided to submit' a detailed programme to the conference. The Italian delegate shared in the general approval of the answer to the German Foreign Minister. Then the conference adjourned for ten days, with the frail hope that something might happen during the recess to restore the situation.

Not everyone was downcast or critical of Hitler's action. George Bernard Shaw, for instance, never at a loss for a publicity-provoking opinion, called Hitler's action in withdrawing from the League 'a master-stroke which completely changed his standing in Europe.' It was evident, said Shaw, that 'Germany needed only a resolute and clear-headed leader to denounce the treaty . . .' Lloyd George considered that 'the whole thing has been very badly muddled, and I think that Germany has a very strong moral case.' Neville Chamberlain asked a Nottingham audience to recall the famous saying of the late Field Marshal Earl Haig: 'No news is ever so good or so bad as it seems at first,' and offered a rebuke to Lloyd George. 'I think all of us,' said Chamberlain, 'whether we are Ministers or ex-Prime Ministers, would do well to refrain from hasty comment and from alarmist speculation.' Professor Gilbert Murray, chairman of the League of Nations Union, expressed his own idealistic sort of optimism. Germany, said Murray, 'possibly imagines that by leaving the League she gains some kind of freedom; but she does not. It is absolutely out of the question that the rest of the League will sit still and allow Germany quietly to rearm or even to go on teaching her youth to look to war as the natural aim and ambition of the country. She does not escape from the control of European public opinion or even of European diplomatic action.' Gilbert Murray, who held his office in the League of Nations Union for fifteen years until 1938, was to learn how little Hitler cared for any opinion but his own, and how emasculate and ineffectual the diplomatic pressure to which he was subjected.

Five days after the dramatic telegram to Henderson, Berlin sent to Geneva its formal notification of withdrawal from the League. In a semi-official statement issued at the same time, the Germans sought to put the blame on the British, for having yielded to French demands. This followed the line taken from the moment of the walkout at Geneva, the Germans trying to suggest that their withdrawal was a direct consequence of Simon's report to the bureau on the Saturday morning: Neurath had made a personal attack upon the Foreign Secretary. That pose carried little credit, for it was abundantly clear that the German decision had been taken at the meeting of the German Cabinet which Hindenburg had attended and Hitler had been working up to it well before that. Yet, as he has revealed in his memoirs, Anthony Eden was one of those who, at the time, felt that Simon had a lot to answer for, most particularly for not having done more to bring about an agreement on disarmament while Brüning was still in power.

Public opinion in Britain was agitated by the breakdown at Geneva. The Government suffered an appalling by-election defeat at East Fulham when a Tory majority of 14,521 was turned into a Labour one of 4,800. It is very likely that, as in all British elections, domestic issues, like unemployment and the 'means test,' played a significant part in determining the way people voted, and that the result was something less than the victory for pacifism acclaimed by politicians and commentators alike at the time. Nevertheless, the despondency induced by the news from Geneva must have infected the electorate and it certainly allowed Labour to make all the running. After the disastrous defeat, the Government set itself to the task of rebuilding confidence in its honourable intentions. In a Commons debate on November 7th, 1933, Simon said, 'At a time like this, when the international system set up since the war is in jeopardy, we declare ourselves, without any qualification, believers in and upholders of the League of Nations as the best available instrument of peace.'

The next day, in Munich, Hitler made a speech to party comrades to celebrate the tenth anniversary of the 1923 putsch when he and Ludendorff had tried to seize power in the city as a first step to a march on Berlin. Hitler offered little comfort to those who hoped to see the Germans at Geneva again. 'The League of Nations,' he said, 'will never see us again until the last vestige of discrimination is removed.' On November 12th, the plebiscite which Hitler declared would give the German people their chance to say whether or not they approved his action showed, as expected, an overwhelming majority behind him.

On November 15th, the Foreign Secretary brought his Cabinet colleagues back to the topic of the Disarmament Conference as a matter of urgency. Understandably, most countries regarded a disarmament conference without Germany as empty of meaning and all the major ones withdrew their ministers, leaving only officials to represent them. Simon and Eden had come home, too. But now, it seemed, Henderson, the president of the conference, was talking of resigning, and it was possible that Benes and Politis, the bureau's rapporteurs, would follow his example because, finding no-one capable of responsible discussion, they could not do the job they had been asked to do. The British Government could not afford to seem indifferent; it must try to find a way of getting talks going again. Reports in that morning's newspapers of a speech by Mussolini, disparaging the League, accentuated the need. The Prime Minister had by now convinced himself, and so set about trying to persuade his Cabinet, that the Germans had withdrawn because they had misunderstood the Foreign Secretary. They had supposed that the British had agreed to the French desire to modify the draft convention by inserting the four-year trial period, whereas, said MacDonald, all the

Foreign Secretary had done, in his speech to the bureau, was to give a factual report of conversations and to indicate the sort of amendments that were likely to be moved.

Simon went to Geneva and reported back to the Cabinet a week later. There was no misapprehension about where Britain stood; no need for any speeches or public statements. The Disarmament Conference had been suspended until after the January meeting of the League Council, but Henderson was not likely to resign. What worried Simon much more was Italy's attitude towards the League, which went far beyond the issue of disarmament. His concern was confirmed on December 5th, when a meeting in Rome of the Fascist Grand Council decided that Italy would remain in the League only if it was radically reformed in the shortest possible time, reformed in ways which must affect its constitution, its aims and its methods of working.

During that winter, the Austrian crisis deepened, with the Germans increasing the political and economic pressure, fostering sabotage. Dr. Dolfuss was again threatening to appeal to the League, a possibility which the Foreign Secretary saw as 'a dangerous test' for the League, especially when Italy's attitude was so uncertain. Few members of the Cabinet emerged with much distinction from their exchanges over Austria. The quality of Ramsay MacDonald's attachment to the League, for example, was harshly exposed. He wanted to avoid the Austrian question coming before the League, and suggested that the Four-Power Pact might be invoked—despite the fact that it had not yet been ratified. Ormsby-Gore, the First Commissioner of Works, who had once been Britain's official representative on the permanent mandates commission of the League of Nations, ventured to question the propriety of referring a question to the Four-Power Pact when it was about to be referred to the League. The minutes record MacDonald's reply:

'The Prime Minister said that, putting all cards on the table, ought the question not really to be kept away from the League? We should have the same old trouble there with the small Powers as in the case of the Japanese difficulties.'

Then the Cabinet turned to the possibility of economic assistance to Austria:

'Sir John Simon asked if it was possible further to encourage the tourist traffic to Austria. It was a very pleasant place for a holiday.

'The Prime Minister said his information was that the attempt to stimulate the tourist industry had not been a success, owing to the volume of the normal German tourist traffic.'

Austria was back on the agenda a week later. The Foreign Secretary reported that he was still being pressed by Dr. Dolfuss.

'. . . he felt that if Austria appealed to the League of Nations the situation would be somewhat embarrassing, though he had done nothing to discourage them from doing so. It might be that the assistance we could give would not make much difference in the long run, but if Austria should turn Nazi we ought to be in a position to show that we had done all that was possible to avert it.'

The President of the Board of Trade, Walter Runciman, said he had been examining for the third time what could be done to help Austria. 'The only trade matter in which we could give help was in velour hats . . .'

The Chancellor of the Exchequer, Neville Chamberlain, urged that we should do anything we could. 'We had a considerable amount of money in Austria. Though he would not go so far as to say that this would be jeopardised if the Nazis came to power, he could not forget that the Nazis had criticised these loans.'

At the Cabinet of February 14th, following more discussion of Austria, the question of selling aero-engines to Germany came up again. Armstrong-Siddeley wanted to sell 118, and there was the probability of a further order for 260. Runciman said his department had made inquiries and discovered that both the American and French industries were selling aero-engines to Germany.

The Prime Minister, the minutes record, 'while admitting that the proposal was rather repugnant to him personally, said that if the Cabinet wished the order to be accepted we ought to make sure of as large a proportion of the order as possible, and not place obstacles which would result in our obtaining only a small proportion of the orders.'

In May, the Cabinet recalled its offer the previous summer to ban sales of aircraft or aero-engines to Germany unless the Nazi Government gave a written assurance about the use they would make of them; the proposed ban had been conditional upon other governments taking similar action. The majority of those approached had agreed, but the American and Italian governments had refused. The Prime Minister 'thought it important that the story of what we had proposed and how we had been thwarted by other countries should be published'; it was also suggested 'that some means ought to be found to let the general public know the large amounts of war material that were being sent to Germany by other countries: for example, the USA and Sweden . . .'

The truth was that German rearmament was going ahead at a rapid rate and in a formidable manner. This made discussions of disarmament even more unrealistic, and made the French even more determined to keep the arms and the men they had, while increasing still further their desire for an effective system of security. The British Government shied away as usual from any risk of 'new obligations' and persisted with efforts to reconcile French and German differences and bring the Germans back to Geneva. As Anthony Eden has recorded, the British Ambassador, Sir Eric Phipps, saw Hitler on December 8th, 1933, and asked him about the training of para-military organisations in Germany and what their functions were. Hitler told the ambassador that the SS and SA might be compared with the Salvation Army.

In February, 1934, Eden himself went to Berlin, Rome and Paris, in search of some acceptable formula for disarmament, but his journeys were fruitless. It was all very well for the British Government to revert to the original draft convention—or to pretend that it had never been prepared to insist on the trial period—but the French were in no mood for concessions and German demands grew tougher with each month that passed. The British efforts were a response, in part, to their appreciation of the consequences of the final breakdown of the Disarmament Conference. There would be a return to competitive rearmament, which was regarded as a 'very serious' prospect for Britain.

The British Government had to admit failure, however, and Arthur Henderson summoned a meeting of the disarmament conference for May 29th, 1934. The spokesmen of the big powers went through the motions of debate. Norman Davis offered the widest degree of co-operation on behalf of the United States, stopping short at any commitment to use armed forces as a means of settling disputes; Davis also spoke of Britain's labours in terms which brought a glow to MacDonald's heart. Litvinov recognised the hopelessness of the situation but proposed, nevertheless, that the conference should translate itself into a permanent commission for keeping of the peace. The Foreign Secretary's report to the Cabinet on June 6th presented a cheerless characterisation of the French position and of the conference itself:

'. . . the position at Geneva was now quite clear. The French did not want a Disarmament Agreement. In no circumstances would they agree to a Convention which would allow of any rearmament to Germany. They gave the following reasons. First, they wished to preserve their own existing military superiority, and they preferred, if Germany was to rearm, that it should be in breach of the Treaty of Versailles and not as the result of a new Convention, which they did not think Germany would observe or could be compelled to keep by means of supervision. Secondly, they were full of the idea of an Eastern "Locarno" . . . Thirdly, they anticipated a break-up of Hitlerism, which was possibly due to the fact that Paris was full of emigrés. Fourthly, they did not think it was necessary to pay court to us because they believed that the UK must, by force of circumstances, come in on the side of France: in fact, the Secretary of State recalled that the first remark that M. Barthou had ever made to him was "Your country is more afraid of Germany than we are." To France security meant an alliance to encircle Germany. . . .'

Louis Barthou was a man whose personal qualities, particularly his courage, revealed themselves after longer acquaintance. But he had a loose temper and he was careless in his use of his mordant wit, lacerating his fellow-delegates, apparently indifferent to the effects upon his country's foreign relations. Simon's report to the Cabinet described Barthou's prodigal behaviour at the conference:

'A foreign representative at Geneva had remarked on the first day M. Barthou had estranged the UK; on the second day, the six Small Powers; and on the third day, the President of the Conference. The Lord Privy Seal [Eden] had sent him [Simon] a message that day indicating that the situation was probably beyond mending. He thought that Mr Henderson would probably adjourn the Conference. A cause of satisfaction in a somewhat gloomy situation was that there had been no breach between the UK delegation and the President of the Conference: in fact they had worked very closely, and the UK delegation had helped Mr Henderson to draft the resolution that had been rejected by M. Barthou on the previous day. That was important from the point of view of domestic politics . . .'

The Disarmament Conference was dead, but no-one wished to be responsible for signing the death certificate. It broke up on June 11th, 1934. No date was set for a further meeting, but nor was there any formal statement dissolving the conference. Indeed, various committees went on with their specialised work on such aspects as bombing from the air, control of manufacturing and trading in arms, and ending secrecy about armaments budgets. But none of these could have any significance except under the umbrella of a universal disarmament convention; and that was now beyond hope. Yet, politically, it was impossible to admit it.

Four months after the Geneva meeting, on October 29th, the Foreign Secretary, in a Note to the Cabinet, analysed the difficulties facing the Government:

'(1) The prospect of securing at the present time a Disarmament Convention . . . does not exist.

'(2) Although this melancholy fact is everywhere recognised, the formal admission by the Conference that it cannot attain its object might have serious additional consequences. For example, article 8 of the Covenant requires that plans should be formulated for the reduction of armaments, etc. If it were conceded that no plans could be formulated, that would be a direct denial of the Covenant. Consequently, some mode of postponement in the hope of trying again later on would be of practical utility . . .

'. . . The Secretary of State for Foreign Affairs thought that while it was clear that there was no immediate prospect of securing a Disarmament Convention, the results of saying so publicly might be very serious, having regard both to the commitments under article 8 of the Covenant and to the probability that Germany would repudiate Part V of the Treaty of Versailles. There was a large and growing number of persons who, in the circumstances, were disposed to think that Germany's rearmament was justifiable as well as inevitable . . .'

A demonstration of the sort of political minefield in which the National Government was now tip-toeing was given on December 5th, 1934, when the Cabinet took extremely cautious note of a question Cecil was to ask in the House of Lords that afternoon on the subject of German rearmament:

'To ask whether the President of the Council [Baldwin] was correctly reported as saying that a collective system is impracticable in view of the fact today that the United States is not yet a member of the League of Nations and that Germany and Japan have both retired from it, and whether that means that it is the policy of the Government to abandon so much of the system of the League of Nations as is contained in Article 16 of the Covenant and to revert in that respect to the pre-war international system: and to move for Papers.'

Robert Cecil, who knew his Baldwin from the frustrating days he had spent trying to serve his government at Geneva in the 1920s, was wholly justified in his suspicions. That, exactly, was what Stanley Baldwin believed ought to happen. It was what many of his Cabinet colleagues, too, believed ought to happen. But they were not going to be caught out saying it. It would happen just the same. Time would take care of all things— except disarmament.

That dream, however impracticable it might have been, however remote from fulfilment; that dream which had sustained the survivors of the world war and inspired their children; that dream died a lingering, miserable death in the committee rooms of Geneva, degenerating in its last days to an exercise in conscious futility, a mocking echo of what might have been.

One of the few men to emerge with any reputation was Arthur Henderson. In 1934 he was awarded the Nobel Peace Prize; in 1935, he died.

14

'Shifting sands of verbal promises and declarations'

In the course of his broadcast of October 14th, 1933, announcing Germany's withdrawal from the Disarmament Conference, Hitler made what was meant to be a soothing and reassuring reference to Franco-German relations. 'There are no more territorial conflicts as far as Germany is concerned,' he said. 'After the return of the Saar to the Reich only a madman could believe in the possibility of war between the two states—for which, as we see it, no moral or reasonably justifiable ground exists.' The Saar did return to Germany and the way this was handled and the achievements of the League commission which had administered it offer a moment's escape from the pervasive melancholy of the 1930s.

After the war, France had demanded that the Saar territory, a rich industrial area lying on her north-eastern frontier, should be her consolation prize for the devastation inflicted by the German Army. Britain and America refused to give in to the French, but did agree that they should be given ownership of the coal-mines there and that the Saar should be placed under the government of a League commission for the next fifteen years, at the end of which the Saarlanders would be free to determine their own future. German miners working for the French; a population deprived of normal opportunities to participate fully in running their homeland: the dangers of such an arrangement were obvious and real. There was much resentment among the Saarlanders; the feeling of being second-class citizens did rankle; yet the territory enjoyed efficient and, for the most part, trouble-free rule during those fifteen years. The only serious phase of unrest and conflict came in the early years, under the commission's first chairman, the somewhat despotic Frenchman, Victor Rault, and especially immediately following upon the French invasion of the Ruhr in 1923.* But the reunion of the Saar with the Fatherland was a recurrent theme of German nationalism and it was one to which the Saarlanders themselves—there were some three-quarters of a million—responded with a patriotic warmth which increased as the time when they would be able to choose their own destiny drew nearer.

Until 1933, that is. With the coming to power of Hitler and his thugs, bullying, terrorising, persecuting, murdering real and imagined enemies, the only attractions left for the Saarlanders in the thought of rejoining the Reich were the ties of blood and history; powerful ties, to be sure, but they were a pacific, moderate people, predominantly Roman Catholic, who felt an intense antagonism towards the ideology and the practices of the Nazis. The Saar had become the base for thousands of refugees working against Hitler. Many Saarlanders began to wonder whether the devil they knew—the League commission—might not be preferable to the devil they feared to know.

The Nazi disease spread to the Saar, where the local brand of bully-boy in his brown shirt started strutting and swaggering about the streets, threatening and intimidating. From Germany came an accompanying assault of propaganda for the regime and warnings of what would happen to any who dared to oppose or defy it. Daily life within the Saar became nervous and treacherous and, for the commission and its British chairman, Geoffrey Knox, increasingly difficult and unpleasant. Knox was a particular target for vilification. Hitler would have liked to make the work of the commission so impossible that the League would surrender its power to govern the territory. But Knox, who had come to the Saar commission from the British Diplomatic Service, gave back as good as he got and the commission did its best to protect the people under its care from the Nazis.

* See Chapter 5.

That was very much the concern of the League Council, too, when it came to consider the arrangements to be made for the holding of a plebiscite, which would offer the Saarlanders the choice of remaining under the commission, returning to Germany or joining France. If the plebiscite was to have validity, they must be able to cast their votes, free of fear, both at the time of polling and in the future. The Italian, Aloisi, helped by the Spanish and Argentinian representatives, who had been given the complex task of organising the plebiscite, managed to persuade the German Government, as well as the French, to give written guarantees not to put the voters under pressure of any kind and not to victimise anyone after the campaign. To help to make sure the Nazis kept their word, a special tribunal was created, with branches throughout the territory to hear complaints from individuals who considered they were being maltreated; the tribunal was to go on operating for the first twelve months of the new government chosen by plebiscite.

There was also a need for a more positive and immediate assurance of safety and law enforcement during the run-up to polling day, which, as a reward to the Germans for promising to behave themselves, had been fixed, with minimal delay, as January 13th, 1935. At one time, it seemed as though French troops might be given the job of policing the Saar, at the invitation of the League commission, inflammatory though this must be to the Germans. This, in the eyes of the commission, was very much second best to the initial idea of having an international force, which would include British troops. That, however, was not at all to the taste of the British Government. On November 15th, 1934, Anthony Eden told the Commons the sending of British soldiers to the Saar was out of the question and had never been contemplated. Six days later, the Cabinet was in general agreement that 'it would be most undesirable to entertain the suggestion of M. Laval [who was now the French Foreign Minister] that if French troops were sent into the Saar there should be a 'token' British contingent to indicate the international character of the force.' The Cabinet was warned, says the official minute, 'that any such participation as was suggested by the French would certainly lead us into a position of grave difficulty and embarrassment.' But under pressure from

Laval, and knowing that the question must soon be settled by the League Council, the British Government did a rapid about-turn. It was still not prepared to fall in with the proposal to contribute a token force, whose function would be to lend respectability to the French troops' presence in the Saar; but nor did it palate the possibility of French troops going in alone. On November 28th, the Cabinet agreed that the best course would be to send to the Saar a bona fide international force. This force 'should be on the lines of similar forces employed in the Silesian plebiscite and on other similar occasions, e.g., a number of countries (other than French or German) should each contribute to it a military unit of the order of a battalion.'

That was the proposal Eden was authorised to put to his surprised Council colleagues on December 5th. They were happy to accept and the German Government gave the consent which Eden had insisted was essential. The international force was formed, more than 3,000 strong, with contingents from Sweden, Holland and Italy, but Britain made the biggest contribution; its commander was also British.

On the eve of the plebiscite bonfires were lit in Germany. Trainloads of Saarlanders went home to vote. Walls bore the slogan, 'The Saar is German.' The international police force had protected the people from open intimidation during the campaign and now ensured their freedom to vote. When the polling booths closed, British soldiers, with fixed bayonets, guarded the ballot papers as they were taken in lorries to the Wartburg to be counted. The count was conducted in a building whose security was guaranteed by British arms.

Throughout the campaign, on polling day itself, during the count and after the result was declared—the signal for a wholly illegal but quite irresistible outburst of wild enthusiasm for Germany and Hitler—the dangers of violence were ever-present. Without the presence of the international force, the plebiscite could never have been held at all, or, if it had been attempted, it would certainly have provoked one more Franco-German, and therefore international, crisis. The foreign troops themselves might have inflamed the tension had they behaved insensitively. The Italians, indeed, made a bad first impression. But as an example of the international ideal in practice, it was a total success. The troops were welcomed by the Saarlanders, and the fact that they were there, on the ground, was enough to ensure order. And, after it was all over, they were cheered.

In the last months before the plebiscite, Hitler had changed his tune. He played now upon the pan-Germanic theme, appealing to the Saarlanders to remember they were Germans and that, by returning to the Fatherland, they would be helping to build a greater Germany. A movement did build up in the Saar in favour of staying under the government of the League commission; it seemed at one stage to have achieved really significant support. But when it came to the vote, the vast majority, some ninety per cent, chose to reunite with Germany. There was rejoicing in Berlin, and something less than enthusiasm in France, for whom fewer than half of one per cent of the Saarlanders had voted. The Council in Geneva could only accept the verdict and take satisfaction in the League's part in the story of the Saar.

On March 1st, Germany took over a well-ordered, prosperous territory. The transition from one form of government to another went smoothly. Hitler was co-operative and he also kept the promise he had made before the plebiscite to allow any people who wanted to leave the Saar and made their intention known within six months of the transfer of power to take their property with them. About 8,000 did so.

The League's service to the people of the Saar was at an end. It had deserved their thanks. The troops who had kept the peace during the plebiscite were only the most conspicuous evidence of an international operation. Several hundred men and women had been needed to prepare and conduct the poll and to staff the tribunals: all of them had come from outside the Saar; none, of course, from Germany or France. There was a lesson to be learned, but the world did not heed it. As Eden wrote in his memoirs:

'The machinery in the Saar both before and during the plebiscite gave a glimpse of a supra-national salvation to a world which was imprisoning itself all the while more closely within the confines of the national state . . .'*

* Op. cit. p. 106.

Just two weeks after the Saar became part of Germany again, the German Government published a new army law under which it intended to form a conscript army of thirty-six divisions— more than half a million men. It was Hitler's most eloquent gesture of contempt for the Versailles Treaty. It was this open defiance which outraged Germany's former enemies, particularly France, not the fact of rearmament itself, of which the French were already all too well aware.

Laval sent a telegram to Geneva asking the Secretary-General to call a special meeting of the League Council; it was arranged for early April. While the British made a formal protest, they were still much more concerned to find the formula which would bring the Germans back to Geneva. That was the purpose of the visit Sir John Simon and Anthony Eden were about to make to Berlin. It was a visit which the French and Italians anticipated with deep distrust. There were doubts, too, inside the British Cabinet, as the record of the discussion at the March 20th meeting reveals. Neville Chamberlain said that if, as Goering and Ribbentrop had suggested, the German idea was to get closer to this country at the expense of other countries, the sooner Hitler was disillusioned the better. He agreed that Hitler ought to have brought home to him what the consequences were likely to be to himself and his country, if he was not prepared to co-operate, but he was also concerned about the distress the visit had awakened in France and Italy. MacDonald said it was because we had been so accommodating to other countries that we had reached the present pass. 'He did not mind much what was said in France and Italy in the interval before the Berlin visit. When they heard what had been said there they would be satisfied.' Walter Elliot, Minister of Agriculture and Fisheries, suggested that the touchstone was whether Germany was going to rejoin the League. 'Hitler would have to eat some of his words to do this,' said Elliot. MacDonald said that what had to be done was to go to Berlin and make Hitler face the facts of the European situation. How far Simon and Eden failed in that objective or caused Hitler to change his attitude towards the League may be measured by reading these extracts from the record of those conversations in Berlin on March 25th and 26th, 1935:

'Sir John Simon: Herr Hitler must know how sincerely the

British Government was attached to this new conception of a League of Nations. It provided an essential meeting-place where the discussion of difficulties might take place and where it had been possible to reach adjustments about many matters which might otherwise have become dangerous.

'Even recently, the value of the League had been made manifest in the question of the policing of the Saar. There, it was true, the British Government had taken the initiative, but the other national contingents could not have been so easily secured or general agreement reached without the useful machinery of the League. Sir John Simon wished to acknowledge the Chancellor's prompt reply about the British proposal for the international force for the Saar . . .

'The British Government knew that the German Government felt that they had criticisms to make of the League of Nations, and he had heard that the German Government thought that the League Covenant should be modified.

'In England they were deeply attached to the League, and they did not wish to see it used on behalf of one side or the other. That was one reason why they attached such importance to the German return to the League, for in the present circumstances they had not the same contact with Germany as they had with the Powers at Geneva.

'Sir John Simon explained that the British Ministers wished particularly to mention the League on this occasion because the German return to the League was a great pre-occupation to the average British citizen, who wanted to do what was fair and right, and who wanted to facilitate Germany's return to the League.

'That feeling was very widespread in Britain, and it was a feeling of regret to very many British people that Germany was not at Geneva. In these circumstances anything Herr Hitler could tell the British Ministers on this matter would be very helpful to them because they wanted to be "honest brokers," as Herr Hitler himself had said a little earlier in the meeting.

'Herr Hitler said that the League of Nations was the most difficult of the matters they had to discuss, because Germany, in the belief she had in the League of Nations in 1918 had laid down her arms. The League had been one of President Wilson's 14

Points, "a society of free nations where there should be no victors and no vanquished, and which should unite all the nations to prevent the recurrence of war."

'Although all the nations had suffered from the war, none had suffered like Germany with her two million dead in battle and 800,000 who had died from starvation. In Germany opinion had at the end of the war been more favourable than in any other country to the League because German opinion thought that the League would be a way to solve all these problems.

'Then came great disillusionment owing to the coupling of the Covenant with the Treaty of Versailles. German opinion had realised that the League, in which it had placed such high hopes, was the only organ by which the Treaty was to be executed. That Treaty had classified the nations as victors and vanquished, as the superior and the inferior.

'Certain German Governments had accepted that classification; but the German people had never accepted it . . .

'The Treaty of Versailles had imposed upon the German nation an inferiority which they had never recognised. The imposition of that inferiority was the greatest mistake in the Treaty. It was not the territorial changes imposed by the Treaty or the reparations; but it was the inferiority which rankled, the division into two classes of nations.

'Once the League of Nations had associated itself with that system, it was impossible for any honest and truth-loving German to associate himself with the League. If Britain wanted relations with Germany, she must want them with the good and honest Germans and not with the bad Germans; the good Germans would not have accepted the idea of inferiority . . .

'Mr. Eden wished to emphasise once more what Sir John Simon had said about the British Government's belief in the League. The British Government were convinced that some such organisation was indispensable in the modern world. The only alternative was the alliances etc. which did not prevent the war of 1914 . . .

'Mr. Eden did not follow Herr Hitler's argument about the victors and the vanquished. It was true that the Covenant was born of the Treaty of Versailles, but technically one could divorce the two. He wished to emphasise that in the minds of the British Government there could never be any conception

303

but that Germany was the complete equal of the other Powers in the League itself and on the Council.

'Germany had entered the League after the Locarno Treaty. One service of that Treaty had been that it had brought to an end the conception of victors and vanquished. Then Germany took her place at the Council as one of its permanent members. There was no inferiority about that, and Germany had certainly been treated with full equality at Geneva ...

'Sir John Simon enquired if the separation of the Covenant from the Treaty of Versailles would help to bring Germany back to Geneva. No doubt there were other points; but there was no use in spending time on formalities if that would not help.

'He fully appreciated the point of view that the Covenant would be better as a self-contained document standing by itself. He was sure that the founders of the League did not regard the Covenant as part of the Treaties. They were trying to create a world-wide thing. If the separation of the Covenant from the Treaty would alter Germany's point of view that would be a new reason for seeing if it could be done. If that matter would have a substantial influence, then they must try and cut the two documents adrift so that there should be no question of tying the Covenant to the tail of the Treaty.

'Herr Hitler said that as regards the League of Nations he had defined the German position in May, 1933 ...

'On that occasion he had made it clear that Germany would not continue to participate in a disarmament conference and the League of Nations etc, if she was to remain a country of inferior right. That was still the position. He agreed with Mr Eden that the problem was partly one of the technical separation of the Covenant and the Treaty. But what remained over and beyond that was the actual fact of Germany's position of inferiority on all those points which she had not rectified for herself.

'Germany had rectified for herself the question of conscription and military equality which touched her honour. He did not refer to European territorial questions. He knew that it was difficult to modify the statute of Europe, unless Germany was ready to face the danger of the whole structure tumbling.

'He would give one illustration of the German position of inferiority. Suppose that Germany returned to the League and that Japan was still not a member. That Germany would still not be thought fit to administer a colony while Japan would administer a former German colony. What a clear illustration of German inferiority! . . .

'Sir John Simon wound up by saying Hitler seemed almost inviting Britain to regard France as less associated with her than Germany. The British Government wished to have the closest association with Germany, but they wanted that without prejudice to their relationship with France . . .'

Simon and Eden experienced what many other, more desperate European statesmen were to experience in the next four years— Hitler's practice of shifting the bases of his arguments so that it was never possible to engage him successfully. But, fruitless though their talks may have been, certainly in terms of getting Germany back into the League, they now had the task of persuading the French and Italians that they were innocent of any underhand dealings. That was not made any easier by the attitude of *The Times*, which had described the French intention to denounce the Germans at Geneva as 'profoundly regrettable,' and which identified the British Government with its own advocacy of coming to terms quickly with Germany. The Cabinet considered that the effect of articles appearing in that newspaper at the time of the Berlin talks was 'deplorable'— especially in countries where *The Times* was taken to represent Government opinion. A memorandum from Eden ended: 'If . . . we appear to the outside world to be weak and vacillating, if we allow *The Times* to continue to preach defeatism and to continue to be regarded as the organ of HMG, then we shall encourage Germany's demands, and, no less serious, encourage the weaker Powers to take refuge with her, in the belief that the collective police system can never be effective because England will never play her part in its support.' The Foreign Secretary was authorised by the Cabinet to make clear, by a statement in Parliament, that what *The Times* had been saying did not represent the opinion of the Government.

When Mussolini suggested that the Italians, French and British leaders should meet in advance of the Council meeting, MacDonald and Simon were only too ready to accept; a get-together of that kind offered an excellent opportunity for repair work on

Britain's relations with the other two countries. The three-power conference turned out to be what would be described today as one of the great non-events of the 1930s. The site of the meeting was Stresa, on the shores of Lake Maggiore. Or, rather, that is where the British and French delegations were housed; for security reasons, the actual talks were held in a palace on an island, a hundred yards or so from the shore. That was where Mussolini was staying and motor launches ferried his guests each day from the shore. The conference, which began on April 11th, had all the trappings of a momentous occasion: scores of jumpy plain-clothes policemen; journalists from all over the world; banquets and pompous junketings.

All that was lacking was either purpose or achievement. Not a word was uttered in public—which was just as well, perhaps, for the emptiness and futility of the discussions might have been too brutally exposed. At the end of three days, a limp, worthless communiqué was issued, proclaiming the unanimity of view on all topics which had been discussed. MacDonald gave a rambling, often unintelligible commentary to the press. If the talks had had any function, it was to co-ordinate the responses of the three big powers to Germany's refusal to be tied any longer by the disarmament clauses of the Versailles Treaty. They now agreed to oppose 'with all suitable means the unilateral repudiation of treaties calculated to endanger the peace of Europe.' But what was meant by 'all suitable means'? When the Council met, summoned immediately after Stresa to suit their convenience, the British, French and Italians invited their colleagues to subscribe to their condemnation of Germany and to accept their proposal for economic and financial sanctions to be applied against any nation which was found guilty in the future of jeopardising European peace by violating its treaty obligations.

The manner in which the Stresa powers presented their resolution, full as it was of solemn declarations of principle and, potentially at least, also of solemn undertakings, was peremptory. Their fellow-members were already resentful of the secrecy with which the big three had conferred in advance of the Council meeting; they were apprehensive of the true purposes of the Stresa talks: now they felt themselves under the strongest pressure to acquiesce in a resolution they had played no part in formulating and of whose implications they were extremely suspicious and dubious. They were not even given the satisfaction of explanation. Laval, Simon and Aloisi showed a total indifference to their doubts and largely ignored their questions. Never had the smaller powers on the Council been called upon, with quite such cynicism, to act as a rubber-stamp; the behaviour of the British, French and Italian delegates mocked at all the League had aspired to be and the traditions of open consultation it had laboured to build up. But, with only the Danish delegate abstaining, the Council passed the resolution. The value of it and of the communiqué issued after Stresa was soon to be demonstrated in an astonishing and dramatic way.

A minute for the Cabinet of April 17th says: 'The main problem at Stresa had been to renew the confidence of the French and Italians in this country, which had been somewhat impaired. This had been successfully accomplished . . .'

In June, to the shock and outrage of her European friends, above all of France, Britain negotiated a naval agreement with Germany, whereby the German surface fleet should be limited to 35 per cent of the Royal Navy's strength and her submarines to 45 per cent. German acceptance of these restrictions might be pleasing to the British, but the agreement was tantamount to approval of a German warship construction programme, an explicit repudiation of the Versailles Treaty, and a knock-out blow at the enfeebled concept of disarmament. It made nonsense of the denunciation of Germany's army law and compounded the very sin against which the Council resolution had inveighed. Responsibility for it must lie with Simon, although he had left the Foreign Office by the time of its formal signing; it was among the more disastrous of his actions. Perfidious Albion has betrayed us again, cried the French. But they were flattering the National Government, whose leaders were incapable of any such positive, resolute and coherent policy as was ascribed to them. Like others who were to follow, they thought they were making the best of a bad job. As Germany is rearming, anyway, they argued, is it not wiser to face facts and do a deal with Hitler? The pattern of Britain's future policy towards Nazi Germany was rapidly taking shape.

* * *

The Nazis, too, were perfecting the techniques they were to employ with more and more success, and it was often the people who had most to fear and to lose who, unwittingly, helped them. In the Free City of Danzig, it was the Poles. Although, in the Peace Treaty, Poland had been denied her demand to annexe Danzig, she had been given distinct and important privileges within the autonomous state: Danzig came under Polish customs and had to bow to Poland in determining its external relations. The Free City was intended to enjoy the permanent protection of the League, symbolised by the presence there of a high commissioner; it would, however, elect its own government.

In the early years of its creation, Danzig caused the League a disproportionate number of headaches. One of the high commissioner's functions was to try to sort out disputes and conflicts between the Poles and the Danzigers; some, however, had to be referred to the superior authority of the League Council. The Poles resented the occasions when they had to plead their case at Geneva, just as they felt aggrieved by the frequency with which they were called upon to defend their treatment of minorities. Their pride told them they would do better to settle any differences directly, nation between nation. That was given the stature of a formal agreement between Poland and Germany in January, 1934, and, for a while, relations between the two countries, and between Poland and Danzig, seemed to improve. But the Nazis were very much at work in Danzig.

From the time they won power in the local parliament in May, 1933, the Nazis were intent on bringing the Free City as much under their own kind of rule as any part of the Reich. They were frustrated by the Danzig constitution, which protected its citizens—with ultimate appeal to the League—against the totalitarian repression and persecution practised throughout Germany. They tried, in the spring of 1935, to win the two-thirds majority which would allow them to discard the constitution. Yet, despite the importation for the campaign of some of the highest-ranking Nazis from Berlin—Hess, Goering, Goebbels, for instance—they were returned to power still lacking the necessary majority. The Danzig Nazis were led now by a man whose name was to become notorious and synonymous with barbaric brutality: Arthur Greiser. Greiser spurned the constitution, and Sean Lester, the Irish High Commissioner, was at the receiving end of increasing numbers of complaints of ill-treatment and injustice. When he found that Greiser was ignoring him, or making quite inadequate redress, Lester could do no other than call in the aid of the Council. What everyone at Geneva recognised, however, was that, if the Nazis chose to defy the constitution and the League's appointed representative, there was, practically, little the Council could do. Certainly, there was little it was prepared to do, beyond expressing its stern disapproval. The Poles, as represented by Colonel Josef Beck, a clever but arrogant man, were slow to recognise the danger to themselves, a danger which was not confined to the destruction of their rights in Danzig.

The attitude of the leading members of the Council was characterised by the Foreign Secretary when the question of Danzig came up in Cabinet on January 15th, 1936. He anticipated that, at the next meeting of the Council, Danzig was likely to be the most troublesome item on the agenda. The Nazis, he said, had wilfully infringed the constitution in various ways and his policy was to bring home to the Polish Government the fact that it must shoulder the responsibility. After all, he suggested, Danzig was a free city for the benefit of the Poles; if they wanted it to continue to exist as a free city, it was up to them to accept responsibility.

The Poles were interested, not with the rights and liberty of the citizens of Danzig, but with the maintenance of their own privileged position there. The Germans were happy to play with the Poles along those lines, so long as it suited their own purposes; meanwhile, they showed more and more contempt for the constitution of the city and, therefore, for the League. In what was now becoming a familiar tactic, they subjected the High Commissioner to a sustained campaign designed to make his task intolerable and to devalue his status.

Greiser, as president of the Danzig senate, was called before the Council more than once. His conduct and his explanations became less and less palatable, but the climax was reached on July 4th, 1936, an already black day in the history of the League because of the decision taken over Abyssinia.* Greiser's speeches to the Council were florid with truculence and invective. From

* See Chapter 15.

the press and public galleries came murmurs of protest. When Eden, as chairman, formally ended discussion of the Danzig question and moved on to the next business, Greiser stood up and moved from his place at the Council table. On his way out of the room, he gave the Nazi salute in all directions, ending his demonstration of defiance by putting his thumb to his nose and slowly cocking a snook at the Council. All pretence to decorum was abandoned. The galleries were standing up and shouting. A British journalist called down to Eden, who had not been watching Greiser, and told him—imitating the gesture—what the Nazi had done. Eden, who was to describe Greiser to the Cabinet a couple of days later as 'a bully,' appealed to everyone to ignore the insult and get on with the next item on the agenda. Outside the chamber, it looked for a while as though Greiser, still in an aggressive mood, was going to provoke the journalists, who had followed him out, into violence; but he was persuaded to leave quietly under escort.

Although the League continued to be represented in Danzig by a high commissioner, his ability to protect Jews and other opponents of Nazism from persecution dwindled. The Nazis took no notice of the League, denying its right to interfere. Danzig's last function was to provide Hitler with the pretext for invading Poland.

* * *

The Russians were acutely conscious of Hitler's eastern ambitions and their fears and suspicions were sharpened by the Polish-German pact of January, 1934. Some months before, Litvinov had renewed, with the Nazis, the treaty of neutrality between Russia and Germany, signed in 1926. But he had no illusions about the value of it, if Hitler determined to expand his eastern frontiers.

The Soviet leadership had concluded numerous non-aggression and neutrality pacts over the years, particularly with her neighbours to the west, but now the Kremlin saw the need for some stronger, more comprehensive insurance policy. The League of Nations was seen as the answer, at once the source and the instrument of collective security. Japan's and Germany's withdrawal from the League made it seem all the more attractive and necessary to the Russians. The old rigid hostilities of Chicherin must be abandoned. In 1933, Stalin gave the *New York Times* man in Moscow, Walter Duranty, a Christmas message. 'The League may become something of a check to retard the outbreak of military actions or to hinder them,' said Stalin. 'If historical events should follow such a course, then it is not impossible that we should support the League of Nations despite its colossal defects.' Not the warmest or purest declaration of affection, perhaps, but a hint that the past was the past and the USSR was ready to forgive and forget, if other countries could do the same. Indeed, it was the logical destination of a more flexible foreign policy which had brought her delegates to the disarmament and economic conferences. But she needed a friend at court to urge her admission as a member of the League: that friend was France, over-zealous in her quest for security, and seeing in the entry of Russia a chance to make the League machinery for peace enforcement really effective.

The man who set about organising support was the French Foreign Minister, Louis Barthou, a man of the right, but one who knew very well where France's interests lay. Although he was now in his seventies, he took himself off in the spring of 1934, on a diplomatic tour, whose objective was to put back life into the Little Entente and to reforge traditional links with Russia. With the full backing of Britain and Italy, the French lobbied other members of the League to approve the idea of sending an invitation to Russia to join them at Geneva. It was important there should be no bungling of the kind that had marred Germany's admission in 1926; the Russians would not tolerate any rebuff. As with Germany, Russia must be assured of a permanent seat on the Council. There were a few nervous moments. A deal had to be done with the Poles, freeing them from supervision in their treatment of minorities in return for their vote for Russia. Eamon de Valera, the Irish Minister for External Affairs, proved embarrassingly awkward, insisting upon the Assembly's full rights to consider the proposition, as normally, in the special committee which dealt with new memberships. There was considerable opposition from other countries, notably Switzerland, Portugal and Holland, to the acceptance of a power which practised Communism, plotted international subversion and discriminated against religion; de Valera was especially concerned that Russia should permit freedom of worship. But the difficulties and objections were sufficiently overcome for an invitation, signed by thirty-four member-nations, to be sent to Moscow. The unambiguous response from the Russians, welcoming the invitation and undertaking 'to observe all the international obligations and decisions binding upon members of the League, in conformity with Article 1 of the Covenant,' smoothed the way in. On September 18th, 1934, the Assembly approved Russia's admission by thirty-nine to three, with seven abstentions. No attempt was made to block her election to the Council.

Maxim Litvinov led the Russian delegation to the Batiment Electoral—which had housed the disarmament conference—and addressed the Assembly for the first time. Understandably, confronted by an audience which he knew was critical of the Soviet Union and suspicious of it, however much its membership of the League was desired, he took the opportunity to proclaim the virtues of the new state. He did so in terms some of his listeners found indigestible, but what he had to say about the League itself found an enthusiastic response.

'One thing is quite clear to me,' said Litvinov, 'and that is that peace and security cannot be organised on the shifting sands of verbal promises and declarations. The nations are not to be soothed into a feeling of security by assurances of peaceful intentions, however often they are repeated, especially in those places where there are grounds for expecting aggression or where, only the day before, there have been talk and publications about wars of conquest in all directions, for which both ideological and material preparations are being made . . .

'Far be it from me to overrate the opportunities and means of the League of Nations for the organisation of peace. I realise, perhaps better than any of you, how limited these means are. I am aware that the League does not possess the means for the complete abolition of war. I am, however, convinced that, with the firm will and close co-operation of all its members, a great deal could be done at any given moment for the utmost diminution of the danger of war, and this is sufficiently honourable and lofty a task, the fulfilment of which would be of incalculable advantage to humanity.'

It was a realistic appreciation of the League and yet, at the same time, one which articulated the highest aspirations of those who sat in the hall. The Russians were joining the League for their own good reasons but their participation could contribute significantly to the benefit of all. Litvinov's own performances at Geneva were frequently distinguished and, as the years went by, increasingly embarrassing to his Council colleagues, who had no stomach for the way he reminded them of the obligations imposed by the Covenant. As Robert Cecil wrote of Russia's membership, it was 'only fair to say that until her monstrous invasion of Finland she co-operated loyally with other members of the League who strove for the maintenance of peace.'*

*   *   *

Louis Barthou's success in bringing about Russia's entry was potentially of the highest importance to the League and to the peace of Europe. There was much more he might have done, for he was still a man of restless intellectual energy and remarkable physical stamina, whose reputation for work was prodigious. But he was not to have the time in which to complete or consolidate his diplomatic designs.

On the afternoon of October 9th, 1934, Barthou waited on the quayside at Marseilles to greet Alexander, the dictator-king of Yugoslavia, a country which Barthou saw as one more link in his security chain. As the King came ashore from his destroyer, there were the usual ceremonials, a guard of honour, national anthems, the formal welcomes. Then, Alexander, an austere, withdrawn-looking figure, the gold braid of his admiral's uniform gleaming in the autumn sunshine, was led to the car that was to take him to tea at the prefecture. It was a somewhat venerable landaulette, open at the back. The grizzled, bearded Barthou sat beside the King, who acknowledged the cheers of the crowd with a sort of salute to his cocked hat. The car crawled along and had gone only a short distance when a man ran from out of the crowd, dodging the accompanying horses, and jumped on to the running-board of the car. He fired several shots at the King who, as the doctors said later, was killed instantly. Barthou

* Op. cit. p. 262.

was wounded in the upper arm. The entire incident was marked by appalling confusion, by fatal bungling and inefficiency on the part of the authorities, and by elements of black farce as well as tragedy. When the King's body was brought to the prefecture, it was to the accompaniment of cheering crowds and shouts of 'Vive le roi'; inside the building, still ignorant of what had happened, they were waiting tea. Barthou, who had staggered out of the car at the height of the panic, was left lying in the street, bleeding dreadfully from a severed artery. Even when he was given medical assistance, it was performed with gross incompetence. By the time he received proper attention, it was too late.

The assassin, who also died—he had been slashed by a colonel's sabre, shot in the head by a policeman, and kicked and trampled on by a shrieking mob—turned out to be a Macedonian, a member of a revolutionary organisation, in this instance acting as the agent of a band of Croatian terrorists. It was one more bloody episode in the turbulent story of the Balkans, ugly, ruthless, fanatical and perilous for the peace of the rest of Europe. It concerned not Yugoslavia alone, but Hungary and Italy as well, for those two countries had been exploiting Alexander's difficulties in welding together the Serbs, Croats and Slovenes, harbouring dissidents and furnishing them with the money and arms for terrorism, training them in the arts of killing and sabotage. The Hungarians dreamed of recovering the territories they had lost at the peace; Mussolini saw a splintered Yugoslavia as serving his ambition, reducing that country's potency as a rival, and damaging to French interests. Some of the terrorists involved in the assassination had come from a farm in Hungary, close to the border with Yugoslavia; but later investigations suggested strongly that Mussolini wanted Alexander dead, and that, while he probably had no direct hand in plotting the murder, it was done in accordance with his general instruction.

The horror and the anger of the Yugoslavs might well have sought its release in belligerent action against the Hungarians, but the regency, appointed to run the country on behalf of the boy-king, Peter, who had succeeded his father, was persuaded to seek peaceful redress of the nation's grievance. Pressure behind the scenes also saved Italy from being formally accused by the

Yugoslavs before the League Council. Mussolini, for his part, told the world of the repulsion provoked in him by the vile deed, and used his navy to express his grief and respect as the King's body was carried back, by sea, to his own country.

Yugoslav faced Hungarian at Geneva for the second time in seven months. In May, it had been Hungary which had taken the initiative complaining of the wild behaviour of Yugoslav frontier guards and charging them with the deaths of fifteen Hungarians. The following month the Yugoslavs counter-attacked with allegations about the succour given by Hungary to the terrorist enemies of Yugoslavia, naming the very farm from which members of the assassination team were subsequently proved to have come. In that summer confrontation, Hungary protested total ignorance and innocence; the delegates parted with promises that their two countries would work to remove the causes of conflict. When they came together again in December, it was different. This time the world did not need to be exhorted to take it seriously. Journalists attended in force; Geneva was at its most fevered.

The debate itself was largely a recapitulation and a repeat performance of previous engagements between Yugoslavia and Hungary. Now, however, the Yugoslavs could point to the terrible fact of Marseilles, and produce the evidence to prove where those responsible had come from. The Hungarians' parade of astonishment and innocence of what had been going on inside their own country was something less than plausible.

The tension was sustained, while members of the Council tried in private to arrive at a formula which would keep the peace and yet be acceptable to the two countries. Anthony Eden was everyone's choice as rapporteur: Britain could take a detached view. Eden moved from delegation to delegation, feeling out the ground, using his considerable skill to produce a consensus. He delivered his proposed solution at midnight on December 10th, five days after the Council had come together in special session to deal with the appeal from Yugoslavia and the arrangements for the plebiscite in the Saar. History might have found a more dramatic figure than Eden, but the situation was dramatic enough and his manifest moderation, his clichés and his soporific voice, had their own value at that moment. His recommendations were as anodyne as his manner. He proposed a public declaration of the responsibility of all countries to stamp out political terrorists and a condemnation of Hungarian neglect. Certainly no-one could disagree with that. Nor did Hungary object to the suggestion that she should make her own investigation of terrorist activities and report back to the League. She did so the following month, acquitting herself of any official complicity or responsibility, but reporting that certain police officers had been punished for not having kept a close enough eye on Croatian refugees.

And that was that, so far as the specific issue was concerned. But with Alexander's assassination, as with the murder of the Austrian Chancellor, Dolfuss, by the Nazis some three months before, Europe had taken another violent lurch towards war. The death of Barthou was even more serious—for France, for Europe, and emphatically for the League. His death removed a force which might have been capable, at the crucial moment, of providing France with the leadership and example to reject squalid compromises and backstairs dealings and thus of underpinning the League itself when it faced its climactic challenge, reinforcing the collective will to resist and denounce aggression. Barthou's death not only deprived the League of his positive strength; it brought on to the stage, as France's chief spokesman, Pierre Laval. Laval, immediately upon succeeding Barthou, was a major influence in persuading Yugoslavia not to make any public accusation against Mussolini over the assassination. That was but a taste of what the French Foreign Minister was prepared to do to appease the Italian dictator, as the League was about to discover.

15

'The very midsummer of madness'

At the invitation of the president, the slight, diminutive figure made his way to the rostrum. He was wearing white, with a dark, silk cloak flowing from his shoulders. The harsh lights of the newsreel cameramen revealed the sharp, semitic features above the black beard. The Conquering Lion of the Tribe of Judah, Haile Selassie the First, Elect of the Lord, Emperor of Ethiopia, was about to address the Assembly. The date was June 30th, 1936.

As the Emperor began to speak, there was an outburst of whistles and catcalls and shouts of 'murderer,' 'slaver,' and 'bandit.' They came from what *The Times* described as a 'brawling claque of Italian journalists.' Defying regulations, other journalists in the press gallery and people in the public gallery countered with loud applause. The Rumanian delegate, Titulescu, called upon the Belgian president to silence the rabble. Van Zeeland banged his gavel on the table, but it was the police who restored order by removing the Italian journalists, some struggling and kicking, to the accompaniment of cheers. Throughout the incident, such as the League had never before experienced, Haile Selassie, the first head of state ever to address the Assembly, remained impassive.

His speech was a long one, delivered in Amharic, a language none of the other delegations understood, and translated into French and English. It was a moving appeal, heard in silence, for League members to 'fulfil those guarantees' in which his people had placed their faith, and not to abandon his country.

'I ask the 52 nations,' said the Emperor, 'not to forget today the policy upon which they embarked eight months ago and on the face of which I directed the resistance of my people against the aggressor whom they had denounced to the world.' His indictment of the League was all the more effective for the dignity with which it was delivered.

'I was defending the cause of all small peoples who are threatened with aggression. The Ethiopian Government never expected other governments to shed their soldiers' blood to defend the Covenant when their own immediate personal interests were not at stake. Ethiopian warriors asked only for means to defend themselves. On many occasions I have asked for financial assistance for the purchase of arms. That assistance has been constantly refused me. I assert that the problem submitted to the Assembly today is a much wider one than that of the situation created by Italy's aggression . . . It is the very existence of the League of Nations . . . In a word, it is international morality that is at stake . . .'

Haile Selassie's words matched the occasion all too well. In his conclusion he asked questions which none could answer with an easy conscience, questions which were to have their tragic echoes in the years ahead:

'God and history will remember your judgement . . . Placed by the aggressor face to face with the accomplished fact, are states going to set up a terrible precedent of bowing before force? Representatives of the world, I have come to Geneva to discharge in your midst the most painful of the duties of a head of state. What reply shall I have to take back to my people?'

Manchuria had been the first great test of the League and it had failed it. That failure undoubtedly influenced the future course of events, encouraging the belief that if a nation were strong enough and ruthless enough it could get away with aggression. But the League could have survived Manchuria. It was possible to make all manner of excuses for inaction at that time, and, while most of them were poor excuses, they could be assembled to argue plausibly that Manchuria represented a special case. It was impossible to say the same about Ethiopia. The challenge by Italy to the League's authority was brazen. There was more than enough time to prevent the invasion of Ethiopia ever happening at all. Even after it, the means existed to force Italy to call it off. It was the supreme and crucial test for the League. Pass it, and the League would demonstrate that the new system of international law and order was not only a desirable ideal but an essentially practical one. Fail it, and the faith of mankind in a better way of running the world must collapse. That measure of the challenge is not just the product of hindsight. Contemporary speeches and records show that statesmen and ordinary people the world over knew very well what was at stake.

The Italian lust for Ethiopia was of long standing. It went back to the latter part of the nineteenth century when the European powers were ruthlessly creating and expanding their African empires. Italy came out poorly. The territories she had managed to grab, Eritrea and Somalia, two unhealthy strips of land on the Red Sea and the Indian Ocean, offered none of the riches of the British, French or German colonies. But across their borders lay Ethiopia, with much fertile land and with the possibility of vast, unexploited mineral deposits. The Italians invaded, but, in 1896, her army suffered an appalling defeat at Adowa. Ten years later, they signed a treaty with the British and French to maintain the territorial and political integrity of Ethiopia. After the war, Italy felt justifiably cheated of the colonial reward she had been promised for joining the alliance against Germany.

Mussolini determined to take Ethiopia. As was the invariable custom of the European dictators, his aggression was preceded by florid professions of friendship and innocent intent. But he was preparing the Italian people for war. He took as his pretext a clash in December, 1934, between Italian and Ethiopian troops at the oasis of Wal-Wal, some fifty miles inside the somewhat vaguely defined frontier of Ethiopia. The two governments accused each other. The means of settling the dispute peacefully lay to hand in the treaty of friendship the two countries had signed in 1928 and which prescribed arbitration to deal with any issue causing friction between them. Mussolini would have none of it. He claimed that Wal-Wal was part of Italian Somaliland and the Ethiopians were clearly in the wrong. He demanded a formal apology, compensation in cash and punishment for the offenders; he backed up his demand with a show of strength by Italian military aircraft. The Emperor refused to yield and sent telegrams to the Secretary-General asking the League Council to act to keep the peace.

That call from Haile Selassie evoked a response from Britain and France which was to be characteristic of their behaviour from the beginning of the Ethiopian crisis to the end. There were two basic reasons why Mussolini managed to get away with his rape of Ethiopia. The first was the belief in Paris and London that Mussolini could and should be attached as an ally against Hitler, for the privilege of which, they realised, they must be ready to make generous concessions to the Fascist dictator. The second, which was to show itself later, was the refusal of the American people to accept any international obligations and the consequent failure of the United States to provide any effective co-operation with the League to check or deter Mussolini. The need for American help would never have arisen, however, if Britain and France had acted decisively when the crisis arose. Instead, they played into Mussolini's hands and encouraged him to believe they would acquiesce in his aggression. Their attempts to find a solution by direct negotiation jammed the machinery of the League and bought Mussolini the time he needed to complete his preparations for the invasion. There were rumours, indeed, which reached the State Department in Washington, that during his talks in Rome in January, 1935, Laval had promised the Italians a clear run in Ethiopia: everything that happened there-after lent conviction to the story. Britain contributed her share, in a negative sense at least, at the Stresa Conference. Greatly to the astonishment of Anthony Eden, who was ill and unable to attend the talks himself, MacDonald and Simon never raised the subject of Ethiopia with Mussolini. In their agreement to oppose the unilateral repudiation of treaties, the big three powers added the qualifying clause, 'calculated to endanger the peace of Europe.' Why only Europe? Many people—Litvinov among them—wanted to know. That conference was held more than three months after the Wal-Wal incident and at a time when evidence of an Italian build-up of troops and arms left no doubt of the imminence of an invasion of Ethiopia.

Month after month, and Council after Council, went by with the dispute no nearer solution and the League seemingly in-different to the mounting danger of war. The Italians had achieved a diversion at the beginning of the year by saying that, after all, they were entirely willing to submit the matter to arbitration, as required by the 1928 treaty. For the next four months, despite further appeals to the Council from the Emperor, the Italians were allowed to pretend to be negotiating while at the same time continuing their demands; and the British and French played along with them. They expressed their satisfaction when, at the April Council, Aloisi announced that Italy was about to appoint two members of the arbitration commission as required by the friendship treaty. But, even then, the Italians made a fuss because the Emperor appointed, not two Ethiopians, but an American and a Frenchman to represent his country's interests.

As the time for the May meeting of the Council approached, Haile Selassie showed his desperate anxiety in further appeals. The Italian press was carrying on a propaganda campaign against him, alleging that he was about to attack the Italian colonies—a transparent cover for Mussolini's own fevered preparations in Africa. At last, the British Cabinet began to appreciate the seriousness of the situation. It recognised the dangers of allowing the Italians to drag out the conciliation procedure with the aim of baulking any action at Geneva until September and the end of the rainy season, when Mussolini could order the invasion. Yet at the Cabinet of May 15th, 1935, there seemed to be almost as much concern over Ethiopia's wish to import arms through British territory: Italy wanted all such consignments stopped.

One of the most surprising parts played in this story was that taken by Sir Eric Drummond. Drummond had displayed many virtues as the first Secretary-General of the League. He had certainly won the confidence of member-nations and attracted to his office an international respect which was reflected upon the Secretariat under his command. Who better, it might have been thought, as British Ambassador in Rome, to hold up to Mussolini the imperative importance of fulfilling his obligations under the Covenant? Any such hopes were to be dashed. Drummond's attitude and behaviour offered a wry contrast with that of Sir Sidney Barton, the British Minister in Addis Ababa, the Ethiopian capital. When the crisis first broke, Barton sent a telegram, in which he told his government, '. . . I can think of only one course likely to prevent perpetration of what may be widely regarded as an international crime and that would be for England and France to tell Italy that she cannot have Ethiopia.' When Drummond went to see Mussolini in February, with instructions to make it clear how disquieting and unsatisfactory Britain found the lack of progress in the negotiations with Ethiopia, his manner was almost apologetic; he disclaimed, on the part of the British Government, any wish to criticise the Italians.

Just before the May Council meeting, Drummond came back to London and, on the 17th, reported directly to the Cabinet upon the situation as he viewed it in Rome. He was to return, briefed to 'communicate directly and urgently' with Mussolini, and it may be that, for all the Cabinet's apprehensions about the way things were developing, he found his cue in the following extract from the official summary of the Cabinet's attitude and aims:

'Great Britain attaches and has always attached a value which cannot be exaggerated to the intimate and long-established character of Anglo-Italian relations, of which the conclusions at Stresa recently furnished so conspicuous and so useful an example. It is therefore of the utmost importance that the course of procedure at the meeting of the Council should be such as shall satisfy the due discharge of the duty of the United Kingdom as a member of the Council without impairing in the least degree the friendly co-operation between the United Kingdom and Italy in all matters.'

It is clear, however, that Drummond needed no urging to deal gently with Mussolini. Whether his assessment of the dictator's mind was accurate or not, it is difficult to understand how a man who had been Secretary-General of the League of Nations for fourteen years could have delivered himself of this advice to the Cabinet:

'. . . His own view was that within six weeks or two months M. Mussolini might realise that he was adopting a dangerous course and might be willing to find a way out, provided he could save his face, by obtaining some real economic advantages . . . Within six weeks or so he thought the Italian Government might possibly ask us to make a démarche at Addis Ababa, and at the appropriate moment we ought to tell them that we were ready to do so. We ought also to warn them that if they proposed anything affecting the independence or territory of Ethiopia we must insist on being consulted in accordance with the provisions of the Treaty of 1906. He thought it was useless to proceed on the lines of the Kellogg Pact or the Covenant, and that the Treaty of 1906 was a better basis. He did not think that Mussolini had decided exactly what he wanted in Ethiopia, but if we insisted on our rights under the Treaty of 1906 that would place us in a strong position, and force the Italians to disclose their hands. . . .

'. . . Sir Eric Drummond commented that there was not much chance of a settlement either by conciliation procedure or through action by the League of Nations. He was convinced that at some point pressure would have to be put on the Emperor to afford some economic advantages to Italy, as had been suggested. If that failed he feared we were in for trouble. He thought that the Italian attitude was likely to be immovable both on the Ethiopian nominations of foreigners (to the Conciliation Commission) and on the terms of reference. Notwithstanding the strong feeling in Italy against the expedition he thought it certain that Mussolini would not give way at the present time to pressure from the League . . .'

Small wonder that when confronted again by such a man, Mussolini put on his most belligerent pose, declaring that he was ready for war, that collective security was something for Europe, not Africa—as agreed at Stresa—and that he had not gone to all this trouble and expense merely to settle the Wal-Wal affair. The most charitable comment upon Drummond's role is that it was one perfectly attuned to the policy pursued by two Foreign Secretaries, Simon and Hoare, by the permanent head of the Foreign Office, Sir Robert Vansittart, who was obsessed by the idea of using Mussolini against Germany, and by the overwhelming majority of the Cabinet.

Mussolini did concede an inch of his position. After days of private talks with the Italian delegation, Laval and Eden did win acceptance for the Ethiopian nomination of two foreigners on the arbitration commission. Italy also agreed that, if the arbitrators had not reached a settlement after two months, the Council should take another look at the issue, and similarly after three months. And that was the sum achievement of the May Council in dealing with the Ethiopian appeal.

The following month saw important changes in the British Government. Ramsay MacDonald made way for Baldwin as Prime Minister, Simon left the Foreign Office for the Home Office and was succeeded by Hoare, and Eden became Minister of League of Nations Affairs—a new office—with a seat in the Cabinet. Coincidentally, came a new urgency about the Ethiopian crisis. At the first meeting of the new Cabinet on June 19th, 1935, Hoare said that, since the discussion with Drummond, the situation 'had deteriorated very seriously.'

'There was no sign, as had then been anticipated, that Mussolini's enthusiasm was waning. On the contrary, large Italian forces were proceeding to the Red Sea, and Italian public opinion appeared to have accepted the situation as inevitable. The French Government, who, according to previous expectations, should in the last resort have supported the League in the event of a clash, were showing every sign that in that case they would be on the side of Italy. There was every prospect, therefore, of our being placed in a most inconvenient dilemma. Either we should have to make a futile protest, which would irritate Mussolini and perhaps drive him out of the League and into the arms of Germany, or we should make no protest and give the appearance of pusillanimity . . .

'The Foreign Office were opposed to Sir Eric Drummond's proposals that we should countenance any proposal that involved the abolition of the sovereignty of Abyssinia, which, in spite of our opposition, had become a member of the League . . .'

It was at that Cabinet the idea was put forward of buying off Mussolini by persuading Ethiopia to make some concessions to him in return for compensatory concessions by Britain. Understandably, there was some reluctance within the Cabinet to make any such proposal, but it was realised 'that the only chance of persuading Mussolini to desist from military operations was to take action at once.'

This was the mission on which Eden was sent to Rome. The package the British Government had designed might have been expected to appeal to both the Ethiopians—who would have

been ceded part of British Somaliland and given direct access
to the sea—and to the Italians, who would have received a
substantial chunk of Ethiopian territory and also the chance she
had long wanted of establishing a rail link between Eritrea and
Italian Somaliland. But Mussolini was in no mood for compromise solutions. He gave Eden a curt rejection. Eden, for his part,
told Mussolini of Britain's grave concern for the League and the
system of collective security, which was imperilled by the
possibility of war in Africa. Mussolini showed himself indifferent
to the dangers: there must be a 'final solution' to the Ethiopian
question, he said.

Throughout the crisis, public opinion exercised a significant
influence upon the policies pursued by the governments of the
United States, France and, not least, Britain. Just three days
after Eden left Rome, the results were published of what came
to be miscalled the 'Peace Ballot'; Lord Beaverbrook called it the
'Ballot of Blood.' This was an opinion poll, organised by the
League of Nations Union and carried out by half a million
volunteers canvassing from house to house. The ballot paper
contained five questions, designed to find out what people felt
about membership of the League, the obligations of the Covenant
and what action should be taken against an aggressor. The poll
was astonishingly successful, both in terms of the numbers taking
part and also in providing the sort of answers for which, no
doubt, the Union was hoping. Upwards of eleven and a half
million people returned their completed ballot papers. Just over
ten million of them declared themselves in favour of stopping an
aggressor by economic and non-military measures, and more
than six and a half million were prepared to go even further:
'if it should prove essential, by military measures.' Over two
million said 'No' to military action.

It would be wrong, some 40 years later, to interpret that poll
too logically, because the general condition of public opinion
at that time was not subject to logic. The result certainly did
not mean that the majority of those taking part were prepared to
go to war, to submit to bombing of their homes and to risk their
own lives and those of their children, to check the dictators.
Most people were confused enough to believe they could be in
favour of the League and against the Fascists and Nazis without

subscribing to the use of force. That was a reality with which any government of the day was faced and, obviously, it influenced policy decisions. Yet the poll did reveal an incipient recognition of what was going to be necessary one day and a government with the will to do so could have harnessed that mood, could have made it articulate and given it definition and direction. But the Baldwin government was not made of such stuff.

As it was, the results of the ballot did act as an admonitory memorandum to ministers who knew they must soon offer themselves for the approval of those voters at a general election. They nudged the Government more positively in the direction of the Covenant, but they were not enough to bring about the sort of resolute attitude which alone could have been effective at that time. Throughout July, meetings of the Cabinet revealed still a hesitancy, a wish to avoid any action, or even words, which might offend Mussolini. There was anxiety about the French position, and voices were raised in caution against the idea of Eden asking Laval whether France would be ready to impose sanctions, in the event of an Italian invasion of Ethiopia, lest news of the conversation should leak to Mussolini, or, worse, lest Laval himself should tell Mussolini and take credit for having blocked any British proposal for sanctions. It was agreed that, while consignments of arms should be allowed to cross British territory to Ethiopia, in accordance with obligations under a 1930 treaty, no licences should be issued for the export of arms to either Italy or Ethiopia, a form of 'equal treatment' which could only perpetuate Ethiopia's military inferiority. Other major European arms-manufacturing countries had already banned sales to Ethiopia. At the Cabinet of July 24th, there was 'general acceptance of the view that there were advantages in playing for time.' The longer the catastrophe was averted, ran the argument, 'the greater would be the realisation by Italy of the difficulties by which she was confronted from many directions and the hope of a weakening on her part,' which, as an example of collective moonshine and political miscalculation, must deserve the highest historical distinction.

At no time was either the Foreign Secretary or Eden instructed or authorised to make unambiguously clear to Mussolini that, if he were to go ahead with his invasion of Ethiopia, Britain would take the lead in calling for sanctions against Italy, as required by the Covenant. At the Cabinet of July 31st, 1935, Hoare made a request to other ministers that, in speeches about the Italo-Ethiopian dispute:

'they should be careful not to convey any idea that the situation was hopeless'; and

'they should be extremely cautious in any references as to what this country would or would not do in the event of an outbreak of hostilities.'

That was the day the Council met again, following a deadlock in the arbitration commission because the Italians said it had no right to determine whether Wal-Wal was in Ethiopia or in Eritrea—which is what the Ethiopian nominees wanted the commission to do. Like a householder worrying about a hot cinder burning a hole in his carpet, while a time-bomb was ticking away in the cellar, the Council confined itself to discussion of this single incident at Wal-Wal and the procedure to be adopted by the commission; not a word was said of the impending disaster which could imperil the peace of much of the world. True, the Council did agree that there should be a general debate on the tension between Italy and Ethiopia when it met again in September, but that meant that eight months would have passed since the Ethiopian Government had first formally brought the issue before the League. Ethiopia had cited Article 11 of the Covenant, which declared that in the event of any war or threat of war . . . the League shall take any action that may be deemed wise and effectual to safeguard the peace of nations.' Far from doing anything 'wise and effectual,' the Council had stood aside, deliberately procrastinating, while Mussolini had shipped a vast army to East Africa and whipped the Italian people into a temper for war. The League had not even acted upon Haile Selassie's request that official observers should be sent, at his country's expense and with the offer of full assistance, to see for themselves what was happening on the spot; the Council made no attempt to adopt the practice which had served it so well in earlier disputes.

What did emerge from the Council which met at the end of July was that there were to be talks between Britain, France and Italy, the three signatories to the 1906 treaty, which had carved up Ethiopia into zones where each could try to exercise its influence and further its economic interests. Ethiopia was to have no part in the discussions. The idea was entirely contrary to the big three's obligations under the Covenant and in defiance of the basic concept of open negotiation. But these secret talks were what several members of the British Cabinet had suggested and they were very much to the French taste; the other members of the Council offered no resistance. Laval and Eden set to work to fashion a new gift to place before Mussolini. They took as their starting-point the Eden package, which Mussolini had rejected in June, and persuaded the Emperor to agree to some costly additions: Italy was to be given special economic privileges in Ethiopia and he was to accept comprehensive reform of his country, according to a plan framed and carried out by foreigners. Eden and Laval need not have wasted their time, nor subjected Haile Selassie to the pain of submitting to their proposals. It was plain almost from the moment they met Aloisi in Paris in the middle of August that his instructions were to take up a wholly negative attitude. Mussolini wanted the lot. Not even he could expect to be given it, with a ribbon around it and a card bearing the Emperor's love: so he must take it by force.

Upon his return to London, Eden reported to a special meeting of senior ministers, who were joined by Vansittart and Sir William Malkin, the Foreign Office legal adviser. The record of the meeting, held on August 21st, 1935, was classified 'Most Secret.' It was to be kept under lock and key. Eden told his colleagues how Aloisi's demands had amounted practically to giving Italy a mandate over Ethiopia. It was with much reluctance that Aloisi agreed to send a draft of the Anglo-French proposals to Rome. When the reply came on the 18th, the Italian had separate interviews with Eden and Laval. He told Eden that the proposals were unacceptable to Italy from every point of view. To Italy, he said, Ethiopia 'represented a menace to be destroyed,' whereas 'the Anglo-French view was apparently that Abyssinia should be given increased authority and placed on an equality with the three powers now in Conference'—an interpretation of the proposals which grossly flattered their authors. Eden asked Aloisi if he had any alternative to suggest and was told the Italian attitude was what it had been earlier in the year. Eden reminded his colleagues that 'the Italian proposal, as Signor Mussolini had developed it in the spring of the present year, had been that Italy should acquire the sovereignty over a circular area including about two-thirds of the population of Abyssinia—in fact over all Abyssinia except a central plateau. Over this plateau Italy wished for a protectorate. These were Mussolini's proposals for a peacefully negotiated settlement. On the other hand, he had said that if it came to a war he would wipe Abyssinia off the map.' That statement shows once more how, during those months of inaction and delay, the British Government had been well aware of the extent of Mussolini's ambitions and the dangers to which they must lead if he were not checked. Vansittart, who had been in Paris with Eden, told the meeting about the way the Italians were making propaganda in Paris. 'They were going about speaking of Abyssinia as the first stage in their African conquests, of seizing domination in the Mediterranean from British hands, and in general of renewing the glories of the Roman Empire.'

At that August 21st meeting, the British Government began to consider seriously for the first time the possibility of sanctions and the manner in which they should be imposed, and how the Council meeting, which was due to start on September 4th, would be likely to develop if war were to break out while it was going on. This was a preliminary skirmish, with much detailed discussion about the proper interpretation of the Covenant and, in particular, of Article 16. Would it be legitimate to introduce sanctions in stages, building up to the more stringent ones, or must the other members of the League subject the aggressor, as Article 16 stated, 'to severance of all trade or financial relations, the prohibition of all intercourse between their nationals and the nationals of the Covenant-breaking state, and the prevention of all financial, commercial or personal intercourse between the nationals of the covenant-breaking state and the nationals of any other state, whether a member of the League or not.'? The Foreign Secretary suggested that it would be legitimate to interpret the sweeping phrases of Article 16 'in the light of the glosses of 1921'—when the Assembly had adopted certain resolutions which were intended to become amendments to the Article, although they had never come into force, because not enough states had ratified them. On this basis, said Hoare ingeniously, it would be legitimate, for example, 'to refuse to receive Italian imports while continuing to export to Italy.' Simon, Hoare's predecessor at the Foreign Office, and now Home Secretary, was also anxious about Article 16, but his concern was about the very first words of it, which said that 'Should any member of the League resort to war in disregard of its covenants under Article 12, 13 or 15, it shall *ipso facto* be deemed to have committed an act of war against all other members of the League . . .' According to the record, Simon 'wondered if it was possible to get round' those words.

The meeting was summed up as follows:

'1. Even the mildest sanction might in the end lead to war.

'2. If this were true, steps ought to be taken to put our armed forces into a state of readiness.

'The Secretary of State for Foreign Affairs agreed: Mussolini in his present frame of mind was not a normal man, and it was conceivable that some apparently innocuous action on our part . . . might be taken as *casus belli*.'

The following day a long emergency meeting of the full Cabinet was called—Parliament was in recess—to discuss the possibility of sanctions and of war with Italy. There was emphasis upon Britain's military weakness and, as at the previous meeting, anxiety lest Britain should find herself leading the charge, with nobody following. Certain of the decisions taken by the Cabinet that day are of central importance for understanding what happened later. It was agreed that the British delegates at Geneva

'should keep in step with the policy of the French Government, particularly in the matter of sanctions. They should avoid any commitment which France was not equally prepared to assume . . .

'. . . should aim at following closely procedure laid down in the Covenant (with the interpretations adopted by the Assembly in 1921) not in any quixotic spirit and with due regard to the many difficulties. They should be careful to avoid trying to force nations to go further than they were willing, and generally should make it clear that the question of sanctions was one which the members of the League had to examine in co-operation, and with a view to collective action. They should be on guard against the possibility that other nations might not in practice fulfil their commitments.'

During these Cabinet discussions, the question was raised more than once of what co-operation the League could expect from the non-member states, like Germany and Japan, Brazil and, especially, the United States. Hoare told the Prime Minister he thought the Americans might go along with the less stringent sanctions. He was wrong. America was turning its face farther and farther away from Europe and from any responsible form of international action. The year, 1935, had begun with a slap in the face for Roosevelt and Cordell Hull, when they tried, as Harding had first tried in 1923, and successive Presidents had tried after him, to get the Senate's approval for American membership of the World Court. The outlook seemed promising at first, but then the propagandists of xenophobia and isolation got to work and the Senate failed to provide the two-thirds majority which was needed. Then in the summer, the State Department, with Roosevelt's approval, drafted legislation which would have given the President wide powers of discretion in time of war. He would have been free to decide whether to apply an arms embargo and, if so, whether it should be imposed on both countries or only on the aggressor. He could have exercised his discretion in applying all manner of other restrictions or sanctions. But Roosevelt lost that battle, too, and found himself, instead, deprived of discretionary powers by a neutrality bill which made mandatory the imposition of an arms embargo on all belligerents, whether they were aggressors or victims of aggression. Cordell Hull was disappointed, but managed to convince himself that, if war did come, an indiscriminate arms embargo must favour Ethiopia, because Italy had the money to buy arms and Ethiopia did not. It was becoming more and more plain that the American Government, no doubt unwillingly, would run a long way to avoid any suggestion of collusion with the League. It was already running away from its minimal obligations under the Kellogg Pact, the treaty the Americans had bestowed upon the world and which, in Stimson's time, had seemed to offer, at least, the certainty of 'consultation' when peace was threatened. But now, when war seemed almost inevitable, Washington turned down flat any suggestion that concerted action might be taken by the signatories to the pact. Not even the suggestion of a conference was acceptable. And Haile Selassie's request for American mediation was rejected—to the accompaniment, it is true, of grandiloquent pieties from Hull—on the grounds that the creation of the League had rendered such old-fashioned practices as mediation obsolete.

On the eve of the September 4th meeting of the Council, the arbitration committee, set up under the Italo-Ethiopia friendship treaty, and now under a neutral chairman, reported that neither side had been to blame for the Wal-Wal incident. Any who hoped that the crisis might be quickly ended were suffering from an arrant delusion. The Italians swept the report aside as irrelevant to the issues between themselves and the Ethiopians. When the Council met, Aloisi presented a comprehensive indictment of Ethiopia, accusing her, in massive detail, of aggression, treaty-breaking, obstructive attitudes and barbarity. The Italians had done an impressive job of manufacturing a document which must put the Ethiopians on the defensive and give any nation seeking one a good excuse for turning its back on the dispute. On the basis of the alleged evidence against her, the Italian delegate denied Ethiopia's right to continued membership of the League or to equality with Italy before the Council. It now became Italy's righteous duty, on behalf of the League and of civilisation, to put an end to the monstrous Ethiopian regime, restoring its subject and enslaved peoples to freedom and bringing them the compassion and efficiency of a European administration. There were, indeed, serious shortcomings in Ethiopia, despite the Emperor's reforms. There was still slavery and the slave-trade still went on. But the Italians had nothing to learn in the ways of cruelty and inhumanity, as they were soon to demonstrate. What had to be said, but what only Litvinov said in unambiguous terms, was that, however true the Italian allegations against Ethiopia might be, nothing could justify direct action against her by Italy. The invasion of Ethiopia would be a gross breach of the Covenant and a repudiation of all the machinery which existed under the League for the peaceful settlement of disputes and the outlawing of aggression. The reality was that no words, no formula for conciliation, would have been acceptable now to Mussolini. The months during which he might have been checked had been dissipated. Now he had gone too far to pull back. The Council set up a committee of five, under the chairmanship of the distinguished Spaniard, Madariaga, to go into the issue more deeply and to try again to find the means of saving the peace; but their task was foredoomed.

The certain failure of conciliation did not spell the certain collapse of the League. The world knew what was at stake. Eden had delineated the dangers at the Council. Many countries declared their formal readiness to stand by the League at its moment of greatest challenge. From all over Europe came manifestations of faith in the League and support for the necessary action to defend its authority, echoing and reinforcing the resolution of the British people, as demonstrated in the peace ballot. It is easy now to be sceptical about the real value of those declarations, to question whether those who subscribed to them had really considered what the consequences of collective action against Italy might be but no politician looking for encouragement from public opinion could have wished for more.

The British Foreign Secretary might be thought to have been intoxicated by it. Eden and Lord Cranborne, the Foreign Office parliamentary under-secretary, were astonished, when Hoare joined them in Geneva, by the draft of the speech he proposed to make at the Assembly. Eden had heard in Cabinet the many ministerial apprehensions. If there was recognition of the need to carry out Britain's obligations under the Covenant, it was a reluctant one. The emphasis throughout had been on caution, a caution which must have led to legitimate doubts among Eden's colleagues on the Council about Britain's intentions. Now, here was Sir Samuel Hoare assuming the mantle of St. George, fearing no man, no nation, come to fight for the honour and the very life of the League.

Hoare was the first to speak in the Assembly debate on September 11th, and no other speech was awaited with such anticipation. Would Great Britain give a clear lead, at last, or would she once more resort to reservations and qualifications, refusing to commit herself? Hoare would have been less than human had he not revelled in it. Speaking with the authority of his Cabinet colleagues, he pledged his country to the defence of the Covenant, the whole Covenant and nothing but the Covenant, in terms which none would dare to misunderstand. It was not a speech hostile to Italy. It showed a readiness to salve Italian grievances, but only if the Covenant was respected and the peace kept. The prime concern of the British Government and the British people was the League of Nations.

'The nation supports the Government in the full acceptance of the obligations of League membership,' the Foreign Secretary declared. 'In conformity with its precise and explicit obligations, the League stands, and my country stands with it, for the collective maintenance of the Covenant in its entirety, and particularly for steady and collective resistance to all acts of unprovoked aggression. The attitude of the British nation in the last few weeks has clearly demonstrated the fact that this is no variable and unreliable sentiment, but a principle of international conduct to which they and their Government hold with firm, enduring and universal persistence.'

Hoare won the reception he undoubtedly deserved. It was a speech of magnificent clarity and resolve, which at once lifted and restored his country's reputation and gave back to those who heard it the courage to believe again in the League they had come to Geneva to serve. Lester Pearson, then a civil servant in the Canadian delegation, has described the reaction of the Assembly: 'I remember the Foreign Minister of the United Kingdom moving us to cheers and almost to tears when he pledged the policy of His Majesty's Government to steady and collective resistance against aggression.'*

Delegate after delegate followed the lead given by Britain, until it seemed that the League of which the idealists had dreamed was really coming to pass. Even the French promised to honour their obligations. When Laval mounted the rostrum, two days after Hoare, it was obvious where his sympathies lay: France still wanted friendship with Italy above all else. But if the Council, through the committee of five, should fail to find a peaceful solution, then France would stand by the Covenant.

The committee did fail. It worked quickly and brought forward a scheme which would have meant, in practical terms, an erosion of Ethiopian sovereignty. To carry out the sort of reforms which would meet Italian criticisms, and indeed would

* BBC Reith Lecture, 1968.

achieve some of the results the Emperor himself wanted to see, the committee proposed that the League should send in its own representatives, who would be responsible, not to the Emperor, but to the Council. Yet Haile Selassie was willing to accept the committee's scheme as a basis, at any rate, for negotiation. Mussolini was not. He rejected it on September 22nd, four days after it had been submitted to him.

The following day, the British Cabinet had before it a draft Note, which Hoare was to send to the French ambassador. The powerful, excessively self-confident terms in which it was couched, carry an irresistible conviction of Britain's determination to go all the way in defence of the League; it is not until one reaches the concluding sentences that the frailty of the pledge is revealed. The French ambassador had asked Vansittart, with the Ethiopian dispute in mind, how far the French Government could be assured of 'immediate and effective co-operation' from Britain in the event of a violation of the Covenant and a resort to force in Europe. Hoare referred the ambassador to his Assembly speech:

'I then declared,' wrote Hoare, 'that His Majesty's Government in the United Kingdom would be second to none in their intention to fulfil, within the measure of their capacity, the obligations which the Covenant lays upon them, and I added that the ideas enshrined in the Covenant, and in particular the aspiration to establish the rule of law in international affairs, had appealed with growing force to the strain of idealism in the British national character, and that they had indeed become a part of the national conscience.

'. . . I further took the opportunity in the course of my speech to repudiate any suggestion that the attitude of His Majesty's Government had been one of other than unwavering fidelity to the League and all that it stands for, and I drew attention to the fact that the recent response of public opinion in this country showed how completely the nation supported the Government in the full acceptance of the obligations of League membership, which was the often proclaimed keynote of British foreign policy. I added that to suggest or insinuate that this policy was for some reason peculiar to the Italo/Abyssinian conflict would be a complete misunderstanding. Nothing, in fact, could be further from the truth. I said, and I sincerely welcome this opportunity to repeat with full responsibility, that it is the principles of the League and not to any particular manifestation thereof, that the British nation had demonstrated its adherence. Another view would at once be an underestimate of British good faith and an imputation upon British sincerity. In conformity with its precise and explicit obligations, I pointed out and I re-emphasise, that the League stands, and this country stands with it, for the collective maintenance of the Covenant in its entirety, and particularly for steady and collective resistance to all acts of unprovoked aggression.'

There was much more in this vein, stressing and underlining Britain's commitment to the League, a commitment which over-ruled all other international obligations. Hoare said he spoke not only for the present Government, but that, given the overwhelming support of the British people, it was inconceivable that any future Government could depart from that same policy. As he came to the end of the Note, the Foreign Secretary expressed his country's faith that the League 'would remain' an effective body, which was the only condition for Britain's persistent and enduring loyalty to it.

'His Majesty's Government have no doubt that this will prove to be the case. They believe that an organism, which, in the considered opinion of this nation, represents the one and only real hope of avoiding the senseless disasters of the past and ensuring world peace by collective security in the future, will not lightly invalidate itself by lack of faith in, and effective action on behalf of, its own ideals. But that faith and that action must, like the security, be collective. The point is so vital, and I must venture, in conclusion, once more to quote my words at Geneva, "If risks for peace are to be run they must be run by all." So long as the League preserves itself by its own example, this Government and this nation will live up to its full principles.'

There, in those last sentences, was the escape-hatch through which the British Government would squirm. But, at the time, the world was not looking for it: Hoare's brave and noble words, proclaiming Britain's commitment, had made eyes misty with admiration. In Cabinet, however, the Lord President of the Council, Ramsay MacDonald, was rather more clear-eyed. He thought that the Note 'set forth our view with too much warmth.' He took as a particular example the following passage:

'That policy seems, moreover, to be the only one consonant with the fulfilment of the obligations contained in the Covenant, obligations which were deliberately given the most solemn form and title and made to over-rule all other international obligations, and consequently it is difficult to conceive of future Governments adopting a different policy.'

A French critic, MacDonald suggested, might say 'What about Japan?' He thought the passage sound in substance but too enthusiastic in expression. But Hoare seemed to be carried away by his new role. It was as though he had just discovered the beauties of the League idea. He observed, with apparent surprise, 'that the Covenant was shown, by the outburst of public opinion, to have greater validity in this country than had been thought.' Than had been thought by the British Foreign Secretary, anyway.

The Cabinet met again the next day, and Hoare made a somewhat pessimistic survey of what other nations might be likely to do if the question of imposing economic sanctions were to arise; but he seemed certain that Laval, 'after vacillating,' had come round to the British view. There was general agreement that we must be sure, before we would do anything, that other members of the League would honour the principle that an attack on any one of them was an attack on them all. The British Government was particularly concerned because it believed that Mussolini might retaliate against sanctions by attacking the British fleet. A French assurance was needed that the Royal Navy would be able to use French ports.

The policy pursued by the British Government at this stage was dangerously uncertain and often self-contradictory. For instance, it sent reinforcements to the Mediterranean fleet— ostensibly in response to the menacing noises being made against Britain in the Italian press. Hoare reported to his colleagues upon a meeting between Mussolini and the French Ambassador in Rome, in which Mussolini expressed the 'curious belief' that the British Admiralty was determined to destroy the Fascist fleet and the British Government equally determined to humiliate Italy before the world. Having made an obvious impression on

Mussolini by the show of naval strength, the Government promptly rendered it worthless by instructing Drummond to go to Mussolini and tell him in the nicest possible way that Britain had not the smallest desire to humiliate Italy.

Hoare made clear that, when he talked of possible sanctions, what he had in mind were the mildest sort of economic sanctions, such as banning certain exports to Italy and refusing to accept Italian goods. But he thought there would have to be some form of sanctions. If the League were to confine itself to a moral condemnation, he said, its futility would be exposed. If sanctions were imposed, Italy would probably withdraw from the League. Collective security ought to be tried out, the Foreign Secretary considered. It was essential to employ the machinery of the League; any other course would be impossible to explain to the country. If the experiment were to be successful, the League would be greatly strengthened. If collective security was not going to be effective, the sooner they found out the better. Nevertheless, until Italy actually committed aggression, British policy must still be geared to trying for further conciliation, and Eden, at Geneva, must not allow himself to be manœuvred into advocacy of immediate strong measures against Italy, as some members would probably urge.

The last Cabinet before the Italian invasion began was held on October 2nd, when Hoare showed plainly how he hoped the Ethiopian crisis would really be settled ultimately and the true value to be placed upon his speech at the Assembly. An advisory committee, which had been looking into the question of sanctions, recommended that, if the aim was to strengthen the League and prove its efficiency, then the toughest sanctions on which agreement could be reached ought to be applied. The Foreign Secretary showed no enthusiasm. He was doubtful whether Laval would agree to truly severe measures and convinced that he would never take them to the point of a blockade or military sanctions. So that, Hoare implied, was that. But, never mind, remembering Italy's weak economic condition, even minor economic sanctions would have some value. It was possible that, fairly soon, Italy would find herself in great difficulties and be ready to make some sort of settlement. 'At that point he hoped that the powers would not be too intransigent and would be willing to consider a settlement which, without destroying Abyssinian independence, would give Italy some satisfaction.' At Eden's urging, ministers agreed that, in their speeches in Britain, they would stress that the Ethiopian dispute was not a British concern but a League of Nations matter, and that the future of the League would depend upon the way it was handled.

On October 3rd, 1935, Italian infantry and motorised columns crossed the frontier into Ethiopia. Italian aircraft bombed two towns. The Emperor had ordered a general mobilisation a few days earlier; the Italians took this as a pretext: the invasion was an act of self-defence. Tribesmen, armed with spears and ancient rifles, prepared to fight a modern army.

On October 5th, the League Council issued its report on the dispute, following Italy's rejection of the settlement proposed by the committee of five. It might have seemed irrelevant to many in the outside world, but, like any institution, the League had to observe the proper constitutional processes and it was important to establish the legitimacy of any future action. The report was to the point. There was nothing, said the Council, in the accusations made by Italy against Ethiopia, to justify the Italians seeking redress outside the machinery of the League. On October 7th, the Council voted unanimously to accept the report; the Italian vote against, coming from a country directly involved in the dispute, did not count. Now the Council caught up quickly with events in Africa and pronounced its verdict upon the invasion: '. . . The Italian Government has resorted to war in disregard of its covenants under Article 12 of the Covenant of the League of Nations.'

There was no doubt about what had to happen next: Article 16, including the words which Simon had hoped it might be possible to find a way round, must come into force: 'Should any member of the League resort to war in disregard of its covenants under Articles 12, 13, or 15, it shall *ipso facto* be deemed to have committed an act of war against all other members of the League.' The obligation upon all members was clear: to apply sanctions. A League committee would have to be set up to consider what sanctions should operate and how.

The Cabinet met on October 9th. At that time, Hoare was still showing some of his Assembly spirit. He had seen the Italian ambassador and had told him that the deeper the penetration of Ethiopia, the more difficult it would be to negotiate. The ambassador had passed on the contents of a long private letter from Mussolini, in which the dictator complained that the British understood so little of the Italian position and suggested some kind of negotiation; he also proposed some demobilisation in the Mediterranean. The Cabinet agreed that any idea of negotiations outside the League must, for the present, be given a cool reception, and, led by Hoare, that there could be no question of cutting our Mediterranean naval forces. The Foreign Secretary suggested that Eden, at Geneva, should try to get a collective decision to lift the embargo on arms to Ethiopia. In its detailed discussion of possible sanctions, however, the Cabinet was definitely against such severe measures as the closing of the ports of League members to Italian shipping, and was insistent throughout that Britain should act only in concert with other nations; she must not find herself alone, and Eden must not take any decisions without referring back to London.

At Geneva, the Assembly was called together again. Of the fifty-four delegations there, only four failed to support the verdict reached by the Council. Italy, of course, voted against. So, too, did Hungary, Albania and Austria, which were not prepared to apply sanctions against Italy. The sanctions conference was set up and immediately went to work. The machinery of the League was functioning smoothly and quickly. The Assembly radiated an atmosphere of self-confidence, a certainty that the League would meet the challenge and prove its efficiency. Curiously, however, the proceedings were conducted in a remarkably low key. The condemnation of Italy was not accompanied by any thoughts of banishing her from respectable international society; indeed, the breaking-off of diplomatic relations, although suggested at one time by the South African delegate, was never seriously considered: the British Cabinet had dismissed the possibility without a second thought. As in London, many of the national delegations at Geneva hoped to do their duty as League members without damaging their relations with Italy. It was left to the delegate from a small, remote, unimportant country—Alfred Nemours of Haiti—to sound an unfashionably dramatic note: 'Great or small, strong or weak, near or far, white or coloured, let us never forget that one day we may be somebody's Ethiopia.'*

Eden showed himself a most positive influence in the sanctions conference. The first major decision was taken upon his proposal to stop all exports of arms to Italy at once, while allowing them to go to Ethiopia. He it was who made the suggestion, which was also accepted, to ban all loans or credits to the Italians. When he proposed an end to all Italian imports, he encountered rather more resistance. This was understandable. Mussolini could be expected to retaliate and that must mean some countries, especially the smaller, weaker ones, would get hurt. Such a sacrifice was especially hard to make, when certain other countries, notably Switzerland, Austria and Hungary, had made clear they could not go along with the embargo. The proposal was accepted, however, on the understanding that the sanctionist states would do all they could to help each other with increased trade, at the expense not only of Italy but of those countries which would not join in the collective embargo.

Within the first few days of its existence it had also agreed upon sanctions which would have the effect of depriving Italy of vital materials, such as rubber, tin and other metals, and although no date was set when this ban should begin to operate, and although the list did not include steel, coal or oil, the conference had done quite enough to convince world opinion that the League was serious in its intention to check Italy's aggression and to force her to a settlement.

But while Eden was so active in Geneva, opinion in the Cabinet at home was beginning to undergo a radical change. At the October 16th meeting, Hoare held the view that the time had not come for a change in policy—yet. But many of the doubts, hesitations and anxieties, which had been evident at earlier meetings but had been smothered, now showed themselves again. The cause of their revival was, in a word, Laval. At the Foreign Secretary's suggestion, Eden had won the support of the states supporting sanctions for a resolution committing

---

* The earlier meeting of the Assembly, before the Italian invasion, had provided for a present-day audience a portentous quotation from the South African, Charles te Water: 'The long memory of Black Africa never forgets and never forgives an injury or an injustice.'

them to the carrying out of the third paragraph of Article 16 of the Covenant. This was a most important paragraph from Britain's point of view, for it prescribed that 'the members of the League agree . . . that they will mutually support one another in resisting any special measures aimed at one of their number by the covenant-breaking state, and that they will take the necessary steps to afford passage through their territory to the forces of any of the members of the League which are co-operating to protect the covenants of the League.' But Hoare still had doubts about how far French support could be relied upon in the event of an Italian attack upon British ships or interests, and he had good reason. He had asked Laval, through the British Ambassador, for an assurance. Laval, in reply, had said that France fully supported paragraph three—but with a worrying and most surprising reservation.

'In the actual situation as presented by the British Government,' Laval had said, 'the circumstances are such that they oblige the French Government to make a reservation as to the presence in the Mediterranean of British naval forces much in excess of the effectives normally stationed in that sea. The covenant-breaking state, actually Italy, could in effect allege that it was justified in seeing in this concentration a step going beyond the application of the step actually agreed upon at Geneva for the execution of Article 16.'

Added to this, said the Foreign Secretary, the French Admiralty had refused to discuss the question of co-operation with the British naval attaché. Hoare also recalled earlier talks with Laval, and his comments take on especial interest in view of his own actions so soon afterwards.

'. . . He had on record Laval's expression of surprise that our reinforcements had not been sent earlier. Mussolini had also said that in our place he would have done the same. In these circumstances Laval's reservation was quite unjustifiable and made a deplorable impression. He seemed constantly to be intriguing behind the back of the League of Nations and ourselves with a view to some accommodation with Mussolini.' It could not be said that Hoare had not got the measure of his man.

Ministers seemed generally to agree that there could be no question of withdrawing British warships from the Mediterranean, while there was any doubt of French help and co-operation in the event of an Italian attack. One recalled French treachery at Chanak; another was in favour of instructing the French in a little hard logic, by pointing out that if they thought the British fleet reinforcements provocative enough to justify an Italian attack, then it could also be held that French fortifications and other defensive preparations were equally provocative to Germany. At which point, Baldwin urged caution, lest Britain should find herself quarrelling with France as well as Italy and all because of what was happening at Geneva. There was already a widespread impression that Eden was making the running on sanctions and, although the Foreign Secretary had said such reports were inaccurate, it was agreed that, until the doubts over the French attitude had been cleared up, 'we must go slow at Geneva.'

Eden was back in London when the Cabinet next discussed the Ethiopian issue a week later, October 23rd. Hoare had had a long and 'satisfactory' reply from Laval, but it was plainly not specific enough in its assurances of French action if the Italians were to attack the British. There was no certainty, for instance, that the French ports of Toulon and Bizerta would be open to the Royal Navy. But talk of a military détente in the Mediterranean was in the air, and, in Rome, the French had been discussing ideas for a settlement. The Foreign Secretary asked for, and received, the authority of the Cabinet to start talking at once with the Italians because 'matters were moving so fast.' But he would lay down the condition that any settlement must be within the framework of the League, a condition which Eden was to stress when he spoke in Parliament that same afternoon. For a Government about to fight a general election and whose Foreign Secretary had inspired such wild enthusiasm by his Geneva speech only six weeks before, it was the very minimum reassurance that could be offered to the electorate.

By this time, Hoare could no longer have any illusions about the American attitude. The State Department had no intention of being discovered in the act of collusion with the League. And when the Foreign Secretary again raised the question of action under the Kellogg Pact, Hull told him that the time for that had gone by, or, as Roosevelt said to the Secretary of State, such action seemed 'somewhat farfetched after the horse is out of the stable.'* The American Administration officially discouraged trade with both Italy and Ethiopia, but it had no legal powers to stop businessmen trading with whatever country they liked and the value of 'discouragement' was proved to be negligible.

The Cabinet felt that, despite the election campaign, Eden could not be spared from Geneva. Even Hoare himself went there. He joined Laval at the sanctions conference. Any delegates who rejoiced at their presence did so prematurely. True, they said the right things in support of the resolution embodying the decisions about sanctions and fixing the date on which they should start, but that was not their real purpose in being there. They wished with their presence to muffle criticism of their talks with the Italians. They were successful. The other delegates were surprised to be told that talks were going on at all, and their suspicions of what the big powers were doing were alert, but they could hardly come out openly against another attempt to settle the dispute, particularly when Hoare and Laval proclaimed their ardent loyalty to the League and the Covenant, for whom they were but as agents in treating with Mussolini.

There was some short, probably unavoidable delay in imposing the more severe of the sanctions, banning Italian imports and the sale to Italy of important metals and materials. They could not start until November 18th. Nevertheless, a serious beginning had been made, and Mussolini had worse to fear when the Canadians proposed extending the embargo to cover materials vital both to the Italian economy and to his ability to wage war: iron and steel; coal and coke; and, above all, oil. It is as certain as anything can be that, even without American co-operation, the imposition of such an embargo would have had a most effective influence upon Mussolini, the war, and hence upon the future of the League and perhaps of European and world peace. No immediate decision was taken on the Canadian proposal, but the possibility of it being accepted when the conference met again towards the end of November remained a real one. World opinion was mobilising against Italy. Here and there, its hostility was translated into action, when workers took restrictive action against Italian goods or Italian orders. In Ethiopia, although the Italian

* Op. cit. p. 433.

army had advanced with predictable ease, it was taking its time about it and, to Mussolini, it looked as though time was one thing he had not got. Imaginative, hyperbolic newspaper stories from the front about the glory, the courage and the chivalry of the Italian conquerors were all very well for popular consumption, but what he needed was a quick and total victory. Even in a dictatorship, people could tire of being fed on rhetoric; they wanted solid evidence of the new Roman empire to justify the risks and the sacrifices. Mussolini could feel the pressure on him.

Laval came to the rescue. He bought Mussolini an important fortnight's respite by asking for the Geneva meeting to consider the much tougher sanctions to be put off until December 12th. Every day that went by meant another day for Italy to build up her supplies. And, if the attitude of certain members of the British Cabinet were to prevail, the oil sanction would never be imposed at all. Now that the general election was behind them, they felt no longer the need to pretend. The National Government had won the election with a very substantial majority. The British people had given their confidence to the men who had proclaimed their dedication to the League and collective security: to solid Stanley Baldwin; to Neville Chamberlain, that epitome of straight-dealing who spoke with a depth of passion about the shame that would fall upon generation after generation of Englishmen and women if Britain were to betray Ethiopia; to Samuel Hoare, a gentleman of culture and honour. The Opposition parties did not stand a chance against such competition and, indeed, the Labour party was rent with such confusion—some, like Attlee, supporting the ideal of collective security, but denying the need to rearm; some, like Lansbury, incorrigible pacifists; some, like Cripps, associating the League with the evil machinations of western capitalism—it was incapable of a coherent foreign policy.

When the new Cabinet met on December 2nd, the Foreign Secretary analysed the pros and cons of an oil embargo with such subtlety and such tortuousness that no-one could have accused him fairly of having a definite opinion on the subject. There was a risk, said Hoare, that Mussolini would react to an oil embargo like 'a mad dog.' On the other hand, Britain must not adopt a negative attitude. 'It might be said that all the member-states of the League of Nations except ourselves had expressed their willingness to support the oil sanctions and of the non-member states the only one that counted [America] was bringing pressure to bear' on the oil companies. Propaganda was being made in the United States and France, said Hoare, for the British failure to define their position. '. . . We were being reproached that we led in sanctions until the moment when our own interests were affected.' On the other hand, there were serious gaps in Britain's defence system, compared with an Italy prepared for war. On the other hand, 'rather to his surprise, he had learned that the Governor of the Bank of England was favourable to strong sanctions on the ground that they would bring the matter to a head rapidly and that the long drawn-out application of sanctions would bring about a serious situation.' He had also had a message from Sir Austen Chamberlain, who had had a talk with Herriot, at that time a minister without portfolio in the French Government; Herriot had said that Laval and Parisian opinion, in their opposition to sanctions, were not representative of France, and that Britain should go ahead with an oil embargo. On the other hand, it might be better to keep the threat of an oil sanction hanging over Mussolini's head. The important thing, said Hoare, was to press on with the peace negotiations as rapidly as possible. Hoare, who had not been well, was going to Switzerland for a holiday, but he proposed to stop off on his way in Paris, to talk about possible terms for a settlement with Laval.

Several voices at that Cabinet urged caution and talked of the weakness of the Royal Navy and the RAF in the Mediterranean. Baldwin was all for postponing the oil embargo, to gain time for peace talks. It had to be remembered, said the Prime Minister, 'that in dealing with Mussolini we were not dealing with a normal kind of intellect. . . .' One Cabinet minister expressed his concern lest Mussolini should be forced to surrender and disappear from Italian politics, because he would be succeeded by a communist government. Only two men spoke in the pre-election spirit: Duff Cooper, who had joined the Cabinet as war minister, and Eden, who faced the unpleasant prospect of stalling for time at Geneva.

Hoare told the Cabinet that talks in Paris at the official level— the Foreign Office man there was Maurice Peterson—were not making much progress. But when he arrived in Paris five days later, there was little more he was expected to do beyond approving the package placed before him. As Eden has written in his memoirs, 'To this day I am unable to understand how Hoare could think that the proposals he agreed with Laval were compatible with his own speech, so much a personal declaration of faith and action, made to the Assembly at Geneva only three months before.'*

Eden might well have been as incredulous, as the rest of the world was appalled, by the terms of the settlement which Hoare was prepared to put to Haile Selassie as the price for buying off Mussolini. They demanded far greater sacrifices by the Emperor than the settlement proposed by Laval and Eden in August. He was to be asked to give Italy a large part of his territory in the north and south-east, where it was adjacent to the Italian colonies, and, in addition, about half of the country would be reserved exclusively for Italian exploitation and settlement, the top administrators coming from Italy, ostensibly on behalf of the League. The only compensation for Ethiopia would be an outlet to the sea. Haile Selassie was being called upon to pay a crippling bill for the privilege of being invaded by Italy and protected by the League of Nations.

To make matters worse, details of the plan were leaked to the Paris press, even before they were known to the British Cabinet. But the Cabinet was more fortunate than the Emperor. It had been Laval's idea that Mussolini should have a chance of considering the proposals first, before they were revealed either to the League Council, on whose behalf the British and French were supposed to be negotiating, or to Haile Selassie, who was supposed to be the victim of aggression. It was only after pressure from London that Laval agreed that the terms could be communicated to Addis Adaba at the same time as Rome. In doing so, he implied that he had made a big concession, and, indeed, he first offered it only on condition of a British Government pledge not to support any extension of sanctions if, as Laval expected, Ethiopia turned down the settlement. The Cabinet

* Op. cit. p. 310.

refused to give such a binding undertaking, and Laval at last consented to the Emperor being told at the same time as the Duce. The British Cabinet, while being generally agreed that this was only fair to the Emperor, also agreed that he should be 'strongly pressed' to accept the proposals as a basis for discussion or, at least, not to reject them.

With Hoare, after spending two days in Paris, now off on holiday, it fell to Eden to explain the proposals to the Cabinet on December 9th. 'Eden, while supporting the Foreign Secretary's proposals,' says the official record, 'felt bound to warn his colleagues that some features of the proposals were likely to prove very distasteful to some state members of the League of Nations, including states represented on the committee of five. He said also that Laval, while stating that France would honour her obligations to the League and its member states in the event of an Italian aggression as the result of further sanctions, had made clear in the conversations that sanctions were unpopular to an important section of French public opinion.'

In the light of what is now known, it is clear that with Vansittart (who was in Paris) and the Foreign Office pushing him on from one side, and with Laval on the other, threatening to drop sanctions if Britain should refuse to agree the terms and making quite plain that, if it came to war with Italy, French help would be minimal, Hoare was bound to abandon any resistance. And, until it proved expedient to abandon him, his Cabinet colleagues in London also approved the proposals.

Eden supported them, too, in so far as he did not actively oppose them. But he was well aware of the storm building up, not only in England, where newspaper speculation about the terms had already started the alarm bells ringing, but also in the world at large. Malcolm MacDonald, Ramsay's son, who had become Dominions Secretary in the new Government, told the Cabinet on December 11th of the concern felt by all the high commissioners in London, except the Australian, about the effect the terms of the settlement would have upon public opinion in their own countries, and upon their governments. It may be presumed that Eden was most acutely conscious that it would be his job to present the proposals at Geneva and, on the eve of his departure, he discussed with the Cabinet the line he should take.

He said he hoped he would not be expected to champion the proposals in detail. What he did ask for, and receive, was the authority to resist any attempt by Laval—who had told him of his intention—to weaken the proposals still further in Italy's favour. But when he said that, if it should come to a choice between risking an attack by the Italians or the collapse of the League, he would consider the former the lesser evil, he was reminded that there must be no question of becoming involved in hostilities without the French.

As the Cabinet had hoped, Eden and Laval managed to avoid any talk about an oil embargo when they attended the meeting of the 18-nation sanctions committee. It was agreed that, as the Italians and Ethiopians were considering the Anglo-French proposals and the Council itself must soon meet to discuss them, it would be unwise to examine the possibility of extending sanctions.

The Council was to meet six days later, on December 18th. In the course of those six days, the death of the proposed settlement as a basis for fresh negotiations became certain. The Ethiopian Emperor asked for the League Assembly to be called together for a public debate on the proposals. The Cabinet was told on the 17th of a telegram from the British Minister at Addis Ababa stating that the Emperor and his advisers were 'bewildered' by the British Government's association with such terms. Eden also told of a talk between Vansittart and the Italian Ambassador, who gave the impression that Mussolini 'was not very enamoured,' either. That was a very discreet version of what Mussolini felt and said in public in Italy about the proposals.

When the details of the Hoare-Laval plan were published for all the world to see, the effect upon confidence in the League, which had been so buoyant, was disastrous. The reputation of the British Government suffered similarly. The Cabinet discussed arguments by which the proposals—and therefore the Government's good name—might be defended. Chamberlain had talked to Hoare and reported his views to the meeting. It was evident that the Foreign Secretary was out of touch with public opinion. He took up a somewhat truculent attitude, saying that the League of Nations must face the realities of the situation. There was no chance of getting anything much better than the Paris terms because the League could not dictate to Mussolini. It was impossible to contemplate sterner sanctions or the risk of war unless all members of the League were ready to contribute to collective action. That, the Cabinet agreed, might be an argument for not extending sanctions or risking war, but it was no justification for the terms put forward in the Hoare-Laval plan. After some discussion, the Cabinet recognised, in effect, that the terms were not capable of being justified. Eden was left to make the best of a bad job. He had to go back to Geneva to try to save what he could, by adopting the argument that Britain and France had never had any vested interest in the proposals: they had merely been carrying out the invidious task, entrusted to them by the League, of trying to find a formula to restore peace; it was for the three parties concerned, Italy, Ethiopia and the League, to decide whether the plan offered any basis for conciliation.

The formal answer to that came at the public meeting of the Council. Laval's pretence that a decision must rest upon the replies of Italy and Ethiopia was soon shattered by a comprehensive criticism of them, verbally and in a prepared paper, by the Ethiopian delegate, Wolde Mariam, who also expressed the resentment and shock felt by his countrymen. He ended with an appeal, not for military help, but for money to help Ethiopia to buy the arms with which to defend herself. There were no other speeches, no further discussion of the plan, no vote upon it: it just died.

In Britain, the Government faced formidable opposition, even within the Conservative party, where it sought the leadership of Austen Chamberlain to give it coherence and a name still respected by the people and feared by the Cabinet. Chamberlain, the epitome of British integrity in international affairs, was appalled by Hoare's behaviour, and went to Baldwin, with a League of Nations Union delegation, for an explanation. Austen Chamberlain might, had he chosen, have led a revolt to bring down the Government. He decided otherwise, but the violent sense of outrage in Parliament and in the country at what was seen as an act of blatant treachery towards the League by a Government newly elected to sustain it, had to be appeased. Hoare was sacked. Eden became Foreign Secretary.

Anthony Eden has explained why he did not resign at the time of the Hoare-Laval proposals: he had not had control of policy or the power to affect decisions in the earlier stages of the dispute. It is easy to believe that he would have taken a stronger line on sanctions and would not have acquiesced in the decision to leave Ethiopia virtually unarmed. By the time he became Foreign Secretary, it was too late for one man to repair the damage. The League, like the British Cabinet, was demoralised by the Anglo-French attempt to force Ethiopia into surrender. There was, momentarily, a hope that Eden, who represented, in Britain as at Geneva, a positive belief in the Covenant, would restore a sense of leadership. But it was impossible to recapture the impetus and self-confidence with which the sanctions conference had set about its work in the period immediately following upon the Italian invasion, and, at home, the forces of caution and inaction within the Cabinet always managed to stifle any impulse towards tougher sanctions. Even now, there were senior members of the Government who believed it possible for Britain to do her bit as a good member of the League and also to retain the friendship of Italy. The Cabinet was not even willing to help Ethiopia financially. The means of doing so had been provided by the League Assembly in 1930—a treaty of financial assistance for the victim of aggression—but the British Government seized on the fact that the treaty had never been ratified as the excuse for instructing Eden not to raise the possibility of aiding Ethiopia nor to support any proposal to do so. The Council, at its January, 1936, meeting, took the same attitude, and the Ethiopian delegation went away empty-handed.

Despite everything, Haile Selassie continued to look to Britain, and to Britain alone, in trust. As the Italians—now commanded by Badoglio, with Mussolini's orders to get on with the job—began to make significant advances, the Emperor sent a telegram to His Britannic Majesty, combining a reproach with an embarrassing suggestion that his country, without yielding its independence, should be tied to Britain by a mandate or as a protectorate. The telegram was dated February 20th, 1936, and it contained this passage:

'Because England has been the main defender of the case we were hoping England would have aided us in a way which would not have touched her honour integrity or armed forces by giving us arms ammunition and loans to carry on our defensive fight. But though it has been judged against Italy that she was an aggressor she has not found a way to help the aggressed state neither to stop the war nor to strengthen us.'

Eden made very plain, through the British Minister at Addis Ababa, that Britain could have nothing to do with any suggestion for a British mandate or protectorate over Ethiopia. Nor was he keen to get mixed up in playing, as the Emperor also suggested, the role of conciliator, bringing together the two sides with the aim of agreeing an armistice. That sort of work, Eden stressed, must be left to the committee of five appointed by the Council.

Although the Emperor had stated, in his telegram, that sanctions taken against Italy had been both inadequate and ineffective, they had made a definite impact upon the Italian economy. Had they been reinforced and extended early in 1936, it might still have been possible to influence Mussolini's conduct. The question of an oil embargo did come up again in the sanctions committee and a body of experts was set up to examine how effective it might be—a move Baldwin had advocated repeatedly, though probably as a means of procrastination. It was not until February 12th that the experts reported, but what they had to say was most encouraging to those who had been advocating a sanction on oil. The two most important findings in their report were that an embargo could bring about the exhaustion of Italy's resources within a matter of months, and that this could be achieved, even if the United States were to take no action to limit sales to Italy, provided other nations would refuse to allow the Italians the use of their tankers.

The conclusion about American exports of oil was especially relevant and reassuring. For all Cordell Hull's pride in it, the 'moral embargo' on essential war materials, including oil, was not working. Hull had expressed to the British Ambassador his impatience with the sanctions conference for its failure to impose an oil embargo, contrasting the expediency of Geneva with the bold, unselfish attitude of the United States, a non-member. But the American oil companies were indifferent to the concept of morality. Far from restricting oil exports to Italy, they continued to increase them substantially. As Hull himself wrote in his memoirs, 'A moral embargo is effective only as to persons who are moral.'* An attempt by Roosevelt and Hull to get a bill through Congress, making the moral embargo a legal one, and restricting the export of essential war materials to normal levels, foundered in January, 1936. The Secretary of State explained the intensification of isolationist feeling as a reaction to the failure of the League to combat aggression and disgust with Anglo-French ditherings.

Those critical spectators of the European drama would not have found much to dissuade them if they could have eavesdropped upon the British Cabinet meeting on February 26th, when oil sanctions were discussed. True, the Cabinet ended with acceptance of Eden's view that the League ought to impose an embargo. But that conclusion was reached only after an assembly of a formidable list of objections. Among these were that an embargo would not prove effective; that the Americans could not be relied upon to co-operate; that Italy could always get the oil she wanted from Venezuela; that it would necessitate interference with the use of tankers and that carried economic and political risks; that Britain had already borne the principal burden of sanctions; that 30,000 miners were about to lose their jobs because of the loss of coal exports to Italy; and that Britain's aim should be to get into such a position that, 'whenever peace was signed between Italy and Abyssinia we should be strong enough to recover our Italian trade and nothing should be done to jeopardise it.' Eyres-Monsell, the First Lord of the Admiralty, harped on a theme to which he was to return time and again during the coming months: that it was time to reduce naval strength in the Mediterranean and to bring back some of the men who were long overdue for leave.

Not all these objections went unanswered. There would be no interference with tankers of countries which did not agree to co-operate. There was absolutely no question of a blockade. When it came to sacrifices, Britain was not alone in bearing the burden of sanctions: one-third of Yugoslavia's total trade was affected. The coal trade with Italy had been virtually dead even before the start of sanctions, because Italy could not pay her bills. The Dominions would support Britain and failure to apply

* Op. cit. p. 460.

oil sanctions would deal a fatal blow to the prestige of the League. So Eden received his authority to back an oil embargo and to try to get it applied as soon as other members of the sanctions committee of 18 would agree to it. But Monsell and Runciman, the President of the Board of Trade, both asked for their dissent to be recorded, and Eden was asked by the Cabinet to try to avoid taking the lead at Geneva and to carry out the Government's policy 'with as little publicity to himself as possible.' Which was something less than full-blooded support for a new initiative.

Nearly three weeks had passed since the experts had presented their report on an oil embargo, before the sanctions committee met again at Geneva. During that period, the governments of the nations forming that committee had been considering what their attitude should be. When the delegates came together on March 2nd, the only outcome was a further postponement. The cause was France. Laval had gone, but his successor, Flandin, was just as determined upon finding ways of pleasing Mussolini. At Geneva, he proposed that the Council, through its special committee, should make one more effort to end the war by conciliation. While agreeing, Eden did announce Britain's support for an oil embargo, and said she would favour its application if conciliation should fail once more. It was an honourable gesture and one that many of his colleagues probably regarded as gratuitous, but it was to prove the last occasion when the possibility of extended sanctions had really existed. Although both the Emperor and, several days later, Mussolini, accepted the Council committee's call to take part in negotiations, the situation was radically changed by Hitler's denunciation of the Locarno Treaty and his reoccupation of the Rhineland by the German Army.

That happened on March 7th. Had any doubt remained of Mussolini's total victory in Ethiopia, Hitler's action made it certain. The French were now obsessed with the need to get Italian support against the Germans: for that they were prepared to pay almost any price and Ethiopian independence became an irrelevance. The sooner sanctions could be lifted and the war in Africa ended the better. Opinion within the British Cabinet was, sometimes more discreetly expressed, moving towards the same conclusion. The service ministers, in particular, wanted to see an end to the emergency in the Mediterranean so that ships, aircraft and men could be brought back to where the need for them was now greater.

But the British Government had to proceed with circumspection. As Neville Chamberlain pointed out in Cabinet on March 19th, if sanctions were taken off before peace was in sight there would be political trouble in the country. Nor would all members of the League be happy to see the end of sanctions in return for a mere truce. Once raised, the Government recognised well enough, sanctions could never be applied again.

Mussolini's response to conciliation was an intensification of the war against Ethiopia. By now the Italians had discarded all pretence to scruple and in pursuit of their civilising mission they employed indiscriminate bombing of open towns and hospitals and the widespread spraying, by aircraft, of mustard gas, which knew no distinction between women and children and warriors. On April 6th, 1936, Eden reported to the Cabinet on a visit from a special Ethiopian envoy, who had told him his country's situation was now 'desperate.' Eden had set the machinery in motion whereby Madariaga was to call a meeting of the Council committee to discuss conciliation and the use of poison gas by Italy. The Foreign Secretary was to speak in a Commons debate that same afternoon and he wanted to rehearse his statement of what the Government had done and was proposing to do.

He would report, he said, that a meeting would be held to consider the possibility of conciliation. If that did not achieve any result, it would be necessary to summon the committee of 18 to consider further sanctions. 'We were prepared to use any measures of an economic or financial character which the other nations were prepared jointly to apply. He wished to consider at Geneva if anything positive could be done to assist Abyssinia. The only effective action at the moment would be the closing of the Suez Canal. France was likely to oppose further sanctions, but he wished to take the attitude he had suggested in order to satisfy British public opinion.'

Eden was right, of course, to think he could propose almost any step, no matter how bold, because there was no likelihood of it leading to joint action. The Cabinet was now concerned only with the problem of getting out of a disagreeable situation with as much political credit as possible. No measures against Italy which the Government was willing to contemplate could possibly do anything to save Ethiopia. The thought of closing Suez, which would certainly have been, from the beginning, the most effective single act, had never been seriously considered. It would have involved the risk of war with Italy, and Baldwin said repeatedly in Cabinet he was not going to support any action which carried that risk.

For all his efforts, Madariaga, as could have been predicted, failed to find a formula for successful conciliation. Mussolini had been happy to pretend interest in order to give himself more time and protect himself against the possibility, however remote, of an oil embargo. The sanctionist powers had often debated the ifs and buts of an oil sanction on the assumption that time was on their side, because the rains would come again before the Italians had finished their conquest of Ethiopia. But the brave, ill-equipped Ethiopians could not hold back their final defeat.

When the Council met on April 20th, Addis Ababa had still to fall, but it could be only a matter of days. Aloisi came to the Council and demanded, as the price of a truce, the Emperor's acceptance of Italian occupation of the whole of his country. Wolde Mariam, for Ethiopia, called for the League to impose the oil embargo forthwith. There were a few token expressions of willingness to consider an extension of sanctions—Eden's among them—but no serious move was made to do so. At least it could be said that the Council voted almost unanimously to continue with existing sanctions—Ecuador was the only exception—and roundly condemned Italy's use of poison gas, a deliberate breach of the 1925 Protocol, which Italy had signed. That condemnation stung Aloisi, himself a civilised man who had come to the Council to trumpet his country's success in bringing civilisation to Ethiopia. But this was a Council confessing its failure. As Eden said to his colleagues upon his return from Geneva, 'apart from the representatives of Portugal, Denmark and Australia, who shared our general view as to the importance of this matter from the point of view of the future of the League, hardly anyone had been thinking of Abyssinia and Africa at all.' Most delegates were thinking of the European situation and how Italy's victory in Africa would affect it. Eden himself took the opportunity, during a brief talk with Aloisi, to repeat what Baldwin had said in a speech, that the British Government's action in the dispute 'was in no sense anti-Italian, but only a fulfilment of the obligations we bore under the Covenant.'

A week later, on April 29th, the First Lord of the Admiralty, was pleading the need to bring the Home Fleet back from the Mediterranean, now that the danger of war was over. But his colleagues, led by Eden, saw how politically explosive such a move would be. Internationally, it would be interpreted as abandoning Ethiopia to her fate and would have the worst possible effect 'on uninstructed opinion' at home.

At that meeting, Eden posed some questions about the future of the League which, merely by being asked, summed up the futility and impotence to which the League must be condemned for the rest of its life:

'Could it survive the failure of sanctions to rescue Abyssinia? If so, could it survive in its present form? Could it ever impose sanctions again? Probably there had never been such a clear-cut case for sanctions. If the League had failed in this case there could probably be no confidence that it could succeed in the future . . . Should it be made clear that we ourselves, after the failure in the case of Italy, did not feel under any obligation to apply sanctions?' As he looked to the immediate future, Eden saw the position of the League Council at its meeting on May 11th, when he was to take the chair, as a humiliating one.

The speed at which the situation then developed surprised even those who, like Eden, had already accepted that the Italian invasion of Ethiopia had been completely successful. There had been a general expectation that the Emperor, although he might be forced to quit the capital, would carry on the fight, in guerrilla fashion, in those parts of the country which were almost impossible of occupation by a modern European army. Such a fight did continue, but without Haile Selassie's personal leadership. On May 2nd, he left his kingdom. On May 6th, Italian forces went into Addis Ababa. Three days later, Mussolini publicly proclaimed the unqualified annexation of Ethiopia and conferred upon King Victor Emmanuel III the title of Emperor of that country. The Duce boasted of the founding of that new Italian empire he had promised his people in so many bombastic speeches.

When the Council assembled in Geneva on May 11th, they heard from Haile Selassie—in a telegram from Jerusalem—his reasons for having chosen exile. 'We have decided,' he said, 'to put an end to the most sweeping, the most unjust, and the most inhuman war of modern times, by leaving the country in order to avoid the extermination of the Abyssinian people. . . . We now ask the League of Nations to pursue its efforts to ensure the respect of the Covenant and to decide not to recognise territorial extensions or the exercise of an alleged sovereignty resulting from illegal recourse to armed force and many other violations of international obligations.'

Even before it had begun its business, the Council was forced to answer that appeal; it was in response to a challenge, not from the Ethiopians, but the Italians. It arose out of a discussion of the agenda. The eighteenth item read: 'Dispute between Ethiopia and Italy'. In accordance with the prescribed practice for dealing with an issue where a party to a dispute was not a member of the Council, Eden, as president, called the Ethiopian delegate, the grey-haired, bearded Wolde Mariam, to take his place at the far end of the Council table.

That single, procedural action provoked another of those dramatic moments which colour the history of the League, although this one was played with few histrionics. In his customary cool and reserved manner, employing neither passion nor emphasis, the Italian delegate, Aloisi, delivered a short statement in French. The Italian delegation, he said, could not consent to the presence of the so-called Ethiopian delegate at the Council table. No sort of organisation existed in Ethiopia and the only existing sovereignty was that of Italy. Any discussion of the Italian-Ethiopian dispute would therefore be purposeless and Italy could have no part of it. When he had finished speaking, Aloisi stood up and walked out of the room, followed by the staff of his delegation. To his departing back, Mariam declared that there was still an Ethiopian government and that Ethiopia, a member of the League, a victim of aggression, had not violated international law. The outburst was understandable, but Eden cut in upon the Ethiopian to point out that the Council's only concern at that moment was to decide whether the item should remain on the agenda. He held that it should. The Spanish and Danish delegates gave him strong support, and there was no opposition. Of little practical value though it was, the Council had refused, at the first bidding, to recognise the *fait accompli* of the Italian conquest. Baron Aloisi returned to his place a short while afterwards, when the Council had moved on to other business. But the following afternoon, acting upon direct instructions from Mussolini, the entire Italian delegation left Geneva by train. Aloisi made a formal call upon Avenol, the Secretary-General, but offered no explanation for his withdrawal.

There was little inclination in Geneva to exaggerate the importance of the Council's gesture in upholding Ethiopia's procedural rights as a member of the League. The Ethiopians themselves were aware—and said so publicly—that they had been abandoned by the League. The smaller powers, which had joined the League for the security against aggression they could not provide for themselves, were conscious that what had happened to Ethiopia could happen just as easily to them. The pretence of resistance by the League to the Italian action was upheld for just a few more weeks. The Council passed a resolution to maintain sanctions while member-governments had a chance to 'consider the situation created by the grave new steps taken by the Italian Government.' The Council would return to the subject in a month's time.

The decencies of burial and mourning were but thinly observed. Pressure built up quickly for a recognition of the facts of life. Governments yielded easily to the tug of national interest. Traditionally neutral nations were anxious to resume their neutrality with the least possible delay, although Switzerland's observance of sanctions, for instance, had, anyway, been considerably less than strict. The Americans were merely waiting for word that the patient was really dead, or, at any rate, was so feeble he would be no trouble to anyone, before lifting the arms embargo. Most outrageously of all, the League's Secretary-General was blatant in his advocacy of acknowledging Mussolini's victory, of forgetting the sometime representatives of a backward African country, and of getting the Italians back to the Council table where they belonged.

The argument was not quite over, however. There were still strong voices—particularly those representing the smaller European powers and the Dominions—insisting that Italian victory could not and must not change or diminish the obligations of other member-countries under the Covenant. The British Cabinet was uncertain of what it should do. There were those who urged, more and more openly as the days and weeks went by, that this country should make a clean end of it all and get back to normal trade with Italy. Others certainly wanted that, too, but were afraid of the political consequences at home of any unseemly haste. Eden led those who argued for keeping existing sanctions and for doing nothing which would imply a weakening of the British position, but he encountered increasingly strong opposition, particularly from the First Lord, who hammered away at the need to relieve the Mediterranean Fleet.

The defeated Emperor, Haile Selassie, presented a particular embarrassment. On May 18th, Eden reported to the Cabinet that 'on enquiry he had established that we had not the right to keep the Emperor of Abyssinia in Palestine. It was not clear, either, how we were to prevent him coming to this country if he wished to do so. The question then arose as to the route by which he should travel. The first possibility was the overland route, but this was difficult because arrangements would have to be made in so many countries. The alternative was by sea, either in a liner or a warship. If he were to travel in a British liner there was danger that the Italians might try to stop him, 'and it would be very awkward if they did.' The Cabinet agreed that Eden should tell Haile Selassie that Britain would not hinder him from leaving Palestine or prevent a visit here, but he would have to make his own arrangements for the journey: it was impossible to place a British cruiser at his disposal.

Two days later, the question came up again and the response was just a shade more gracious. The Foreign Secretary told the Cabinet the Emperor was ill and was proposing to go to a sanatorium in Germany. Eden had let him know that the British Government would not object, of course, and nor would there be any objection to his coming to Britain, so long as he travelled incognito and limited his suite to no more than, say, six persons. The Government was even prepared to offer the Emperor passage in one of HM warships, but only as far as Gibraltar; he would have to work out for himself how he and his party were to get from there to London.

As the time for the June Council meeting drew nearer, the British Cabinet was looking more and more actively for a way to drop sanctions. But it still hoped to save its own face and that of the League by extracting from Mussolini some public declaration of good intent for the future, including, perhaps, a promise to report annually on developments in Ethiopia, an assurance that he would not raise a 'black army,' and, above all, that he would join a united front against Hitler. With fears of a German attack on Austria, this last consideration weighed most heavily in the Cabinet's thinking. As far as Baldwin was concerned, nothing else really mattered. There remained, however, the difficulty of getting out of sanctions without incurring the censure of the rest of the world. In particular, there was a new uncertainty about how the French would react. A new Government had taken over in France, the Popular Front, led by Leon Blum, and representing very different views about sanctions from those of Flandin and Laval. The British Cabinet recognised the risk that if Britain were to call for an end to sanctions, ahead of other nations, the French might then turn round and say they would have been prepared to continue them.

Nevertheless, it was the British Government which did take the initiative, after all. Or, it might be said more accurately, was pushed into it by the extraordinary behaviour of Neville Chamberlain, then Chancellor of the Exchequer. Extraordinary, because Chamberlain turned a political somersault, without warning to his colleagues and, most importantly, without warning to Anthony Eden. At the Cabinet of May 27th, 1936, it had been Chamberlain who had been among the most influential voices in favour of keeping sanctions. Chamberlain had said then that Mussolini might respond and be ready to co-operate with Britain and France in Europe, if we were to offer to raise sanctions. But, he added, this advantage would be offset by the effect on British public opinion. 'The Italians had behaved so badly that it would be impossible morally and, indeed, almost indecent to come to terms with them.'

Chamberlain had thrown out a hint at that meeting of the way his mind might jump, if he should see the French being awkward or if there were a danger of forcing the Italians into too isolated and alienated a condition. He had also indicated that he thought it would be a mistake to refuse to acknowledge Italy's position in Ethiopia. Similar action over Manchuria, he said, had proved a great embarrassment. But none of this could have prepared his colleagues for his speech to a group of Tory MPs on June 10th, only two weeks later, when he held that the maintenance of sanctions would be 'the very midsummer of madness.' He made that speech just five days before the League Council was due to meet again. Eden was saved from the embarrassment of trying to justify it, or of explaining it away, because the Council took up a proposal from Argentina for the Ethiopian issue to be considered by the Assembly of the League and a meeting was called for June 30th.

Chamberlain's view was taken throughout the world, however, as the corporate view of the British Government, and there was no will within the Cabinet to disown it. Indeed, for all his understandable shock and resentment of Chamberlain's action, the Cabinet minutes reveal that at its meeting that same day, June 10th, Eden himself was coming round to much the same decision, if for different reasons. He said that 'the French Government was unlikely to take any initiative at Geneva but was likely to confirm our own attitude. This was as much as could be expected of them. He was rather veering towards the view that if sanctions were to be removed there was something to be said for our taking the initiative.' It was then his intention to meet his French colleagues a few days before the Assembly. On June 17th, however, in advance of any such consultation, Eden received the approval of the Cabinet for an announcement to the House of Commons that Britain would take the lead in proposing at Geneva an end to sanctions. The record states specifically that he was to do so without previous consultation either with the French or the Italian 'or, indeed, any other Foreign Government,' although he did propose to see the French Ambassador and the diplomatic representatives in London of Greece, Turkey and Yugoslavia, to let them know in advance the general line he intended to take in Parliament. Eden's statement, coming as it did from the man who, probably more than any other individual statesman at that time, represented respect for the authority of the League and the obligations of the Covenant, and coming from the Foreign Secretary of the country whose policy, more than any other's, would determine the mood and action of the Assembly, killed off the last frail hopes.

But at the Assembly, especially among the smaller powers, feelings of outrage and betrayal smouldered. They flared up in reaction to the appeal by Haile Selassie, described at the beginning of this chapter. 'I ask the 52 nations not to forget today the policy upon which they embarked eight months ago. . . . It is the very existence of the League of Nations . . . it is international morality that is at stake . . . God and history will remember your judgement . . .' The League, led by Britain, inspired by the noble words of Samuel Hoare, had held out to the Emperor the certain promise to defend him against aggression. Now, so impatient were some countries to have done with the whole embarrassing business, that they wanted to deny him the opportunity of addressing the Assembly at all. There was a move to that effect in the steering committee, and Motta, the Swiss Foreign Minister, spoke in favour of it, but Eden was not prepared to swallow it. As president, he held that the Emperor had a perfect right to speak.

Eden's own speech on the following day was an unconvincing attempt to combine realism with idealism. It was unconvincing because nothing he could have said could have made the decision to end sanctions palatable.

'Had His Majesty's Government,' said the Foreign Secretary, 'any reason to believe the maintenance of existing sanctions, or even the addition to them of other economic measures, would re-establish the position in Abyssinia, then, for their part, they would be prepared to advocate such a policy and, if other members of the League agreed, to join in its application.' Because no such agreement was conceivable there was no danger of Britain's offer being tested; it was, therefore, one which Eden could make without misgiving. In the view of his government, he said, only military action by the League could restore the *status quo* in Ethiopia. 'I cannot believe,' he added, 'that, in present world conditions, such military action could be considered

363

a possibility.' He was right, of course, and it would have been better if he had left it at that. But Eden had to try to rescue some comfort, some easement of conscience from what was, in truth, a situation of moral squalor.

'. . . If I have tried to indicate, with a heavy heart,' he said, 'some of the lessons of recent months, it is not because I believe that His Majesty's Government in the United Kingdom or the League of Nations need proffer any apology for having made an attempt which has no parallel in history. However deeply, however sincerely, we may deplore its outcome, we cannot regret, nor, I think, will history regret, that the attempt was made.'

Eden was trying to turn the facts on their heads. What was to be regretted was not that the attempt at collective action against an aggressor had been made, but that it was not sustained.

Leon Blum made his first speech to the Assembly that same day. His enthusiasm for the League, his support for the principles of the Covenant, his talk of arbitration in international affairs, of disarmament and of a peace guaranteed by collective security, could have been uttered by his celebrated predecessor, Briand. But the year was 1936, not 1926. In Blum's mind, his brave assertion of France's readiness to risk herself in any European conflict for the sake of an 'indivisible peace' was probably more than an oratorical flourish. His audience, understandably, failed to respond.

As so often during the Ethiopian crisis, te Water, the South African delegate, stripped away the humbug. The Covenant was falling to pieces in their hands, he told the Assembly, urging the maintenance of sanctions. Fifty nations, led by the three of the most powerful nations in the world, were about to declare their powerlessness to protect the weakest in their midst from destruction. The authority of the League was about to come to nought. But it was the Irish Prime Minister, de Valera, who put into words the fears that possessed that Assembly.

'Read the speech delivered by the Emperor of Abyssinia,' he said. 'Does any delegate deny that, as far as it relates what has happened here, there is, to his knowledge, truth in every line of it? Is there any small nation represented here which does not feel the truth of this warning, that what is Abyssinia's fate today may well be its own fate tomorrow, should the greed or the ambitions of some powerful neighbour prompt its destruction?'

The Assembly dragged on to its shabby, humiliating, but now inevitable conclusion, although not without some bitter argument within the steering committee. So far as sanctions were concerned, the formal task of ending them was delegated to the sanctions conference. What caused even more acrimony was the demand of the smaller powers, particularly those of South and Central America, for a declaration that member-nations of the League would never recognise Italian sovereignty over Ethiopia, never condone, in other words, a territorial conquest by force. The great powers, especially Britain and France, were anxious not to pass any formal resolution which would make future collaboration with Italy more difficult. The committee arrived at a formula, designed to appease the Latin-American delegates, without giving any explicit undertaking not to recognise the Italian annexation. The fourth paragraph of the resolution declared the League's continuing attachment to the principles of the Covenant, 'principles which also find their expression in other diplomatic instruments, such as the declaration of the South American states of August 3, 1932, which excludes the settlement by force of territorial questions.' The Mexican delegation, however, refused to take any further part in the Assembly as a mark of its disapproval. Panama denounced the resolution as not consistent with international justice or compatible with the prestige of the League.

The Assembly met at noon on July 4th in a morose funereal atmosphere. Yet certain delegations still refused to be hustled through the business of passing the resolution, as the president, van Zeeland, had intended. There might even have been an open revolt had any sufficiently strong leader been forthcoming. As it was, there were more speeches, notably that of the Ethiopian, Ras Nasibu, who insisted on being heard and who made an appeal to the Assembly to express its unambiguous refusal to recognise annexation by military conquest. The president ruled, however, apparently in defiance of standing orders, that the steering committee's resolution must be put first. When it had been passed by forty-four votes to one—Ethiopia—with four abstentions—South Africa, Chile, Panama and Venezuela—van

Zeeland decided there was no need to vote on the Ethiopian resolution, because paragraph four of the adopted resolution already covered the point. He did take a vote on a second Ethiopian resolution, asking the League to guarantee a loan of £10 million to buy arms. Only Ethiopia voted for it. Twenty-three delegates voted against. Yet twenty-five others made their silent comment by abstaining.

Van Zeeland, in his closing speech, said he had examined his conscience and found it clear. He was sure, he said, that if any of the nations represented at that Assembly were to find themselves one day in a situation like that of Ethiopia, they would be glad, 'in default of something better,' to see economic and financial sanctions applied to the aggressor by fifty other countries. It was a speech of stupefying complacency. Yet when, on July 6th, Eden reported to the Cabinet upon the meetings of the Council and Assembly—'the most exacting and the most depressing he had attended'—he praised the Belgian as 'a particularly good president' and claimed that van Zeeland's last speech 'had done something to restore confidence.' The task of the British delegation, said the Foreign Secretary, 'had not been made any easier owing to the speech of the South African representative, which had been rather too strong for the occasion.' Rather too strong for Eden's stomach, at any rate. Altogether, the episode was not one of the more noble in the career of the sometime champion of the League.

There was much talk during the Assembly of the need to 'reform' the Covenant. This, for some, meant they wanted to see their obligations as members of the League reduced. It was a view which had gained more and more favour inside the British Cabinet. It was what the Prime Minister, Baldwin, meant, when he told a meeting of City of London Tories on July 2nd that, if Britain were ever again to be prepared to impose sanctions, it must not be done 'with her eyes shut.' It was not a comment which would bear much examination, implying as it did that Baldwin's own government had subscribed to sanctions —and sent reinforcements to the Mediterranean Fleet—without knowing or seeing what it was doing. But it was plainly indicative of a desire to cast off any international responsibilities which were not chosen as furthering Britain's immediate self-interests.

Others in the Assembly wanted the commitments of member-nations to be strengthened so that, never again, would aggression go unchecked for want of collective action. The Russians' major motive in joining the League had been to further their own security, and this interest, accentuated by Hitler's actions, impelled Litvinov to call for sanctions to be made obligatory upon all member-nations.

'I am far from idealising the Covenant,' said Litvinov. 'Its imperfections lie not so much in its articles as in its reservations and obscurities. Therefore, the thing is not to talk of reforming the Covenant, but of making it explicit and stronger ... Assurance is needed that in all cases of aggression, irrespective of the degree of concern in the conflict, sanctions will be applied by all, and this can be achieved only if sanctions are made obligatory.

'To strengthen the League of Nations,' the Russian declared, 'was to abide by the principle of collective security, which is by no means a product of idealism, but is a practical measure towards the security of all peoples ...'

There were also those who recognised that there was nothing wrong with the Covenant as an instrument, only the way in which members discharged their responsibilities under it. Stanley Bruce, the Australian delegate, who had supported the immediate abolition of sanctions, admitted frankly that if sanctions had been properly applied, Italy's aggression would not have succeeded. 'There is no defect in the system embodied in the Covenant,' said Bruce, 'if it is fully implemented.'

Eden had told the Assembly not to lose heart because of this failure to make the rule of law prevail over the rule of force. 'How many efforts have been needed in history to realise objectives of far less significance to the ultimate destiny of the human race? With such an objective as this before us our endeavour must be centred upon the task of reconstruction.' But Eden was more aware than most of the moral sickness with which the League was infected and which rendered it incapable of collective action when the crucial challenge came. It was a sickness to which Britain had contributed. As he was to reflect as he looked back, the British Government's failure had been a failure of will, which itself was the product of a conflict within the Cabinet between those whose first objective was to keep intact the so-called Stresa front and those who put the League first.

The former American Secretary of State, Stimson, looked at his own country's role in the crisis and found that its failure had two main causes. There was the narrowness of the neutrality legislation which denied the President the discretion and the authority to give the League powers effective co-operation in their efforts to impose economic sanctions. There was also Roosevelt's own failure to offer leadership to the American people by appealing to them on basic moral and political grounds, spelling out the issues involved. Had he done so, said Stimson, the President would have been able to achieve a general, though voluntary, trade embargo against Italy.

Haile Selassie went into exile in Britain, where he was to find much sympathy but where he was to seem, as he must, a lonely and pathetic figure. He was to present himself once more at Geneva, but he had to wait five years until the war, which the League's failure to save his country had made all the more certain, was to enable him to return to Addis Ababa.

16

'The epidemic of world lawlessness is spreading'

Even before the Italian conquest of Ethiopia was complete, Europe had begun to pay the price of betrayal. In the years that followed it, not only Europe but the whole world was to go on footing the bill.

Sean Lester, the League's High Commissioner in Danzig, was one of those who made an accurate assessment of what was at stake in Ethiopia at a time when decisive action by the League was still possible and still credible. Eden has recalled a long talk with Lester during the earliest days of the Italian invasion. 'His view,' says Eden in his memoirs, 'supported by our Embassy in Berlin, was that if the League succeeded in Abyssinia, Nazi policy would probably follow a moderate course for several years. If, on the other hand, Mussolini showed that the League could be flouted with impunity, then Nazi demands in other countries would come fast and furious.'*

On March 7th, Hitler denounced the Locarno pact and German troops re-occupied the demilitarised zone of the Rhineland. It was a direct consequence of the failure of the Hoare-Laval plan and the subsequent vacillations at Geneva. The remilitarisation of the Rhineland was at once a breach of the Versailles Treaty and a blatant challenge to the other Locarno powers, whose paper obligations demanded a military response

* Op. cit. p. 267.

to Germany's armed aggression. Hitler ordered the action against the warnings of his service chiefs, who told him the German Army was not yet strong enough for such an adventure. Hitler was ready to retreat again, at speed, should his bluff be called. But he got away with it. The three signatories to Locarno who had the capacity to check Hitler had no heart for it. The Italians, who, anyway, were moving towards an ever closer accord with the Nazis, were busy elsewhere. It is just one more example of the fantasy in which the second half of the 1930s was enveloped that Italy, a nation found guilty by the League of the most flagrant violation of the Covenant, should have sat down solemnly with the other Locarno powers to discuss how to deal with the German law-breaker.

On March 5th, Eden had reported to the Cabinet that, in the event of a German move in the Rhineland, France would not act alone. Flandin had been pressing Britain for an assurance that, even if Italy were to renege, the British would still honour their Locarno obligations. The French, for their part, while taking necessary steps as a preliminary to military action, intended to make their first move through the League Council. That is what happened. Preparatory measures taken by the French Army led to speculation that France intended to drive the German troops out of the Rhineland again, as she was entitled to do under the Locarno agreement. But her government went to the League instead. That decision, and the inaction which followed upon it, proved to Hitler that he had been right in taking a gamble and his advisers had been wrong and, until September, 1939, he was to repeat the lesson over and over again.

Flandin, for France, and van Zeeland, for Belgium, the other Locarno signatory which could regard the Rhineland action as an invasion, called upon the Secretary-General to summon the Council urgently. It did not meet until March 14th in London, and was preceded by talks between the Locarno powers, which gave the French little comfort. Flandin had no success in persuading Britain and Belgium, let alone Italy, to join in sanctions against Germany. Sir Austen Chamberlain, for whom Locarno was not only an unforgettable personal triumph but a practical promise of European security, was among those who were shocked by his country's failure to carry out its unambiguous commitments. Chamberlain continued to embarrass the Conservative Government with his reminder of the principles which were supposed to inspire British policy and of the obligations which accompanied membership of the League. As he observed the denial of those obligations and the indifference to principle, he offered the House of Commons a sharp and fearful vision of what lay ahead. The theme of his speech on April 1st was that the Rhineland and Ethiopia were just the beginning.

'What attitude shall we take if Austrian independence be threatened or destroyed, whether by an attack from outside or by a revolution fostered and supported from outside like that which caused the death of Dollfuss? If we mean anything at all by the declarations that our policy is founded on the League and that we shall fulfil our obligations, possibilities of this kind must give food for thought to every British citizen. For we may have to intervene at any moment. The independence of Austria is a key position. If Austria perishes Czechoslovakia becomes indefensible. Then the whole of the Balkans will be submitted to a gigantic new influence. Then the old German dream of a Central Europe ruled by and subject to Berlin will become reality from the Baltic to the Mediterranean and the Black Sea, with incalculable consequences not only for our country but for our whole Empire.'

Austen Chamberlain is easily mocked for his patrician manner and his concept of Britain's attachment to the League was always a limited one. Yet he had an understanding, founded on principle and national self-interest, of the place of honour in international relations. He believed in the sanctity of treaty obligations. If he resisted the persuasions of other countries to extend Britain's commitments, it was because he took existing ones seriously. To talk in such terms to the British Governments of the late 1930s was to speak in a foreign language. Austen Chamberlain, the last of the three great men of Locarno and Geneva, died in 1937. He was spared the sight of his fearful vision coming to fulfilment. He was spared the pain of seeing his brother, Neville, actively helping it to come about.

Widespread in Britain was a feeling that, although technically in breach of treaties, Germany was committing no great crime in sending troops into territory which was, after all, German. A government which was moving rapidly towards acceptance of

Italy's indisputable aggression was not likely to choke over swallowing an act that involved no annexation of territory and no loss of life. It seized hopefully upon Hitler's declaration of good intentions, of his willingness to conclude new security pacts, of his readiness to return to the League of Nations. He had, he said, no further ambition but to live in peace and friendship with the rest of the world.

The other members of the Council were in no mood, either, for dramatic action against Germany. It was one thing to agree that the Locarno treaty had been broken; it would be something very different to participate in any form of collective action against Germany. Flandin, who had rediscovered the beauties of a Covenant he was content, over Ethiopia, virtually to ignore, could expect nothing more than a vote formally confirming Germany's misconduct. Litvinov inveighed against 'collective capitulation' when confronted by the violation of treaties and offered Russia's fullest co-operation in any common action. Such a speech came fittingly from the foreign minister of a country which could see in every aggressive act by Germany a threat to itself and which, in May, 1935, had signed a treaty with France, a treaty Hitler had taken as an excuse for his denunciation of Locarno.

Neither the Council meeting nor the separate discussions between the Locarno powers led to any material or co-ordinated action against Germany. Belgium's withdrawal from the Locarno treaty a few months later merely confirmed a death most people had already taken for granted. For much of that summer, however, the British Cabinet was considering seriously the possibility of a meeting in Brussels of the Locarno powers, to which Germany would be invited, with the object of devising a new Locarno treaty. It was also trying to find out, not very successfully, what Hitler's terms would be for returning to the League.

The futility of these activities, as of the efforts, by conciliation and surrender, to draw Mussolini into a defensive grouping against Germany, was to be swiftly demonstrated. In the autumn of 1936, the Rome-Berlin Axis, the recognition, by the conclusion of secret agreements, of the aims and interests linking the two dictatorships, was born. In November that year, Germany and Japan signed the anti-Comintern Pact—to which Italy adhered a year later—thereby giving titular identity to the theme which all three powers were to pursue into war. The common enemy of mankind was communism. The League of Nations was an instrument of the communist conspiracy, therefore the League was also the enemy of mankind.

If Europe had any doubts of what it was in for, Spain provided a hideous illustration. The Spanish civil war began on July 18th, 1936, just two weeks after the League Assembly had voted for the lifting of sanctions against Italy. The value of all those professions of Italian good faith, and of their promises of a return to the law-abiding fold once the Ethiopia affair was settled, was now to be tested. On August 17th, Ciano, who had become Foreign Minister two months earlier, gave the British Ambassador 'the most formal and categorical assurances' that neither the Italian Government nor any Italians had had dealings with General Franco. At that time, Italian fighter-aircraft were already helping Franco, and Italian troops, whose numbers built up to a peak of 50,000, were soon to play a major part on the rebels' side.

This book is about the League of Nations and will say little in detail about the Spanish civil war because the League had little to do with it. Almost from the outset the view of the League was that, while the time might come when the Council could offer its 'good offices' to bring about an end to the fighting, the war was an internal matter for the Spanish people and all other countries should mind their own business. This policy of 'non-intervention' was initiated by the French Government which, although itself broadly sympathetic to the Spanish Republicans, was dependent upon support of the Radicals, who opposed the idea of helping the Madrid Government, and had to contend with a country violently divided on the issue. There is no cause to think the British were reluctant to follow the French lead. Indeed, an international agreement to ban the sale of arms to either side in Spain might have been proper enough, however strongly the Spanish Government might feel it was deserving of preferential treatment. But, in practice, the agreement permitted a flow of war materials to Franco and largely denied them to the legitimate Government. Britain and France kept the embargo; Italy, Germany and Portugal sent massive aid to the insurgents;

the Russians joined in with help to the Republicans, but not on the same scale.

The committee which was supposed to see that the principle of non-intervention was honoured, was established, not in Geneva, but in London, and its existence owed nothing to the League. The fact that several countries which were members of the League Council were also represented on the non-intervention committee only made it that much more certain that, wherever possible, the issue of the Spanish war would be skated over, if not actually ignored, at Geneva. The British and French governments were determined to steer clear of the fighting. They feared any possibility of a head-on collision with the Germans and Italians. In the face of irrefutable evidence of mounting Axis involvement in Spain—as a 'dummy-run' for the Luftwaffe it combined maximum realism with minimum loss of men and aircraft—the British and French continued to ask for assurances that the Republican allegations were untrue or, even if there were some substance to them, the malpractices would cease henceforth. The soil of Spain had become a battleground where thousands of foreign 'volunteers,' armed with foreign equipment, rehearsed for the second world war, in the name of justice, democracy, civilisation, communism and anti-communism, fascism and anti-facism. The committee in London became the scene of accusation and counter-accusation by the Germans and Italians on the one hand and the Russians on the other. Still, London and Paris persisted with their pretence that the policy of non-intervention was working, if not perfectly, then at least partially. But when, in November, 1936, Hitler and Mussolini recognised Franco as head of state and his government as the nationalist government of Spain, even the Anglo-French willingness to be duped was strained.

Until then, Eden and Delbos, the French Foreign Minister, had been successful in dissuading the Spaniards from making any formal appeal to the League and thus had prevented the war, which had engaged the political passions of men and women the world over, from being discussed seriously in the body which had been created with the ideals before it of open debate and the collective enforcement of peace. (Against the background of everything else happening at that time, it was but a minor irony that the September, 1936, meeting of the League Council should have been the first to take place in the Palais des Nations, the splendid new home of the League, first planned when there were young hopes of a different kind of world, completed in time to serve as an ornate mausoleum.) Now the Republican government held up the Italo-German recognition of Franco as evidence of the aggression of those two countries against Spain, and asked for an urgent meeting of the Council. It was nearly two weeks before the Council did meet, and during that time the non-intervention committee had been conferring and had decided that no more volunteers must go to Spain and that entry into Spain must be strictly checked.

The Council at Geneva was happy to go along with what a majority of its own governments had agreed in London. The Spanish representative at Geneva, Alvarez del Vayo, did make out his case against the inequitable effects of non-intervention and gave the Council vivid and circumstantial illustrations of the activities of German and Italian troops, guns, bombers and submarines. Neither Eden nor Delbos thought it necessary to attend the meeting. Their belief in non-intervention was genuine enough and, had they been able to do so, they would certainly have enforced it: Eden was overruled in the Cabinet when he suggested that British warships should patrol the Spanish coast. But the British Foreign Secretary was not prepared—and even less the British Government—to abandon non-intervention, when it failed, for a more positive role for either Britain or for the League. British foreign policy was now concentrated upon appeasement of the dictators and, in that context, Spain was almost irrelevant and certainly not worth the risk of an open clash with Hitler and Mussolini.

The Germans and Italians gave their new assurances to the non-intervention committee and they turned out to be as worthless as all previous ones. They intensified what Litvinov described as the 'attempt to force upon the Spanish people a Fascist government with the aid of bayonet, hand-grenade and bomb.' The peoples of the world sat in their cinema-seats and watched the newsreels which gave them a preview of what the next war was going to be like, and the Spanish nation endured three years of the vilest barbarities. Spokesmen of the Spanish government took every opportunity to catalogue the crimes perpetrated

375

against their countrymen. In a leading article on January 7th, 1937, the *Manchester Guardian* commented: 'The Foreign Minister of Spain possesses, like the Emperor of Abyssinia, a faculty for writing Notes to the League of Nations which, granted the principles of "collective security", are unanswerable. If they accomplish nothing, at least they will stand as historical records of appeals vainly made to the international conscience.' At Geneva, del Vayo stirred the consciences of his fellow-delegates sufficiently for the May, 1937, Council to pass a unanimous resolution which said that all foreigners fighting in Spain must leave the country at once. The Spaniard, who claimed that there were between 75,00 and 80,00 Italian troops in his country, told the Council that if the League were to have a future the struggle in Spain could not end without the League adopting a clear and firm position.

'For some time,' said del Vayo, 'the League, ignoring the enormous force of world public opinion on which it ultimately depends, has taken a road that may become fatal.' He aimed a shaft directly at Britain and France. Often, he said, the League was more concerned with its enemies than with its friends. 'I believe the time has come to halt on this path, because the moral ruin of the League of Nations would do incalculable damage to the cause of world peace. The principle which could be applied to put an end to this fatal drift is, in my opinion, very simple. It is that those who are present should never be sacrificed to those who are absent.' He was speaking at a time when Franco could send a protest to the Secretary-General against the claim of the Valencia government—the Republicans had been driven out of Madrid—to represent Spain.

Delbos spoke sympathetically of the friendship of the French people. He never, he said, put the two sides in the civil war on the same level. He spoke of the need to withdraw the 'foreign combatants.' Eden referred to the 'volunteers on both sides' and reiterated the British Government's objectives: to make sure the Spanish conflict did not spread to envelop all Europe and to ensure that, whatever the final outcome of the civil war, the territorial integrity of Spain should be preserved. Throughout the Foreign Secretary's speech the Italian journalists ostentatiously read their newspapers.

Litvinov once again championed the Spanish Government's right to help from the League. What was happening, he said, was a threat to the very existence of the League, and he chided those so-called supporters of the League who thought that it could be kept alive only on condition that nothing was asked of it and it was not expected to do anything. 'These people would like to change the League into a universal mummy and admire its inertness and imperturbable calm.'

The Council's resolution demanding the withdrawal of all foreigners was a forceful one and sounded as though it meant what it said. But the non-intervention committee, whose members were charged by the Council to see the resolution made effective, behaved as though the resolution itself was action enough. Foreign troops stayed in Spain in contempt of the League. The Italians, in particular, were now fighting an open, full-scale war on behalf of Franco; there were times, indeed, when, so great was the Italian participation and so dominant their role, they might have been there as an invading army of conquest. Their methods were almost as unscrupulous as they had been in Ethiopia. The conduct of their warships, in enforcing a boycott of Republican ports, amounted to unbridled piracy. Any ship was a potential target for their torpedoes, whatever its nationality, and there were stories showing their total indifference to the fate of the crews of ships they had sunk. But it was these activities which, at last, provoked the British and French into their one really effective move.

So far as Britain was concerned, the ultimate provocation came when a submarine made an unsuccessful torpedo attack upon a British destroyer. The French agreed there must be a conference. Even that was not held at Geneva, or under League auspices, but at Nyon, a few miles away. The theory was that Nyon would be a more palatable location than Geneva for the Germans and Italians, but they did not attend, anyway. The conference was held, nevertheless, and the other European powers attending it quickly reached the decision that naval patrols must operate under orders to retaliate against any attacks on shipping by warships or aircraft. This work would fall to the British and French navies. Faced, for once, with determined action and the obvious danger to their own 'pirates,' the Italians said their fleet would co-operate in patrolling the Mediterranean. The offer was accepted and the piracy ended. That result was, in itself, satisfactory to the Spanish Government, but it raised a most justifiable objection to the fact that the Nyon agreement excluded Spanish ships from the protection of the patrols; theoretically, that meant they were still exposed to German aircraft and Italian ships. The Nyon powers refused, however, to extend the agreement.

The Nyon Conference was held in September, 1937, just before the League Assembly. At the Assembly, the Spanish Government, as represented by its Prime Minister, Juan Negrin, and del Vayo, successfully capitalised upon the new determination shown at Nyon, upon the instinctive sympathy of many—though not all—of the delegates, and upon the sense of outrage fired by Mussolini's braggart rantings in Germany, where he had been fêted and where he had been awed by demonstrations of German military strength and professionalism. Mussolini used the occasion to let the world know that Italian troops were in Spain, as in Ethiopia, to save civilisation. At the Assembly, the Spaniards appealed to the League to recognise the truth of what was happening in their country and to allow them to buy war materials without restriction. A resolution, delicately worded but clear enough in its intent, was passed by a large majority. Unless all foreign troops were cleared out of Spain immediately, the League must consider putting an end to non-intervention. Although a unanimous vote was needed for the resolution to carry any obligation upon League members, it seemed as though the Spanish Government had achieved an important breakthrough, the more so because the British and French had voted in favour. That was soon to be written off as just one more lakeside hallucination.

Mussolini spurned an Anglo-French suggestion for talks about pulling out foreigners from the fighting in Spain. Eden made public noises of impatience and exasperation. But he was Foreign Secretary of a government which had lost all interest in the League and retained only the flimsiest of pretences to uphold its principles. Any issue which involved a risk of conflict with the dictatorships but did not impinge directly and immediately upon British interests was certain to be shelved.

The determining influence was that of Neville Chamberlain,

who had succeeded Baldwin as Prime Minister at the end of May, 1937. In the earlier years of the 1930s Chamberlain had filled out the part of strong man of the Cabinet from time to time, counselling a show of bulldog, or, at any rate, terrier resolution. As Prime Minister, he courted the dictators, bidding them to state their price for peace, deluding himself that their lusts for power were finite and that, once satisfied, they would take their place again as law-abiding members of international society. He placed an inordinate value upon paper declarations of honourable intentions and debased his country in quest of them. His chief disciple and frequent courier was Lord Halifax. One of his most disastrous journeys took Halifax to Germany in November, 1937. On the 19th, he met Hitler at Berchtesgaden and, while urging him to seek a solution to the 'outstanding questions' of Danzig, Austria and Czechoslovakia through the League, encouraged the Nazi leader in the belief that the British would not really mind how those questions were solved, so long as it was done peacefully. In reporting to the Cabinet on the friendliness and desire for good relations he had encountered in his meetings with the likes of Goering, Goebbels and Schacht, and his warm reception by crowds of ordinary people, he gave his view that, while the Germans were too busy building up their country for any immediate adventure, he would expect them to show 'a beaver-like persistence in pressing their aims in Central Europe, but not in a form to give others cause—or probably occasion—to interfere.'

When Halifax had raised the question of the League, Hitler had said he regarded 'the present system and conception as unworkable and unreal.' This struck a chord with the Prime Minister, who said he took the same view as Hitler about the League. 'At present it was largely a sham,' runs the Cabinet record, 'owing more particularly to the idea that it could impose its views by force. As long as the League had attached to it powers that it could not use it would be of little value.' If the League were reformed, said Chamberlain, it might become a great moral force and then, although the Americans might not be willing to join it, their attitude towards it might become much more benevolent.

Anthony Eden had done his own share of fetching and carrying around the European capitals in pursuit of appeasement. If he had doubts about the wisdom of such a policy, he seemed prepared most of the time to suppress them. Whenever he did propose a stronger line, he was always in a minority in Cabinet. Despite Mussolini's blank refusal to pull his troops out of Spain, the British Government did not drop the policy of non-intervention. Eden stomached what was, by any measure, one more deflation of his authority as Foreign Secretary. His conduct in office had followed a pattern familiar to any in political life. Having failed to resign over Ethiopia, when resignation might have influenced future policy and when it would certainly have evoked a popular response, he thereafter condoned a course of policy which, at heart, he probably disapproved. Time and again, he saw his proposals turned down or, worse perhaps, so diluted as to make them innocuous and futile. Yet he hung on, believing that, so long as he was there, he might be able to do something useful, to influence the direction of policy in some small way. It is an argument which is advanced by many men of conscience as well as by those who will offer any justification for clinging to office. For some, the process of acquiescing in disagreeable policies seems to become easier the longer it goes on. For others, there comes a moment of ultimate revulsion. For Eden, who had swallowed so much, this came over a proposed pact, favoured by Chamberlain, between Britain and Italy which would have granted *de jure* recognition to Mussolini's conquest of Ethiopia and, in effect, sanctioned the employment of Italian troops in Spain. Chamberlain had gone too far in his willingness to believe in Mussolini's good faith. His Foreign Secretary was quite prepared to recognise the annexation of Ethiopia as an accomplished fact, but he was not ready to put his name to a deal which would give Mussolini both the respectability he craved for his new African empire at the same time as ignoring what the Italians were doing in Spain. On February 20th, 1938, Eden—along with Lord Cranborne, his junior colleague at the Foreign Office—resigned. The Anglo-Italian proposal lapsed.

That proposed agreement with Mussolini was only one, perhaps not even the most important, reason for Eden's resignation Indeed, for all the indignation the deal might have aroused, Eden's own attitude towards Italy was, by that time, not so radically different from Chamberlain's. What had become intolerable was the Prime Minister's habit of going over Eden's head or neglecting to seek his opinion. Eden felt his authority shrinking.

The previous month had provided an example of Chamberlain's arrogance—or insensitivity—which had bitten deeply into Eden's pride. Early in January, 1938, President Roosevelt sent Chamberlain a message in which he outlined his 'Plan for World Peace' and invited Britain's support. The details of Roosevelt's plan are not now important; in short, he would ask all nations to reach unanimous agreement upon certain highly desirable aims, including 'most effective methods for achieving limitation and reduction of armaments'—that same objective which had frustrated so many good men at Geneva for so many years. If he received enough encouragement, the President proposed to go ahead, not by calling an immediate world conference, but by inviting to Washington representatives of certain smaller governments, such as Sweden, Holland and Switzerland, to negotiate on the issues raised by his plan.

He received something very like a snub from Chamberlain. Eden was on holiday in the south of France. The Prime Minister, without consulting his Foreign Secretary, told Roosevelt, in effect, that Britain was engaged in direct contacts with Italy and Germany to try to bring about 'a general appeasement,' and that the President's plan was more likely to hinder than help those efforts. Roosevelt, not unnaturally, was disappointed. There were rows in Cabinet and private talks and Chamberlain was persuaded to soften his line in later exchanges, if only for the *de jure* recognition of Italy's annexation of Ethiopia—a proposal which shocked Cordell Hull and his President.

Chamberlain now encouraged Roosevelt to take the initiative, at the same time making clear that the British had criticisms of the proposals. There was guile behind this new approach, the Cabinet was told. Chamberlain wanted to be sure it was the President himself who was clearly seen to have initiated the idea. If it then flopped, Britain would not share responsibility for it, and nor could Roosevelt say he had not been given any warning of what might happen. Chamberlain's own opinion of the plan had not changed, as he showed when he analysed for the Cabinet the 'dilemma' facing the Government. We wanted American co-operation and to have closer relations with the United States, said Chamberlain, but the Government was being asked to give its whole-hearted support to these 'rather preposterous proposals.' The President's scheme offered nothing new and it would be unpalatable to the dictatorships. As for summoning representatives of certain small states to Washington—that was not likely to bring about world appeasement. In the event, Roosevelt went no further with his plan. It is extremely doubtful whether it could have had any useful effect; there was no suggestion that the Americans would be any more ready than before to back up their words with the kinds of action likely to impress the dictatorships and deter them from new aggressions; nevertheless, Eden and Summer Welles, who had acted as a go-between for the President, both reckoned, perhaps for personal reasons, that the Roosevelt plan had represented the last chance of dragging the world back from war.

The impotence of the American Administration at this time must go a long way towards explaining the obsession of both President and Secretary of State for high-minded pronouncements—just such a one as issued forth from the State Department, in July, 1937, six months before the still-birth of the Roosevelt plan. It amounted to a formal statement of the American stance in international affairs, and every other government in the world was asked to say whether it agreed with what the Americans were advocating. This code of conduct included the abstinence by all nations from use of force in pursuit of policy and from interference in the internal affairs of other nations; adjustment of international problems by peaceful negotiation and agreement; and faithful observance of international agreements with modification of treaties, where necessary, by 'orderly processes in a spirit of mutual helpfulness and accommodation.' But that did not prevent Germany, Italy and Japan from adhering to it. Nor did their adherence shake Cordell Hull's conviction of its supreme value or of his own service to humanity in having presented these tablets to the world. Only Portugal dared—or bothered—to object to 'the habit of entrusting the solution of grave external problems to vague formulae,' an observation which nettled Hull. However, no good supporter of the League would find fault with the American statement of aims and principles, even if, unlike the Covenant, it contained no provisions for dealing with transgressors. It showed the Americans—or some Americans, at least—had their hearts in the right place.

Yet the attempts at co-operation between the United States and the League powers were not fruitful. That was proved when, in the summer of 1937, the Japanese Army—interpreting the will of the militarists and extremists who had become more and more powerful in Japan—exploited a brush between Chinese and Japanese troops to make war upon China. It was a war marked by savage battles, resulting in appalling losses on both sides, by indiscriminate bombing of Chinese towns by a Japanese air force which, like every other arm of Japan's war machine, enjoyed a terrible superiority, and by the perpetration of barbarous cruelties by the invading troops. There was no lack of sympathy in the world for the Chinese, as their appeal to the League, in September, 1937, showed. But their delegates, Wellington Koo and Quo Tai-chi, found much more difficulty in persuading those who sympathised to translate their feelings into practical help.

The body which was given the task of dealing with the Chinese appeal was the Far East committee, established after the 1933 Assembly resolution on Manchuria—the resolution which had led to Japan's walk-out. The Americans were represented on this committee by an observer. The committee was forthright in its condemnation of the Japanese bombings and of their violation of treaties. But members of the Assembly, while approving the committee's findings, were much less willing to meet the Chinese request, if not for material help, then at least for a stop on all help to Japan. As certain countries most intimately concerned recognised, to grant the Chinese request might well mean cutting off particular kinds of trade with Japan, and any restrictive action might provoke Japanese hostility. The Assembly agreed to a lame proposal that each country should see what, if anything, it could do to help the Chinese.

China must have looked forward more hopefully to a meeting of the countries—Japan was one of them—which had signed the Nine-Power Treaty to respect the territorial and administrative integrity of China. And Chinese expectations had every reason to rise when reports came in of a speech made in Chicago, on

October 5th, by President Roosevelt. This speech, which became known as Roosevelt's 'quarantine' speech, was one which seemed to indicate a radical departure in American policy towards Japan

'The peace, the freedom, and the security of 90 per cent of the population of the world, is being jeopardised by the remaining 10 per cent, who are threatening a breakdown of international order and law,' said the President. 'Surely the 90 per cent who want to lie in peace under law and in accordance with moral standards that have received almost universal acceptance through the centuries, can and must find a way to make their will prevail . . .

'It seems to be unfortunately true that the epidemic of world lawlessness is spreading. When an epidemic of physical disease starts to spread, the community approves and joins in a quarantine of the patients in order to protect the health of the community against the spread of the disease.' The peace-loving nations, said Roosevelt, must make a concerted effort to uphold laws and principles on which peace alone could rest secure; there was no escape through mere isolation or neutrality.

What could this mean if it did not imply America's willingness to join in collective action against the Japanese? Did it not signify a new resolution on the part of the United States Government to call a halt to aggression? In Europe, there was a brief period of optimism. In America, there was a vociferous reaction against the President's apparent wish to get his country mixed up in dangerous actions which might lead to war. The reaction was not confined to the isolationists. Inside the State Department, there was consternation. Cordell Hull felt that the speech, by engaging the isolationists head-on, must have set back the work of those, like himself and the President, who had been trying, by stealth, to nudge their compatriots, step by little step, into accepting a wider concept of American responsibilities. Both Hull and Norman Davis, who was to represent America at the Nine-Power Conference in Brussels, had seen the draft of the President's speech and had discussed it with him three weeks before it was delivered. At that time, the 'quarantine' passage did not exist. Roosevelt had put it in himself without further reference to his colleagues. When he got back from Chicago,

Davis asked him why. The President's explanation, as related by Davis in private conversations at Brussels, was telegraphed back to the British Cabinet in a report from its own representative at the conference, Malcolm MacDonald:

'Mr. Roosevelt explained that he wished to find some phrase which conveyed a certain impression without implying hostility against Japan. Therefore he did not want to use the word "sanctions," nor any other words which might seem to indicate that hostile action was a possibility. "Quarantine" was the best word that he could find. He instanced the case of a community in which there was an outbreak of some fell disease, red flags were put on the houses of the victims, so that everyone might know what places to avoid. Mr. Davis had replied that in those cases of course the red flag was very effective; but supposing a brigand armed with a machine gun entered the street, it was not much good putting a red flag on him.'

It would seem that Roosevelt, by an injudicious choice of phrase, had at once been credited with a measure of political backbone he did not possess, while alienating powerful sections of American opinion. His speech did anything but help at the Brussels conference, because Davis's hand, however palsied it would have been, anyway, was weakened still further by awareness of reactions on the other side of the Atlantic. Wellington Koo and Quo Tai-chi went from delegation to delegation, pressing their country's case, but with no success. None was willing to risk involvement in the war by discriminating against Japan, or by doing too much too openly to help China. Davis said if the American Government tried to organise a supply of arms to China, there would be immediate demands for a strict application of the neutrality legislation. The British explained that if large quantities of supplies were to go through Hong Kong to China, then the Japanese would declare a formal state of war and impose a blockade and China would be worse off than ever. The Americans were most anxious to prevent the question going back from the conference to Geneva, and the British were only too ready to co-operate in devising ways of adjourning the conference indefinitely. It broke up with empty promises to see what could be done to help China and with expressions of hope that the Chinese and Japanese would work out a solution to the conflict between them. The war went on.

The League Council meeting of January, 1938, was the last which Eden attended before resigning as Foreign Secretary. He went there armed with the Cabinet's thoughts about how the League should be 'reformed'. The general conclusion was that the original concept of the League was 'impracticable,' because of the absence from Geneva of so many important countries. The Government recognised the political risks in calling for the Covenant itself to be amended, but there ought to be a resolution whose effect would be to water down the obligations of League members, when faced with aggression. The Cabinet wanted membership to involve 'a general obligation to consult, and an additional obligation to take coercive action when, but only when, consultation between members of the League indicated that coercion might profitably be employed.'

If adopted, that formula would certainly have reflected current League practice. It was a line of thought which found favour even with Avenol, the Secretary-General It could also have had the incidental virtue of meeting a small domestic political difficulty recognised by Sir John Simon, who was now to be found at the Treasury. Simon said that, in Britain, 'confidence in the League had been rather shaken by the long explanations that were given as to why in particular questions it did not prove effective.' But during the January Council, Eden found there was not only total opposition to any changes in the Covenant, but also—from France, Soviet Russia and the Little Entente— to any suggestion of a 'facultative solution of the sanctions question.' The matter was postponed until September. When Eden reported this to the Cabinet on February 2nd, the Prime Minister said the consequence was that, 'if another difficult situation should arise before September the position of the League would be as unsatisfactory as ever.' The present weakness, he said, became greater after each failure. What Chamberlain meant was that if, no matter what sort of breach of the Covenant were committed, you intended most resolutely to do nothing about it, it would be better to admit it in advance: that was his way of protecting the prestige of the League.

At that same Cabinet, Eden gave his general impression of the Council as 'one of bewilderment rather than anxiety.' He had

had conversations with eight foreign ministers, he said, and found much less immediate anxiety about possible action by Germany. The Polish Foreign Minister had seen Hitler and had come away with the feeling that Germany was experiencing considerable internal difficulties and the German Army was not yet ready for a foreign adventure. This view, said Eden, had been confirmed by his talk with the Danzig high commissioner. The Foreign Secretary had found a very real desire at Geneva for better relations with Germany.

On March 12th, Hitler sent his troops into Austria, and announced its annexation. Another of those 'difficult' situations, which Chamberlain had feared, had now arisen. He himself, in the House of Commons, expressed his angry shock at Hitler's act. But the Prime Minister made no effort to invoke the joint guarantees given by Britain, France and Italy in February, 1934, to protect Austria's independence. Austria did not try to resist the German invasion. Her Government did not appeal to the League. No other country seemed to think any good could come out of doing so, either. And that, unfortunately, was by now an entirely accurate as well as realistic appreciation of the League's effectiveness. The League, like Austria, had been let down too often by the only powers that could have made it effective.

Hitler's annexation of Austria momentarily intruded upon the British Government's preoccupation with Mussolini. Chamberlain and Lord Halifax, Eden's successor as Foreign Secretary, had been preparing carefully for the final betrayal of Ethiopia. An agreement was framed whereby Italy would withdraw her troops from Spain as soon as the war had been won for Franco and, in return, Britain would recognise the annexation of Ethiopia. This was known in Cabinet terminology as 'clearing up' the situations in Spain and Ethiopia. The Anglo-Italian deal was done on April 16th, and all that remained was to clear the way at Geneva for recognition. Halifax said at the Cabinet meeting of April 27th that he had warned the Italians they must expect 'a certain number of unpleasant things' to be said about them at the May Council. He thought they understood the position. The Foreign Secretary also reported on his talks the day before with the League Secretary-General, who was visiting London. On the Ethiopian question, 'M. Avenol had adopted rather a cynically helpful and hopeful manner. His main object appeared to be to protect the League of Nations against having to decide any very difficult questions of principle.' Avenol did not think it would be necessary to remit the question to the Assembly. He even thought the Council would probably decide that Haile Selassie 'was not a person to whom an invitation to attend the League could properly be sent'. After some discussion in Cabinet, however, Halifax said he might propose that, as a matter of courtesy, a representative of the Emperor should be allowed to make a speech at the Council.

The reaction in Britain, among supporters of the League, to the news that the British Government was smoothing the path for recognition of the Italian conquest was swift and loud. It expressed itself in many forms of protest all over the country. In London, a meeting of the British executive of the International Peace Campaign, attended by Lord Cecil, Philip Noel-Baker and Megan Lloyd George, among others, passed a strong resolution. In Crewe, the local branch of the Peace Council issued a manifesto. 'More than 25,000 people in the Crewe parliamentary division expressed their firm belief in the League of Nations when they signed the "Peace Ballot" in 1935,' it said. 'Of the 21,729 electors in the division who voted for the present Member of Parliament doubtless most believed that the Government's promises in regard to the League of Nations were genuine. . . . The only way in which the British Government can regain the confidence of the thousands of electors in this division who voted for their policy in 1935 is to withdraw their request for the League to clarify the situation—a request that implies the Government's intention that Abyssinia, a fellow-member of the League of Nations, shall be wiped off the map.' At a big meeting in the Central Hall, Westminister, Haile Selassie's daughter, the Princess Tsahai, pleaded, as well she might, for stronger proof of interest on the part of the British Government in her country's fate. The Women's Peace Crusade sent a letter of protest to the Prime Minister and Foreign Secretary. But, like the protests that poured into the Palais des Nations at Geneva, those in Britain were powerless to make the Government change course.

And so, in brilliant May sunshine, with the chestnut trees in blossom around the lake, the delegates began to arrive for the

Council meeting at which the last act of the Ethiopian tragedy was to be played. Halifax went quickly into private and informal huddles, testing the attitudes of the other delegates. The Emperor had nominated his permanent representative in Geneva, Dr. Taezaz, with a technical committee of British experts to help him; this committee included Norman Angell, whose writings had helped to promote the League idea before its actual creation and who had fought for it with savage despair in its years of decline. It was by no means sure, however, that the Council would admit the Ethiopian delegation. Five of the Council's fourteen members, and twenty out of the League's total membership of fifty-one, had already recognised Victor Emmanuel as Emperor of Ethiopia. It was a delicate situation for men of sensibility, and Haile Selassie, who was in arrears in paying his dues to the League, had not made things any easier by sending 10,000 Swiss francs—about £200—as a token contribution for 1935. How could the League refuse to accept it? On the other hand, did not acceptance imply recognition of Haile Selassie as the Emperor and of Ethiopia's right to independent representation at Geneva? In the end, after a stormy, secret meeting, which lasted three hours, and at which Litvinov and William Jordan, the New Zealand delegate, insisted on Ethiopia's rights, the Council managed to devise a formula which permitted the Ethiopian delegates to present themselves and to speak. For its part, the Ethiopian delegation refused absolutely to acquiesce in a move to hustle through the question regarding the status of their country with the minimum of debate. With a deal of impatience and bad grace among certain of the delegates the Council agreed that one day, but one day only, should be set aside.

Then came another piece of news which heightened the tension at Geneva. The Emperor had not intended to attend the Council himself. According to his legation in London, he saw no object in going there. 'It is hopeless; our written appeals have been almost ignored.' Less than an hour before the boat train was due to leave Victoria, Haile Selassie changed his mind. When he arrived at Geneva late on the night of May 11th, a large crowd pressed around him, with such shouts as 'Long live Ethiopia.' He was looking pallid and tired.

The next morning, when the Council had assembled, Munters,

the Latvian president, whose own country had already recognised the Italian annexation, invited the exiled leader to take his seat, addressing him not as 'the Emperor of Ethiopia,' but simply as 'His Majesty, Haile Selassie.' There was a pause, and then the Emperor entered the chamber, followed by his delegation, and walked slowly to his seat. The delegates might have been expected, as by diplomatic custom, to have risen in the presence of a head of state and have bowed to him. But for Haile Selassie they stayed in their seats. Only Halifax, it seems, half-rose, half-bowed to the Emperor, looking embarrassed for himself.

It was Halifax who was to speak first, and charitable observers, regarding him as a good and decent man, however misguided, pictured him as the unhappiest member of the Council, a man struggling with his conscience. Yet, afterwards, he was widely accused of gross hypocrisy. With only the words of his speech to judge by, it is hard to see what other view could be taken. In his efforts to appease his own doubts, perhaps, he constructed a justification which was sophistic and offensive in its pieties.

'Those who seek to establish a better world on the basis of universal acknowledgment of League principles,' said Halifax, 'are really right to feel reluctance to countenance action, however desirable on other grounds, by which they may appear to be infringed. But when, as here, two ideals are in conflict—on the one hand the ideal of devotion, unflinching but unpractical, to some high purpose; on the other, the ideal of some practical victories for peace—I cannot doubt that the strongest claim is that of peace. Life is, indeed, perpetually confronting us with difficulties not dissimilar, whether in the affairs of nations or of individuals. Each one of us knows by painful experience how consistently it is necessary to recognise that which may be ideally right and what is practically possible.' The Foreign Secretary wound his tortuous and torturing way towards his conclusion. It was the considered opinion of His Majesty's Government that, for practical purposes, Italian control over virtually the whole of Ethiopia had become an established fact. '. . . Sooner or later, unless we are prepared by force to alter it, unless we are to live in an unreal world, that fact, whatever be our judgement of it, will have to be acknowledged.' He played with the antithesis of 'practical' and 'unreal' to arrive at the conclusion, which presumably satisfied himself, that the question of whether to recognise the Italian annexation was not a moral one but merely one of timing, of political calculation. Of course, the British Government did not condone the manner by which the Italians had taken over in Ethiopia and its respect for the principles of the League and the Covenant were as great as ever, but no cause was served by vain lamentations. 'Nothing is gained, and much may be lost, by the refusal to face facts. Great as is the League of Nations, the ends that it exists to serve are greater than itself, and the greatest of these ends is peace.' It was a preposterous conclusion, but it was one which provided the basis of the policies pursued by Halifax and Chamberlain, who believed they were saving the peace of Europe, making the lesser sacrifices for the greater good.

The Emperor was called upon to speak immediately after Halifax. He said that, although recovering from a chill, he had come to Geneva to defend in person the cause of his people. He asked, however, that Taezaz should read his speech for him. If Halifax had indeed been conducting a struggle of conscience, then Haile Selassie must have reawakened his shame. After expressing his regret at finding himself in opposition to a government he greatly respected and whose hospitality he was then enjoying, the Emperor appealed to 'its generosity, its loyalty and its honour' to re-examine its attitude He protested against any attempt to recognise the conquest of Ethiopia.

'Even if Italy had full possession of the country, the British proposals should be refused. We do not expect any material assistance from the League, but I ask that Ethiopia shall be allowed to remain among you as an image of violated rights.' He referred to the peoples throughout the world who were watching the League at work: were they to witness the Council tearing up the Covenant with their own hands?

'The suggestion of Great Britain is to favour general appeasement by the sacrifice of a people. This is contrary to the ideals of the Covenant and those ideals so constantly proclaimed by Great Britain and France . . . It is sheer hypocrisy to attempt to strangle a people by procedure.'

What Halifax had asked for from the Council was not a resolution embodying formal recognition of the Italian conquest, but agreement that each member should be free to make a decision for itself whether or not to recognise. It was obvious from the debate that most delegates shared his view. Litvinov made a strong speech condemning the Italians and extolling the principle of non-recognition, but he left a final impression of sitting on the fence. Only the Bolivian and New Zealand delegates, and Wellington Koo, for China, sounded as though they would have cast a definite vote against any motion. Koo said that what they were being asked to do would establish as part of the approved practice of the League, 'the unilateral repudiation of pledges collectively given.' But all the other delegates, the French, Rumanian, Swedish, Belgian, Peruvian, Ecuadorian, Persian and Latvian, supported the British line. No vote was taken. Technically, because unanimity was required, a resolution would have been defeated. But none could disagree with Munters, the chairman, when he announced that the great majority of members felt, despite regrets, that individual countries should be left free to recognise or not to recognise as they thought fit. Emperor Haile Selassie, who had listened throughout with eyes cast down and an impassive expression, rose in silence and walked out of the chamber without a backward glance.

The *Manchester Guardian*'s correspondent wrote: 'We have assisted today at one of the most discreditable episodes in the history of the League of Nations, which was also, to quote a famous phrase, "grotesque and ridiculous." The Council dealt with the question of Abyssinia at two public meetings and arrived at no decision. The question remains exactly where it was before. Abyssinia is still a member of the League of Nations . . .' But the futility, the worthlessness of that membership, had been made manifest.

Two other nations demonstrated that truth at that same meeting of the League Council in May, 1938, although their past experience had been such their delegates could not have presented themselves at the Council table with any hope that their appeals would evoke a practical response. For those other delegates who were still capable of feeling anything but despair, however, the words of del Vayo and Wellington Koo could not be other than painful. The setting for these tragically hopeless appeals to the international conscience was the council chamber of the Palais des Nations, with its murals executed in sepia and gold, depicting mankind's magnificent struggle towards the unity symbolised on the ceiling. The murals were a gift from Spain.

At the public meeting of the Council, it was the Spanish delegate who lashed the policy of non-intervention and asked the League to restore Spain's right to buy war material. He asked nothing of the League, he said, except that it should give back to Spain the right to free commercial relations. 'Let us put an end to this sham non-intervention whose sinister spectre taints the international atmosphere,' said del Vayo, 'and let us restore the question to its natural jurisdiction—namely, the League of Nations.' He warned his audience of the violent, expansionist ambitions of Germany and Italy, but in doing so he was merely underlining the reason why neither France nor Britain was likely to hear his appeal.

Halifax once more defended non-intervention and denied that Britain had ever minimised the breaches which had taken place on both sides. 'If in our second object—the leaving of the Spanish people to decide for themselves—we have only partially succeeded, our first and primary object—the maintenance of European peace—has been wholly successful.' The Foreign Secretary was not only capable of uttering those words; he could even believe them. The Spanish proposal was put to the Council and it was lost. Nine countries abstained; only Russia voted with Spain; Britain and France had the distinction of finding themselves in the same bed with Poland and Rumania.

Dr. Koo was no more successful in presenting the Chinese Government's appeal against Japanese aggression, or in asking for effective, material aid. As usual, there was no lack of sympathy for China; intellectually, there was acceptance of his argument that a defeat for the forces of disorder, and violence in the Far East, would lessen the tension in Europe. None could dispute his contention that for nations which had undertaken the obligations of the Covenant there could be no neutrality. But China was not likely to receive any help that might provoke Japan into retaliatory action.

Whatever newspapers might have said about the Council proceedings and whatever the response of public opinion, Lord

Halifax felt able to tell the Cabinet on May 18th that the Council meeting 'had been got through reasonably well.' So far as the issue of Spain was concerned, he considered the results had been 'somewhat deplorable.' He seemed content that a resolution had been passed condemning the use of poison gas in the Sino-Japanese conflict—'if it should be resorted to.' As for Ethiopia, the Foreign Secretary appeared generally satisfied with the way things had gone, but he was obviously displeased with the behaviour of the New Zealand High Commissioner, Jordan, whose speech had been critical of the British proposal, 'in spite of efforts to induce him to modify its terms.' Halifax pointed out that the New Zealand representative was due to take the chair at the next meeting of the Council, and that, unless Jordan altered his attitude, 'this might be an embarrassment.' The Cabinet agreed that Halifax and Malcolm MacDonald, the Dominions Secretary, should consider drawing up a message which could be sent to the Governor-General of New Zealand, to be passed on, at his discretion, to the New Zealand Prime Minister, calling attention to the 'inconvenience' that might result from Jordan's chairmanship if he did not modify his attitude.

Jordan did take the chair at the September meeting of the Council, a meeting at which China employed a procedure which was bound to end in the application of Article 16 against Japan. The Chinese began by invoking Article 17, under which a non-member in dispute with a League member could be invited to accept the obligations of membership. The invitation was sent to Japan and, as everyone knew it would be, was rejected. For the first time in the Sino-Japanese dispute, the Council was forced back upon Article 16. It made a formal pronouncement authorising League members to carry out sanctions—if they wished. Many countries had already given public notice that, for the time being, they had abandoned their obligations under Article 16.

What was happening at Geneva had become wholly academic, anyway. There was no likelihood of effective action by the League in any dispute involving major powers; the crisis now catching the breath of Europe was not even under discussion by the League. At no time was Czechoslovakia placed on the agenda of the Council. Neither the Czechs themselves nor any of those other countries pledged specifically by treaty, like France and Russia, or by the Covenant, like Britain, to defend Czech integrity, ever referred the issue to the League. Once more, the negotiations to try to resolve an international dispute were kept away from Geneva, not because the Czechs were afraid to bring the conflict into open debate but because they were persuaded by their powerful friends that their best interests would be served elsewhere. The pathetic humiliations of Chamberlain's meetings with Hitler, culminating in the climactic delusion of Munich, are not the stuff of this book, except in so far as they illustrate how complete was the abandonment of the League idea and how bereft of meaning the concept of collective security had become. The Russians, now acutely apprehensive of the German threat to themselves, did declare their readiness to honour their treaty obligations to Czechoslovakia. Litvinov, the only foreign minister of a major power to attend the nineteenth Assembly of the League, on September 31st, 1938, eight days before the Munich agreement was signed, stated what was bitterly obvious to the representatives of those smaller powers gathered together in the grandiose Assembly Hall.

'The League was created,' said Litvinov, 'as a reaction to the world war . . . its object was to make that the last war, to safeguard all nations against aggression, and to replace the system of military alliances by the collective organisation of assistance to the victim of aggression. In this sphere the League has done nothing.'

Nor did the League do anything in the following twelve months which ended with the German invasion of Poland. In March, 1939, the Germans invaded Czechoslovakia, thus carrying out the murder, which Munich had made only a matter of time. In April, the Italians invaded and annexed Albania. At its May meeting, the Council considered, not Czechoslovakia, not Albania—despite protests from their exiled leaders—but the Aaland Islands, which the Finns and Swedes wished jointly to fortify. Historians may find a pleasing symmetry in observing that these islands, which had been the subject of the first important political dispute resolved by the Council in 1920, should now be on the agenda of what was to be the last Council before the second world war. The issue was again of some moment to

Sweden and Finland, but that it should have engaged the Council's time, while the real matters of peace and war were ignored, can only emphasise the ultimate enfeeblement of the League. Delegates to that May Council were even spared the ritual embarrassment of listening to Spanish reproaches, for the Franco-Mussolini-Hitler alliance had finally crushed the Republicans and on May 9th, 1939, the new ruler of Spain announced his country's withdrawal from the League.

The League virtually ceased to be mentioned in the minutes of British Cabinet meetings in that last year of peace. There were longish discussions in June and July, 1939, concerning Palestine and Britain's difficulties in failing to persuade the Permanent Mandates Commission that her proposals, put forward in a white paper in May, for settling the conflicting aims and demands of Jews and Arabs, were consistent with the terms of her original mandate. The British Government was preparing its case for the September meeting of the Council, and planning diplomatic action to rally support, when war broke out, leaving the Palestine question to be dealt with another day.

It is a curiosity—and one worth remarking briefly—that as the League showed itself less and less capable of effective action to save peace in Europe, the countries of the Middle and Near East looked to Geneva with the kind of respect and for the kind of conciliation which the League's creators had wished for it. When Britain at length reached and agreement with Egypt, which would allow British forces to be stationed in the Suez Canal and bring the Egyptians to full independence, there was a provision for the Council to decide what should happen if, at the end of the prescribed period of twenty years, the two countries could not agree whether the troops should remain. Furthermore, as they had aspired to do for so long, the Egyptians entered the League— in May, 1937. It was to Geneva that Persia and Iraq brought a dispute over frontiers, and the Council was called upon to deal also with a dangerous-looking conflict on the frontier between Turkey and Syria. The machinery of international conciliation was still working and was still useful, in other words. In its special committees and departments for promoting health and economic development, for the relief of hunger, for aid to refugees, for the resolution of all manner of impediments to

396

good relations between nations, the League was proving that the countries of the earth could work together effectively, with common purpose, to the common good. It was work to which the United States contributed more and more positively, serving on these committees as well as becoming an active member of the International Labour Organisation.

But all that constructive, hopeful effort was nullified by the failure of the major powers to use the League and to observe their obligations under the Covenant to check the aggressions of the totalitarian powers. The desperate attempts by the British and French, in the late spring and summer of 1939, to convince Hitler, by means of the alliance with Poland and the guarantees to Greece and Rumania, that they were, after all, prepared to go to war, came too late. So did their moves to make common military cause with Russia. The Russians had given up their search for security through the League and hence through collaboration with the western democracies. Litvinov, the instrument of that search, was discarded as Foreign Minister in May, 1939. Anglo-French-Soviet talks looked for a while as though they might bear fruit; the British Government even thought of dignifying any defensive agreement against Germany as in line with obligations under article 16 of the Covenant: but they fizzled out.

In August came the non-aggression pact between Russia and Germany. The League High Commissioner—Carl Burckhardt succeeded Sean Lester in February, 1937—stayed in the free city of Danzig until the end, and there is no doubt that, by his presence and his own determination, he did much to mitigate the suffering of the Jews. But his role as the League's watchdog, the visible guarantor of the peculiar status of Danzig or of the rights of the Danzigers, had evaporated years before. He was ignored as a mediator between Danzig and Poland. The Poles, misled by the arrogance of Josef Beck, disdained to refer to Geneva Hitler's demand for the return of Danzig or to have their behaviour towards the German minority in Poland examined by the League. Poland reckoned she was big enough, as well as proud enough, to deal direct with Germany. Germany dealt direct with Poland on September 1st, 1939.

The unreality of so many of the League's activities, the necessity for those at Geneva to go about their daily tasks as though the world was inhabited by sane men conducting their affairs according to reason, ought now to have ended but the months of the 'phoney war' did something to protract the pretence to normality. And there was one last scene to play.

On November 30th, 1939, the Russians invaded Finland. The Finnish Government appealed to the League. The resistance offered by the Finns won an emotional response throughout the world, a surge of sympathy going out to the little nation fighting for its life. There was, too, the fear and hatred of Communism which had remained quiescent during Soviet Russia's membership of the League, but had never died. And so the Assembly of the League met once more. Russia refused an invitation to attend, but in her absence she was condemned for her violation of the Covenant. The Council followed up the Assembly's resolution and on December 14th, 1939, seven members—including Britain and France—cast positive votes to expel the USSR from the League, using the powers conferred upon the Council by Article 16, powers which had never been invoked before, not against Japan, nor against Italy. No word was spoken in either the Assembly or the Council about Germany. The Assembly's condemnation of Russia was fully justified. So was the action of the Council in excluding her from the League. But when viewed against the omissions, the evasions, the failures of the past, and the reality of the world scene at that moment, the incident must seem like no more than an irrelevant piece of play-acting.

17

'The League is dead'

The Palace of Peace came to life again. Shutters were taken down. Hundreds of charwomen swept and dusted offices which had not been occupied for nearly six years. Electricians fitted new lights and telephones. In the great rectangular Assembly Hall, which had seen the last, ignoble days of the League before the outbreak of war, microphones were being tested. National flags flew once more over the hotels of Geneva. Delegates began to arrive for the formalities of winding up the League. On April 7th, 1946, Lord Cecil of Chelwood, now in his eighty-second year, one of the men whose work and ideas had helped to create and shape the League, flew in from London. Heading the British delegation was Philip Noel-Baker, a member of the League Secretariat at the start of its life, now a minister of state at the Foreign Office in the Labour government elected at the end of the war. A white-haired Paul-Boncour came by train from Paris. The mood was one of nostalgia and reflection.

It was impossible to deny the ultimate failure of the League: the horrors through which the world had passed were too recent and the living evidence of them too grotesque. But there were memories also of what had been accomplished. The League had survived the almost mortal blow of America's rejection. Without the United States, without Germany, without Soviet Russia, the nations had come together at Geneva and had begun to build that new system of conciliation and arbitration which promised to safeguard peace by the assertion of reason and by collective security. It was a new world the men of Geneva began to build, still an imperfect world, still a world which fell short of mankind's aspirations, but one which, in the midst of famine, disease, poverty and unemployment, held out the fragile hope that things could be different.

Essentially through the exercise of Anglo-French power, but by the demonstration, too, of a common will within the League Council, disputes like those about Memel and the Aaland Islands were resolved peacefully; dangerous conflicts like the Greco-Bulgarian one were checked; a settlement was found to the territorial and ethnic tangle of Upper Silesia. For years the League prevented Balkan rivalries and the friction between Poland and Lithuania from erupting into full-scale wars and protected the status of the free city of Danzig and the rights of its citizens. The League stood as the champion of minorities. From the vindictive follies of Versailles, the atavistic lunacies of Chanak and the bitterness of the Ruhr occupation, the British and French moved falteringly towards a better understanding of the League they had done so much to bring into being and which depended so heavily upon them for its continued existence. While still employing the methods of old-fashioned diplomacy they began to fashion a faith in the League as the final court of appeal and in the Covenant as the instrument by which all nations should order their relationships. They might still make their treaties behind closed doors but they would exhibit them, for approval, upon the open stage of Geneva. And when the German delegates took their place, for the first time, in the Assembly, the slap in the face Mussolini had given the League over Corfu could be disregarded, if not completely forgotten. With Chamberlain, Briand and Stresemann so conspicuously devoted to the League ideal, who could doubt that the League must grow ever stronger, that one day the Americans would take up the responsibilities Woodrow Wilson had designed for them and that one day all the countries of the world might disband their armies and destroy their armaments.

The withering of that faith began with the economic depression. Then came Manchuria and the brazen challenge to the League's authority by the Japanese who, throughout the 1920s, had worked so loyally to establish it. The League condemned Japan but the Japanese quit Geneva with their conquest an accomplished fact. At last the great Disarmament Conference assembled, but after nearly two years the only outcome was Nazi Germany's withdrawal from the League to continue openly the rearmament she had been practising secretly for several years. The dictators were now preparing to parade their total contempt for the principles of international behaviour enshrined in the Covenant, but there were yet moments when supporters of the League could delude themselves that all would come out right in the end. They could brush off the frustrations of the Chaco and point to the League flag flying over Leticia. The increasing degree of American co-operation in the work of various League committees, combined with Russia's entry after a long period of hostility, were solid reasons for optimism; so, too, was the peaceful conduct of the Saar plebiscite, under the protection of an international force. While the Italian threat to Ethiopia was still ripening, the League—or, rather, the Council, under the irresistible Anglo-French influence—procrastinated. When Italian ground and air forces went into the attack, the League, led by Britain, looked as though it was prepared, by mobilisation of the collective will, to implement the letter as well as the spirit of the Covenant. The League and Europe could have been saved. But the tepid reaction of America to feelers for co-ordinated action with the League nations drained what little courage had been conjured in the British and French governments. The Hoare-Laval pact, although disowned, ensured the abortion of sanctions. Mussolini got away with it and the Rhineland, Spain, China, Austria, Czechoslovakia and Poland followed predictably.

The League had died years before the official funeral of 1946, but it was *The Times*, which had played its own part in bringing about its death, which found the right words among all those valedictory editorials which accompanied the last gathering of the delegates at Geneva:

'. . . To mourn the League immoderately would be to fall into the very fallacy that was responsible for most of the disappointments of its later years, that of attributing to the League a will and a power of its own, distinguishable from the collective will and collective power of the States that fashioned it as an instrument for preserving the peace of the world. In truth it was only by a metaphor, easily misunderstood or abused, that the League was ever capable of either success or failure; rather was it the members who might succeed or fail in using its machinery in proportion as they maintained the essential unity of purpose . . .'

What can be done even more usefully today than in 1946 is to ask why the collective will failed and why the machinery of the League was left to rust. The apologists for those pre-war governments in Britain say there was really no choice: they did not have the material power with which to offer credible resistance to the dictators and therefore, goes the argument, to talk of their implementing the Covenant is unrealistic. To be called 'realistic' is one of the highest medals of praise one can receive from most professional practitioners of politics in Britain. Realism is the recognition of what is possible, as compared with what might be desirable, all other things being equal which they never are. But the challenges which faced the democratic governments in the late 1930s cannot be seen in isolation. The choices which lay open to them then were themselves the product of their responses—or failures to respond—to other challenges in earlier years. In other words, every evasion, every compromise, every hesitation, every betrayal of faith or principle, contributed to the ultimate surrender at Munich.

No doubt, as many politicians have witnessed in their memoirs, it is a chastening experience to exchange the luxury of opposition for the responsibilities of office. Of course, not all those things that have been promised are possible; bold, radical plans have to be trimmed and modified; circumstances dictate compromise. But circumstances should never be allowed to dictate to the point where basic principles are not merely shelved, but repudiated. Great men can dominate circumstances and they can carry their fellow-countrymen along a path of seemingly unpopular action, if their will and their dedication to an avowed principle is determined enough and is matched by their capacity to light up the imagination with their words. Did Franklin Roosevelt and Cordell Hull really do all that was in their power to drag the American people out of their isolationist torpor, or did they submit to popular opinion with an insignificant struggle, living to hold office another day, and, in Cordell Hull's case, to lecture the people of other countries upon their folly?

Leadership is a word which has become dirtied by association with the dictators; it is still a quality which should enhance and ennoble political action. It may be said that Woodrow Wilson is a prime example of a political leader bashing his head against popular opinion and losing despite all his idealism and all his personal magnetism. Wilson failed to lead America into the League of Nations, not because the people were unwilling to follow him, not because they rejected his leadership, but because of his own pig-headed arrogance. The principles of international conduct to which he dedicated himself have survived his personal failure. So, too, with the League of Nations. The Covenant, which Wilson did so much to frame, did not perish with the outbreak of war. The ideal of a League of Nations was not tarnished by the betrayal of Ethiopia, the mockery of non-intervention in Spain or the ignominy of Munich. 'It,' the League, did not fail the Ethiopians, or the Spaniards, or the Chinese, or the Czechs; the blame for those betrayals must lie with the political leaders of the democracies and their foreign offices.

It is convenient for the little-minded nationalists in all countries to be able to explode their grievances for everything that goes wrong in the world against some impersonal organisation, against some 'it.' But the truth is there is no 'it,' whether it be the League of Nations or the United Nations, each is or could be only as strong or as weak as we allow it to be, for there is only 'us,' the collectivity of peoples and of the governments we elect. Much facile cynicism has been expended over the corpse of the League because 'it' failed to live up to the aspirations expressed by men like Woodrow Wilson, Robert Cecil and Norman Angell, and by some who were mouthing words they had no serious intention of honouring. Yet even those who merely mimicked the idealists were, almost despite themselves, reaching out towards a different, better, more rational way of conducting man's affairs.

As Philip Noel-Baker said at Geneva in April, 1946, 'We know now that we who stood for the collective system were always right and that our opponents who attacked and ridiculed us were always fatuously, but catastrophically wrong. We know that the world war began in Manchuria fifteen years ago. We know that four years after we could easily have stopped Mussolini if we had taken the sanctions that were obviously required—if we had closed the Suez Canal to the aggressor and stopped his oil. Geneva has been the first parliament of the world. Our work has not ended, it has only just begun, and this time both the governments and the peoples are resolved not to struggle only but at last to win.'

But as if to prove that struggle there must certainly be, not even the formal burial of the League could pass off without a note of disharmony. The first business was to close the twentieth Assembly which had adjourned on December 14th, 1939, and to open the twenty-first. Vice-presidents of the new Assembly were elected by secret ballot in secret session. The Argentine delegation, having failed to secure one of those elections, a matter it considered of great importance to national prestige, walked out. That did not prevent the Assembly, under the presidency of the Norwegian, Dr. Carl J. Hambro, from getting on with the practical business of liquidating the League, handing over the Palace to the United Nations, settling its debts, and handing back its reserve funds to those countries which had provided them. On April 18th the delegates of thirty-four nations came together in the Assembly Hall for the last time. They were outnumbered by spectators in the public galleries and journalists, including many who had watched the rise and fall of the League. One by one the delegations answered 'yes' to a roll call on a motion which provided that 'with effect from the day following the close of the present session of the Assembly, the League of Nations shall cease to exist except for the sole purpose of the liquidation of its affairs.' Hambro tapped his gavel and announced, 'I declare the twenty-first and last session of the General Assembly of the League of Nations closed.' And so, on April 19th, 1946, the League formally ended, and the man who had been there at the beginning was the one who, during that last Assembly, spoke the words which must have summed up the feelings of all those present.

'Let us boldly state,' said Robert Cecil, his voice occasionally trembling, 'that aggression wherever it occurs and however it may be defended, is an international crime, that it is the duty of every peace-loving state to resent it and employ whatever force is necessary to crush it, that the machinery of the Charter, no less than the machinery of the Covenant, is sufficient for this purpose if properly used, and that every well-disposed citizen of every state should be ready to undergo any sacrifice in order to maintain peace . . .

'I venture to impress upon my hearers that the great work of peace is resting not only on the narrow interests of our own nations, but even more on those great principles of right and wrong on which nations, like individuals, depend.

'The League is dead. Long live the United Nations.'

APPENDIX

THE COVENANT OF THE LEAGUE OF NATIONS

Preamble

THE HIGH CONTRACTING PARTIES,

In order to promote international co-operation and to achieve international peace and security

by the acceptance of obligations not to resort to war,

by the prescription of open, just and honourable relations between nations,

by the firm establishment of the understandings of international law as the actual rule of conduct among Governments, and

by the maintenance of justice and a scrupulous respect for all treaty obligations in the dealings of organized peoples with one another,

Agree to this Covenant of the League of Nations.

Article 1

1. The original Members of the League of Nations shall be those of the Signatories which are named in the Annex to this Covenant and also such of those other States named in the Annex as shall accede without reservation to this Covenant. Such accession shall be effected by a Declaration deposited with the Secretariat within two months of the coming into force of the Covenant. Notice thereof shall be sent to all other Members of the League.

2. Any fully self-governing State, Dominion or Colony not named in the Annex may become a Member of the League if its admission is agreed to by two-thirds of the Assembly, provided that it shall give

effective guarantees of its sincere intention to observe its international obligations, and shall accept such regulations as may be prescribed by the League in regard to its military, naval and air forces and armaments.

3. Any Member of the League may, after two years' notice of its intention so to do, withdraw from the League, provided that all its international obligations and all its obligations under this Covenant shall have been fulfilled at the time of its withdrawal.

Article 2

The action of the League under this Covenant shall be effected through the instrumentality of an Assembly and of a Council, with a permanent Secretariat.

Article 3

1. The Assembly shall consist of Representatives of the Members of the League.

2. The Assembly shall meet at stated intervals and from time to time as occasion may require at the Seat of the League or at such other place as may be decided upon.

3. The Assembly may deal at its meetings with any matter within the sphere of action of the League or affecting the peace of the world.

4. At meetings of the Assembly, each Member of the League shall have one vote, and may have not more than three Representatives.

Article 4

1. The Council shall consist of Representatives of the Principal Allied and Associated Powers, together with Representatives of four other Members of the League. These four Members of the League shall be selected by the Assembly from time to time in its discretion. Until the appointment of the Representatives of the four Members of the League first selected by the Assembly, Representatives of Belgium, Brazil, Spain and Greece shall be members of the Council.

2. With the approval of the majority of the Assembly, the Council may name additional Members of the League whose Representatives shall always be members of the Council; the Council with like approval may increase the number of Members of the League to be selected by the Assembly for representation on the Council.

The Assembly shall fix by a two-thirds majority the rules dealing with the election of the non-permanent members of the Council, and particularly such regulations as relate to their term of office and the conditions of re-eligibility.

3. The Council shall meet from time to time as occasion may

require, and at least once a year, at the Seat of the League, or at such other place as may be decided upon.

4. The Council may deal at its meetings with any matter within the sphere of action of the League or affecting the peace of the world.

5. Any Member of the League not represented on the Council shall be invited to send a Representative to sit as a member at any meeting of the Council during the consideration of matters specially affecting the interests of that Member of the League.

6. At meetings of the Council, each Member of the League represented on the Council shall have one vote, and may have not more than one Representative.

Article 5

1. Except where otherwise expressly provided in this Covenant or by the terms of the present Treaty, decisions at any meeting of the Assembly or of the Council shall require the agreement of all the Members of the League represented at the meeting.

2. All matters of procedure at meetings of the Assembly or of the Council, including the appointment of Committees to investigate particular matters, shall be regulated by the Assembly or by the Council and may be decided by a majority of the Members of the League represented at the meeting.

3. The first meeting of the Assembly and the first meeting of the Council shall be summoned by the President of the United States of America.

Article 6

1. The permanent Secretariat shall be established at the Seat of the League. The Secretariat shall comprise a Secretary-General and such secretaries and staff as may be required.

2. The first Secretary-General shall be the person named in the Annex; thereafter the Secretary-General shall be appointed by the Council with the approval of the majority of the Assembly.

3. The secretaries and staff of the Secretariat shall be appointed by the Secretary-General with the approval of the Council.

4. The Secretary-General shall act in that capacity at all meetings of the Assembly and of the Council.

5. The expenses of the League shall be borne by the Members of the League in the proportion decided by the Assembly.

Article 7

1. The Seat of the League is established at Geneva.

2. The Council may at any time decide that the Seat of the League shall be established elsewhere.

3. All positions under or in connexion with the League, including the Secretariat, shall be open equally to men and women.

4. Representatives of the Members of the League and officials of the League when engaged on the business of the League shall enjoy diplomatic privileges and immunities.

5. The buildings and other property occupied by the League or its officials or by Representatives attending its meetings shall be inviolable.

Article 8

1. The Members of the League recognize that the maintenance of peace requires the reduction of national armaments to the lowest point consistent with national safety and the enforcement by common action of international obligations.

2. The Council, taking account of the geographical situation and circumstances of each State, shall formulate plans for such reduction for the consideration and action of the several Governments.

3. Such plans shall be subject to reconsideration and revision at least every ten years.

4. After these plans shall have been adopted by the several Governments, the limits of armaments therein fixed shall not be exceeded without the concurrence of the Council.

5. The Members of the League agree that the manufacture by private enterprise of munitions and implements of war is open to grave objections. The Council shall advise how the evil effects attendant upon such manufacture can be prevented, due regard being had to the necessities of those Members of the League which are not able to manufacture the munitions and implements of war necessary for their safety.

6. The Members of the League undertake to interchange full and frank information as to the scale of their armaments, their military, naval and air programmes and the condition of such of their industries as are adaptable to war-like purposes.

Article 9

A permanent Commission shall be constituted to advise the Council on the execution of the provisions of Articles 1 and 8 and on military, naval and air questions generally.

Article 10

The Members of the League undertake to respect and preserve as against external aggression the territorial integrity and existing political independence of all Members of the League. In case of any such aggression or in case of any threat or danger of such aggression the Council shall advise upon the means by which this obligation shall be fulfilled.

Article 11

1. Any war or threat of war, whether immediately affecting any of the Members of the League or not, is hereby declared a matter of concern to the whole League, and the League shall take any action that may be deemed wise and effectual to safeguard the peace of nations. In case any such emergency should arise, the Secretary-General shall on the request of any Member of the League forthwith summon a meeting of the Council.

2. It is also declared to be the friendly right of each Member of the League to bring to the attention of the Assembly or of the Council any circumstance whatever affecting international relations which threatens to disturb international peace or the good understanding between nations upon which peace depends.

Article 12

1. The Members of the League agree that if there should arise between them any dispute likely to lead to a rupture, they will submit the matter either to arbitration or judicial settlement or to inquiry by the Council, and they agree in no case to resort to war until three months after the award by the arbitrators or the judicial decision or the report by the Council.

2. In any case under this Article the award of the arbitrators or the judicial decision shall be made within a reasonable time, and the report of the Council shall be made within six months after the submission of the dispute.

Article 13

1. The Members of the League agree that whenever any dispute shall arise between them which they recognize to be suitable for submission to arbitration or judicial settlement, and which cannot be satisfactorily settled by diplomacy, they will submit the whole subject-matter to arbitration or judicial settlement.

2. Disputes as to the interpretation of a treaty, as to any question of international law, as to the existence of any fact which if established would constitute a breach of any international obligation, or as to the extent and nature of the reparation to be made for any such breach, are

declared to be among those which are generally suitable for submission to arbitration or judicial settlement.

3. For the consideration of any such dispute, the court to which the case is referred shall be the Permanent Court of International Justice, established in accordance with Article 14, or any tribunal agreed on by the parties to the dispute or stipulated in any convention existing between them.

4. The Members of the League agree that they will carry out in full good faith any award or decision that may be rendered, and that they will not resort to war against a Member of the League which complies therewith. In the event of any failure to carry out such an award or decision, the Council shall propose what steps should be taken to give effect thereto.

Article 14

The Council shall formulate and submit to the Members of the League for adoption plans for the establishment of a Permanent Court of International Justice. The Court shall be competent to hear and determine any dispute of an international character which the parties thereto submit to it. The Court may also give an advisory opinion upon any dispute or question referred to it by the Council or by the Assembly.

Article 15

1. If there should arise between Members of the League any dispute likely to lead to a rupture, which is not submitted to arbitration or judicial settlement in accordance with Article 13, the Members of the League agree that they will submit the matter to the Council. Any party to the dispute may effect such submission by giving notice of the existence of the dispute to the Secretary-General, who will make all necessary arrangements for a full investigation and consideration thereof.

2. For this purpose the parties to the dispute will communicate to the Secretary-General, as promptly as possible, statements of their case with all the relevant facts and papers, and the Council may forthwith direct the publication thereof.

3. The Council shall endeavour to effect a settlement of the dispute, and if such efforts are successful, a statement shall be made public giving such facts and explanations regarding the dispute and the terms of settlement thereof as the Council may deem appropriate.

4. If the dispute is not thus settled, the Council either unanimously or by a majority vote shall make and publish a report containing a state-

ment of the facts of the dispute and the recommendations which are deemed just and proper in regard thereto.

5. Any Member of the League represented on the Council may make public a statement of the facts of the dispute and of its conclusions regarding the same.

6. If a report by the Council is unanimously agreed to by the members thereof other than the Representatives of one or more of the parties to the dispute, the Members of the League agree that they will not go to war with any party to the dispute which complies with the recommendations of the report.

7. If the Council fails to reach a report which is unanimously agreed to by the members thereof, other than the Representatives of one or more of the parties to the dispute, the Members of the League reserve to themselves the right to take such action as they shall consider necessary for the maintenance of right and justice.

8. If the dispute between the parties is claimed by one of them, and is found by the Council, to arise out of a matter which by international law is solely within the domestic jurisdiction of that party, the Council shall so report, and shall make no recommendation as to its settlement.

9. The Council may in any case under this Article refer the dispute to the Assembly. The dispute shall be so referred at the request of either party to the dispute, provided that such request be made within fourteen days after the submission of the dispute to the Council.

10. In any case referred to the Assembly, all the provisions of this Article and of Article 12 relating to the action and powers of the Council shall apply to the action and powers of the Assembly, provided that a report made by the Assembly, if concurred in by the Representatives of those Members of the League represented on the Council and of a majority of the other Members of the League, exclusive in each case of the Representatives of the parties to the dispute, shall have the same force as a report by the Council concurred in by all the members thereof other than the Representatives of one or more of the parties to the dispute.

Article 16

1. Should any Member of the League resort to war in disregard of its covenants under Articles 12, 13 or 15, it shall *ipso facto* be deemed to have committed an act of war against all other Members of the League, which hereby undertake immediately to subject it to the severance of all trade or financial relations, the prohibition of all intercourse between their nationals and the nationals of the covenant-breaking State, and the prevention of all financial, commercial or personal

intercourse between the nationals of the covenant-breaking State and the nationals of any other State, whether a Member of the League or not.

2. It shall be the duty of the Council in such case to recommend to the several Governments concerned what effective military, naval or air force the Members of the League shall severally contribute to the armed forces to be used to protect the covenants of the League.

3. The Members of the League agree, further, that they will mutually support one another in the financial and economic measures which are taken under this Article, in order to minimize the loss and inconvenience resulting from the above measures, and that they will mutually support one another in resisting any special measures aimed at one of their number by the covenant-breaking State, and that they will take the necessary steps to afford passage through their territory to the forces of any of the Members of the League which are co-operating to protect the covenants of the League.

4. Any Member of the League which has violated any covenant of the League may be declared to be no longer a Member of the League by a vote of the Council concurred in by the Representatives of all the other Members of the League represented thereon.

Article 17

1. In the event of a dispute between a Member of the League and a State which is not a member of the League, or between States not members of the League, the State or States not members of the League shall be invited to accept the obligations of membership in the League for the purposes of such dispute, upon such conditions as the Council may deem just. If such invitation is accepted, the provisions of Articles 12 to 16 inclusive shall be applied with such modifications as may be deemed necessary by the Council.

2. Upon such invitation being given the Council shall immediately institute an inquiry into the circumstances of the dispute and recommend such action as may seem best and most effectual in the circumstances.

3. If a State so invited shall refuse to accept the obligations of membership in the League for the purposes of such dispute, and shall resort to war against a Member of the League, the provisions of Article 16 shall be applicable as against the State taking such action.

4. If both parties to the dispute when so invited refuse to accept the obligations of membership in the League for the purposes of such dispute, the Council may take such measures and make such recom-

mendations as will prevent hostilities and will result in the settlement of the dispute.

Article 18

Every treaty or international engagement entered into hereafter by any Member of the League shall be forthwith registered with the Secretariat and shall as soon as possible be published by it. No such treaty or international engagement shall be binding until so registered.

Article 19

The Assembly may from time to time advise the reconsideration by Members of the League of treaties which have become inapplicable and the consideration of international conditions whose continuance might endanger the peace of the world.

Article 20

1. The Members of the League severally agree that this Covenant is accepted as abrogating all obligations or understandings *inter se* which are inconsistent with the terms thereof, and solemnly undertake that they will not hereafter enter into any engagements inconsistent with the terms thereof.

2. In case any Member of the League shall, before becoming a Member of the League, have undertaken any obligations inconsistent with the terms of this Covenant, it shall be the duty of such Member to take immediate steps to procure its release from such obligations.

Article 21

Nothing in this Covenant shall be deemed to affect the validity of international engagements, such as treaties of arbitration or regional understandings like the Monroe doctrine, for securing the maintenance of peace.

Article 22

1. To those colonies and territories which as a consequence of the late war have ceased to be under the sovereignty of the States which formerly governed them and which are inhabited by peoples not yet able to stand by themselves under the strenuous conditions of the modern world, there should be applied the principle that the well-being and development of such peoples form a sacred trust of civilization and that securities for the performance of this trust should be embodied in this Covenant.

2. The best method of giving practical effect to this principle is that

the tutelage of such peoples should be entrusted to advanced nations who by reason of their resources, their experience or their geographical position can best undertake this responsibility, and who are willing to accept it, and that this tutelage should be exercised by them as Mandatories on behalf of the League.

3. The character of the mandate must differ according to the stage of the development of the people, the geographical situation of the territory, its economic conditions and other similar circumstances.

4. Certain communities formerly belonging to the Turkish Empire have reached a stage of development where their existence as independent nations can be provisionally recognized subject to the rendering of administrative advice and assistance by a Mandatory until such time as they are able to stand alone. The wishes of these communities must be a principal consideration in the selection of the Mandatory.

5. Other peoples, especially those of Central Africa, are at such a stage that the Mandatory must be responsible for the administration of the territory under conditions which will guarantee freedom of conscience and religion, subject only to the maintenance of public order and morals, the prohibition of abuses such as the slave trade, the arms traffic and the liquor traffic, and the prevention of the establishment of fortifications or military and naval bases and of military training of the natives for other than police purposes and the defence of territory, and will also secure equal opportunities for the trade and commerce of other Members of the League.

6. There are territories, such as South West Africa and certain of the South Pacific Islands, which, owing to the sparseness of their population, or their small size, or their remoteness from the centres of civilization, or their geographical contiguity to the territory of the Mandatory, and other circumstances, can be best administered under the laws of the Mandatory as integral portions of its territory, subject to the safeguards above mentioned in the interests of the indigenous population.

7. In every case of mandate, the Mandatory shall render to the Council an annual report in reference to the territory committed to its charge.

8. The degree of authority, control, or administration to be exercised by the Mandatory shall, if not previously agreed upon by the Members of the League, be explicitly defined in each case by the Council.

9. A permanent Commission shall be constituted to receive and examine the annual reports of the Mandatories and to advise the Council on all matters relating to the observance of the mandates.

Article 23

Subject to and in accordance with the provisions of international conventions existing or hereafter to be agreed upon, the Members of the League:

(a) will endeavour to secure and maintain fair and humane conditions of labour for men, women, and children, both in their own countries and in all countries to which their commercial and industrial relations extend, and for that purpose will establish and maintain the necessary international organizations:

(b) undertake to secure just treatment of the native inhabitants of territories under their control;

(c) will entrust the League with the general supervision over the execution of agreements with regard to the traffic in women and children, and the traffic in opium and other dangerous drugs;

(d) will entrust the League with the general supervision of the trade in arms and ammunition with the countries in which the control of this traffic is necessary in the common interest;

(e) will make provision to secure and maintain freedom of communications and of transit and equitable treatment for the commerce of all Members of the League. In this connexion, the special necessities of the regions devastated during the war of 1914–1918 shall be borne in mind;

(f) will endeavour to take steps in matters of international concern for the prevention and control of disease.

Article 24

1. There shall be placed under the direction of the League all international bureaux already established by general treaties if the parties to such treaties consent. All such international bureaux and all commissions for the regulation of matters of international interest hereafter constituted shall be placed under the direction of the League.

2. In all matters of international interest which are regulated by general conventions but which are not placed under the control of international bureaux or commissions, the Secretariat of the League shall, subject to the consent of the Council and if desired by the parties, collect and distribute all relevant information and shall render any other assistance which may be necessary or desirable.

3. The Council may include as part of the expenses of the Secretariat the expenses of any bureau or commission which is placed under the direction of the League.

Article 25

The Members of the League agree to encourage and promote the establishment and co-operation of duly authorized voluntary national Red Cross organizations having as purposes the improvement of health, the prevention of disease and the mitigation of suffering throughout the world.

Article 26

1. Amendments to this Covenant will take effect when ratified by the Members of the League whose Representatives compose the Council and by a majority of the Members of the League whose Representatives compose the Assembly.

2. No such amendment shall bind any Member of the League which signifies its dissent therefrom, but in that case it shall cease to be a Member of the League.

The original text of the Covenant was approved by the Peace Conference on April 28th, 1919. The text given here as an appendix is as amended in later years by the League Assembly. But the amendments were few. The second paragraph of clause 2 of Article 4 was added in 1921, as was clause 5 of Article 6, although neither came into force immediately because of delays in their formal ratification by individual countries. The only other amendments followed the setting-up, in 1921, of the Permanent Court of International Justice, as required in Article 14. The amendments—to Articles 12, 13 and 15—simply provide for the possibility of submitting disputes to the Court and refer to its powers to make judicial decisions and settlements.

INDEX